POSTAL OFFICIALS
OF THE CAPE OF GOOD HOPE

POSTAL OFFICIALS
OF THE CAPE OF GOOD HOPE

A book of data, including lists of postmasters,
early visitors to the Cape, licensed stamp vendors,
main post and sub-post offices, railway stations
and returns of post office property

Franco Frescura

Phansi Museum Press
Durban

2022

"What is the use of a book," thought Alice,
"without pictures or conversations?"

This book is dedicated to readers
of directories, genealogies, catalogues, inventories,
registries, thesauruses, gazettes, lexicons, grocery lists,
train schedules, telephone books, dictionaries,
almanacs, ledgers and government statistical returns

Whatever their reasons

Published under the patronage of the Phansi Museum, Durban, https://phansi.com
in association with the Philatelic Society for Greater Southern Africa, https://www.psgsa.org

The opinions expressed here are those of the Author

© Copyright Franco Frescura 2022

All rights reserved.

No part of this book may be reproduced or transmitted in any form
or by any means, electronic or mechanical, including photocopying, recording,
or by any information storage and retrieval system,
without prior permission in writing from the Author.

ISBN 978-0-620-95924-7
First Edition 2022

Edited and text typeset by Peter Thy in Garamond 12 pt using Adobe Indesign
Front cover illustration by the Author
Back cover contemporaneous satiric drawing of
Postmaster General G.W. Aitchison (1873-92) delivering the mail

Available in South Africa from Phansi Museum, https://phansi.com
or for the rest of the World from Amazon.com, https://www.amazon.com

Printed in South Africa by Digniti Press, Durban

CONTENTS

	Introduction	vii
1.	Biographical Listing of Postal Officials 1792-1910	1
2.	Diary of Early Visitors to the Cape 1530-1646	191
3.	Licensed Stamp Vendors at the Cape	205
4.	Return of Cape Post Office Buildings 1899	225
5.	Head and Subsidiary Post Offices 1886	229
6.	Main Posts 1903	235
7.	Index of Railway Stations 1862-1910	243
8.	Growth of Railway Infrastructure 1862-1910	261
9.	Listing of Field-Cornet Mails 1877-1910	267
10.	Departmental Income: Annual Returns 1873-1910	275
11.	List of Literary Publications, 1909	277
12.	Divisional House Duties Returns for 1870	281
	Abbreviations	285
	Bibliography	289

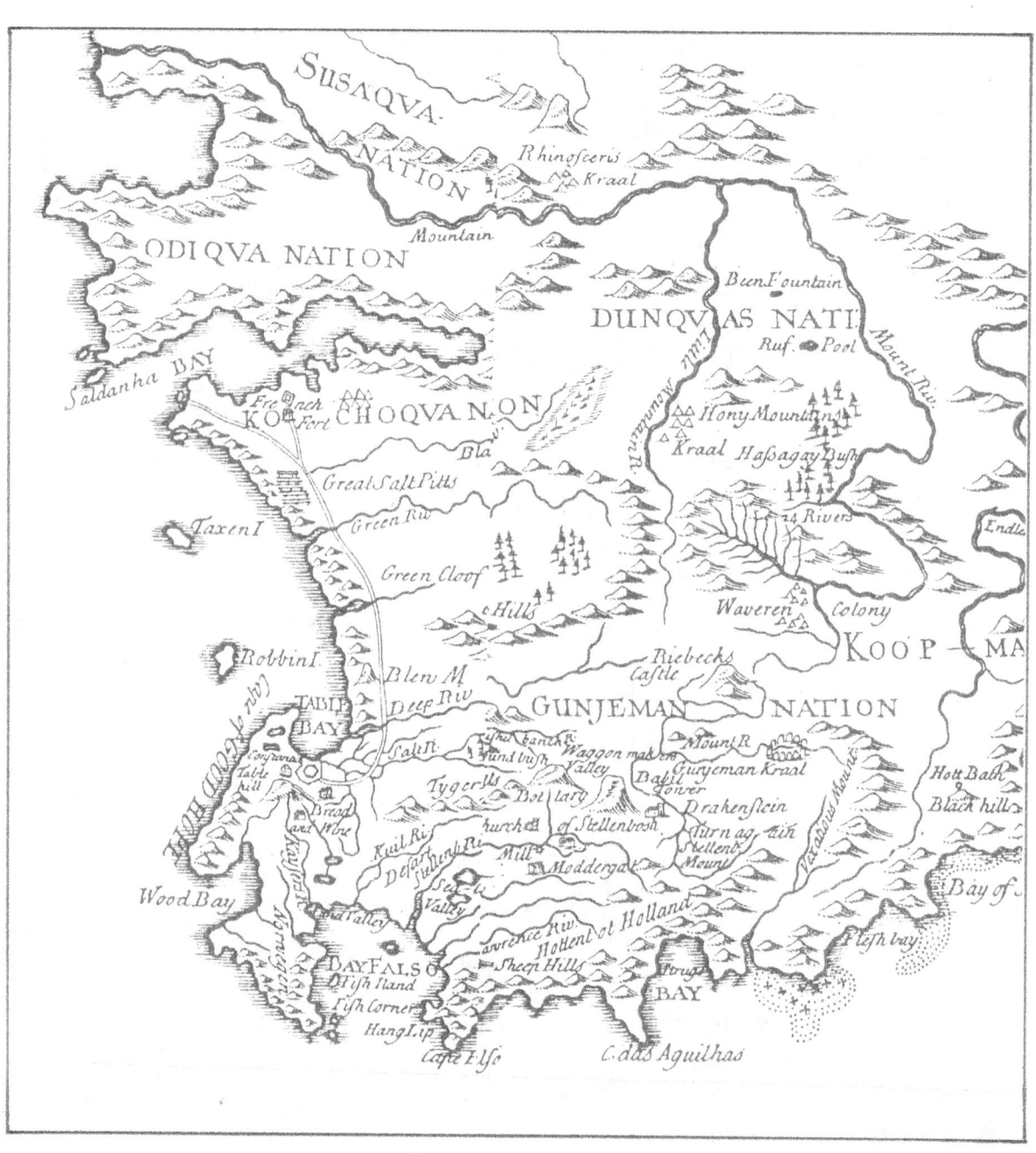

Map of the Cape of Good Hope from Peter Kolbe, 1727. Beschryving van de Kaap de Goede Hoop. Amsterdam: Hakeman

INTRODUCTION

There is much about this little volume which will recommend itself to an audience whose ancestors once found employment in the postal establishment of the Cape of Good Hope. Admittedly this is not a book that many members of the Westville Book Club will purchase. Indeed, as some people will sadly attest, it is woefully lacking in plot, it has no romantic heroines, and its list of protagonists is boringly long. On the other hand, it has been pleasingly laid out by my friend Peter Thy who, as well as being a most agreeable fellow, is also a highly regarded Professor of Geology at Davis University. Under his capable guidance the text has been set in Garamond 11pt which, as all people of unquestionable good taste agree, is an elegant face immensely superior to Times New Roman, which is vulgar and quite horrid. Not my type, if you know what I mean.

Although my editor has assured me that we should have no difficulty in selling 20 copies of the book to various members of my family, I have little doubt that once free copies have been distributed to the Fourth Estate, even without the R100 note that we propose to attach, the reviews will find sufficient interest in its content to recommend the book to a wider literary public. This may be a boring book, but then every self-respecting home also has its own copy of a thesaurus.

As is only to be expected, a research project that has taken 43 years of my life to complete will have a number of unfinished issues to deal with. These, like dangling participles, are lists of data that have taken hundreds of loving hours to compile but have never been disseminated to anyone other than a few interested friends. At the time they were a necessary means to an end, but now that the letters QED have been inscribed at the bottom of my thesis, they are in great danger of being abandoned to gather metaphorical dust in some long-forgotten electronic file.

Not so, oh ye of little faith! Enter stage left St Thomas the Doubtful and his comrade, St Jude the Obscure who, as patron saints of forgotten manuscripts have decided to lend a hand. Thanks to the open wallet policy of a generous donor, the Phansi Museum has been able to print a limited run of this book for the benefit of scholars. May the information it contains make it possible for you to explore new by-ways of knowledge without having to undergo the tedium of beating the same path.

During the course of this research the following libraries and institutions were consulted. Many of these names have now changed, and I apologise in advance for any omission I might have made. This has been owed to a factor of time, and may not reflect changing national circumstances.

 Africana Municipal Library, Johannesburg
 Albany Museum, Grahamstown

Amathole Museum, King William's Town
Atholl H Murray Personal Archive
Barrie Biermann Architectural Library, UKZN
Cape Archives, Cape Town
Cory Library, Rhodes University, Grahamstown
David Mordant Personal Archive
Fort Beaufort Museum
KwaZulu-Natal Museum in Pietermaritzburg
Lovedale Mission Records, University of Fort Hare, Alice
McGregor Museum, Kimberley
Mafeking Museum
Mervyn Emms Personal Archive
Museum Africa, Johannesburg
National Cultural History Museum, Pretoria
Nelson Mandela Metropolitan University Library
Post and Telecommunications Museum, Pretoria
South African Cultural History Museum, Cape Town
South African Library, Cape Town
South African Railway Museum, Johannesburg
Union Archives, Pretoria
War Museum of the Boer Republics, Bloemfontein
Sir John Inglefield-Watson Personal Archive
William Cullen Library, University of the Witwatersrand

I wish to pay special thanks to Peter Thy who, as Editor of Forerunners, an especially fine journal of postal matters published in California, has quietly become one of the foremost promoters of research into the fields of postal history and all matters in the transmission of mails. His journal continues to publish papers on an eclectic range of subjects which challenge the boundaries of conventional postal research and it is thanks to his enthusiasm that this, and another book that is soon to follow, will see the light of day. I thank him for his patience in editing this work.

No research project can survive without an infusion of life-giving funds, and for this I am indebted to the Federation of South African Philatelists as well as the Post Office department formerly known as the Museum of Posts and Telecommunications in Pretoria, who made available a number of small financial grants or grants-in-kind to make this research possible. In this respect I also wish to remember Jonas Michelson and Mervyn Emms for their friendship and good humour throughout these efforts. This volume is only a small part of their legacy to this country.

Franco Frescura
University of the Witwatersrand
Johannesburg, April 2022

ONE

BIOGRAPHICAL LISTING OF POSTAL OFFICIALS 1792-1910

A

ABBOTT, Mary A, Postmaster at Hopetown, 16 January 1865
ABBOTT, T, Postmaster at Hopetown, 15 June 1861
A'BEAR, E, Postmaster at Sneezewood, 15 March 1897
ABINGTON, SJ, Clerk to the Civil Commissioner and postmaster at Alice, 1 January 1848
ABURN, S, Postmaster and station master at Blue Cliff, 1 May 1878
ACKER, HO, Postmaster at Mossel Bay, 1835
    Postmaster at Mossel Bay, 1 February 1844
ACKERMAN, CT, Postmaster and field-cornet at Richmond, 20 October 1854
ADAMS, H, Postmaster at Woodstock Station, 17 April 1863
ADAMS, J, Postmaster at Victoria West, 23 November 1858
ADAMS, Mrs Margaret, Postmaster at Windvogelberg, 1 November 1863
ADAMS, T, Postmaster at Modderfontein, Division of Clanwilliam, 24 August 1877
ADAMS, TCP, Postmaster at Blaauw Krantz, Cradock, 4 May 1857, service provided for free
ADCOCK, G, Postmaster at Burghersdorp, 1 March 1871
ADCOCK, William, Postmaster at Amsterdam Flats, 23 December 1854
    Postmaster at Zwarte Koppen, 11 January 1855
ADDEY, John, Postmaster at Wellington, 25 March 1846
ADENDORFF, M, Postmaster at Jansenville, 1 January 1876
ADEY, E, Postmaster at Tsolo, 1 September 1883
ADEY, E, Postmaster at Tsomo, 1 September 1883
ADEY, TH, Postmaster at Elujilo, 1 October 1875
ADKINS, GCS, also listed as GS, born in about 1860
    Postmaster at Heidelberg, 1880
    Postmaster at Malmesbury, 1 May 1885
    Postmaster at Barkly East, 1 October 1887
    Postmaster at Alice, 1 June 1895
    Postmaster at Stellenbosch, 1 November 1895

Postmaster at Uitenhage, 1 December 1903

Soon thereafter Mr Adkins appears to have taken early retirement for in the Pension Lists of 30 November 1909 he is recorded at the age of 49 to be on a pension of £113.6.0 pa

ADKINS, H, Postmaster at Fort Jackson, 1 July 1865

Postmaster at Cathcart, 1 November 1879

AHERN, William, Postmaster at Eerste River Station, 1 March 1909

AHLBOM, A, Postmaster at Riebeek West, 1883

AINGER, JH, Postmaster at Maitland, 1 November 1898

Postmaster at Maitland, 1 February 1900

AINSLIE, HM, Postmaster at Umzimkulu, 1 May 1906

AINSLIE, W, Postmaster at Kowie East, 10 May 1858

AITCHISON, George William, began his career in the Cape's postal service on 23 September 1850 when he was appointed to the position of Additional Clerk in the General Post Office, Cape Town, with a fixed annual salary of £90. This was raised to £100 in 1852. The following year he was seconded to the Audit Office, and on 18 July 1857 he was promoted back to the GPO as Accountant to the Postmaster General with an annual salary of £250. In 1860 his duties were extended to include the work of Secretary to the Postmaster General, thus effectively making him Le Sueur's deputy. This involved a commensurate increase in annual salary to £300. Despite his senior position, he was not implicated in the financial scandal of 1864 and his reputation appears to have escaped unscathed by the subsequent dismissal of Le Sueur. Nonetheless, on 1 January 1869 he was transferred to Tulbagh where he spent the next four years as its Civil Commissioner and Resident Magistrate. In 1873 he returned to the postal service as Postmaster General, and remained in office until his sudden death on 26 January 1892.

Aitchison's tenure marks a key period in the development of the Colonial Post Office. Under his leadership the postal system was modernized, with the rationalization of the field-cornet's posts, the appointment of career post office administrators to key provincial positions, the extension of the postal network from 379 to 718 post office, and the merger of the post and telegraph systems. His administration laid the groundwork for subsequent events that allowed the transformation of the Cape Postal Establishment from its colonial roots into a modern and efficient service. However many of the important innovations achieved by his administration were probably owed to Somerset French, an expert in the British postal system who was seconded by the Colonial Service to the Cape Post Office in 1880

AITCHISON, WF, Clerk, GPO, Cape Town, in about 1880

ALBERTS, Jesse, Postmaster at Two Waters, c May 1879

On 1st May 1879 Jesse Alberts, postmaster at Two Waters, addressed a letter to the Postmaster General in Cape Town, requesting clarification over current postal tariffs (Athol H Murray personal communication). The Cape's postal records make no mention of such a post office before 1882 and no trace of a Jesse Alberts has been found to date in the Colonial Blue Books of that era. This letter therefore not only establishes that the post office at Two Waters was already open by 1879 but, in view of Alberts' enquiry, it is also obvious that, at that stage, he had not been a postmaster for very long. It is probable therefore that the post office at Two Waters was only opened shortly before the dispatch of this letter

ALBERTYN, F, Postmaster at Zuurbraak, 1881

ALBERTYN, H, Postmaster at Saldanha Bay, 29 May 1858

ALBERTYN, JJG, Postmaster and field-cornet at Kruisman's Rivier, 8 November 1860

ALCOCK, Mrs Frances, Postmaster at Simonstown, 29 November 1811
Postmaster at Uitenhage, 19 March 1823

ALCOCK, Mrs Harriet H, Postmaster at Uitenhage, 2 June 1853

ALDEMAN, A, Postmaster at Drooge Vlei, 1 January 1877

ALDEN, D, Postmaster at Matjesfontein, Division of Worcester, 1 July 1892

ALDRICH, G, Postmaster and field-cornet at Baviaans River, 21 March 1850

ALHEIT, Rev CW, Special Justice of the Peace and postmaster at Carnarvon, 20 August 1858, service provided for free in 1858-61
Postmaster at Saron, 1 November 1875, service provided for free

ALHEIT, JH, Postmaster at Saron, 1882

ALLISON, H, Postmaster at Kariega Station, 10 September 1859, deceased while in office

ALLISON, J, Postmaster at Faure Siding, 24 January 1857

ALLMAN, TE, Postmaster at Ladismith, 1880

ALTENSTED, Miss ML, Postmaster at Adderley Street, Port Elizabeth, 1 February 1909

AMBLER, GM, also listed as GS, Postmaster and station master at Coega, in about 1875
Postmaster and station master at Sandflats, 1 April 1877
Postmaster and station master at Glenconnor, in about 1878
Postmaster and station master at Mount Stewart, 1 September 1878

AMOS, A, Postmaster at Witteklip, 1 December 1907

AMOS, J, Postmaster at Upper Tyumie, 7 October 1863, service provided for free
Postmaster and field-cornet at Lower Tyumie, 31 May 1866, service provided for free

AMYS, Oswald John, Postmaster at Delport's Hope, 1 June 1906
Postmaster at Longlands, 1 January 1909
Postmaster at Marydale 1 April, 1910, salary £180 pa

ANDERHOLD, GE, Postmaster at Riversdale, 15 March 1846

ANDERSON, CL, Postmaster at Venterstad, 1880
Postmaster at Calvinia, 1881

ANDERSON, CWP, Postmaster at Adelaide, c1874
Postmaster at Cradock, 1 November 1875. Dismissed from office on about 1 February 1877

ANDERSON, D, Postmaster at Karroo Poort, 26 November 1864, service provided for free
The post office at Anderson's, Karroo Poort, was opened on 26 November 1864. It took its name from Mr D Anderson, its first postmaster, whose hotel was located at the head of the Hottentot's Kloof

ANDERSON, G, Postmaster at Matjesfontein, Division of Worcester, 1881

ANDERSON, Mrs H, Postmaster at Somerset East, 1 March 1873

Assistant postmaster at Somerset East, 1 April 1880

Postmaster at Spring Valley, 1 October 1900

ANDERSON, J, Postmaster at Conradie's, 12 May 1862, service provided for free. His tenure was not long-lived and in 1864 the office was abolished

Postmaster at Klipheuvel, 1882

Postmaster at Kalabas Kraal, 1882

ANDERSON, James, Postmaster at Victoria West, 7 May 1849

Postmaster at Victoria West, 15 September 1853

ANDERSON, JP, Postmaster at Highlands, 1 April 1900

ANDERSON, LFN, Postmaster at Idutywa, in about 1879

ANDERSON, John Pears, Station master at Middleton, 1 September 1904, salary £203 pa

ANDERSON, S, Postmaster at Kariega Station, in about 1877

ANDERSON, W, Postmaster at Napier, 1 December 1893

ANDERSON, WG, Postmaster at Stal Street, Cape Town, 1 January 1889

ANDERSON, WS, Postmaster and station master at Addo, 1 July 1877

Postmaster and station master at Coega, in about 1877

Postmaster and station master at Blue Cliff, in about 1878

ANDREW, Richard Lidsey, Postmaster at De Doorns, 1 August 1894

Station master at Huguenot, 11 July 1908, salary £270 pa

ANDREWS, J, Postmaster at Vlakfontein, Division of Albert, 18 December 1867, service provided for free

ANGUS, John, Postmaster at Delport's Hope, 1905

Postmaster at Sydney, 1 June 1906, salary £185 pa

APRIL, T, Post Office Messenger, Uitenhage., The Pension Lists of 30 November 1909 record that in 1910 Mr April, age 55, was retired on an annual pension of £35.11.6

ARCHER, Thomas, Postmaster at Lawrence Street, Port Elizabeth, 1909, salary £300 pa

ARCHIBALD, R, Postmaster at Kruisfontein, 5 June 1849

Postmaster at Gamtoos River Ferry, 26 May 1852

ARMSTRONG, CWP, Postmaster at Adelaide, in about 1874

Postmaster at Cradock, 1 November 1875, dismissed from office

ARMSTRONG, Mrs E, Postmaster at Wynberg, 6 March 1851

ARMSTRONG, J, Postmaster at Baroe Kraal, 1 July 1877

ARMSTRONG, J, Clerk, seventh class, GPO, Cape Town, 23 October 1858

Clerk, fifth class, 1863, dismissed from office 1864

ARMSTRONG, P, Postmaster at Zoute Kloof, 1 December 1875

ARNOLD, Miss Margaret E, Postmaster at Bathurst, 1 June 1896

Postmaster at Bathurst Station, July 1896

Postmaster at Koonap, 17 April 1897

Postmaster at Seymour, 1 May 1902

Postmaster at Bayville, 1 August 1902

Postmaster at Kowie West, 1908, salary £115 pa

ASCHEN, Miss MA, also listed as ASCHMAN, Postmaster Stal Street, Cape Town, 1 March 1891
Postmaster at Stal Street, Cape Town, 8 March 1899

ASCHMANN, JC, Postmaster at Modder River, Division of Kimberley, 1 September 1896
Postmaster at Kenhardt, 8 January 1898
Postmaster at Griquatown, 1 June 1899

ASHBY, Charles, Acting postmaster at Belmont, 1 September 1906

ASHMAN, A, Postmaster at Palmietfontein, 1880

ASHTON, CH, Postmaster and station master at Blaney Junction, 13 April 1879

ASPINALL, Frank Stancliff, born in about 1859
Imperial Telegraph Service, 2 February 1876
Telegraphist, Colonial Service, Port Elizabeth, 29 October 1880
Telegraphist, Colonial Service, Kimberley, 16 September 1882
Telegraphist, Colonial Service, Port Elizabeth, 1 September 1888
Acting Assistant Surveyor, Midland District, 1 December 1894
Assistant Surveyor, Midland District, 1 May 1895
Surveyor and District Engineer, Eastern District, 1 July 1898
Postmaster at Umtata, 1 December 1902
Retired from service in about 1908 on an annual pension of £252.0.3

ASPINALL, W, Postmaster at Houw Hoek, 1880
The postal agency at Houw Hoek was located on the grounds of the Houw Hoek Inn, a coach halt on the road between Cape Town and Swellendam. Its first postmaster, John Aspinall, was also the innkeeper and, by all accounts, ran *a quality establishment*

ATKINSON, RH, Assistant Conservator, Crown Forests, and postmaster at Knysna, Woodside, 15 May 1846, service provided for free in 1846-60 and again in 1867-72

ATMORE, W, Postmaster at Tabankulu, 10 October 1900

ATREE, ES, Postmaster at Gamtoos River Ferry, 1880

ATTRIDGE, J, Postmaster at Klapmuts, 1 October 1866
Postmaster and station master at Wellington Station, 1 June 1873

ATTWELL, Miss J, Postmaster at Salem, 1 June 1902

ATTWELL, Miss O, Postmaster at Salem, 1 December 1908, salary £60 pa

AURET, EB, Postmaster at Durbanville, 11 May 1860
Postmaster and field-cornet at Pramberg, 1 October 1862

AURET, JB, Postmaster at Beaufort West, 1 January 1842
Postmaster at Beaufort West, 18 June 1853

AURET, Peter Oloff Alexis, Postmaster at Belmont, 1 April 1889
Postmaster at Fraserburg, 1 March 1893
Postmaster at Carnarvon, 1 October 1900
Postmaster at Sterkstroom, 1 February 1909, salary £280 pa

AUSTEN, AG, Postmaster at Orange Grove, Division of Victoria East, 1880

AUSTEN, J, Postmaster at Kraai River, 10 May 1858
AUSTIN, HAW, Postmaster at Douglas, in about 1882
    Postmaster at Langford, 1882
AVERSON, HS, also listed as AVESON
    Postmaster and station master at De Doorns, 20 October 1878
    Postmaster at Klipheuvel, 23 September 1879
    Postmaster at Matjesfontein, in about 1879
AYLIFF, Rev John (1797-1862). John Ayliff immigrated to the Cape in 1820, as a member of Willson's party. He married Jane Dold and settled with her parents at Beaufort Vale. In January 1822 he moved to Somerset Farm, where he was given charge of its stores and of the post office. He was accepted as an assistant missionary by the Wesleyan Mission in Grahamstown in 1827, and after spells at Salem, Somerset East, Butterworth, Peddie and Wesleyville, he took charge of the new mission at Haslope. He is credited with the founding in 1848 of a mission to the Mfengu, which subsequently developed into Healdtown. Suffering from failing health, he retired to his son's farm near Fauresmith, where he died in 1862
AYLING, JR, also listed as RJ, Postmaster at Tsolo, 1 July 1902
    Postmaster at Mount Ayliff, 1 March 1903, salary £210 pa
AYRE, R, Postmaster at Blue Cliff, 1880

B

BACHELOR, HH, see under BATCHELOR, HH
BAELSTON, J, Postmaster at Wynberg, 1 February 1827
BAILEY, D, Postmaster at De Doorns, 1 July 1896
    Postmaster and station master at Retreat, 14 July and 15 July 1899, salary £265 pa
BAILEY, GH, Postmaster and station master at Woodstock Station, 14 April 1874
BAILEY, HE, Postmaster at Postmasburg, 1 March 1901
    Postmaster at Schmidt's Drift, 1 June 1902
    Postmaster at Postmasburg, 1 August 1902
BAILEY, W, Postmaster at Riversdale, 1882
BAILIE, Jane A, Postmaster at Alice, 25 March 1862
BAILIE, WA, Postmaster at Simonstown, 9 October 1875
BAIN, G, Postmaster at Redhouse, 6 December 1897
BAINBRIDGE, G, Postmaster at Berlin Station, in about 1877
BAIRD, RJ, Postmaster at Mount Ayliff, 1 July 1902
    Postmaster at Schmidt's Drift, 1 December 1903
BAKER, F, Postmaster at Witteklip, 1883
BAKER, J, Postmaster at Grabouw, 2 October 1857, service provided for free
BAKER, J, also listed as BUTLER, Postmaster at Palmiet River, 2 October 1857
BAKER, M, Postmaster and field-cornet at Blinkwater, 29 April 1871
BAKER, WA, Postmaster at Klipheuvel, in about 1883.

On 17 February 1884 Mr WA Baker, former postmaster of Klipheuvel Station, was charged in the Supreme Court, in Cape Town, with the theft of two letters in August 1883. He was found guilty and sentenced to twelve months imprisonment with hard labour

BAKKEN, C, Postmaster at Kenhardt, 1 December 1880

BALDWIN, Herbert, Postmaster at Mossel Bay, 1909

BALE, SHJ, Postmaster at Kariega Station, 1 May 1879

Postmaster at Middleton, 1881

BALL, HS, Postmaster at Toise River, 1 August 1889

BALLOT, HW, Postmaster at Vlakteplaats, 10 June 1868, service provided for free

BALSTON, FE, Postmaster at East London, 4 November 1848

BALSTON, Isaac, Church clerk, Postmaster at Wynberg, 1 February 1827

BAM, Christian Jacobus, Postmaster at Upington, 10 April 1886

BAMBERGER, AN, Postmaster at Robertson, 9 February 1859

BANNETT, H, Postmaster at Norval's Pont, 1 November 1896

BANTJES, C, Postmaster at Zeekoegat, Division of Prince Albert, 1 April 1878

BANTJES, M, Postmaster at Zeekoegat, Division of Prince Albert, 1 May 1873, service provided-for free

BAQUEY, GA De Lanjeac, Postmaster at Maseru, in about 1880

BARBEY, George William, Postmaster at Daniel's Kuil, 1 November 1899

Postmaster at Taungs, 1 October 1902

Postmaster at Queen Street, Port Elizabeth, 1 April 1903

By 1910 George Barbey was an Assistant Postmaster in Port Elizabeth at a salary £235 pa

BARENDSE, Mr, Letter carrier, GPO, in about 1863, deceased while in office in 1863

BARENDSE, HJ, Postmaster at Woodstock Station, 23 November 1857

BARKER, E, Clerk to the Chief Magistrate, Griqualand East, and postmaster at Kokstad, 15 August 1876

BARKER, EL, Station master at Mafeking, 21 June 1907, salary £288 pa

BARKER, G, Postmaster at Clarkebury, 1 August 1878

BARKER, JM, Postmaster at Lusikisiki, 1 March 1900

BARKER, Mrs S, Postmaster at Molen River, 1 July 1876

BARKER, W, Postmaster and field-cornet at Blood River, 1 March 1870

BARKER, WH, Postmaster at Glenconnor, 1880

BARNARD, F, Postmaster at Steenberg's Cove, 7 August 1862

BARNARD, JH, Postmaster at Armoed, 1 August 1897

BARNARD, Mrs MJ, Postmaster at Villiersdorp, 25 June 1900

Postmaster at Philadelphia, 14 April 1903

BARNARD, PH, Postmaster at Storm's Vlei, 1 March 1904

BARNES, C, Surveyor, Provincial Post Office, Deceased. In November 1909 his widow was receiving a pension of £17.16.8d pa

BARNES, G, Surveyor of Provincial Post Offices, GPO, 17 March 1881

BARNES, JB, Post Office Agent for the Orange Free State, and postmaster at Aliwal North, 18 November 1856

BARNES, SR, Postmaster at Bolotwa, 1883

BARNES, WA, also listed as BURNESS, Postmaster at Hanover, 6 September 1855

BARNETT, Charles, Postmaster at Ibeka, in about 1879

BARNETT, HRC, Postmaster at St Marks, 1 October 1894

BARNHARDT, A, Postmaster at Klaarstroom, 1 September 1873

BARR, D, Postmaster at St Marks, 10 September 1874

BARRABLE, DS, Postmaster at Queenstown, 5 December 1860

BARRABLE, W, Postmaster at Molteno, 1881

BARRABLE, Walter Eric, Postmaster at Clarkebury, 1 September 1906

    Postmaster at Cofimvaba, 1 December 1908, Salary £160 pa Civil Service records show that this appointment may have been made much earlier, on 1 March 1904

BARRETT, AH, Postmaster at Touws River, 1 October 1883

    Postmaster at Fraserburg Road, 1888

    Postmaster at Carnarvon, 1 September 1888

    For further details see also under GC Geyer, station master at Montagu Road and Touws River

BARRETT, Edward, Served in Postal Department from 10 April 1894 to 1 July 1901

    Postmaster at Middledrift, 1 November 1896

    Postmaster at Herschel, 1 June 1897

    Postmaster at Rosebank, 1 May 1899

    Passed the Civil Service Law Examination, probably in about 1900 or early in 1901

    Clerk to the Resident Magistrate, Mount Ayliff,

    Assistant Magistrate, 1 July 1901

    Transferred to the Prime Minister's Office, Deparment of Native Affairs

    Acting Chief Clerk, Native Affairs Office, 1 June 1907, confirmed 1 Jan. 1908, Salary £400 pa

BARRETT, HR, Postmaster at St Marks, 1 November 1895

BARRETT, John Edward Parker, Postmaster at Wellington Station, 10 April 1899

    Postmaster at Beaufort West Station, 1 January 1904

    Postmaster at Britstown, 1 June 1906

    Postmaster at Vryburg, 1909, Salary £300 pa

BARRON, TJ, Acting postmaster at Lady Frere, 1907

    Postmaster at Lady Frere, 1 June 1907

BARRY, C, Postmaster at Caledon Street, Cape Town, 1 March 1901

BARRY, M, Postmaster at Orange Grove, Division of Victoria East, 26 April 1855

BARRY, Maurice Clifford, Postmaster at Cofimvaba, 1 August 1903

BARRY, P, Postmaster at Whittlesea, 1 December 1894

    Postmaster at Komgha, 1 May 1896

    Postmaster at Calitzdorp, 15 December 1897

BARRY, T, Postmaster at Port Beaufort, 12 August 1853

BARTMAN, LPJ, Postmaster at Hottentot's Kloof, 1 April 1875

BARWELL, AL, Postmaster at Hopefield, 1 January 1897

BASHFORTH, T, Messenger, Post Office, Cape Town. The Pension Lists of 30 November 1909 record that in 1910 Mr Bashforth was retired on an annual pension of £33.15.8

BASSON, JJ, Postmaster at Paardenberg, 1 July 1879

BASSON, T, Postmaster and field-cornet at Paardeberg, 1 July 1879

BASTIAANSE, Geneite, Issuer of Process and postmaster at Porterville 5 March 1875

BATCHELOR, Herbert Henry, also listed as BACHELOR
  Postmaster at Idutywa, 1 May 1882
  Postmaster at Qumbu, 1885
  Postmaster at Butterworth, 15 July 1886
  Postmaster at Barkly East, 1 April 1896
  Postmaster at Alice, 16 June 1896
  Postmaster at Indwe, 1 February 1903, Salary £340 pa

BATEMAN, Postmaster at Porterville Road, 1881

BATHURST, Bartholomew, Postmaster at Nelspoort, 1 September 1896
  Station master at Observatory Road, 25 August 1908, Salary £232 pa

BATTENHAUSEN, C, Postmaster at Philipstown, 1 January 1873
  Postmaster at Britstown, 1 April 1878

BATTY, GM, Postmaster at Hanover, 26 May 1857

BAUMGARDT, GD, Postmaster at Clanwilliam, 7 November 1838

BAUSER, J, Postmaster at Diep River, 15 January 1875

BAYLY, B, Management, Department of Telegraphs, 1880

BAYNE, GC, Clerk, seventh class, GPO, Cape Town, 22 November 1860
  Clerk, sixth class, GPO, Cape Town, 1863
  Clerk, fourth class, GPO, Cape Town, 1864

BEAMISH, Arthur Lenny, Postmaster at Hout Kraal, 1 January 1904

BEAMISH, C, Postmaster at Somerset East, 2 June 1853

BEARDMORE, John Markham, Assistant Postmaster at Muizenburg, ca 1. January 1902, Salary £245 pa

BEARDMORE, WH, Postmaster at Clarkebury, 1 September 1896

BEATTIE, DAG, Caretaker, Post Office, Port Elizabeth. The Pension Lists of 30 November 1909 record that in 1910 Mr Beattie, age 50, was retired on an annual pension of £43.13.11

BEATTY, H, Postmaster at Barkly West, 1 March 1896
  Postmaster at Klipdam, 8 June 1896

BEAUMONT, HG, Postmaster at Kenhardt, 1 April 1892

BECKER, C, Postmaster at Barkly West, 1 January 1896

BECKER, Cecil Francis John, Telegraphist at Fort Beaufort, 12 June 1887
  Postmaster at Belmont, 1 November 1888
  Postmaster at Millwood, Goldfields, 1 October 1889

Postmaster at Calitzdorp, 1 December 1890

Appointed to Fixed Establishment on 1 April 1895

Postmaster at Philipstown, 1 September 1896

Postmaster at St George's Street, Cape Town, 1 March 1898

Postmaster at Fort Beaufort, 1 October 1907, Salary £340 pa

BECKER, Fredric, Postmaster at Burghersdorp, 1 April 1867

BECKER, H, Postmaster at Darling, 1 June 1870

BECKER, J, Postmaster at Riversdale, 3 December 1851

Postmaster at Malmesbury, 1 January 1862

BECKER, JD, Postmaster at Steinkopf, 1 September 1875, service provided for free in 1875-77 and again in 1879-81

BECKER, RS, Postmaster at Worcester Station, before 1896

Postmaster at Laingsburg, 1 June 1896

BECKETT, D, Postmaster at Vlugt, 1 April 1868, service provided for free

BEDGOOD, G, Postmaster and station master at King William's Town Station, 25 April 1879

BEEL, W, Postmaster at Commadagga, 1880

BEERE, CR, Clerk and Controller, Circulation Branch, GPO, Cape Town, 14 June 1870

BEERY, J, Postmaster at Bedford, in about 1878

BEGLEY, DC, born in about 1855

Postmaster at Victoria West, 1 July 1881

Postmaster at Rondebosch, 1 December 1896

Postmaster at Colesberg, 1 July 1898

Postmaster at Fort Beaufort, 1 December 1902

Postmaster at Port Alfred, 1906

Postmaster at Queen Street, Port Elizabeth, 1 November 1906

Postmaster at Port Elizabeth, 1 October 1908

The Pension Lists of 30 November 1909 record that in 1910 Mr Begley, age 54, was retired on an annual pension of £212.11.10

BEGLEY, Vincent Henry, Station master at Blaney Junction, 18 June 1904, salary £255 pa

BEHRENS, JFH, also listed as J and H BEHRENS

Postmaster and station master at Goudini Road, 25 September 1878

Postmaster at Matjesfontein, Division of Worcester, 1880

Postmaster at Calvinia, 1 May 1882

Postmaster at Clanwilliam, 1 July 1891

Postmaster at Somerset West, 1 February 1892

Postmaster at Somerset Strand, 1 May 1892

Postmaster at Piquetberg, 1 March 1897

Assistant Postmaster, GPO, date not known. The Pension Lists of 30 November 1909 record that in 1910 Mr Behrens, age 55, was retired on an annual pension of £139.12.4

BEIMEISTER, JW, Postmaster at Claremont Station, 1 August 1875

Postmaster at Mowbray Station, 1880

Postmaster at Salt River, 1881

BEIMEISTER, WG, Postmaster at Ceres Road, 1 April 1889

BEINEKE, FW, Postmaster at Ebenezer, 15 December 1858, service provided for free in 1870

BEINEKE, FW Jun, Postmaster at Ebenezer, 1 February 1877

BEINEKE, TW, Postmaster at Ebenezer, 1 March 1872, service provided for free in 1872

BEKKER, Miss ME, Postmaster at Bolotwa, 1 April 1901

Postmaster at Jamestown, 1 February 1903

Postmaster at East London Jetty, 1 April 1903

Postmaster at Jamestown, 1 May 1903

Postmaster at Clarkebury, 1 March 1905

Postmaster at Cofimvaba, 1 December 1905

BELL, Charles George Harland, Postmaster at Leribe, 1 February 1875

Postmaster at Advance Post, 1 July 1877

Harland Bell was born in 1825, and entered the British army on 23 March 1843 when he was commissioned an Ensign in the 63rd Regiment of Foot, in Madras, India. When his regiment returned to England in 1844 he was promoted to Lieutenant, and on 5 May 1848 he exchanged to the Cape Mounted Riflemen. He served with distinction on the eastern frontier of the Cape during the war of 1850-53, purchased his Captaincy in 1858, was gazetted Brevet Major on 6 June 1856, and sold out in that rank on 8 August 1862. He would have obtained the regulation £1800 for his commission. He should not be confused with Charles Davidson Bell, Surveyor-General of the Cape 1852-72. On 13 May 1871 the Cape Government appointed Bell as Magistrate of the Leribe District, in northern Basutoland, where he soon gained the reputation of being a just and fair-minded administrator, becoming known as *Majorobello* to local baSotho. The contradictions inherent in the concept of being a respected colonial official were demonstrated a few years later, during the War of the Gun of 1880-81, when Bell commanded the besieged garrison at Leribe, sharing this responsibility with his son, Charles (Tylden 1948). Even though the camp was under constant attack from well-armed baSotho warriors, whenever a dispute arose amongst his opponents over a point of law, a deputation would be sent to Bell under a flag of truce and he would be requested to try the case. After it was heard and sentence was passed, the baSotho would be escorted outside the defensive perimeter and hostilities would be allowed to resume. Bell died on 2 July 1881, probably as a result of physical exhaustion (Tylden 1948)

BELL, Fitzwilliam Edward Carry, Postmaster at Advance Post, 1 July 1876

Postmaster at Maseru, 1 July 1877

First appointed Resident Magistrate at Berea, 26 January 1874, and thereafter acted as Resident Magistrate at various locations in Basutoland, Transkei and Griqualand East. He served in the military during the War of the Gun of 1880-81

BELL, HC, also listed as ER BELL

Postmaster at Queenstown, 5 July 1853

Postmaster at Somerset East, possible date 5 July 1854

Postmaster at Queenstown, 10 February 1855

BELL, Joseph, Postmaster at Struis Bay, 4 August 1854, service provided for free

BELL, James Browne, Emigrated to the Cape in 1898, postmaster at Klaarstroom, 16 May 1899, Salary £13.9.0 pa

BELL, JC, Clerk, second class, GPO, Cape Town, 1 February 1859

Clerk, first class, GPO, Cape Town, 1863

Clerk and Controller, Circulation Branch, GPO, Cape Town, 1867

Civil Commissioner and Resident Magistrate, Stockenstrom, 1870

BELL, Robert, Station master at Vlottenberg, 1 June 1893, salary £235 pa

BELL, Mrs RCE, Postmaster at Napier, 14 January 1878

BELLINGHAM, J, also listed as T BELLINGHAM and as BILLINGHAM, J

Postmaster and station master at Addo, 1 June 1876

Postmaster at Centlivres, 1 July 1877

Postmaster at Zwartkops Station, 22 October 1879

BELLIS, James Henry, Postmaster at Salt River, 1 October 1908

BELSHAW, A, Postmaster at Genadendal, 1883

BELSHAW, Ellen, Postmaster at Genadendal, 6 January 1858

BEMMING, G, Postmaster at Berlin Station, 1 August 1873

BENDELACH, C, Postmaster at Daggaboersnek, 18 November 1859

BENEKE, AH, Postmaster at Kruis River, 1 January 1863

BENEKE, DJ, Postmaster at Kruis River, 4 May 1867

Postmaster at Buffelsklip, 15 January 1868, may not have taken office

BENJAMIN, B, Postmaster at Richmond Road, 1 April 1896

BENJAMIN, Ch, Postmaster at Drooge Vlei, 17 May 1876

BENN, AR, also listed as AB BENN

Postmaster at Vlakteplaats, 1 July 1869, service provided for free

Postmaster at Kruis River, Upper Olifants River, 19 August 1871, service provided for free

BENNECKE, W, Postmaster at Prince Albert, 1 January 1849

BENNETT, A, Postmaster at New Kloof, 9 September 1864, service provided for free

BENNETT, Miss Kate, Postmaster at Kenilworth, Cape Town, 1 April 1895

Clerk in charge of Telephone Exchange, GPO, Cape Town, 1 March 1905, salary £160 pa

BENNETT, R, Postmaster at Matjesfontein, Division of Worcester, 1 June 1893

BENNING, T, Postmaster at Farm No 91, July 1862

BENSUSAN, R, Postmaster at Springbokfontein, 1 September 1870

BENTLEY, T, Postmaster at Tylden, 1 October 1861

BENTLEY, WD, Postmaster at St Marks, 1 November 1886

BERGH, Adriaan Vincent. On 2 March 1792 Acting Governor Johan Isaac Rhenius appointed Adriaan Vincent Bergh the first Postmaster of the Cape. Following the first British occupation of the Cape, on 11 June 1795, he took the oath of allegiance to the British Crown, and was allowed to retain his position until 1798, when he was replaced by John Holland. On 18 October 1820 he was appointed the first postmaster of Clanwilliam, and filled this position until 15 December 1826. Bergh married his first wife, Angelique Wilhelmina Falck, in 1794, and his second, Cornelia Sophia Cruywagen, in 1802. He died in 1852

BERGH, OM, Postal contractor and postmaster at Pakhuis, 1 February 1862, service provided for free in 1870

BERGMAN, Mrs GC, Postmaster at Caledon, 1 October 1823
Postmaster at Simonstown, 25 March 1830

BERGMANN, FW, Postmaster at Rhodes, 1 June 1897

BERLINER, G, Acting postmaster at Peiserton, 13 March 1907
Postmaster at Peiserton, 1 May 1907

BERNBERG, C, Postmaster at Fairfield, 5 March 1861, service provided for free

BERNHARDI, JH, Postmaster at Worcester, 8 March 1854

BERNHARDT, Harold, Postmaster at Glen Lynden, 1 March 1910

BERRINGTON, Miss Ch, Postmaster at Kowie West, 1 September 1853

BERRINGTON, Ch, Postmaster at Port Alfred, 1 September 1853

BERRY, JJW, Postmaster at Port Beaufort, 1 April 1877

BERTRAM, PD, Postmaster at Klopper's Fontein, 1 January 1866

BEST, JE, Postmaster at Kalk Bay, 1 September 1870

BESTER, AE, Postmaster and field-cornet at Brak River West 25, Oct 1858, service provided free

BESTER, AJ, Postmaster at Langebaan, 15 December 1860, service provided for free in 1867

BESTER, C, Postmaster at Genadendal, 1 September 1909

BESTER, Miss HJ, Postmaster at Genadendal, 1 July 1906

BEVAN, James, Postmaster and assistant field-cornet at Balmoral, Division of Uitenhage, 28 September 1863

BEVAN, John, Postmaster at Zwarte Koppen, 16 May 1860
Postmaster and assistant field-cornet at Balmoral, Division of Uitenhage, 1 April 1865

BEYERS, JA, Postmaster at Houw Hoek, 1 January 1863

BICCARD, JJ, Postmaster and field-cornet at Zout Rivier, 1 August 1864, service provided for free in 1867-72, deceased while in office

BIDEN, Arthur E, Employed temporarily at the GPO, Cape Town, 1871, confirmed, 1 Oct 1872
Clerk, second class, GPO, Cape Town, 1 January 1876
Chief Clerk and Assistant Accountant, GPO, Cape Town, 1 July 1881
Postmaster at Grahamstown, 1 May 1892
The Pension Lists of 30 November 1909 record that in 1910 Mr Biden, age 52, was retired on an annual pension of £150

BIDEN, MB, Postmaster at Zoute Kloof, 1 January 1877

BIDDULPH, E, Postmaster at Cuylerville, 11 August 1860
Postmaster at Blaauw Krantz, Division of Cradock, 1 July 1868

BIDDULPH, WB, Postmaster at Colesberg, 24 November 1840

BIEBUYCK, Julian Francoise, Postmaster at Porterville, 1 March 1898
- Postmaster at Montagu, 1 August 1900
- Acting postmaster at Laingsburg, 1904
- Postmaster at Laingsburg, 1 April 1904
- Postmaster at Ceres Road, 1 November 1907
- Postmaster at Wellington Station, 1 October 1908
- Postmaster at Prince Albert, 1 February 1909

BIERMANN, Miss AJ, Postmaster at Van Wyk's Vlei, 1 January 1906

BIGG, JB, Postmaster and field-cornet at Murraysburg, 1 December 1861

BIGGAR, Mrs Mary, was born in England in about 1781 and married Capt Alexander Biggar in about 1800. Over the next twenty years she bore him eleven children, the last of whom was born aboard the *Weymouth* en route to Algoa Bay, where they landed on 15 May 1820. After the death of her husband in Zululand in 1839 she settled in Port Elizabeth where she was appointed postmaster on 17 December 1840, a position she held until her retirement in 1852. During her tenure she conducted all postal business from her home in Chapel Lane, just off Main Street, and although she did move once, on 2 July 1845, this was to another house, only a few doors away in the same street. She died in Grahamstown on 9 February 1855, at the age of 74. Her daughter Ann married Robert Newton Dunn of Port Alfred, where she gave birth to John Dunn, who subsequently worked in Zululand as a hunter and a trader

BIGGS, J, Postmaster at Sandflats, 1 April 1872, service provided for free

BILK, George, Postmaster at Kenhardt, 16 May 1899
- Postmaster at Hopetown, 1 July 1902
- Postmaster at Lawrence Street, Port Elizabeth, 1 June 1903
- Postmaster at Douglas, 1 April 1904

BILLINGHAM, J, see under BELLINGHAM, J

BING, W, Postmaster at Bathurst, 1 February 1894

BIRBECK, Mason, Postmaster at Witmoss Station, 20 November 1894
- Station master at Adelaide, 1 November 1903, salary £232 pa

BIRCH, J, Postmaster and station master at Kariega Station, 1 January 1878
- Postmaster and station master at Glenconnor, 1 February 1879
- Postmaster at Zwartkops Station, 1880

BIRD, TC, Clerk to the Civil Commissioner and postmaster at Burghersdorp, 21 February 1848

BIRKETT, CJBF, born in about 1857, Postmaster and station master at Bedford, 6 May 1879
- Postmaster at Naauwpoort, 1 September 1899
- Postmaster at Graaff-Reinet, 1 July 1906
- The Pension Lists of 30 November 1909 record that in 1910 Mr Birkett, age 52, was retired on an annual pension of £280.4.5

BIRKETT, JP, Postmaster at Beaufort West, 1881
- Postmaster at Queenstown, 1 March 1890, deceased while in office. On 30 November 1909 his widow, EW Birkett was receiving an annual pension of £21.14.8

BIRT, Mrs, see under SCOTT, Mrs

BIRT, J, also listed as Widow R BIRT, Postmaster and field-cornet at Gwelegha River, 1 October 1870

BIRT, J, Postmaster at Birt's Farm, 1 October 1879

BIRT, R, Postmaster and field-cornet at Gwelegha River, 1 July 1862

BISHOP, GD, Postmaster at Draghoender, 1 March 1901
Postmaster at Draghoender, 1 August 1902

BISSET, Alexander, Postmaster at Bathurst, 1 January 1825
Alexander Bisset was a member of the Willson party, which sailed to the Cape in 1820 on the *Belle Alliance*. His son, Sir John Bisset, was prominent in the military defence of the eastern frontier, and was appointed Lt-Governor of Natal in 1865

BISSETT, JW, Postmaster at Malmesbury Station, 1882

BLACK, Capt, Postmaster at Boetsap, 1881

BLACKBURN, GS, Postmaster at Carlisle Bridge, in about 1910

BLACKWELL, Arthur, Postmaster at Witteklip, 1 November 1909
Postmaster at Thornhill, Division of Herbert, 1 February 1910

BLAKE, John, Postmaster at Colesberg, 1 September 1843, possibly acting

BLAND, JA, Postmaster at Gouritz River, 1835

BLANDFORD, William George, Postmaster at O'Okiep, 1 August 1902

BLANKENBERG, D, Clerk to Civil Commissioner and acting postmaster at Cradock, June 1849

BLATCHFORD, WL, Postmaster at Durbanville, 1873

BLATHERWICK, Miss Julia Florence, Postmaster at Vredenburg, 1 February 1904
Postmaster at Kuils River, 1 April 1906

BLATT, JD, Postmaster at Hutchinson, 1 July 1890
Postmaster at Matjesfontein, Division of Worcester, 1 February 1892

BLECKSLEY, A, Postmaster at Paarl Station, 1881

BLEKSLEY, ARH, Postmaster at Springbokfontein, 8 June 1864

BLEKSLEY, Herbert Harold, Postmaster at Qumbu, 25 June 1898
Postmaster at Matatiele, 1 June 1899
Postmaster at Elliot, 1 April 1902
Postmaster at Umzimkulu, 1 July 1904
Postmaster at Matatiele, 1 October 1905

BLIGNAUT, J, Postmaster at Gamka's Vlakte, 31 July 1867, service provided for free
Postmaster at Calitzdorp, 31 July 1867, service provided for free

BLOCK, W, Postmaster at Maraisburg, 1 March 1879

BLYTH, Charles Archibald, Postmaster at West Bank, 1 November 1908

BLYTH, Capt MT, Government Agent to Fingoland, c1877 (SESA 1972)

BOASE, Henry, Postmaster at Somerset West, 1 January 1846

BOBBERT, J, Postmaster at Ladismith, 29 August 1857

BODEN, FW, Postmaster at Kei Road, 1 January 1907

Assistant postmaster East London, date of appointment not known, retired on pension in 1909

BOHM, J, Postmaster at Walfish Bay, 1883

BOKWE, John Knox, (1855-1922). On 1 July 1895 the Rev John Knox Bokwe was appointed Postmaster and telegrapher at Lovedale, thus becoming South Africa's first known black Postmaster (PMG 1895, POC 163). However this was not his first appointment and by the time he resigned this post in 1897 the Rev Bokwe had been associated with the Cape Postal Establishment for nearly twenty-four years. It is probable therefore that he was appointed Lovedale's first postmaster when its post office was opened in 1873. Apart from his skills as a postal administrator the Rev Bokwe was also a leading member of the Lovedale intellectual elite. He was an accomplished composer and is remembered for his many songs and hymns in Xhosa, while during the 1870s and 1880s he assisted Dr Stewart in editing *The Christian Express* and *Isigidimi*. He was ordained into the Presbyterian Church late in life, and eventually retired to minister to the racially mixed congregation at Ugie, in the Eastern Cape. When he resigned from the Post Office in 1897, the Cape's Postmaster General, Somerset French wrote that *"I regret to see that it is necessary for you to sever your connection with this Department after so many years of service ... I would ask you to accept my thanks for the very efficient and satisfactory manner in which the Lovedale Office has been conducted by you"* (Lovedale Annual Report, 1897)

BOLTMAN, Mrs C, Postmaster at Wynberg, 9 June 1837

BOLTMAN, C, Postmaster at Villiersdorp, 16 February 1873

BOLTMAN, FJ, Postmaster at Villiersdorp, 1 October 1877

BOND, Charles Alfred, born in about 1856
   United Kingdom Telegraph Service, Southampton, 1871
   Cape Government Telegraphs, Cape Town, 1879
   Postmaster at Worcester, 13 December 1880
   GPO, Cape Town, in about 1883
   Postmaster at Worcester, 1 March 1886
   Assistant Accountant, GPO, Cape Town 1893, post relinquished for reasons of health
   Postmaster at Queenstown, 16 May 1897
   Postmaster at Kimberley, 1 November 1903
   GPO, Cape Town, probable date 1 September 1908
   Retired from service, in about 1909

BOND, Gerald William, Postmaster at Muizenberg, 1 July 1890
   Postmaster at Hutchinson, 1 February 1892
   Postmaster at Prieska, 1 December 1893
   Postmaster at Observatory Road, 1 August 1908

BOONZAAIER, JH, Postmaster and field-cornet at Voor Riebeek's Kasteel, 29 May 1858, service provided for free in 1867-73

BOOTH, B, Postmaster and field-cornet at Koonap, in about 1860, service provided for free

BOOYSEN, Thomas Arnold, Telegraphist at Ceres Road, 1892
   Postmaster at Moorreesburg, before 1895

Postmaster at Balfour, 1 November 1895
Postmaster at Pearston, 1 February 1897
Postmaster at Krakeel River, 1 July 1900
Postmaster at Steytlerville, 1 February 1901
Postmaster at West Bank, 1 October 1902
Postmaster at Komgha, 1 January 1903
Postmaster at Ceres Road, 1906
Postmaster at Laingsburg, 1 November 1907
Postmaster at Richmond, 1 December 1908

BORCHERDS, Carl Gerhard Blanckenberg, Clerk, Customs, Cape Town, March 1873
Provisional appointment, GPO, Cape Town, August 1874
Clerk, third class, GPO, Cape Town, 1 January 1876
Magistrate's Clerk, Carnarvon, February 1877. Eventually rose to Civil Commissioner and Resident Magistrate at Sutherland (1889), Murraysburg (1892), and Uniondale (1896)

BORCHERDS, HJ, Postmaster at Graaff-Reinet, 15 August 1834

BORCHERDS, JG, Clerk to the Civil Commissioner and postmaster at Caledon, 1 January 1848

BORCHERDS, JH, Postmaster at Clanwilliam, 2 June 1853

BORCHERDS, Miss M, Postmaster at Aberdeen, Division of Aberdeen, 1 May 1878

BORCHERDS, Peter Borchardus, Postmaster at Klaarstroom, 1 November 1891
Postmaster at Ladismith, 1 June 1892
Postmaster at Herschel, 1 November 1893
Postmaster at Mount Frere, 1 June 1894
Postmaster at Molteno, 1 December 1895
Postmaster at Calitzdorp, 16 April 1899
Postmaster at North End, Port Elizabeth, 1 April 1902
Postmaster at Vosburg, 1 April 1903
Postmaster at Wellington Station, 1 September 1906
Postmaster at Laingsburg, 1 October 1908

BOSCH, Miss C, also listed as M BOSCH
Postmaster at Riebeek East, 1 January 1896
Postmaster at Waverley Siding, 1 December 1902
Postmaster at Balfour, 1 July 1905

BOSMAN, AD, Postmaster at Bellville, 1 October 1887

BOSMAN, CF, Postmaster at Van Wyk's Vlei, 1 August 1902

BOSMAN, HL, Postmaster at Seven Weeks Poort, 1880

BOSMAN, JC, Postmaster at Steytlerville, 1 September 1879
Postmaster at Porterville, 1 June 1887
On 1 September 1879 a post office was established on the site, with Mr JC Bosman, a local storekeeper, as its first postmaster. It is probable that from 1879 to 1887 the postal affairs of the village were run from Mr Bosman's store.

BOTES, Miss Cora Francis, Postmaster at Dam's Laagte, 1 January 1901
  Postmaster at Albertinia, 1 October 1908, £72 pa
BOTES, DJ, Postmaster at Dam's Laagte, 1 October 1908
BOTHA, C, Postmaster and field-cornet at Stanley, 1 October 1861
BOTHA, DB, Postmaster and field-cornet at Goudini Road, 1 December 1864
BOTHA, F, Postmaster at Van Wyk's Vlei, 1 January 1903
BOTHA, FC, Postmaster at Hout Kraal, in about 1906
  Postmaster at Orange River, 1 November 1906
BOTHA, HPR, Postmaster at Serjeant's River, 1 August 1867
BOTHA, JS, Postmaster at Zout Rivier, 1863
BOTHA, L, Postmaster at Kruis River, Cango, 3 September 1858
BOTHA, P, Postmaster at Stanley, 25 June 1860
BOTHA, ST, Postmaster at Paardeberg, 26 September 1872, deceased while in office
BOTHA, TC, Postmaster at Goudini Road, 10 May 1858, not the same person as the postmaster at Voorste Bosjesveld
BOTHA, TC, Postmaster and field-cornet at Voorste Bosjesveld, 10 May 1858, not the same person as the postmaster at Goudini Road
BOTHA, TC, Postmaster at Rawsonville, 1 January 1898
BOTHA, WJ, Postmaster at Mount Fletcher, 1 November 1902
BOTHAM, C, Postmaster at Tabankulu, 1 April 1900
BOTTING, George, Postmaster at Struis Bay, 26 June 1855, service provided for free
BOURHILL, H Jnr, Postmaster at Caledon, 1 August 1863
BOURHILL, JC, Postmaster at Caledon, 4 December 1851
BOUWER, WC, Postmaster and field-cornet at Mapassa's Leven, 29 September 1858
BOWERS, Albert William, Postmaster at Prince Albert Road, 12 October 1900
  Station master at Claremont, 23 April 1902, salary £247 pa
BOWDEN, FW, Postmaster at Beaufort West Station, 1 November 1899
BOWE, Mary A, Postmaster at Hondeklip Bay, 1 October 1869
BOWERS, Albert William, Station master at Claremont, appointed 23 April 1902, salary £247 pa
BOWIE, J, Inspector, GPO, Cape Town. The Pension Lists of 30 November 1909 recorded that in 1910 Mr Bowie, age 57, was retired on an annual pension of £153.12.2
BOWKER, W, Postmaster and field-cornet at Bowden, 29 September 1859
BOWKER, WM, Postmaster at Bowden, 1 January 1866
BOWLES, AF, Postmaster at Tsolo, 16 May 1899
  Postmaster at Tsolo, 1 November 1902
  Postmaster at Ugie, 1 April 1906
  Postmaster at Tsolo, 1 November 1906
BOWLES, WW, Postmaster at Mqanduli, 1 August 1897
  Postmaster at Tsolo, 16 August 1897
  Postmaster at Umzimkulu, 16 May 1899

BOX, Alfred, Station master at Vryburg, 19 September 1909, salary £248 pa

BOYD, CR, Postmaster at Campbell, 1 June 1893

BOYD, J, Postmaster at Nababeep, before 1907

    Reappointed postmaster at Nababeep, 1 October 1907

BOYES, BJ, Postmaster at Wellington Station, 1 December 1888

    Postmaster at Jansenville, 1 July 1890

    Postmaster at Matjesfontein, Division of Worcester, 1 April 1892

    Postmaster at Laingsburg, 1 March 1893

    Postmaster at Britstown, 1 May 1893

    Postmaster at Hoetjes Bay, 1 July 1894

    Postmaster at Philipstown, 1 September 1894

    Postmaster at Norval's Pont, 16 July 1898

    Postmaster at Klipdam, 1 September 1899

BOYES, RCR, Clerk to the Civil Commissioner and postmaster at Cradock, 23 May 1850

BOYES, Mrs Sarah, Postmaster at Plumstead, 1 October 1841

    Postmaster at Wynberg, 1 November 1841

    On 1 November 1841 Mrs Sarah Boyes was appointed postmaster at Wynberg at an annual stipend of £6, and on 12 March 1846 she was transferred to Plumstead, where a new post office was established. However, given the fact that on 1 October 1841 Mrs Boyes had also been appointed postmaster at Plumstead, it seems probable that, from 1841 to 1846 she ran the postal business of both villages from Wynberg

BRADFIELD, E, Postmaster and field-cornet at Wolvefontein, Division of Albert, 14 September 1864, service provided for free

BRADLEY, Mr, The post office at Fourteen Streams was closed on 31 March 1892. As a result a post office agency was opened sometime between April and June 1892 at Mr Bradley's Store, adjoining the railway halt (POC 124)

BRADLEY, Henry, Colour Sergeant, His Majesty's 6th Regiment, and postmaster at Breakfast Vlei, 27 June 1856

BRADLEY, John Watson, was born in about 1855 and joined the United Kingdom Telegraph Company in 1869, being employed at South Shields. The following year he transferred to Imperial Government Service, and in 1879 moved to the Cape Government Telegraph Service. There he rose to the position of Senior Telegrapher, and remained in Cape Town until 1 September 1882 when he was appointed postmaster at George. Thereafter he served as postmaster at Beaufort West from 1 March 1886, Beaconsfield from 1 December 1888, returned to Cape Town as Superintendent, Circulation Branch on 1 January 1896, and finally became the postmaster for Grahamstown on 1 November 1903. He retired from the Service in about August 1908 (Bennett 1908). The Pension Lists of 30 November 1909 recorded that in 1910 Mr Bradley, age 51, was retired on an annual pension of £353.6.8

BRADY, GV, Postmaster at Rhodes, 1 February 1909

BRAMLEY, H, born in about 1860

Postmaster at Prince Albert, 15 February 1879

Postmaster at Riversdale, 1 March 1883

Postmaster at Mossel Bay, 1 October 1887

The Pension Lists of 30 November 1909 recorded that in 1910 Mr Bramley, age 49, had probably taken early retirement with an annual pension of £52.5.4

BRAND, Peter Christian, Postmaster at Nelspoort, 1 December 1893

Postmaster at Redhouse, 1 June 1899

Station master at Firgrove 23 September 1909, salary £247 pa

BRANFIELD, William, Postmaster at Kalk Bay, before 1885

Postmaster at Porterville Road, 1 April 1885

Station master at Aliwal North, 12 March 1897, salary £297 pa

BRANTHWAITE, JH, Postmaster at Dynamite Factory, 1 September 1902

BRAY, Arthur Rooum, Postmaster at North End, Port Elizabeth, 1 June 1910

BRAY, JS, Postmaster at Philipstown, 1 March 1896

BRAY, James Kirkwood, Born in Glasgow, Scotland, and emigrated to the Cape in 1889

Postmaster at Caledon Street, Cape Town, 1 December 1902

BRECHER, Ferdinand, Postmaster at Steinkopf, 9 December 1859, service provided for free. Reappointed postmaster at Steinkopf in 1881

The village of Steinkopf was established in 1818 as a station of the London Missionary Society. Within a few years members of its congregation, which consisted largely of migrant-pastoralist Khoikhoi, had slowly migrated away in their search for water and fresh grazing. As a result the station was moved to a new site known as Kookfontein, and in 1840 its control was transferred to the Rhenish Missionary Society. In about 1859 the missionary Ferdinand Brecher restored its name to Steinkopf and on 9 December 1859 he was appointed its first postmaster (SESA 1972)

BREEDE, JE, also listed as BRIELE, Postmaster at Prieska, 1 December 1895

Postmaster at Wellington Station, 1 May 1896

BREMNER, DC, Postmaster and jailer at Fort Beaufort, 2 August 1853

BREMNER, G, Clerk, GPO, Cape Town, 12 February 1874

BRENNER, J, Postmaster and police constable at Fort Beaufort, 9 December 1865

BRESLER, FO, Clerk to the Civil Commissioner and postmaster at Mossel Bay, 27 April 1848

BRESLER, G, Postmaster at Durbanville, 15 April 1847. Salary £7.10.6.

BRETT, FR, Postmaster at Villiersdorp, 7 March 1850

BRETT, J, Postmaster at Laingsburg, 3 April 1875

BRIDGER, WJ, Acting postmaster at Carnarvon, in about 1874

Postmaster at Carnarvon, 1 May 1875

BRIDLE, Edward, Postmaster at O'Okiep, 1 May 1899

Postmaster at Clanwilliam, 1 July 1900

Postmaster at Riversdale, 1 September 1900

BRIELE, JE, see under BREEDE

BRIEN, J, Postmaster and station master at Cambridge, 1 May 1877

BRIGHT, HER, Postmaster at Maseru, 1 February 1872

BRILL, W, Postmaster at Somerset West, 1876

BRIMACOMBE, Miss Eliza, see under MORRIS, Mrs Eliza

BRINE, Charles Frederick James, Station master at Fort Beaufort, 14 Oc 1904, salary £201 pa

BRINK, A, Postmaster and field-cornet at Achter Zwartland, 27 January 1862, service provided for free in 1867-71

BRINK, C, Postmaster at Molen River, 1 March 1870

BRINK, CP, Postmaster at Philadelphia, 1880

BRINK, D, Postmaster and field-cornet at Groot Berg River, 1 September 1861

Postmaster and field-cornet at Paardeberg, Division of Malmesbury, 1 June 1874

BRINK, DPS, Postmaster at Riebeek West, 1 October 1871

BRINK, F, Postmaster at Ladismith, 1 August 1861

BRINK, J, Postmaster at Durbanville, 1856

BRINK, JH, Postmaster at St Helena Bay, 1 September 1879

BRINK, John James, Postmaster at Ceres Road, 1 October 1890

Postmaster at Laingsburg, 1 February 1891

Postmaster at Sutherland, 1 July 1891

Postmaster at Britstown, 1 June 1894

Postmaster at Newlands, 1 August 1908

Postmaster at Sea Point, 1 December 1908

BRINK, Ludolph Christian, Postmaster at Krakeel River, 1 October 1893

Postmaster at Steytlerville, 1 June 1894

Postmaster at Deelfontein Station, 16 July 1900

BRINK, PAP, Clerk, second class, GPO, Cape Town, 2 January 1849. Salary £130 pa

BRINK, Tobias Mostert, Postmaster at Nieuwe Rust, 1 July 1905

BRISTOW, L, Assistant Postmaster, King William's Town. The Pension Lists of 30 November 1909 recorded that in 1910 Mr Bristow, age 54, was retired on an annual pension of £145.15.0

BRITTAIN, J, Postmaster at Wellington, 18 September 1858

BRITTAIN, J, Postmaster at Fraserburg, 15 December 1870

BROAD, G, Postmaster at Aliwal North, 1852

BROADWAY, Mrs A, Postmaster at Kuils River, 1 January 1863

BROCKLEBANK, JM, Postmaster at Prince Albert, 1882

BROCKMAN, Ernest Edward, Postmaster at Mowbray, 1 February 1902

Postmaster at Lower Paarl, 1 October 1903, probably never took office

Postmaster at Upper Paarl, 1 October 1903

Postmaster at the Houses of Parliament, 1 July 1906

Postmaster at Montagu, 1 October 1908, salary £245 pa

BRODERICK, PJ, Postmaster at Carnarvon, 1880

BROEDELET, O, Postmaster at Panmure, 1 September 1866

BROEKHUIZEN, G, Postmaster at Grahamstown, 1818

BROLE, CR, Postmaster at Leeuwfontein, Division of Bedford, 1 April 1866

BROLE, CW, Postmaster at Leeuwfontein, Division of Bedford, 14 February 1859

BRONK, Geo, Postmaster at Daggaboersnek, 1 January 1863

BROOK, HK, see under KAYE-BROOKE

BROOKS, J, Postmaster at Campbell, 1 April 1896

BROOKS, Sidney, Telegraphist at Alfred Docks, 1882
  Postmaster at St George's Street, Cape Town, 1909

BROWN, Mr, Postmaster at Claremont, 27 May 1846

BROWN, A, Secretary to the Divisional Council and postmaster at Aliwal North, 1 January 1863
  The Pension Lists of 30 November 1909 recorded that in 1910 Mr Brown was retired on an annual pension of £30

BROWN, Andrew, Postmaster at Moshesh's Ford, 2 September 1899
  Controller, Central Telegraph Office, Johannesburg, date of appointment not known

BROWN, CCH, First Superintedent of the Travelling Post Office.

BROWN, D, Postmaster at Tulbagh Road Station, 1 April 1908

BROWN, FWS, Postmaster at Kuils River, 1881

BROWN, H, Postmaster at Greytown, in about 1874

BROWN, J, Postmaster and Issuer of Stores at the Katberg Convict Station, 23 March 1867, service provided for free

BROWN, J, Postmaster at Richmond Road, before1895
  Postmaster at Retreat, 1 August 1895

BROWN, JT, Postmaster at Trumpeter's Drift, 31 August 1858

BROWN, M, Postmaster and station master at Fort Jackson, 18 December 1876
  Postmaster at Blaney Junction, 1 May 1877
  Postmaster and station master at King William's Town Station, 1 November 1877

BROWN, Miss Mary Munsie, Postmaster at Douglas, 1 July 1885
  Postmaster at Campbell, 1 September 1886
  Postmaster at Douglas, 15 January 1891
  Postmaster at Campbell, 1 May 1892
  Postmaster at Britstown, 1893
  Postmaster at Griquatown, 1 June 1893
  Postmaster at Sutherland, 1 August 1893
  Postmaster at French Hoek, 1 December 1893
  Postmaster at Griquatown, 1 May 1894
  Postmaster at Seymour, 1 October 1895
  Postmaster at Tsomo, 1 December 1895
  Postmaster at Springbokfontein, 1 January 1899
  Postmaster at Middledrift, 1 October 1902
  Postmaster at Kuruman, 1 March 1906
  Postmaster at Marydale, 1 November 1906

    Postmaster at Libodi, 1 December 1907 paid 9s6d daily
BROWN, T, Postmaster at Plettenberg's Bay, 16 April 1857
BROWNING, Mrs ME, born in about 1828
    Postmaster at Fort Beaufort, 1 April 1871
    Postmaster at East London, 24 June 1874
    Postmaster at West Bank, East London, 1 June 1877
    The Pension Lists of 30 November 1909 recorded that in 1910 Mrs Browning, age 81, was retired on an annual pension of £88.19.10
BROWNING, WA, Postmaster at East Bank, East London, 9 June 1879
BROWNLEE, William Thompson, Clerk to the Fingo Agent, Idutywa, 1 May 1876
    Postmaster at Nqamakwe, 1 December 1876
    His postal appointments appear to have been incidental to his other duties as a colonial administrator. During the Gcaleka War of 1876 he was in charge of Fingoland and served with the military in the field, thereafter supervising the removal of Gcaleka clans from Bomvanaland to the Willowvale district; during the Mthembu uprising of 1880 he had charge of a section of the Mfengu-Mthembu border, and commanded Mfengu forces; and during the South African War of 1899-1902 he was appointed Lieut-colonel in command of Mthembu and Mfengu levies. Thereafter he served as Assistant Chief Magistrate for the Transkeian territories and Resident Magistrate for Umtata
BRUNETTE, S, also listed as BURNETTE
    Postmaster and station master at Goudini Road, 1 December 1876
    Postmaster and station master at Klipheuvel, 29 September 1878
BRUNETTE, WK, Postmaster at Serjeant's River, 1 May 1879
BRUSSEL, G, Postmaster at Onderstedoorns, 1 April 1876
BRUTON, Arthur, Postmaster at Greefdale, 1 February 1891
BRUTON, T, see under BURTON, J
BUCHANAN, CK, Postmaster at Alicedale, 1882
    Postmaster at Alexandria, 5 January 1883
BUCHNER, MJ, Postmaster at Nieuwoudtville, 1 February 1900
BUDDLE, CW, Assistant Postmaster at King William's Town. The Pension Lists of 30 November 1909 recorded that in 1910 Mr Buddle, age 36, had taken early retirement on an annual pension of £100.11.7
BUDGE, HW, Postmaster at Mill Street, Gardens, Cape Town, 1 June 1903
    Postmaster at Kloof Street, Gardens, Cape Town, 1 October 1908
BUDLER, W, Postmaster at Upington, 1 February 1896
BUGLASS, Thomas, Postmaster at Eerste River Station, 1 September 1882
    Postmaster at Cathcart, 1 September 1887
    Postmaster at Sandflats, 1 January 1893
BULT, CM, Postmaster at Beaconsfield, 1881
BUNN, CH, Postmaster at Lusikisiki, 16 June 1900

Postmaster at Ugie, 1 March 1901

Postmaster at Elliot, 1 September 1902

BUNN, CJ, Postmaster at Elliot, 1 May 1904

BURGER, A, Postmaster at Tulbagh Road Station, 1 February 1910

BURGER, N, Postmaster at Houw Hoek, 1 September 1899

Postmaster at Vanrhynsdorp, 1 November 1903

BURGER, PJ, Postmaster at Uitvlugtfontein, Division of Victoria West, 16 October 1874

BURGER, RN, Postmaster at Port Nolloth, 31 October 1855

BURGER, SW, Postmaster and field-cornet at Vette Rivier, 31 August 1859, service provided for free 1867-74

BURGER, SW, Postmaster at Patatas River, 31 July 1862, service provided for free

BURGER, W, Postmaster at Brand Vlei, 1 July 1876

BURGESS, Mr, Postmaster at Colesberg, 1854

BURKE, Miss KS, Postmaster at Greyton, 1 September 1904

Postmaster at Barrydale, 1 February 1906

Postmaster at Grabouw, 1 May 1906

Postmaster at Houw Hoek, 1 August 1908

Postmaster at Barrydale, 1 October 1909

BURKE, Miss Patience A, Postmaster at Garies, 1 April 1892

Postmaster at Springbokfontein, 1 April 1903

On 12 September 1901 Republican forces entered Garies and ransacked its post office, inflicting extensive damage upon its establishment. Despite the presence of some Republican soldiers in her office, the postmaster, Miss Patience Burke, managed to save valuable mails, but the remainder of the post, as well as some stores, were set alight and destroyed. Thereafter she was detained as a prisoner in her quarters under armed guard

BURKE, M, Postmaster at Bowesdorp, 1 November 1876

BURKE, T, Postmaster at Kuils River, 7 August 1850

BURKE, WR, Postmaster at Bowesdorp, 1 August 1871, service provided for free

Postmaster at Garies, 1 January 1889

BURNESS, CL, Postmaster at Sunday's River Ferry, 7 March 1854

BURNETT, HIR, Postmaster at Fraserburg, 16 June 1857

BURROUGHS, W, Postmaster at Seven Fountains, 1 January 1867

BURTON, BG, Postmaster at Spring Valley, 1 February 1903

BURTON, J, also listed as BRUTON, T, Postmaster at Riet Vlei, Division of Uitenhage, 14 October 1858

BURTON, JH, Postmaster at Belmont, 1 January 1907

BUTCHER, J, Postmaster and station master at Blue Cliff, 1 July 1877

BUTCHER, JJ, Postmaster at Somerset Strand, 1 May 1897

BUTLER, J, Postmaster at Somerset Strand, in about 1875

BUTLER, Rev JF, Postmaster at Saron, 6 November 1853, service provided for free in 1853-57

and again in 1867-73

BUTLER, MJ, Postmaster at Mowbray, 1 March 1846

BUTLER, MT, Letter Carrier, GPO, Cape Town, 18 August 1866

BUTLER, T, Postmaster at Observatory Road, 9 Jan 1866, service provided for free in 1866-67

BUTLER, Thos, Postmaster at Aliwal North, in about 1851

BUTLER, WJ, Postmaster and station master at Rondebosch Station, 16 September 1868
Postmaster and station master at Rondebosch, 5 April 1879

BUTT, C, Postmaster and field-cornet at Salem, 1 July 1869

BUXTON, F, Postmaster at Fraserburg, 1880

BUYS, SA, Postmaster and field-cornet at Brak River North, 25 October 1858

BUYSKES, Dirk Egbert, Clerk, GPO, Cape Town, 1 January 1889
Transferred to Surveyor-General's Department, 1 October 1889

BUYSKES, PL, Postmaster at Bathurst, 14 June 1851
Clerk, fifth class, GPO, Cape Town, 2 June 1853

BYNON, WJ, Postmaster at Ceres Road, 1 June 1888
Postmaster at Touws River, 1 April 1889
GPO, Cape Town, 1 March 1891
Postmaster at Mowbray, 1 October 1903
Postmaster at Simonstown, 1909
For further details see also under GC Geyer, station master at Montagu Road and Touws River.

BYRNE, A, Postmaster at Kruis River, Upper Olifants River, 19 Aug 1870, service provided free

BYRNE, Alex, Postmaster at Oudtshoorn, 25 April 1855

BYRNE, Miss E, Assistant Postmaster at Wynberg. The Pension Lists of 30 November 1909 recorded that in 1910 Miss Byrne, age 52, was retired on an annual pension of £71.10.0

BYRNE, Mrs FM, Postmaster at Bell, 25 June 1900

BYRNE, P, Letter Carrier, GPO, Cape Town, in about 1880

BYRNE, R, Postmaster at Wynberg, 1 February 1865

BYRNE, WA, Postmaster at Wynberg, 1 March 1883

C

CADLE, H, Postmaster at Witteklip, 7 August 1861, deceased while in office

CADLE, Mrs Hannah, Postmaster at Witteklip, 1 July 1864. In 1862 Mr H Cadle of Witteklip (Van Staaden's River) was granted a license to run an *"accommodation house"* on the Cape Town road. In view of the fact that in 1861 Mr Cadle had been appointed the postmaster for Witteklip, and that in 1864 he was succeeded to this post by his wife, Hannah, it can be assumed that between 1862 and 1874 the Witte-klip post office was located at Cadle's Hotel, and was run by the Cadles as an adjunct to their establishment.

CAIRLEY, Harry, Postmaster at Klein Boetsap, 1 September 1903
Postmaster at Richmond Road, 1 March 1906
Postmaster at Biesjespoort, in about April 1906.

Cairley was born in about 1883. His last posting as postmaster was at Biesjespoort, a small railway siding located on the farm Noblesfontein, where he died suddenly on 2 May 1906, at the age of 23. He was buried in the small cemetery attached to the station, where the personnel of the Department of Posts and Telegraphs erected a fine tombstone in his memory

CAIRNCROSS, Edward George, Postmaster at Wellington, 1 April 1886

CAIRNCROSS, JC, Postmaster at Porterville Road, 1883

CAIRNCROSS, ME, Postmaster at Wellington, 20 March 1879

CAIRNCROSS, Seton Falkenberg, Postmaster at Steytlerville, 1 November 1898
  Postmaster at Whittlesea, 1 May 1899
  Postmaster at Houw Hoek, probable date 1 February 1901
  Postmaster at Calitzdorp, 1 April 1902
  Postmaster at Steytlerville, 1 December 1905

CAIRNCROSS, T, Postmaster and field-cornet at Montagu, 29 Nov 1858, suspended from duty

CAIRNCROSS, TLL, Postmaster at Steytlerville, 1 May 1890

CAIRNS, Alfred James, Postmaster at Krakeel River, 1 May 1894
  Postmaster at Hankey, 1 June 1896
  Postmaster at Jansenville, 1 April 1900
  Postmaster at Port Alfred, 1 August 1900
  Postmaster at Avontuur, 1 March 1902
  Postmaster at Pearston, 1 January 1903

CAIRNS, James Francis, also listed as J and JS, Postmaster at Eerste River Station, 1 Dec 1892
  Postmaster at Darling, 1 May 1893
  Postmaster at Hopefield, 1 June 1893
  Postmaster at Klipdam, 1 July 1894
  Postmaster at Murraysburg, 1 August 1895
  Postmaster at Hutchinson, 1 December 1897
  Postmaster at Fraserburg, 23 April 1898
  Postmaster at Worcester Station, 1 May 1900
  Postmaster at Murraysburg, 1 July 1903

CAIRNS, TG, also listed as TC, Postmaster at Alicedale, 1885
  Postmaster at Bellville, 1 April 1886

CAIRNS, Thomas Bewick, Station master at Kalk Bay, 21 July 1908, salary £247 pa

CAITHNESS, Mrs P, Postmaster at Simonstown, 18 March 1844

CALDWELL, no first name recorded, Postmaster at Swellendam, in about 1835

CALDWELL, Mrs Catharina. Catharina Hendrina Bletterman married William Caldwell on 12 February 1796, less than a month after his arrival at the Cape, and during the course of their marriage bore him two daughters. She must have been a vigorous and enterprising woman in her own right. Not only does she appear to have taken an active hand in her husband's business affairs, but on 8 May 1808 she was appointed postmaster at Stellenbosch with Mrs AC Hudson as her deputy. She filled this post for the next 38 years, with only a brief break in 1829, and retired from the Post Office in 1846, when she must have been close to 70 years old (Philip 1981: 51-2). After Caldwell's death in Cape Town on 2 July 1816, she continued to provide lodgings at their old house at 7 Bergh Street, as well as at 30 Strand Street, while also retaining her position as postmaster at Stellenbosch

CALDWELL, William, was born in May 1758 in Inverness, Scotland. Having served for a time in India as a Lieutenant in the Bengal Artillery, he arrived at the Cape on 26 January 1796 aboard the Danish ship "*Johanna*". On 12 February 1796, less than a month after his arrival, he was married to his second wife, Catharina Hendrina Bletterman, who bore him two daughters. On 7 May 1798 he requested the Cape Government for permission to settle in the Colony, and on 5 January 1799 he signed the Loyal Address to Gen Sir Francis Dundas, then Lieutenant-Governor of the Cape

During the twenty years of his life at the Cape, Caldwell appears to have led a busy, and perhaps even convoluted, business life. On 30 August 1800 he was recorded to be running a warehouse at 25 Shortmarket Street, Cape Town, and on 16 January 1802 he moved to 32 Berg Street where he opened a hotel. On 13 November 1802 he moved to 4 Strand Street where he ran a retail store beneath his dwelling and boarding house, but on 10 September 1803 he sold off his stock and moved to Stellenbosch where he ran a boarding house from a dwelling owned by Mr Wolfferum. On 20 November 1803 he signed an oath of submission to the Batavian Republic, and on 15 February 1806 he expressed his intention of remaining in Stellenbosch. However two months later, on 1 April 1806, he was appointed Deputy Postmaster General for the Cape, a position he held until 2 December 1807 when Matthew Gall, the new Postmaster General, arrived from England. On 9 August 1806 he moved back to Cape Town where, from 11 April 1807, he resided at 8 Strand Street. On 5 March 1808 he was running a general merchandise store at 7 Bergh Street, with a branch in Stellenbosch. On 19 September 1808 he purchased the home of the widow J Bernhard in Stellenbosch. However on 11 January 1812 he announced that "*his public duty obliges him*" to move back to Cape Town and on 25 January he sold off his Stellenbosch house and effects. He probably retained his property at 7 Bergh Street for in 1815 he was reported to be acting from there as the agent for a London property firm. On 3 January 1812 he was appointed Wine Taster for all Cape Wines, a position he held until his death in Cape Town on 2 July 1816, at the age of 58. Although Caldwell's career in the Post Office was relatively brief, he is credited with the re-organization of the local postal service, the spread of new postal routes into the interior of the country, and the revision of postal charges

CALITZ, Frederick Jacobus, Postmaster at Draghoender, 1 January 1898

Postmaster at Pearston, 1 January 1896

CALLAGHAN, C, Postmaster at Adelaide, 1 October 1865

CALLAGHAN, Honora, Postmaster at Voor Hantam, 16 August 1865

CALLAGHAN, J, Postmaster at Voor Hantam, 1 September 1858

CALLAGHAN, J, King William's Town's post office agent at Alice, 21 October 1859

CALLAGHAN, J, Postmaster, police constable and field-cornet at Beenleegte, 31 August 1857, service provided for free

CALLAGHAN, JH, Postmaster and field-cornet at Klein Poort, 1 March 1875
CAMBRIDGE, Frederick William, Postmaster at Rosebank, 1 September 1898
CAMP, J, Postmaster at Plumstead, 1 June 1875
CAMPBELL, Arthur, born in Belfast, Ireland, and emigrated to the Cape with his family in 1895
   Postmaster at Port Alfred, 1 March 1907
CAMPBELL, D, Postmaster at Prince Albert, 1882
CAMPBELL, David, Station master at Modder River, 28 September 1908, salary £220 pa
CAMPBELL, F, Postmaster at East London Jetty, 1 July 1903
   Postmaster at Witteklip, 1 April 1906
CAMPBELL, J, Postmaster at Bedford, 18 August 1854, dismissed from office
CAMPBELL, Mrs Mary Anne, Postmaster at Fort Beaufort, 1 October 1846
CAMPBELL, R, Letter carrier, GPO, Cape Town, 1 April 1848. Salary £45 pa
CAMPBELL, Sarah LC, Postmaster at Alice, 16 March 1872
CAMPBELL, Thomas, Postmaster at Trappes Valley, 1 June 1901
CAMPHER, RP, Postmaster at Doorn River, 15 February 1847
CAMPTON, H, Postmaster at Katberg, 1881
CANNELL, W, Postmaster and police constable at Kowie West, 16 June 1870
CAPPER, J, Postmaster at Sunday's River Ferry 25 June 1852
CARDINAL, Mr, Postmaster at Breede River Station, in about 1877, deceased while in office
CARDWELL, HB, Postmaster at Beaufort West, 1 June 1855
CARLISLE, WM, Postmaster at Mohaleshoek, 1 January 1876
   Postmaster at Mafeteng, 1 July 1877
   Postmaster at Mohaleshoek, 1 March 1879
   Postmaster at Quthing, 21 November 1881
CARNEY, D, Postmaster and station master at Salt River, 12 May 1864
   Postmaster and station master at Wynberg Station, 1 June 1877
   Postmaster at Rosebank, 1881
CARNEY, Thomas H, Postmaster at Bellville, 1 January 1887
CARPENTER, FM, Postmaster and station master at Eerste River Station, 20 February 1877
   Postmaster at Fraserburg Road, 1881
CARPENTER, TM, Postmaster at Fraserburg, 1881
CARR, J, Letter Carrier, GPO, Cape Town, 8 February 1849, Salary £45 pa
CARROLL, JV, Postmaster at Palmietfontein, before 1896
   Postmaster at Douglas, 1 June 1896
CARRUTHERS, Arthur, Postmaster at Pearston, 1 May 1885
CARSTENS, E, Postmaster at Pearston, 16 November 1858
CARSTENS, F, Postmaster at Concordia, 15 March 1895
CARSTENS, FG, Postmaster at Kuils River, 1 March 1909
   Postmaster at Steinkopf, in about 1910
   Postmaster at Bowesdorp, 1 January 1910

CARSTENS, JC, Clerk, GPO, Cape Town, 15 September 1867
    Clerk, GPO, Cape Town, 24 March 1871
    Clerk and Controller, Circulation Branch, GPO, Cape Town, 16 February 1874
    Postmaster at Cape Town, 16 February 1874
CARTER, Thomas, Postmaster at Coerney, 1 May 1891
CARTER, WH, Postmaster at Tafelberg, 1 August 1892
CARVER, JF, Assistant Postmaster at Grahamstown. The Pension Lists of 30 November 1909 recorded that in 1910 Mr Carver, age 54, was retired on an annual pension of £94.4.1
CASTLE, Alfred Thomas, Station master at Richmond Road, 16 July 1904, salary £186 pa
CASTLES, GA, Postmaster at Delport's Hope, 1 January 1903
    Postmaster at Kenhardt, 1 April 1904
    Acting postmaster at Kenilworth, Kimberley, 1 June 1905
    Acting postmaster at Hutchinson, 1 August 1906
    Acting postmaster at Kenilworth, Kimberley, 1908, confirmed in 1909
    Postmaster at Philipstown, 1 September 1909
CATTO, GT, Junior assistant, Money Order Branch, GPO, 1 September 1897
    Postmaster at Kenilworth, Cape Town, 1 April 1898
CAVANAGH, F, Postmaster at Ndabakazi, in about 1878
CAVELL, HC, Postmaster at Bellville, 1 March 1900
    Postmaster at Mill Street, Gardens, Cape Town, 1 March 1900
CAVERS, Frank Robert, Postmaster at Vosburg, 1 October 1908
CAWOOD, J, Postmaster at Varkenskop, 29 April 1864, service provided for free
CAWS, Ernest William, Postmaster at Schmidt's Drift, 1 June 1904
CELLARIUS, JR, Postmaster at Vlakteplaats, 1 January 1871
CENTLIVRES, Ms E, Postmaster at Hanover, 1 September 1871
CENTLIVRES, FCRJ, Postmaster at Hanover, 10 August 1859
CHABAUD, Claude Wright, Clerk to the Resident Magistrate and postmaster at St Marks, 1881. Went on to serve in various magisterial capacities at Xalanga (1883), Elliot (1894), Barkly East (1900), Lusikisiki (1902), Calvinia (1902), Robben Island (1904), and Glen Gray (1907)
CHALMERS, F, Postmaster at Ccrcs, 1 July 1879
CHAMBERLAIN, Geo, Postmaster at Swellendam, 1 April 1854
CHAMBERS, WA, Postmaster at Mount Fletcher, 1 August 1906
CHAMEN, George C, Telegraphist at Adelaide, 1886
    Postmaster at Lawrence Street, Port Elizabeth, 1 August 1896
    Postmaster at Adelaide, 1906
CHARLES, C, Postmaster at Waterford, Division of Jansenville, 1 May 1879
CHARLTON, J, Acting postmaster at Port Alfred, 1 April 1871
CHARLTON, R, Postmaster at Port Alfred, 1 July 1870, dismissed from service
CHARLTON, R, Postmaster at Bathurst, 23 May 1867
CHASE, EH, Postmaster at Hondeklip Bay, 12 December 1860

CHEEVERS, TS, Assistant Postmaster at Port Elizabeth. The Pension Lists of 30 November 1909 recorded that in 1910 Mr Cheevers, age 65, was retired on an annual pension of £112.10.0

CHEZE, EF, Postmaster at Krakeel River, 1 October 1875

CHOWLES, C, Postmaster at Paarde Poort, 1 September 1874

CHRISTOPHERSON, H, Postmaster at Panmure, 1874

CHURCH, C, Postmaster at Worcester Station, 1 March 1896

CHURCH, GR, Postmaster at Daniel's Kuil, 1 May 1907

CHURGWIN, C, Postmaster and station master at Observatory Road, 1880

CILLERS, JD, Postmaster at Wellington, 2 February 1859

CILLERS, Ms JD, Postmaster at Wellington, 1 November 1877

CILLERS, JF, Postmaster at Wellington, 1 March 1863

CILLERS, Susannah, Postmaster at Wellington, 1 November 1867

CILLERS, Ms SS, Postmaster at Wellington, 1 January 1874

CLAASEN, JG, also listed as KLAASEN, JC
  Postmaster and field-cornet at Upper Gouritz River, 1 October 1870
  Postmaster at Langtown, 1880

CLACK, A, Postmaster at Sidbury, 1 June 1908

CLAPHAM, CH, Postmaster at Matjesfontein, Division of Worcester, 1883

CLARK, A, Postmaster at Nanaga, 1 July 1872

CLARK, J, Postmaster at Matjesfontein, Division of Worcester, 1 July 1893

CLARK, JW, Postmaster at Zwarte Koppen, 1 June 1865

CLARK, SJ, Station master at Coerney, 1 June 1893, salary £264 pa
  Postmaster at Coerney, 1 October 1893

CLARKE, AE, Acting postmaster at Pearston, 1909
  Postmaster at Pearston, 1 January 1909

CLARKE, Dudley Stewart, Postmaster at Papkuil, 1 April 1905
  Postmaster at Daniel's Kuil, 1 January 1906

CLARKE, J, Postmaster at Woodstock Station, 1883

CLARKE, JC, Postmaster and field-cornet at Zuurbron, 1 October 1864

CLARKE, James, Station master at New Brighton, 21 February 1907, salary £198 pa

CLAY, CJ, Postmaster at Hondeklip Bay, 3 April 1868

CLEMENTSON, S, Postmaster at Hoetjes Bay, 1883

CLEMENTSON, T, Postmaster at Hoetjes Bay, 6 January 1865

CLEMITSON, William Fred, Postmaster at Bowesdorp, 1 May 1909

CLEVERLY, JJ, Resident Magistrate and postmaster at Walfish Bay, 1885
  Resident Magistrate and postmaster at Walfish Bay, 1901

CLINKNALES, Postmaster at Boetsap, 1882

CLOETE, E, Postmaster at Bowden, 14 July 1864
  Postmaster and field-cornet at Bowden, 1 July 1874

CLOETE, JEG, Postmaster at Bowden, 1 January 1869

CLOETE, JG, Postmaster at Swellendam, 1 February 1827

CLOETE, JH, Postmaster and field-cornet at Camdeboo, 30 Nov 1858, service provided free

CLOETE, DHG, Clerk, fourth class, GPO, Cape Town, 18 June 1856
    Clerk, third class, GPO, Cape Town, 1857
    Clerk, second class, GPO, Cape Town, 1858

CLOETE, GWA, Clerk, GPO, Cape Town, 1 February 1872
    Clerk, Money Order and Stamp Branch, GPO, Cape Town, 1 January 1876

COCK, GH, Postmaster at Glen Lynden, 1 April 1904
    Postmaster at Koonap, 1 April 1905

COCKER, Miss Amy Winifred, also listed as AM
    Postmaster at River Zonder End, 1 September 1902
    Postmaster at Philadelphia, 1 July 1904

COCKING, Henry Reginald, Postmaster at Taungs, 1 October 1908
    Postmaster at Philipstown, 1 July 1910

COCKROFT, W, Postmaster and field-cornet at Funah's Kloof, 21 June 1869, service provide free

COCKSON, William VS, Postmaster at Engcobo, 1 December 1893
    The Pension Lists of 30 November 1909 recorded that in 1910 Mr Cockson, age 52 was retired on an annual pension of £67.7.8

COE, EB, Postmaster at Tylden, 11 August 1859

COE, JB, Postmaster at Daggaboersnek, 1 March 1861

COETZEE, Alfred Mills, Postmaster at Modder River, Division of Kimberley, 1 January 1910

COETZEE, G, Postmaster at Kamnassie, 24 July 1858

COETZEE, Johannes Christoffel, Postmaster at Aberdeen, Aberdeen Division, 1 March 1902

COETZEE, Mrs M, Postmaster at Krakeel River, 1 October 1876

COFFE, Miss J, see under McNAMARA, Mrs J

COFFEY, Mr C, Postmaster at Kenhardt, 1 August 1889

COGHILL, AR, Postmaster at Ceres Road, 1882

COGHILL, WH, Postmaster at Diep River, 1 September 1861, service provided for free

COLDREY, A, Postmaster at Houw Hoek, 1 April 1902

COLDREY, Aubrey Vincent, Postmaster at De Rust, 1 March 1904

COLE, AB, Postmaster at Kentani, January 1883

COLE, FH, Postmaster at Grahamstown, 1 June 1842, deceased while in office

COLE, HT, Postmaster at Grahamstown, 26 May 1866

COLE, James. Riverside was a trading station providing staple goods to a predominantly rural indigenous clientele. It was already well-established when it was purchased by James Cole, an eccentric trader who settled in Griqualand East in the 1860s and made his home at Riverside. A notorious miser whose mode of dress was more suited to the life-style of a homeless pauper, he soon accumulated a vast fortune through a string of trading stations and extensive dealings in land. At one stage he also issued his own coinage, small brass disks imprinted "*James Cole.1s. Mealies*", which remained in local circulation until 1935 when they became illegal (Coulter 1988)

COLE, Mrs Louisa, Postmaster at Piquetberg, 1 May 1885

COLE, L, Postmaster at Somerset West, 1880

COLEGATE, Miss Florence, Postmaster at Lawrence Street, Port Elizabeth, 1 July 1886

COLEMAN, GH, Postmaster at Aliwal North, 11 September 1855

COLEMAN, J, Postmaster at Diep River, 1 July 1903

COLEMAN, William Alfred, Postmaster at Sterkstroom, 1 April 1895
    Postmaster at Stutterheim, 1 November 1896
    Postmaster at Sea Point, 1 September 1899
    Postmaster at Observatory Road, 1 July 1902
    Postmaster at Claremont Station, 1 August 1908, salary £360 pa

COLEMAN, WH, Postmaster and storekeeper at the Boontjes River Convict Station, 1 Sept 1853

COLLARD, Mrs TW, Postmaster and field-cornet at Petersburg, 14 February 1867, deceased while in office

COLLETT, J, Postmaster at Zoutpans Drift, October 1869

COLLEY, EH, Postmaster at De Rust, 1 January 1879

COLLIER, Miss E, see under COLLINS, Emily

COLLIER, LC, Postmaster at Gwelegha River, 1 January 1875

COLLING, G, Postmaster at Sunday's River Ferry, 7 April 1853

COLLING, T, Postmaster at Paarde Poort, 1 December 1863, listed in 1865

COLLINGS, WT, Postmaster at Flagstaff, 1 December 1903

COLLINS, DJ, Postmaster at Whittlesea, 5 July 1853

COLLINS, Miss Emily, also listed as COLLIER, born in about 1849
    Postmaster at Murraysburg, 1 May 1885
    Postmaster at Alice, 1 March 1887
    Postmaster at French Hoek, 1 Decembr 1894
    Postal assistant, third class, Burghersdorp, 16 February 1899
    The Pension Lists of 30 November 1909 recorded that in 1910 Miss Collins, age 60, was retired on an annual pension of £84.2.5

COLLINS, E, born in about 1853
    Postmaster at Bedford, 1 March 1872
    Postmaster at Middelburg, 10 September 1884
    Postmaster at Paarl, 1 July 1894
    Postmaster at Burghersdorp, 1 January 1899
    Postmaster at Somerset East, 1 September 1899
    Postmaster at Uitenhage, 1910
    The Pension Lists of 30 November 1909 recorded that in 1910 Mr Collins, age 56, was retired on an annual pension of £213.15.7

COLLINS, Frederick, Postmaster at Omdraai's Vlei, 10 November 1900
    Postmaster at Papkuil, 1 October 1902
    Assistant Engineering Division, Cape Town, salary £235 pa

COLLINS, RC, Postmaster at Dohne, 1883

COLLYER, JH, Postmaster at Balfour, 1882

COLYN, A, Postmaster at Grey's Pass, 19 December 1866, service provided for free

COMADU, DJ, Postmaster at Jan Foure's Kraal, 1881

CONGDON, CE, Postmaster at Laingsburg, 1 September 1898
- Postmaster at Kei Road, 1 October 1892
- Postmaster at Caledon Street, Cape Town, 1 September 1900
- Postmaster at Kloof Street, Gardens, Cape Town, 1 December 1900
- Postmaster at Bellville, 1 January 1904

CONHAM, CS, Postmaster at Egoso, 22 October 1878

CONLON, WBP, Assistant Postmaser at Kimberley. The Pension Lists of 30 November 1909 recorded that in 1910 Mr Conlon, age 47, probably took early retirement on an annual pension of £168.0.10

CONNELL, James, Postmaster at Eerste River Station, before 1891
- Postmaster at Bellville, 1 February 1891
- Postmaster at Fraserburg, 1 February 1892
- Postmaster at Prieska, 1 March 1893
- Postmaster at Hutchinson, 1 December 1893
- Postmaster at Modder River, Division of Kimberley, 1 January 1895
- Postmaster at Tsolo, 1 December 1895
- Postmaster at Mount Ayliff, 16 August 1897
- Postmaster at Tabankulu, 1 July 1902

CONNOCK, Frederick William, Station master at Grahamstown, 24 Sept 1905, salary £300 pa

CONNOCK, J, Postmaster at Tsomo, 1882

CONRADIE, FD Snr, Postmaster and field-cornet at Achter Hex River, 10 May 1858

CONRADIE, FD Jnr, Postmaster at Zaaiplaats, 1 July 1863

CONWAY, John Jenkins, Postmaster at Hout Kraal, 1 August 1909

COOK, Edward Altham. Prior to his arrival at the Cape, Edward Cook had served in India, where he had held high office, both in the military and in the civil service. He was also well educated, and during his stay there he had gained for himself a reputation as a "*capital Hindustani scholar*". Late in 1855 he was given the post of Clerk, fifth class, at the GPO, in Cape Town, and on 23 February 1856 he was appointed postmaster at Port Elizabeth, much to the dissatisfaction of its citizens, who had favoured one Nathaniel Randall, a local shopkeeper who had previously acted in that position. Ultimately the notoriously xenophobic public of Port Elizabeth had its way, for Cook died suddenly in September 1858

COOK, GH, Postmaster at Barkly East, 1881

COOKE, J, Postmaster at Seven Fountains, 1 January 1872

COOPER, George, Station master at Cathcart, 11 January 1899, salary £265 pa

COOPER, George, Postmaster at Bowesdorp, 1 November 1909
- Postmaster at Steinkopf, 1 January 1910

COOPER, Geo C, Postmaster at Stapleford, 1 July 1855
    Postmaster at Balmoral, Division of Uitenhage, 15 February 1861
COOPER, George Herbert, Postmaster at Moshesh's Ford, 1 April 1905
COOPER, GS, Postmaster at Port Alfred, 1 March 1902
COOPER, H, Postmaster at Nelspoort, 1 December 1894
    Postmaster at Nelspoort, 1 November 1897
COOPER, HWA, Postmaster at Willowmore, 21 September 1864
COOPER, Henry, Station master at Porterville Road, 1 February 1903, salary £294 pa
COOPER, JC, Postmaster at Glen Lynden, 31 May 1855
COOPER, JD, Postmaster at Naauwpoort, 28 July 1861, service provided for free
COOPER, JF, Postmaster at St Helena Bay, 1 July 1863
COOPER, JS, Postmaster at Moshesh's Ford, 1 May 1903
COOPER, RH, Postmaster at Langford, 1881
COOPER, WG, Postmaster at Maclean Town, 1 September 1863
COPENHAGEN, John William, also listed as VAN COPPENHAGEN
    Postmaster at Pearston, 1 May 1890
    Postmaster at Kalk Bay, 1 October 1895
    Postmaster at Woodstock Station, 1 July 1906
    Postmaster at Aberdeen, Division of Aberdeen, 1 August 1908
CORBETT, TA, Postmaster at Fraser's Camp, 28 December 1858
CORBEY, Alfred Charles, Postmaster at Daniel's Kuil, 1 November 1909
CORDNER, WT, Postmaster at Omdraai's Vlei, 1 September 1897
CORDNER, William Townley, Postmaster at Eerste River Station, 1 March 1904
    Postmaster at Fraserburg, 1 March 1909
CORDY, EJ, Postmaster at St Helena Bay, 1882
CORNELIUS, Miss M, Postmaster at Peiserton, 1 December 1907
CORRIGAN, T, Postmaster at Patatas River, 27 May 1861, service provided for free
COSGRAVE, J, Postmaster at Zwarte Koppen, 29 May 1857
COSGROVE, Elizabeth, Postmaster at Nanaga, 26 May 1860, service provided free in 1867-78
COTTERILL, R, Postmaster at Dordrecht, 1 May 1869
COURTENAY, Mrs L, Postmaster at Simonstown, 1 July 1847
COURTENAY, William H, Postmaster at Stutterheim, 16 July 1885
    Postmaster at Britstown, 1 August 1889
COVE, Philip Ernest, Postmaster at Kimberley Station, 1 March 1910
COWAN, D, Postmaster at Victoria West, 5 August 1852
    Postmaster at Victoria West, 5 November 1855
COWAN, D, Postmaster and field-cornet at Nieuwveld No 3, 1 April 1863, service provided for free in 1867-68
COWAN, Ellen, Postmaster at Victoria West, 1 July 1862
COWAN, W, Postmaster at Victoria West, 14 June 1862

COWARD, James Evans, Postmaster at the Houses of Parliament, 1 April 1905
COWARD, Mrs MA, Postmaster at Alice, 1 April 1886
   Postmaster at Seymour, 1 February 1888
COWDEROY, J, Postmaster at Kowie East, 1830
COWDEROY, T, Postmaster at Kowie East, 1833
COWDEROY, TF, Postmaster at Kowie East, 6 June 1823
COWIE, J, Postmaster at Farm No 239, Kei River, 1 July 1862
COX, H, Postmaster and station master at Sandflats, 15 June 1878
COX, T, Postmaster at Klein Poort, 1880
   Postmaster at Redhouse, 1881
CRAFFORD, CW, Postmaster at Ladismith, 1 November 1890
   Postmaster at Klaarstroom, 1 June 1893
   Postmaster at Ladismith, 19 December 1899
CRAMER, R, Postmaster at French Hoek, 1 October 1875
CRANE, EHG, Acting postmaster at Post Retief, 1 May 1906
CRANKSHAW, G, Postmaster at Mount Stewart, in about 1879
CRANKSHAW, JC, Postmaster and station master at Aberdeen Road, 1 December 1879
CRANKSHAW, JFW, Postmaster at Prince Albert Road, 1880
CRAWFORD, A, Postmaster at Cyphergat Station, 15 December 1889
CREE, Hugh Donald, Postmaster at Prince Albert Road, 1 February 1903
CREED, HL, Postmaster at Karree Kop, 1881
CREIGHTON, Archibald A, Postmaster at Balfour, 1 October 1886
CRERAR, John William, Postmaster at Upper Kloof Street, Cape Town, 1 November 1907
   Postmaster at Caledon Street, Cape Town, 1909
   Postmaster at Caledon Street, Cape Town, 1910
CRITTALL, A, Postmaster at South End, Port Elizabeth, 1 March 1903
CROCKER, AE, Postmaster at Ashton, 1 May 1900
CROCKER, Henry, Station master at Wynberg 22 October 1901, salary £300 pa
CRONK, J, Postmaster and field-cornet at Gwelegha River, 1 January 1877
   Postmaster at Silvervale, 1881
CROSBIE, Frederick William, Postmaster and station master at East Bank, East London, 18 December 1876
   Postmaster and station master at Dohne, 1 January 1879
   Postmaster at Fort Jackson, in about 1880
   Postmaster at Imvani, 1881
   Postmaster at Tylden, 1883
   Postmaster and station master at Kei Road, 1 November 1888
   Station master at East London, 1 February 1893, salary £360 pa
CROSBIE, JTS, Assistant, Second Class, at Beaufort West, date of appointment not known
   Postmaster at Tylden, 1 May 1894

Postmaster at Tylden, 1 March 1895

Postmaster at Kloof Street, Gardens, Cape Town, 1 December 1897

Postmaster at Mill Street, Gardens, Cape Town, 1 December 1900

Postmaster at Clarkebury, 1 October 1909

Assistant Postmaster at the GPO, Cape Town

The Pension Lists of 30 November 1909 recorded that in 1910 Mr Crosbie, age 47, was retired on an annual pension of £103.4.0

CROSBIE, MJ, also listed as M and MM

Postmaster at Wellington Station, 18 December 1867, service provided for free in 1867-68

Postmaster and station master at East Bank, East London, in about 1878

Postmaster and station master at Kei Road, 1 January 1879

Postmaster at East London Station, 7 May 1879

Postmaster at Imvani, 1883

CROSOER, Joshua, Station master at Oudtshoorn, 21 July 1903, salary £285 pa

CROSSLEY, J, Postmaster at Highlands, in about 1878

CROWE, J, Postmaster at Debe Nek, 1 February 1869, service provided for free

CROWLEY, BL, Assistant Postmaster at Port Elizabeth. The Pension Lists of 30 November 1909 recorded that in 1910 Mr Crowley, age 42, was retired on an annual pension of £126.0.2

CROZIER, Dupre C, deceased in office in about 1862

Clerk, third class, GPO, Cape Town, 10 April 1844

Clerk, first class, GPO, Cape Town, 2 January 1849. Salary £150 pa

Chief Clerk, GPO, Cape Town, 1 April 1856. Salary £300 pa

CROZIER, R, Sergeant Major, 27th Regiment, and postmaster at Fort Beaufort, 1843

CROZIER, Robert. Robert Dupre Crozier was born in Caledon, County Tyrone, Ireland, in about 1785, the son of John Crozier and his wife Mary Henderson. His father was an Ensign in the 29th Regiment from the Estate Strathmore, near Gilford in County Down, Ulster. When Dupre Alexander, Earl of Caledon, was appointed Governor of the Cape early in 1807, he invited Crozier to join his administration, and the party arrived in Cape Town on 22 May 1807. After spending his first week at Government House making copies of dispatches, on 1 June 1807 Crozier was made 8th clerk in the Colonial Secretariat at the Castle, and on 1 September 1808 he was promoted to Cashier in the Lombard and Discount Bank at a salary of £225 per annum. While retaining this position he also served as Acting Postmaster General in 1809-11, and again in 1813-15 in the absence of Matthew Gall. Despite his obviously advantaged social and political connections Crozier's career does not appear to have progressed as rapidly as the young man might have wished, and on 3 April 1812 Lord Liverpool wrote to Governor Cradock requesting that he be found more lucrative employment. This request was repeated on 10 November 1814 when the Secretary of State for War and the Colonies, Lord Bathurst, wrote to Lord Somerset, stating that *"Mr C is represented to be a very meritorious public servant"*. On 3 February 1815 Crozier was appointed agent to the Agricultural Board, and on 13 March he married Johanna Magdalena van Ryneveld, daughter of Chief Justice WS van Rijneveld. In time she bore him three sons, all of whom went on to fill important positions in the British Colonial Administration.

He was appointed Acting Postmaster General for a third time on 21 September 1815, and following the resignation of Matthew Gall on 18 November 1815, was confirmed in this position with an annual salary of £375. For the next thirteen years he continued to work in the Government offices at the top of the Heerengracht, occupying one room as cashier in the morning, and another across the courtyard as Postmaster General in the afternoon. On 1 June 1828 he gave up this dual existence and took up the position of Postmaster General on a full-time basis with a revised salary of £600 pa. This was reduced to £400 when the Whig Party won the British elections in 1834, but was restored to its original level when the Tories returned to power in 1844.

During his term of office, southern Africa underwent a number of major changes, including the British colonization of the eastern frontier, the emigration of dissident Dutch from the Cape, and the expansion of European settlement into the Karroo. Under Crozier's leadership the Cape Post Office opened 73 new offices, introduced prepaid adhesives, and extended its postal routes throughout the southern African hinterland, providing the Colonial Administration in Cape Town with communication links to the troubled Eastern Cape as well as most of the Karroo. Towards the end of his life he was struck by a long and painful illness, and although he took sick leave on 10 April 1851, he did not retire until 4 February 1852. He died in Cape Town on 11 March 1852

CROZIER, Robert J, Clerk to the Civil Commissioner and postmaster at Uitenhage, 8 Feb 1849
  Postmaster at Malmesbury, 4 February 1850
  Postmaster at Stellenbosch, 6 February 1851
CRUICKSHANK, W, Postmaster at Schietfontein Hotel, 1880
CRUYWAGEN, JA, Postmaster at Karroo Poort, in about 1868, service provided for free
CUMBERPATCH, Mr, Postmaster at Centlivres, in about 1877
CUMMING, Miss, Postmaster at Emgwali, 1 October 1875
CUMMING, John Paige, Clerk to the Resident Magistrate, 22 May 1876
  Postmaster at Idutywa, 1 December 1878
  Took part in the Gcaleka War of 1877, and was in charge of the Idutywa lines under Major Elliot. Served in the Pondomise uprising of 1880, and went on to serve as Resident Magistrate at Tsolo (1889), Elliotdale (1900), and Idutywa (1902)
CUMMING, Rev, Postmaster at Emgwali, in about 1875
CUMMING, Frederick Duncan, Postmaster at Pearston, 1 August 1889
  Postmaster at Orange River, 1 March 1895
  Postmaster at Porterville Road, 1 February 1900
  Postmaster at Clanwilliam, 1 March 1902
  Postmaster at Kimberley Station, 1 February 1907
  Postmaster at Willowmore, 1 December 1909
CUMMING, GG, Postmaster at Salem, 1 April 1900

Postmaster at St Marks, 1 September 1900

CUMMING, JP, Clerk to the Government Agent and postmaster at Idutywa, 1 May 1877
Clerk to the Magistrate and postmaster at Tsolo, 24 September 1879
In 1879 JP Cumming, postmaster for Tsolo, recorded that during the year the outgoing mail traffic for this office was 2743 letters, 68 books and 461 newspapers. The majority of these probably originated from the St Augustine's Mission nearby

CUMMING, R, Postmaster at Great Brak River, 1 March 1906

CUMMING, Robert Forbes, Clerk to the Resident Magistrate and postmaster at Maclear, 17 May 1878. Thereafter acted as magistrate at Maclear, Matatiele, Qumbu and Mount Frere. Took part and was decorated for his services as Lieutenant and Adjutant of Streatfeild's levies during the Gcaleka uprising of 1877; served as Captain and Field-Adjutant of the Maclear Constabulary during the Pondomise-Mthembu uprising of 1880-1; and commanded the Matatiele Native Reserves during the South African War of 1899-1902

CUPPLEDITCH, H, born at Stockport, Cheshire, in about 1857
Imperial Service, Manchester, date of appointment not known
French-American Cable Company, date of appointment not known
Emigrated to the Cape in 1881, described by his supervisors to be the most expert telegraphist in the Colony in his time
Superintendent of Telegraphs, CTO, Cape Town, 1897
Postmaster at King William's Town, 18 October 1900
Retired from service August, 1908. The Pension Lists of 30 November 1909 recorded that in 1910 Mr Cuppleditch, age 52, was retired on an annual pension of £295.12.6

CURLEWIS, JW, Postmaster at Petrusville, 1 September 1879

CURNICK, F, Postmaster at Nqamakwe, 15 August 1890

CURNICK, William Norman, Postmaster at Nqamakwe, 1 September 1897
Postmaster at Kentani, 1 March 1903

CURRIE, GV, Postmaster at Prince Albert Road, 1906
Acting postmaster at Schmidt's Drift, 1908
Postmaster at Schmidt's Drift, 1 December 1908

CURTIS, Charles Henry, Station master at Mulder's Vlei, 29 March 1907, salary £189 pa

CURTIS, Ernest Herbert, Postmaster at Rosmead, 1 April 1896

CUSENS, HD, Postmaster at Umtata, 1 December 1879
Postmaster at Dordrecht, 1881
Postmaster at Cookhouse, 1 May 1885
Postmaster at Naauwpoort, 1 October 1892
Postmaster at Middelburg, 1 October 1899
Postmaster at Sterkstroom, probable date 1 July 1900
Retired 1909. The Pension Lists of 30 November 1909 recorded that in 1910 Mr Cuzens, age 47, was retired on an annual pension of £216.10.2

CUSTARD, William Charles Elton, Postmaster at De Doorns, 1 November 1909, salary £245 pa

D

DALLAS, John, Postmaster at Boontjes River, 6 January 1849
    Postmaster at the Buffels River Convict Station, 19 June 1868, service provided for free

DALTON, Patrick Joseph, Postmaster at Jamestown, 1 September 1903
    Postmaster at Hankey, 1 December 1909

DALY, C, Messenger at Port Elizabeth. The Pension Lists of 30 November 1909 recorded that in 1910 Mr Daly. age 51, was retired on an annual pension of £21.13.4

DALY, John, also listed as Johannes
    Postmaster at St Helena Bay, 8 August 1853
    Postmaster at St Helena Bay, 31 August 1857

DALY, RL, Postmaster at St Helena Bay, 21 August 1856

DALY, W, Postmaster at Sandflats, 1 August 1890

DALZIEL, William Cornelius, Station master at Redhouse, 1 November 1908, salary £223 pa

DAM, J, Postmaster at Uitenhage, 1880

DAMANT, FK, Postmaster and field-cornet at Swanepoel's Kraal, 25 January 1862
    Ranger and Receiving Officer at Tsitsikamma, and postmaster at Witte Els Bosch, 1 April 1874, service provided for free
    Postmaster at Hankey, 1 September 1886
    Postmaster at Koonap, 1 April 1903

DAMON, WT, Postmaster and station master at Kalabas Kraal, in about 1877
    Postmaster at Porterville Road, 6 November 1877
    Postmaster at De Doorns, in about 1878

DANIEL, AG, Postmaster at Achter Zuurberg, 1881

DANIELL, C, Clerk to Magistrate at Southeyville and postmaster at Engcobo, 15 October 1879

DANIELL, E, Postmaster and field-cornet at Kariega Station, 1 July 1866

DANIELL, EA, Postmaster at Wooldridge, 1 January 1876

DANIELS, Fred, Postmaster at Hottentot's Kloof, 1 November 1873

DANIELS, J, Acting postmaster at Eerste River Station, 1907
    Postmaster at De Doorns, 1 November 1906

DANIELS, James Samuel, also listed as DANIEL
    Postmaster at Balmoral, Division of Knysna, before 1902
    Postmaster at Great Brak River, 1 July 1902
    Postmaster at Bowesdorp, 1 February 1904

D'ARCY, FH. Assistant Postmaster at Kimberley. The Pension Lists of 30 November 1909 recorded that in 1910 Mr D'Arcy, age 47, was retired on an annual pension of £166.5.0, probably for reasons of ill health

DARLEY, Charles John, Postmaster at Mount Frere, 1 October 1905

DASSONVILLE, H, Postmaster at Two Streams, 16 June 1875

DAVENPORT, J, Postmaster at Kuils River, 1 May 1854

DAVEY, JG, Postmaster at Blaauw Krantz, Division of Cradock, 14 October 1859

DAVIDSON, James Christopher. In 1865 le Sueur was replaced by James Davidson, MP, as Acting Postmaster-General. At the same time the Colonial Administration and instituted a Commission of Enquiry into the system of audit of Post Office accounts. It found that the Post Office's method of handling stamp stocks as well as large sums of money was suspect and recommended sweeping changes to its accounting and reporting structures. Given the nature of the theft, and the fact that the matter was not finally settled until some years later, this must have been a difficult period for Davidson to supervise. Nonetheless he appears to have dealt with this difficult transition successfully and with a certain amount of tact. He certainly came to the post with a notable history of public service, having previously served as the Chair of the Tender Board, the full-time Treasurer and Accountant-General in the Colonial Treasury, a sitting member of the Cape Parliament, and a member of the Executive Council of the Cape Legislature, at a salary of £1000 pa Almost no changes appear to have taken place during his tenure at the GPO, but then given the fact that both le Sueur and Aitchison had been removed, none were probably expected of him

DAVIE, Mrs, Postmaster at Prieska, 1 July 1890

DAVIE, R, Postmaster at Barroe, in about 1879

DAVIES, AE, Magistrate's Clerk with Umhlonhlo and postmaster at Qumbu, 7 January 1879
Postmaster at Engcobo, 1 July 1886
On 23 October 1880 the amaMpondomise, under the leadership of their Chief Umhlonhlo, rose in protest against the annexation of their lands to the Cape Colony. At the time the Resident Magistrate, Mr Hamilton Hope, was travelling to Maclear together with his assistants Messrs Hendley and Warren as well as his clerk, Mr AE Davies. Near the Sulenkama mission station the group was ambushed by a party of Mpondomise and, with the exception of Davies, who was the postmaster at Qumbu as well as the brother of the Wesleyan Missionary to Chief Umhlonhlo, all were killed

DAVIES, EO, Acting postmaster at Mafeteng, 1 October 1877

DAVIES, HL, Postmaster at Maseru, 1 February 1875

DAVIES, HT, Postmaster at Port Alfred, 24 December 1875

DAVIES, John, Postmaster at Upington, 1 March 1886

DAVIES, James David, Postmaster at Mill Street, Gardens, Cape Town, 1 November 1897
Postmaster at Fraserburg Road, 1 November 1899

DAVIES, ML, Postmaster at Kokstad, 1 October 1879

DAVIES, William, Postmaster at Highlands, 1883

DAVIES, WG, Postmaster at Cookhouse, 1 October 1889
Postmaster at Fraserburg Road, 1 July 1890
Postmaster at Ceres Road, 1 June 1891
Postmaster at Belmont February, 1892
Postmaster at Laingsburg, 1 August 1892
Postmaster at Bellville, 1 March 1893
Postmaster at Wellington Station, 1 May 1894

Postmaster at Calvinia, 1 January 1896

DAVIES, WO, Postmaster at Hout Kraal, 15 May 1896

DAVOREN, JA, Postmaster and station master at Kubusie, 1 November 1879

DAVOREN, JW, Postmaster at Dohne, in about 1879

Postmaster at Thomas River Station, 1880

DAWE, WN, Postmaster at Burghersdorp, 1 February 1875

DAWSON, W, Postmaster at Hanover, 9 November 1858

DAY, Samuel Henry, Postmaster at Commadagga, 1 September 1895

Station master at Kimberley, 23 May 1903, salary £295 pa

DAY, WA, Postmaster at O'Okiep, 1879

DEACON, Maria, Postmaster at Alexandria, 23 September 1858

DEACON, John, Postmaster at Herbertsdale, 1 March 1900

DEAS, Henry Peter, Postmaster at Klaarstroom, 1 June 1892

Postmaster at Darling, 1 June 1893

Postmaster at Sutherland, 1 July 1893

Postmaster at Griquatown, 1 August 1893

Postmaster at Britstown, 1 October 1893

Postmaster at Sutherland, 1 June 1894

DE BEER, Mr, Postmaster at Grootfontein, in about 1878

DE BEER, IT, Postmaster at Darling, 16 June 1866

DE BEER, L, Postmaster at Durbanville, 25 April 1846

DE BEER, LGS, Postmaster at Tarkastad, 3 August 1865

DE BENE, Ernest Henry, Station master at Burghersdorp, 1 September 1902, salary £285 pa

DE BENE, Joseph John, Began work as a clerk on the Great Western Railway Co, at Paddington and, after seven years service, emigrated to the Cape, where he was appointed postmaster and station master at Coega, 1 December 1876

Postmaster and station master at Sandflats, 1877

Postmaster and station master at Zwartkops Station, 15 June 1878

Postmaster and station master at Alicedale, 1879

Thereafter served in a variety of railway positions, first at Graaff-Reinet (1883), then Grahamstown (1885), Naauwpoort (1893), Port Elizabeth (1893), Cape Town (1895), returned to Port Elizabeth (1896), and as Traffic Manager at Bulawayo (1902) and Beaufort West (1904)

DE BRUYN, Miss CE, Acting postmaster at Zuurbraak, 1 December 1902

Postmaster at Doorn River, 1 April 1903

Postmaster at Schoemanshoek, 1 December 1903

Postmaster at Barrydale, 1 May 1906

DE BRUYN, Miss Janet Louisa, Acting postmaster at Zuurbraak, 1 April 1903

Postmaster at Schoemanshoek, 1 October 1903

Postmaster at Doorn River, 1 December 1903

Postmaster at Herbertsdale, 1 May 1905

DEELEY, Frederick Horace, Postmaster at Whittlesea, 1 May 1906

DE FIN, J, Postmaster at Stutterheim, 1 May 1862

DE JAGER, JJ, Postmaster at Over Duivenhoks Rivier, 1 October 1865

DE JAGER, PJ, Postmaster at Steyn's Kraal, 14 March 1870, service provided for free

DE JAGER, W, Postmaster at O'Okiep, 1 June 1900. Postmaster at Matjesfontein, Division of Worcester, 1 August 1902. On 4 April 1902 a Republican force under Gen JC Smuts reached O'Okiep and demanded its surrender. The British garrison of 44 men curtly rejected their kind offer and promptly dug in. Smuts' forces surrounded the village and over the next month made numerous attacks upon its perimeter defenses. Their efforts included home-made dynamite bombs, which proved ineffective; a home-made siege gun, which blew itself to pieces; a second home-made siege cannon, which also blew itself to pieces; a train-load of dynamite, which exploded prematurely; and a challenge to a football match, which was politely declined. The siege was raised on 4 May after the arrival of a relief column under Col H Cooper. After the war, Mr W de Jager, postmaster at O'Okiep, received special mention by the British Military for the manner he managed to maintain telegraphic communications between Garies and O'Okiep, often at great risk to his own personal safety (POC 243, 1 February 1902)

DE JONG, Dirk, Postmaster at Cape Town, 1806

DE KOCH, GS, see under DE KOCK, GS

DE KOCK, DJ, Postmaster at Belmont, 1881

DE KOCK, G, Postmaster at Wynberg, 29 November 1853

DE KOCK, GS, Assistant, fifth class, GPO, Cape Town, 17 August 1888
- Postmaster at Millwood, Goldfields, 1 November 1890
- Acting postmaster at Humansdorp, 1 June 1892
- Postmaster at Willowmore, 1 February 1894
- Acting postmaster at Port Alfred, 1 May 1895
- Postmaster at Humansdorp, 1 August 1895

DE KOCK, JH, Postmaster at Philadelphia, 1 July 1899
- Postmaster at Napier, 1 January 1901

DE KOCK, PJ, Postmaster at Drogas River, 20 March 1855

DE KORTE, J, Postmaster at Pearston, 1 September 1869

DE LACY, Capt G, also listed as LACY. Temporary clerk to the Assistant Magistrate with Makaula and postmaster at Mount Frere, 1 September 1876, deceased while in office

DE LA HUNT, AW, Postmaster at Burghersdorp, in about 1877
- Postmaster at Hanover, 1881
- Postmaster at East London, 1 September 1882
- Postmaster at Beaufort West, 1 May 1894
- Postmaster at Queenstown, 1 May 1897
- GPO, Cape Town, 16 May 1897. Possibly appointed to the Telegraph Message Branch. On 30 November 1909 his widow, A De la Hunt, was receiving an annual pension of £27.10.11

DE LA HUNT, JJ, Postmaster at Dordrecht, 1 September 1878

DELGAIRNS, Mrs Agnes, Postmaster at Knysna, 1 May 1854

DE LINT, K, Postmaster at Piquetberg, 8 April 1866

DELY, W, Clerk to the Civil Commissioner and postmaster at Somerset East, 1 January 1848

DEN, John D, General Manager of Telegraphs. In about 1864 Den was employed by the Cape of Good Hope Telegraph Co, where he held the position of General Manager. When the Company was purchased by the Cape Colonial Government in 1873, the new owners retained his services in the same management position. There he *"discharged the responsible duties belonging to that post with great zeal and unwearying industry"* (Bennettt, 1908: 6). In 1877 Den contracted *"a fever"* and died. In a message to the Department, the Commissioner of Crown Lands and Public Works, John X Merriman MLA, stated that *"In Mr Den the Department has lost an efficient officer, and the Colony a conscientious and devoted public servant"* (Bennett, 1908:6)

DENYSSEN, Harry, Postmaster at Malagas, 12 September 1855

DENYSSEN, HJ, Postmaster at Malagas, 3 July 1854

DE OLIVERA, MJ, Postmaster at Klaarstroom, 1 October 1870

DERBYSHIRE, W, Postmaster at Plettenberg's Bay, 9 June 1854

DE ROOS, JL, Postmaster at Claremont Station, 10 May 1869
Postmaster at Bellville, 1 April 1872
Postmaster and station master at Eerste River Station, 17 February 1874
Postmaster and station master at Worcester Station, 1 January 1877

DESCALLY, TD, Acting postmaster at Tylden, July 1891

DE SMIDT, JH, Postmaster at Vredenburg, 1 April 1890

DE SMIDT, WT, Assistant postmaster at George, 1 May 1889
Postmaster at Bredasdorp, 1 September 1898
Postmaster at Woodstock Station, 1 May 1905
Postmaster at Butterworth, 1 July 1906. On 30 November 1909 his widow, FM de Smidt, was receiving an annual pension of £12.16.7

DESSINGTON, JL, Postmaster and station master at Newlands, 23 March 1866

DE STADLER, PJ, Postmaster at Hopefield, 1 March 1895

DEVENISH, C St L, Postmaster and field-cornet at Van Wyk's Vlei, 15 April 1869

DEVENISH, Miss EM, Postmaster at Omdraai's Vlci, 1 October 1899
Reappointed postmaster at Omdraai's Vlei, 1 September 1906.
In colonial times Omdraai's Vlei probably marked the terminal point of an early wagon route. On 22 February 1900 Republican forces occupied the village and, on 4 March, they were reinforced by an additional group of 200 men led by Gen PJ Liebenberg. On 30 December 1901 a visiting Republican commando extensively damaged the post office and looted its mails. After the war the postmaster of Omdraai's Vlei, Miss Devenish, was commended for the courage she displayed during the invasion, when she not only saved her telegraph equipment, but also managed to restore communications with other centres at a time when these were being interrupted repeatedly by enemy forces (PMG 1896; POC 245, 1 April 1902)

DEVENISH, Miss FJ, Postmaster at Omdraai's Vlei, 1 November 1908

DEVENISH, J, Postmaster at Beaufort West, 14 June 1830

DEVENISH, JG, Clerk to the Civil Commissioner and postmaster at Beaufort West, March 1846

DE VILLIERS, AB, Postmaster at Groot Drakenstein, 1 January 1861, service provided for free

DE VIILIERS, AB, Postmaster at Sutherland, 1880

DE VILLIERS, Miss Anna Elizabeth, Postmaster at River Zonder End, 1 September 1906

DE VILLIERS, AH, Postmaster at Wallfontein, 20 April 1852

DE VILLIERS, AP, Clerk to the Civil Commissioner and postmaster at Peddie, 1 February 1848
  Clerk to the Civil Commissioner and postmaster at Graaff-Reinet, 20 March 1852

DE VILLIERS, Miss AT, Postmaster at Durbanville, 1 March 1890

DE VILLIERS, BL, Acting postmaster at Genadendal, 1 April 1895
  Postmaster at Genadendal, 1 September 1895

DE VILLIERS, CC, Postmaster at Paarl, 1 March 1846

DE VILLIERS, CV, Postmaster at Darling, 1 May 1896
  Postmaster at Bellville, 1 February 1897
  Postmaster at Ceres Road, April 1897

DE VILLIERS, G, Postmaster at Prince Albert Road, 1882

DE VILLIERS, Miss HA, Postmaster at Genadendal, 1 July 1904
  Postmaster at Elim, 1 July 1905

DE VILLIERS, Mrs HM, Postmaster at Riebeek West, 1 March 1894

DE VILLIERS, J, Postmaster at Greyton, 1880

DE VILLIERS, J, Postmaster at Kookfontein, 9 January 1859, service provided for free

DE VILLIERS, J, Postmaster at Modder River, Division of Caledon, 29 December 1859, service provided for free

DE VILLIERS, JA, Postmaster at Modder River, Division of Caledon, 11 February 1864, service provided for free
  Postmaster at Springer's Kuil, 1 July 1867

DE VILLIERS, Miss JE, Postmaster at Elim, 1 October 1906

DE VILLIERS, Miss Janetta Francis, Postmaster at Durbanville, 20 January 1900

DE VILLIERS, JJ, Postmaster at Paarl, 2 June 1853

DE VILLIERS, JPG, Station master at Belmont, 7 December 1901, salary £212 pa

DE VILLIERS, MJ, Postmaster and field-cornet at Paardenberg, 7 April 1856, service provided for free

DE VOS, HR, Postmaster and field-cornet at Somerset West, 9 May 1823

DE VOS, J, Postmaster at Haaspoort, 1881

DE VOS, WN, Postmaster at Tulbagh, 7 November 1822
  Postmaster at Tulbagh, 1829

DE VRIES, Catharina S, Postmaster at Clanwilliam, 1 June 1866

DE VRIES, N, Postmaster at Clanwilliam, 17 July 1865

DE VRIES, NA, Postmaster at Clanwilliam, 19 October 1857

DE VRIES, Mrs NA, Postmaster at Clanwilliam, 1 March 1874

DE VRIES, W, Postmaster at Lily Fountain, 1 September 1874

DE WAAL, BJ, Postmaster at Tulbagh, 13 May 1868

DE WET, DJ, Postmaster at Victoria West, 18 January 1847

DE WET, DJ, Postmaster at Sutherland, 1881

DE WET, HWB, Postmaster at Mossel Bay, 21 July 1853

DE WET, JP Jnr, Clerk, fifth class, GPO, Cape Town, 28 January 1865
Moved to Swellendam, 1866

DE WET, PD, Postmaster and field-cornet at Middlebosjesveld, 10 May 1858. The post office of Middelbosjesveld was listed as a field-cornetcy whose mail was forwarded through Worcester

DE WIT, CF, Postmaster and field-cornet at Groot Zwartberg, 31 August 1859, service provided for free in 1867-73

DE WIT, FC, Postmaster at Lady Grey, Robertson, 1 October 1883
Postmaster at Lady Grey, Robertson, 19 May 1890

DE WIT, Frederick Francois, Postmaster at Houw Hoek, 1905
Postmaster at Riebeek Kasteel, 1 April 1905
Postmaster at Genadendal, 1 June 1905
Postmaster at Smith's Mine, 1 April 1910

DE WITT, Miss Wilhelmina du Toit, Postmaster at McGregor, 1 January 1906

DEXTER, Ralph Grenfell, Entered Private Wires Branch, GPO, London, 3 February 1881
Migrated to the Cape and entered Secretary's Office, GPO, Cape Town, 21 November 1882
Principal Clerk, Records Branch, 1 January 1889
Clerk, Inland Mails Branch, 1 July 1897, Principal Clerk, 1 January 1902

DIACK, Charles, Assistant teacher at the Church of England Mission School and postmaster at Bredasdorp, 5 February 1852, dismissed from post

DICK, J, Postmaster and field-cornet at Gonubie, July 1862, service provided for free in 1868-73

DICK, R, Postmaster at Cookhouse, 1 July 1890
Postmaster at Alicedale, 1 February 1891

DICKINSON, J, also listed as DICKENSON, born in about 1852
Postmaster at Molteno, 1 January 1896
Postmaster at Burghersdorp, 1 April 1903
The Pension Lists of 30 November 1909 recorded that in 1910 Mr Dickinson, age 57, was retired on an annual pension of £250

DICKENSON, J, see under DICKINSON

DICKERSON, Walter Edward, Station master King William's Town, 19 Aug 1906, salary £330pa

DICKSON, H, Postmaster at Porterville, 1881

DICKSON, SA, Postmaster at Porterville Road, 17 November 1879

DIRK, J, Postmaster at Lily Fountain, 1880

DIRKER, J, Postmaster at Molen River, 5 May 1857

DISTIN, AS, Postmaster at Daggaboersnek, 1 August 1878

DITHMUS, J, Postmaster at Kendrew Station, 1880

DIXON, J, Postmaster at Lily Fountain, 15 January 1869

DIXON, JH, Postmaster at Cathcart, 1 February 1892

Postmaster at Rosmead, 1 March 1902

The Pension Lists of 30 November 1909 recorded that in 1910 Mr Dixon, age 45, was retired on an annual pension of £152.10.0

DIXON, W, Postmaster at Henderson, 8 June 1877

DOBSON, RJ, Postmaster at Kariega Station, 1 July 1863

DODDS, EH, Postmaster at Van Wyk's Vlei, 1 January 1878

DOMAN, AJ, Postmaster and field-cornet at Steenberg, 17 May 1867, service provided for free

DONALDSON, J, Postmaster at Beaufort West, 1909, formerly Assistant first class

DONALDSON, Walter James, Station master at Maitland, 2 June 1908, salary £274 pa

DONALDSON, William Edward, Postmaster at Tsomo, 1 June 1903

DONGES, M, Postmaster at Carnarvon, 1 October 1865

DONKIN, GT, Postmaster at Kokstad, 1881

DONOVAN, T, Postmaster at Bain's Kloof, 29 August 1850

DOOLITTLE, J, Postmaster and station master at Centlivres, 1879

Postmaster at Highlands, 1 December 1879

DORRINGTON, Neville Windsor, Postmaster at Cofimvaba, 1 January 1897

Postmaster at Seymour, 1 July 1897

Postmaster at Mount Fletcher, 1 April 1899

Postmaster at Peddie, 1 March 1900

Postmaster at Draghoender, 1 June 1900

Postmaster at Peddie, 1 March 1901

DOUGLAS, D, Postmaster at Barroe, in about 1878

DOUGLAS, WM, Postmaster at Clarkebury, 1882

DOVEY, R, Postmaster at Bedford, 1 October 1855

DOWLING, GR, Postmaster at Napier, 24 April 1857, dismissed from office

DOWNING, R, Postmaster and field-cornet at Bland's Drift, 12 September 1861

DOWNING, R, Postmaster at Bland's Drift, 1882

DOWSETT, W, Postmaster and field-cornet at Uitvlugtfontein, Victoria West, 1 August 1870

DOYLE, Frederick, Station master at Willowmore, 24 September 1909, salary £219 pa

DRAPER, Mr, Postmaster at Malmesbury, 1852

DRAPER, Thomas, Postmaster at Claremont Station, 12 April 1853

DREDGE, Mrs, Postmaster at Farm No 53, 1 August 1872

DREDGE, W, Postmaster at Farm No 53, 1 March 1866

DREYER, A, Postmaster at Riversdale, 1880

DREYER, AB, Postmaster at Pampoenpoort, 1881

DREYER, C, Postmaster at Tsomo, 1 September 1879

DREYER, TF, Postmaster at Lily Fountain, 26 June 1867

DREYER, WA, Postmaster and field-cornet at Honingberg, 29 May 1858

DRINKWATER, HF, Postmaster at George, 29 December 1851

DRY, Th, Postmaster at Cradock, 2 June 1853

DRY, Ann, Postmaster at Cradock, 18 May 1860

DRYSDALE, James, Clerk, GPO, Cape Town, 1 February 1888. Moved to Clerk, Civil Commissioner and Resident Magistrate, Knysna, 1 December 1889; eventually appointed Civil Commissioner and Resident Magistrate, Alexandria (1908); served as trooper and Lieutenant, 2nd Brabant's Horse, in the South African War of 1899-1902

DUBLIN, RJ, Postmaster at North End, Port Elizabeth, 1881

DUCK, Walter George Percy, Postmaster at Doorn River, 1 February 1900

    Postmaster at Darling, 1 June 1903. Before his death he may have been appointed Assistant Post Master in Aliwal North. On 30 November 1909 his widow, FM Duck, was receiving an annual pension of £16.17.0

DUDLEY, E Lionel, Postmaster at Cradock Station, before 1905

    Postmaster at Knysna, 1 February 1905

DUDLEY, W, Postmaster at Blanco, 1 March 1862

    Postmaster at Uniondale, 1 June 1866

    Postmaster at Avontuur, 30 October 1871

    Deceased while in office in about 1874

DUFF, Benjamin Michael, ISO, VD, born about 1840

    Acting postmaster at Swellendam, 1 April 1863

    Telegraph Officer under the old Telegraph Company, 1864

    Chief Clerk and Accountant of Telegraphs, Cape Town, March 1875

    Secretary, GPO, Cape Town, possible date 1 April 1875

    Superintendent of Telegraphs, Cape Town

    Management, Department of Telegraphs, 1880

    Acting Postmaster General, 1900

    Acting Postmaster General, 1902, retired in 1904

    Full member, Institute of Electrical Engineers

    Lieutenant-Colonel and Commanding Officer, Cape Town Highlanders

    Awarded the the Imperial Service Order in 1903

    South African General Service Medal

    The Queens Medal, Souith African War

    Companion of the Imperial Service Order

    By 1909, at the age of 69, Benjamin Duff was receiving an annual pension of £633.6.8

DUFFETT, CRJ, Postmaster at Nelspoort, 27 April 1898

DUGGAN, Mr, Postmaster at Richmond, in about 1873

DUGGAN, DJ, Postmaster at Daggaboersnek, 23 May 1868

DUGGAN, John E, Postmaster at Britstown, 16 December 1885

DUGGAN, T, Postmaster at De Aar, 1 August 1908

    Postmaster at Worcester, 1 November 1909

DUGMORE, HE, Postmaster at Pearston, 1 September 1896

DUGMORE, J, Postmaster and field-cornet at Bowden, 1 February 1875

DUGMORE, WF, Postmaster at Spring Valley, 1 September 1899

DUK, Charles William Raven, Postmaster at Mowbray Station, 16 March 1872
  Postmaster at Addo, probable date of appointment 16 May 1872
  Postmaster and station master at Bennettsville, 1 May 1873
  Postmaster and station master at Uitenhage Station, 4 October 1875
  Postmaster at Kariega Station, in about 1876
  Postmaster and station master at Glenconnor, 1 May 1877
  Postmaster and station master at Porterville Road, 1 April 1878
  Postmaster and station master at Ceres Road, in about 1879
  Postmaster and station master at Malmesbury Station, 1880

DUMINY, B, Postmaster at Maitland Road, Eleventh Milestone, 20 December 1853
  The post office at Maitland Road was also known as Maitland Road (Eleventh Milestone), Duminy's, and Eleventh Mile Stone (Maitland Road). On 20 December 1853 Mr B Duminy was appointed as postmaster there and rendered this service gratis. Duminy was a descendant of Francis Duminy, who landed at the Cape in 1771 and settled on a farm near Cape Town now known as Gardens. It seems probable that this post office was abolished in about 1860 when the new village of Bellville was established nearby, on a site previously known as Twelfth Mile Stone, Maitland Road

DUNKLEY, G, Postmaster and field-cornet at Pearston, 6 June 1862

DUNN, H, Postmaster at Eerste River Station, 1 February 1865, service provided free in 1865-67

DUNN, J, Postmaster at Vyge Kraal 29 January 1855, service provided for free

DUNN, T, Postmaster at Kuils River, 1 November 1860

DUNN, William, Postmaster at Port Elizabeth, 1 February 1822
  Post Master at Port Beaufort, 1830, possibly as early as 1 January 1828
  William Dunn was appointed as the first postmaster of Port Elizabeth on 1 February 1822. He was also employed as the port's Collector of Customs, His office was a small wood and iron shed, located close to the beach landing place, at the foot of Jetty Street, which the Government rented from Richard Hunt (Harradine, personal communination), and it is probable that he conducted both his postal business and the collection of custom duties from these premises. In 1830 he moved to Port Beaufort where he was also appointed as its postmaster

DU PLESSIS, CP, Postmaster at Carnarvon, 1 February 1892
  Postmaster at Rosmead, 1 June 1895
  Postmaster at Steynsburg, 1 April 1896
  Postmaster at Rosmead, 1 March 1898

DU PLESSIS, J, Postmaster at Rasfontein, 1 September 1870

DU PREEZ, HM, Postmaster at Middelburg, in about 1875
  Postmaster at Cradock, 15 May 1875

DU PREEZ, HS, Postmaster and field-cornet at Two Streams, 27 April 1859

DU PREEZ, J, Postmaster at Misganst, 16 October 1858

DU PREEZ, JH, Postmaster and field-cornet at Upper Gouritz River, 10 May 1858, removed from office

DU PREEZ, ML, Postmaster and field-cornet at Attaquas Kloof, 1 June 1860

DU PREEZ, Petrus Johannes, Postmaster at Campbell, 1 August 1893

Postmaster at Griquatown, 15 April 1896

Postmaster at Hopefield, 1 November 1898

Postmaster at Hankey, 1902

Postmaster at Steytlerville, 1 June 1903

Postmaster at New Bethesda, 1 December 1903

Postmaster at Jansenville, 1 September 1909

DU PREEZ, WJ, Postmaster and field-cornet at South Middelveld, 1 January 1875

DUTHIE, AH, Postmaster at Belvidere, 12 October 1857

DUTHIE, F, Postmaster at Belvidere, 1 January 1864

DUTHIE, John, Lighthouse keeper and postmaster at Cape St Francis, 1880

DUTHIE, Capt Thomas Henry, Postmaster at Belvidere, 1 February 1844, service provided for free, deceased while in office. Capt Thomas Henry Duthie emigrated to the Cape in 1826. In 1830 he visited Knysna where he was the guest of George Rex, whose daughter Caroline he subsequently married in Cape Town in 1833. He retired to Knysna the following year, where he devoted his time to the development of his estate on the Knysna Lagoon, and to the construction of Belvedere House. The post office at Knysna, Belvidere, was opened on 1 February 1844 with Duthie as its first postmaster. Between 1844 and 1867 the position of postmaster at Belvidere was filled by four members of the Duthie family, two of whom performed their duties gratis. This would explain why, in its early days, this establishment was listed by some sources as Duthie's. It seems probable, therefore, that the postal business of Belvidere was conducted by the Duthies more as a social service than as a commercial activity

DU TOIT, Alida, Postmaster at North Paarl, 1 September 1866

DU TOIT, AH, Postmaster and field-cornet at Over Hex River, 16 May 1863

DU TOIT, AJ, Postmaster at Bellville, 1882

Postmaster at Prince Albert Road, 1882

DU TOIT, Charl, Postmaster at De Keur, 27 February 1855

DU TOIT, DJ, Postmaster at Sir Lowry's Pass, 16 July 1857

Postmaster at Stanford, 20 January 1864

DU TOIT, Miss H, Postmaster at Prince Alfred's Hamlet, 1 June 1906

DU TOIT, HP, Postmaster at Riebeek West, 1 December 1864

DU TOIT, JA, Postmaster at Eendekuil, 1 October 1902

DU TOIT, JAJ, Postmaster at Montagu, 1 May 1885

DU TOIT, Mrs JH, Postmaster at George, 1 October 1816

DU TOIT, Miss MD, Postmaster at Prince Alfred's Hamlet, 1 February 1909

DU TOIT, RJ, Postmaster at Over Hex River, 1 July 1862, deceased while in office

DU TOIT, SH, Clerk to the Civil Commissioner and postmaster at Uitenhage, 1 March 1846
DU TOIT, SP, Postmaster and field-cornet at Voor Zwartland, 29 May 1858
DU TOIT, SPJ, Postmaster and field-cornet at Klaarfontein, 1 Nov 1870, service provided free
DUTTON, WR, Postmaster at Hankey, 1 April 1896
DYASON, Ernest Clement, Clerk, Money Order Office, GPO, Cape Town, July 1890
    Moved to Assistant Superintendent of Convicts, Tokai, 1 February 1899
DYASON, George, Postmaster at Bathurst, 1 April 1821
    Postmaster at Grahamstown, 20 March 1823
    George Dyason was the leader of a party of settlers originating from London who sailed to the Cape in 1820 on the *Zoroaster*. He was subsequently appointed field-cornet for Albany, and Civil Commissioner and Resident Magistrate at Bathurst and, later, at Graaff-Reinet
DYASON, H, Postmaster and field-cornet at Petersburg, 1 June 1863
DYASON, Isaac, Postmaster at Bathurst, 1824
    Postmaster at Beaufort West, 1 September 1836
    Isaac Dyason was a member of a party of settlers originating from London who sailed to the Cape in 1820 on the *Zoroaster*
DYER, Mrs F, Postmaster at Halfmanshof, 12 November 1907
DYKE, Egbert Walter, also listed as DW, Postmaster at Worcester, 1883
    Postmaster at Worcester Station, 4 October 1883
    Postmaster at Naauwpoort, 1 April 1889
    Postmaster at Middelburg Road, 1 June 1890
    Postmaster at Steynsburg, 1 May 1892
    Postmaster at Alicedale, 1 February 1895
    Postmaster at Kenhardt, 1 June 1896
    Acting postmaster at Clanwilliam, 1 August 1897
    Postmaster at Richmond, 1 November 1897
    Postmaster at Klipdam, 1 January 1899
    Postmaster at Norval's Pont, 1 September 1899
    Postmaster at Carnarvon, 1 March 1900
    Postmaster at Barkly East, 1 October 1900
    Postmaster at Porterville Road, 1 October 1902
    Postmaster at Calvinia, 1 February 1903, in 1909 he earned a salary of £220 pa
DYKE, JF, Postmaster at North End, Port Elizabeth, 1 July 1894
DYKE, T, Postmaster at Sandflats, 12 November 1895

E
EADIE, David, Telegraphist, Glasgow, 13 May 1885
    Assistant postmaster at Graaff-Reinet, 23 September 1889
    Postmaster at Barkly West, 1 April 1893
    Moved to Clerk, Civil Commissioner and Resident Magistrate, Cradock, 20 November 1895

Resident Magistrate, Collector of Customs, and postmaster at Walfish Bay, 23 August 1905

Civil Commissioner and Resident Magistrate, Peddie, 9 December 1907

EALES, R, Postmaster at Bedford, 2 August 1856

EAMES, T, Postmaster at Thomas River Station, 12 August 1897

EARL, Arthur Cecil, Postmaster at Delport's Hope, 1 October 1902

Postmaster at Fraserburg Road, 1 January 1907

EARL, Percival, Postmaster at Mount Frere, 1 August 1899

Postmaster at Griquatown, 1 October 1900

Postmaster at Orange River, 1 April 1903

EARLE, EF, Postmaster at Seven Fountains, 26 April 1879

EARLE, William I, Acting postmaster at Bathurst, 1830

Postmaster at Bathurst, 6 June 1832

William Earle sailed to the Cape in 1820 on the *Belle Alliance*, and was married to Mary Boardman. He was killed during the frontier war of 1850-53

EARLE, WJ, Postmaster at Grahamstown, 1 September 1836

EASLEY, F, Postmaster at Coerney, 15 January 1879

EASLEY, J, Postmaster and station master at Uitenhage Station, 15 June 1878

Postmaster and station master at Zwartkops Station, 1 March 1876

EAST, George Robert, Postmaster at Umzimkulu, 1 March 1908

EATON, FJ, Acting postmaster at Drooge Vlei, 1862

EATON, FJA, Postmaster at Steynsburg, 13 August 1875

EATON, HR, Postmaster at Steynsburg, in about 1874

EATON, Oswald, Postmaster at Hanover, 1 August 1908

EATON, WH, Postmaster and field-cornet at Drooge Vlei, 14 June 1856, service provided for free in 1856-60

EATWELL, Albert James, Postmaster at Hoetjes Bay, 1 March 1896

Postmaster at Eerste River Station, 16 November 1897

Postmaster at O'Okiep, 1 January 1904

EBERLIN, J, Postmaster at Uitkyk, 1 July 1875

ECKARD, G, Letter carrier in about 1881

ECKHARD, JC, Letter carrier, GPO, Cape Town, 1 Nov 1871, dismissed from office in 1874

ECKHARD, JJ, Postmaster at Beaufort West, 1 March 1876

ECKLEY, John C, Postmaster at Burghersdorp, 4 December 1855

Postmaster at Vlakfontein, Division of Albert, 3 January 1862, service provided for free

EDDY, James, Postmaster at De Aar, 1 July 1906

Postmaster at Cradock, 1 September 1908

EDGECOMBE, E, Postmaster at Ceres Road, 1885

Postmaster at Hopetown, 1 October 1885

EDGCOME, FJ, Postmaster at Porterville, 23 April 1890

Postmaster at Observatory Road, 1 April 1895

Postmaster at Calvinia, 1 June 1900

EDMONDS, GB, Postmaster at Emgwali, 1 April 1902

EDMONDS, T, Postmaster at Emgwali, 1 September 1909

EDWARDS, JJ, Postmaster at Glen Lynden, in about 1866

EDWARDS, JP, Management, Department of Telegraphs, 1880

Postmaster at Fort Beaufort, 1 March 1886

Postmaster at King William's Town, 1 January 1892

EDWARDS, K, Postmaster at Ceres, 5 June 1852

EDWARDS, W, born in about 1863 in Birmingham, England, joined the Post Office in 1881

Telegraphist at Birmingham, England, 1881, emigrated to the Cape in 1882

Postmaster at Fort Beaufort, 1906

Postmaster at Beaconsfield, 1 October 1907

Retired on pension in 1908. The Pension Lists of 30 November 1909 recorded that in 1910 Mr Edwards, age 46, was retired on an annual pension of £172.5.0.

EEDES, H, Postmaster at Herbertsdale, 1 November 1879

EEDES, M, Postmaster at Little Brak River, 1 April 1871, service provided for free in 1871-73

EHLERS, GL, Postmaster at Malmesbury, 23 August 1853

EHLERS, JG, Postmaster at Malmesbury, 28 January 1857

EHLERS, JH, Postmaster at Veld Drift, 1 January 1866, service provided for free

EHLERS, TL, Postmaster at Zout Rivier, 30 April 1873, service provided for free

EKSTEEN, JH, Postmaster at Napier, 1 April 1902

Postmaster at Moorreesburg, 1 September 1902

Postmaster at Napier, 1 February 1903

EKSTEEN, Michael Jacobus Adriaan, Postmaster at Vanrhynsdorp, 1 July 1894

Postmaster at Calvinia, 1 November 1895

Postmaster at Wellington Station, 1 January 1896

Postmaster at Prieska, 1 May 1896

Postmaster at Carnarvon, 1 March 1897

ELFORT, FA, Postmaster at Amalienstein, 1 January 1864, service provided for free

ELIOT, GA, Sorter, GPO, Cape Town, 16 November 1866, deceased while in office in 1869

ELLIOTT, H, Postmaster at Prince Albert, 6 August 1850

ELLIOTT, JH, Postmaster at Nelspoort, 15 August 1858

ELLIOTT, WT, Postmaster and field-cornet at Nelspoort, 1 February 1877

ELLIS, C, Postmaster at Ibeka, 22 September 1878

Postmaster at Butterworth, 1879

ELLIS, James, born in about 1827

Postmaster at Caledon, 1 May 1874

Postmaster at Montagu, 1 January 1893

Postmaster at Hopefield, 1 January 1896

The Pension Lists of 30 November 1909 recorded that in 1910 Mr Ellis, age 82, was retired on an annual pension of £114.18.11

ELLISON, G, Postmaster at Simonstown, 1 May 1877

ELLMAN, R, Postmaster at Beaufort West, 1882

ELS, RC, Postmaster at Fort Wiltshire, 10 May 1858, service provided for free

ELSLICK, HM, Postmaster at Aberdeen Road, 16 December 1897

ELSON, MM, Postmaster at Grabouw, 1 April 1871

ELTON, H, Boy Sorter, GPO, Cape Town, in about 1880
Superintendent, Registered Letter Branch, GPO, Cape Town, in about 1881

ELTON, WE, Postmaster at Laingsburg, 16 May 1877

ELTRINGHAM, E, born in about 1856
Postmaster at Cradock, 1 May 1883
Reappointed postmaster at Cradock, 1 January 1892
The Pension Lists of 30 November 1909 recorded that in 1910 Mr Eltringham, age 53, was retired on an annual pension of £310

ELTZE, A, Postmaster at Jagersbosch, 1 May 1875

ELY, H, Postmaster at Aberdeen, Division of Aberdeen, 4 March 1859

EMETT, E, Postmaster at Caledon, 1 March 1846

EMMETT, EC, Postmaster at Qumbu, 1 September 1887
Postmaster at Philipstown, 1 November 1888

EMMETT, W, Clerk to the Civil Commissioner and postmaster at Seymour, 8 March 1848

EMMS, J, Postmaster and field-cornet at Fish River Randt, 1 July 1871, service provided for free

EMSLIE, W, Postmaster at Seven Fountains, 1 April 1869

ENGEL, M, Postmaster at Port Beaufort, 1 January 1873

ENGELA, Miss AA, Postmaster at Aberdeen, Division of Aberdeen, 1 April 1886

ENGELA, Carel Andries, Postmaster at Sutherland, 1 October 1886

ENGELA, CJ, Postmaster at Sutherland, 1 November 1885

ENGELA, MJ, Postmaster at Sutherland, 14 November 1897

ENGELBRECHT, C, Postmaster at Spruitdrift, 1 July 1874

ENGELBRECHT, JA, Postmaster at Kookfontein, 15 November 1861, service provided for free

ENGELBRECHT, PG, Postmaster and field-cornet at Uitvlugtfontein, Division of Victoria West, 1 January 1869

ENGELS, A, Postmaster at Petersburg, 1 March 1863

ENGELS, George, Postmaster at Woodstock Station, 29 April 1854
Postmaster at Koopman's Rivier, 6 July 1858
Postmaster at Riebeek West, 9 June 1859

ENGELS, H, Postmaster at Modderfontein, Division of Clanwilliam, 1 May 1904

ENMAN, G, Postmaster at Two Streams, 1 April 1873

ENSLIN, Adriaan Jacobus, Postmaster at Alexandria, 1 April 1905

ENTE, JG, Postmaster at Darling, 1880

ERASMUS, JJ, Postmaster at Petersburg, 1 May 1875

ERFURT, V, Postmaster at Calitzdorp, 1 March 1890
ERRINGHAM, A, Postmaster at Bizana, 1 November 1895
ERSKINE, D, Resident Magistrate and postmaster at Walfish Bay, 1878
ESCOTT, W, Postmaster at Umtata, 1880
ESTERHUIZEN, AE, Postmaster at Merweville, 1 September 1906
EVA, FM, Postmaster at Queen Street, Port Elizabeth, 1 May 1899
EVA, RB, Postmaster at Pavet, 1 October 1875
EVANS, EJ, Postmaster at Kentani, 1 May 1895
EVANS, G, Postmaster at Wolvefontein Station, 1 February 1879
EVANS, JA, Postmaster at Modder River, Division of Kimberley, 1 April 1896
EVE, Frederick James, Postmaster at Rosmead, 1 October 1897
    Postmaster at Steynsburg, 1 March 1898
    Postmaster at North End, Port Elizabeth, 1 June 1903
    Postmaster at Rosmead, 1 August 1908
EVENS, Frederick J, Postmaster at Whittlesea, 1 May 1885
EVERINGHAM, Albert Reginald Ainge, Postmaster at Plumstead, 1909
EVERITT, AE, Postmaster at Barkly East, 16 June 1896
    Postmaster at Claremont Station, 1 April 1899
    Postmaster at Swellendam, 1 October 1902
    Postmaster at Graaff-Reinet, 1 September 1908
EVERITT, Alfred, Postmaster at Willowmore, c1901
    On 1 June 1901 a Republican commando under Comdt Gideon Scheepers attacked Willowmore, but without success. About six weeks later, on 11 August 1901, British forces engaged Scheepers' forces in the vicinity of Willowmore. It is recorded that during this time Mr Everitt, postmaster of Willowmore, rendered exceptional services to the Postal Department. For this he received the specific commendation of the military authorities (POC 245, 1 April 1902)
EVERTON, J, Postmaster and station master at Blue Cliff, 1 October 1879
    Postmaster at Blue Cliff, 1881
EVETT, WH, Postmaster at Zuurpoort, Murraysburg, 18 April 1867, service provided free
EWERS, Miss K, Postmaster at Keiskammahoek, 1 June 1896
EWERS, Miss M, Postmaster at Keiskammahoek, 1 October 1903
EWING, WJ, Postmaster at Murraysburg, 1 April 1890
EYRE, George H, Acting postmaster at Orange River, 1 October 1885.
    George Eyre went become Postmaster General and Commissioner of Mines for Rhodesia
EYRE, Mrs I, Postmaster at Wynberg, 22 August 1836

F

FACHSE, RA, Postmaster at Willowmore, 1 May 1869
FAHEY, Henry James, Postmaster at Van Wyk's Vlei, 1 May 1907
FAIR, Chas, Postmaster at Knysna, 17 November 1852

FAIRBROTHER, JC, Postmaster and station master at Woodstock Station, 1 April 1876

FALCK, DGA, also listed as DA, Postmaster at Middelburg, 15 July 1875

Postmaster at Beaufort West, 1 June 1878

Falck was subsequently appointed Postmaster General of the Orange River Colony in Bloemfontein. He was placed on pension on 31 May 1910 when the Union of South Africa was proclaimed, and the four colonial Post Offices were united under a single management based in Pretoria. In the Parliamentary Election of 1924 for the Constituency of Albert, Mr DGA Falck of the South African Party lost to Mr Lourens Jacobus Steytler of the National Party by 739 votes

FANANT, L, Postmaster at Engcobo, 1881

FARQUHAR, A, Postmaster and field-cornet at Van Putten's Vlei, 1 March 1868

FARQUHARSON, W, Postmaster at Wagenaar's Kraal, 1 August 1874

Postmaster at Beaufort West, in about 1878

FARRELL, John William, born in about 1848

Postmaster at Simonstown, 1 August 1868

Postmaster at George, 1 November 1878

Postmaster at Heidelberg, 1 May 1885, retired in 1901

The Pension Lists of 30 November 1909 recorded that in 1910 Mr Farrell, age 61, was retired on an annual pension of £147.2.7

FARRELL, Miss Kathleen May Emily, Postmaster at Doorn River, 1 May 1906

FAURE, A, Postmaster at Hertzog, 1880

FAURE, JC, Postmaster at Somerset Strand, 1 November 1867, service provided for free

FAURE, JPE, Postmaster at Cape Town, 1823

FEATHERSTONE, JH, Postmaster and field-cornet at East Riet River, 1 April 1866

FELLOWS, Mr, Postmaster and station master at Sandflats, in about 1877

FENIX, G, Clerk to the Magistrate and postmaster at Cofimvaba, 1 January 1879

Postmaster at Southeyville, 1880

Postmaster at Cala, 1883

FENNELL, J, Postmaster at Toleni/Ndabakazi, 1 June 1874.

The post office at Toleni was opened on 1 June 1874, and was probably located on the premises of Mr Fennell's hotel. In May 1907 its establishment was moved to the local station and soon thereafter, in August 1907, its name was changed to Ndabakazi

FENSTONE, J, Postmaster at Nelspoort, 1881

FERGUSON, EA, Postmaster at Yellow Woods, 1 May 1877

FERGUSON, EH, Postmaster at Manly's Flats, 31 May 1859, service provided for free

FERGUSON, Isabella, Postmaster at Cookhouse, in about 1870

FERGUSON, J, Postmaster at Yellow Woods, 1 July 1874

FERGUSON, June, Postmaster at Cookhouse, 1 June 1868

FERNIE, GM, Postmaster at East London Jetty, 1 October 1909

FERNIE, James, born in about 1855

Postmaster at Tarkastad, 1 December 1886
Postmaster at De Aar, 1 February 1896
Postmaster at Cookhouse, 1 January 1902
Postmaster at Vryburg, 1902
The Pension Lists of 30 November 1909 recorded that in 1910 Mr Fernie, age 54, was retired on an annual pension of £264.18.9

FERREIRA, I, Postmaster at Adelaide, 5 May 1859, service provided for free

FERREIRA, Miss M, Postmaster at Peiserton, 1 July 1908

FEUCHT, John A, Acting postmaster at Moorreesburg, before1897
Postmaster at Springbokfontein, 1 July 1897

FFORDE, James, Chief Inspector of Public Works, 1877
Acting General Manager, Telegraphs, held dual appointment in 1877 following the death in office of Mr Den, ans awaiting the appointment of a new Acting General Manager

FICK, Mrs Johanna C, Postmaster at Piquetberg, 18 March 1857

FILMER, Miss E, Postmaster at Libodi, 1902

FILMER, G, Postmaster at Sea Point, 1 October 1870

FINCHAM, FP, Postmaster at Jamestown, 1 October 1875, service provided for free in 1875-76

FINCHAM, G, Postmaster and field-cornet at Roydon, 29 September 1858

FINCHMAN, A, Postmaster at Willow Park, 1882

FINDLAY, J, Postmaster at Lady Grey, Division of Aliwal North, 9 August 1860

FINDLAY, P, Postmaster at Paarl, 11 January 1883

FINLAY, George, Postmaster at Prince Albert Road, 1 December 1895
Station master at Graaff-Reinet, 18 August 1906, salary £285 pa

FINLAY, J, Postmaster at Klipplaat, 1 February 1900

FINLAY, W, Postmaster at Highlands, 1880

FINLAYSON, Ms A, Postmaster at Drie Vlei, 1 April 1874, service provided for free

FINLAYSON, J, Postmaster at Grootfontein, in about 1878

FINLAYSON, R, Postmaster and station master at Mowbray Station, 1 February 1879
Postmaster at Claremont Station, 1880
Postmaster at Newlands, 1881

FINLAYSON, WM, Postmaster at Bushman's River, 1882

FIRTH, William Charles, Postmaster at Mill Street, Gardens, 1 February 1892
Postmaster at Clanwilliam, 1 March 1894
Postmaster at Wynberg, 1909

FISCHER, Miss Andrea Billie, Postmaster at Bolo Reserve, 1 July 1903

FISCHER, Miss CC, Postmaster at Bolo Reserve, 1 November 1892
Postmaster at St Marks, 1 November 1896
Postmaster at Bolotwa, 1 May 1899

FISCHER, Miss EG, Postmaster at Springbokfontein, 1 June 1892

FISCHER, FS, Postmaster at Oudtshoorn, 18 January 1853

FISCHER, JG, Postmaster at Springbokfontein, 1 July 1878
FISCHER, R le Sueur, Postmaster at Malmesbury, 6 February 1851
FISCHER, W, Postmaster at Aliwal North, 31 August 1857
FISHER, JA, Sorter, GPO, Cape Town, 15 April 1854
    Clerk, fifth class, GPO, Cape Town, 18 August 1856
    Clerk, fourth class, GPO, Cape Town, 1857
    Clerk, third class, GPO, Cape Town, 1858
    Clerk, second class, GPO, Cape Town, 1863
    Dismissed from service and convicted of defrauding the Post Office, 1866
FITZGERALD, JP, Postmaster at Fraserburg, in about 1880
FITZHOFF, W, Postmaster at Molen River, 1 June 1873
FITZPATRICK, M, Postmaster at Highlands, 1 December 1878
FLACK, C, Postmaster at Somerset West, 1 February 1877
FLANAGAN, P, Postmaster at Sandfontein, Division of Uitenhage, 1880
FLANAGHAN, G, Postmaster and field-cornet at Farm No 216, 1868, service provided for free
FLAXINGTON, James Charles, Postmaster at Sea Point, 1 April 1902
    Postmaster at Beaconsfield, 1909
FLEISCHER, JH, Postmaster at Somerset East, 28 July 1830
FLEISCHER, Sydney Martin, Acting postmaster at Prince Albert Road, 1906
    Postmaster at Kowie West, 1 July 1906
FLEMING, L, Postmaster at Sandflats, 21 July 1868, service provided for free
FLEMMER, TAA, Postmaster and police officer at Maraisburg, 1 July 1877
FLETCHER, Miss, Postmaster at Millwood, Goldfields, 1 July 1894
FLINT, TCA, Postmaster at Orange River, 1 December 1885
FLORENCE, John, Postmaster at Tylden, 1 April 1897
    Station master at Britstown, 10 March 1904, salary £225 pa
FLOQUET, AF, Postmaster at Windvogelberg, 1 July 1871
    Postmaster at Cathcart, 1 June 1877
FLOWERS, Harry Hamilton, Postmaster at Mafeking, 1 August 1890
    Postmaster at Somerset Strand, 1 February 1898
    Postmaster at Rondebosch, 1 July 1898
    Postmaster at Mafeking, 1 January 1901
FLYNN, HM, Postmaster at Petrusville, 16 August 1898
FLYNN, William Charles, Postmaster at Nqamakwe, 1 November 1906
FORBES, C, Postmaster at Walfish Bay, 1882
FORBES, James Charles, Postmaster at Molteno, 1 November 1909
FORBES, James M, Postmaster at Queenstown, 1 October 1886
FORD, Arthur James, Station master at Hout Kraal, 1 July 1908, salary £280 pa
FORD, AS, Postmaster at Richmond, 3 September 1853
FORD, ET, Clerk to the Civil Commissioner and postmaster at Richmond, 8 March 1848

FORD, H, GPO, Cape Town, 1 February 1868
   Clerk, Deeds Registry Office, 1871
FORD, J, Postmaster and field-cornet at Southwell, 1 July 1871, service provided for free
FORESTER, JF, Postmaster and station master at Porterville Road, 5 May 1876
   Postmaster at Hermon, 1 March 1877
FORGET, Nicholas Gaston, Station master Imvani, 1 March 1902, salary £232 pa
FORRESTER, I, Postmaster at Bellville, 1881
FORRESTER, JAM, Postmaster at Paarl Station, 1883
FORSYTH, R, Civil postmaster at Fort Beaufort, 5 April 1833
FOSTER, E, Postmaster at O'Okiep, 1 October 1895
FOSTER, Charles Hanson, Postmaster at Peddie, 1 August 1908
FORSTER, N, Postmaster at Plat River, 1880
FORSYTH, Alexander, Station master at Addo, 23 September 1909, salary £220 pa
FOTHERINGHAM, Mrs, Postmaster at Millwood, Goldfields, 1 April 1894
FOTHERINGHAM, AA, Postmaster at Wellington, 1883
   Postmaster at Blanco, 15 January 1886
FOUCHE, F, Postmaster at Blaauw Water, 26 August 1854, service provided for free
FOUCHE, JH, Postmaster and field-cornet at Petersburg, 1 July 1864
FOULKES, JF, Deputy Sheriff, Secretary to the Divisional Council, and postmaster at Malmesbury, 1 April 1871
FOULKES, S, Postmaster at Fransche Kraal, 24 November 1858, service provided for free
FOURIE, J, Postmaster at Krakeel River, 1882
FOURIE, JC, Postmaster at Springer's Kuil, 9 November 1861
FOURIE, L, Postmaster at Gamka's Vlakte, 3 September 1858
   Postmaster at Calitzdorp, 3 September 1858
FOURIE, PJ, Postmaster and field-cornet at Van Wyk's Vlei, 30 June 1860, service provided for free in 1867-68
FOURIE, Stephanus Josephus, Postmaster at Philadelphia, 5 May 1897
   Postmaster at Napier, 1 July 1899
   Postmaster at Groot Drakenstein, 1906. Salary £205.
FOURIE, WF, Postmaster at Wolvekop, 11 December 1873, service provided for free
FOWLER, Alfred John, Postmaster at Ugie, 1 January 1902
   Postmaster at Spring Valley, 1 April 1904
   Postmaster at East London Jetty, 1 November 1905
   Postmaster at Sterkspruit, 1 May 1908
FOWLER, J, Postmaster at North End, Port Elizabeth, 1880
FOWLER, T, Postmaster at West Bank, East London, 1 June 1895
FOWLER, TG, Postmaster at Maclear, 1 December 1895
FOX, J, Justice of the Peace and postmaster at Hondeklip Bay, 31 March 1857
FOX, Samuel, Postmaster at Alicedale, 16 December 1897

Postmaster at Prieska, 1 May 1899

On 1 February 1900 a Republican offensive into the north-western districts of the Cape sparked off a popular uprising among the Dutch inhabitants of this region, many of whom were Republican sympathisers. The revolt began at Prieska on 15 February 1900, when Dutch forces under Gen Steenkamp entered the town. It remained in their hands until 19 March when it was occupied by troops under the command of Gen Lord Kitchener. The Postmaster General's report to the Cape Parliament in 1899 made special mention of the postmaster of Prieska, and the manner in which he safeguarded official property during this time

FOX, Thomas Henry, Postmaster at Darling, 1 April 1904

FOXCROFT, J, Postmaster and field-cornet at Karreeboschfontein, 1 June 1875

FOY, L, Postmaster at Umtata, 1 August 1878

FRADGLEY, Edward, born in about 1848

Postmaster at Cala, 1 May 1887

Postmaster at Cala, 1 July 1894

The Pension Lists of 30 November 1909 recorded that in 1910 Mr Fradgley, age 61, was retired on an annual pension of £82.6.5

FRANCIS, AW, Postmaster at Queen Street, Port Elizabeth, 1883

FRANCIS, DN, Postmaster at Funah's Kloof, 10 May 1858, service provided for free

FRANCIS, E, Postmaster at Berlin Station, 1883

FRANCIS, JG, Postmaster at Upper Kloof Street, 1909

FRANCKE, Rev CT, Postmaster at Mamre, 14 March 1849

FRANENDORFER, M, Postmaster at Lady Grey, Division of Aliwal North, 19 July 1861

FRANKEN, PJ, Postmaster at Riebeek East, 1 April 1869

FRASER, John Blackbourne, Telegraphist, George, 1 November 1883

Postmaster at Prince Albert, 1 January 1886

Postmaster at Cathcart, 1 August 1886

Chief Clark, Worcester, 1 August 1887

Chief Clark, East London, 1 August 1889

Moved to Acting Clerk, Magistrate's Office, Queenstown, 23 November 1895, and in due course was appointed Acting Civil Commissioner and Resident Magistrate, Kenhardt, 12 February 1909

FRASER, N, Postmaster at Klaarstroom, 1 March 1890

Postmaster at Maclear, 1 September 1894

FRASER, PS, Postmaster at Mossel Bay, 1 April 1890

Postmaster at Port Alfred, 1 October 1891

FRASER, William, Joined the Cape Civil Service 17 February 1874

Telegraphist at Fraserburg, 1 August 1881

Postmaster at Fraserburg, 1 July 1885

Postmaster at Queenstown, 1 January 1889

Postmaster at Vryburg, 1 February 1896

Postmaster at Oudtshoorn, 1 November 1901

FRAZER, W, Postmaster at Fraserburg, 1 August 1881

FREAN, Miss, Postmaster at Green Point, 15 March 1891

FREEMAN, JJ, Postmaster at Rosmead, 1 March 1893

FREEMANTLE, Oliver Woodland, Postmaster at Elliotdale, 7 June 1897
Postmaster at Elliot, 1 June 1903

FREISLICH, C, Postmaster at Normandie, 11 January 1853

FREISLICH, JDA, Postmaster at Clanwilliam, 1 April 1836

FRENCH, JW, Postmaster at Kenhardt, 1 August 1897

FRENCH, Sir Somerset R. Somerset Richard French was born in England on 31 January 1849, the son of Robert French. He married Josephine Murphy who bore him a daughter and a son. He was educated privately, and on 30 August 1866, at the age of 17, he was appointed to the Money Order Office, at the General Post Office in London. The young man made rapid progress, and in September 1869 he was transferred to the Secretary's Department, Postal Branch. In about 1874 he was placed in charge of the Intelligence Branch, Telegraphs, and in July 1878 was selected to accompany the expeditionary force to Cyprus under Lt-Gen Sir Garnet Wolsley, where his task was to organize a post and telegraph service on the island. By now his reputation as an expert in postal matters was firmly established, and following the successful completion of this mission, he was requested to undertake the re-organization of the Cape's postal system. As a result he was transferred permanently to the Colonial Service and was posted to Cape Town where, on 1 August 1880, he was appointed Secretary and Accountant to the Postmaster General. On 1 January 1884 he introduced a Postal Savings Bank system and, in addition to his other duties, also became its Controller. Following the sudden death of George Aitchison on 26 January 1892, he was appointed Postmaster General of the Cape, as well as General Manager of the Cape, Natal and Basutoland Telegraph Company.

In time his portfolio was enlarged to include a number of additional responsibilities. In 1893 the post office of British Bechuanaland and the Rhodesian telegraphs were brought under his administration; in 1897 he was appointed Postmaster General for the Bechuanaland Protectorate; and from 1893 to 1897 French was also the General Manager of the Transvaal Continental Telegraph Company. As a result French personally came to control the greater part of Southern Africa's postal services, a role which gave him a major voice in the formulation of postal policies for the region and allowed him the scope to realize his vision of a greater southern African postal union. He was responsible for having the Cape Colony admitted to the Universal Postal Union in 1895, and was the major driving force in the introduction of the Imperial Penny Post on 28 December 1898. He represented the Cape, Natal and Rhodesia at the UPU conference in Washington in 1897, and in Rome in 1906. He oversaw the creation of a Southern African Postal Union in 1898, and brought South African postal rates in line with those of the UPU. During the South African War of 1899-1902 he was in control of the British Army Post Office in South Africa, as a result of which he received the special thanks of the Imperial Government and of Field-Marshal Lord Roberts.

A man of great business acumen and organizing ability, French predicted that the telegraph and the telephone would have a major impact upon communications. He also advocated the employment of well-educated men in the postal service, although he opposed the employment of women where office conditions would bring about fraternization between the genders. His administration was marked by a willingness to introduce extensive technical innovation, as well as a process of continual assessment, re-organization, and streamlining of management functions within the Post Office. In 1896 he was conferred the Dignity of Companion of the Most Distinguished Order of St Michael and St George for his services to the Colonial Post Office, and was knighted in 1901. He retired from his post in Cape Town on 31 January 1908, but continued to serve the Cape Colony until 1910, acting as its Agent General in London. He died at Aylwins, Mayfield, in Sussex, on 11 May 1929

FREW, Harry, Postmaster at Barkly West, 18 July 1898

Superintendent, GPO, Cape Town, , salary £360 pa plus £30 overtime.

FRISBY, E, Postmaster at Daggaboersnek, 1 July 1869

FROST, C, Postmaster and station master at Berlin Station, 1 November 1877

Postmaster and station master at Kubusie, 1 May 1878

Postmaster and station master at King William's Town Station, in about 1879

Postmaster and station master at Kei Road, 25 April 1879

FROST, Edward Gilbert, Station master at Klipheuvel, 23 October 1907, salary £223 pa

FROY, A, Postmaster at Kalk Bay, 1 July 1888

Postmaster at Belmont, 1 September 1889

Postmaster at Modder River, Division of Kimberley, 22 September 1889

Postmaster at Port Nolloth, 1 February 1895

Postmaster at Griquatown, 1 November 1895

FRYER, F, Postmaster at Fish Water, in about 1890. The post office at Fish Water was probably a small farm agency run from a rural trading store owned by Mr Fryer. It seems likely that the name of this office was a deliberate pun based upon the name of its postmaster

FUIDGE, ED, Postmaster at Fort Jackson, 1880

FULLER, A, Postmaster at Butterworth, in about 1879

FULLER, J, Postmaster and field-cornet at Blood River, 1 January 1871

Postmaster and station master at Barroe, 1 August 1878

Postmaster at Redhouse, 1 March 1879

FULLER, WJ, Postmaster at Kalabas Kraal, 1883

FULLER, WM, Postmaster at Bontebok Flats, 1 July 1876

FURMIDGE, J, Postmaster at Qunu, possibly acting, 1881

FURMIDGE, W, Postmaster at Fish River, 1 March 1896

FURNEY, W, Postmaster at Darling Bridge, 22 June 1852. It appears that W Furney combined his duties as postmaster of Darling Bridge with those of hotelier

FURNRIDGE, W, Postmaster at Port Alfred, 1 August 1877

FYNN, WW, Clerk to Colonel Eustace and postmaster at Entlambe, 1 October 1876

G

GACE, Francis Joseph, Telegraphist at Aberdeen, 1881
    Postmaster at Wellington Station, 23 December 1884
    Postmaster at Orange River, 1 March 1887
    Postmaster at Hopetown, 1 August 1888
    Postmaster at Lawrence Street, Port Elizabeth, 1 December 1900
    Postmaster at Jansenville, 1 January 1903
    Postmaster at Aberdeen, Division of Aberdeen, before 1908
    Postmaster at Somerset East, 1 August 1908

GALL, Matthew. On 28 August 1806 the British Secretary of State for the Colonies in London wrote to General Sir David Baird, Governor of the Cape, instructing him that, upon the arrival at the Cape of Matthew Gall, he should be appointed Postmaster General for the Colony. Gall arrived at Cape Town on the sailing ship "*London*" on 2 December 1807, and was confirmed to this position the following day. On 11 September 1808 his house in Wale Street was broken into and a murder committed on its premises. On 20 May 1809 he took a prolonged leave of absence in Europe and only returned on 21 June 1811. In May 1813 he again left, returning on 8 September 1815. On both occasions Robert Crozier was left acting on his behalf. He finally resigned on 18 November 1815. In total Gall remained in office for just on eight years, and for four-and-a-half of these he was absent from the Colony. This lack of concern was to have a detrimental effect upon the organization of his department, and by the time he had resigned in 1815, the postal services of the Cape were widely regarded to be in a shambles

GALLOWAY, H, Postmaster at Groot Doorn Pan, 22 August 1862

GALLOWAY, James, Postmaster at Ceres Road, 1 April 1886
    Postmaster at Malmesbury, 1 May 1893
    Postmaster at Middelburg, 4 April 1897

GARCIA, EB, Clerk, third class, GPO, Cape Town, 30 January 1865
    Clerk, second class, GPO, Cape Town, 1866
    Clerk, Money Order and Stamp Branch, GPO, Cape Town, 1867
    Civil Commissioner and Resident Magistrate, Victoria West, 1869

GARCIA, M, Postmaster at George, 1 January 1830

GARDE, Ms T, Postmaster at Bathurst, 1 July 1879

GARDINER, Miss AC, Postmaster at Parow, 1 February 1904

GARDINER, Edward William Francis, Postmaster at Bolotwa, 1 March 1910

GARDINER, WJ, born in about 1860
    Postmaster at Stellenbosch, 1 October 1894
    Postmaster at Kimberley, 1 September 1908
    The Pension Lists of 30 November 1909 recorded that in 1910 Mr Gardiner, age 49, was retired on an annual pension of £286.0.3

GARDNER, William Calvert, Postmaster at Wagenaar's Kraal, 1 July 1892
    Postmaster at Moshesh's Ford, 1 February 1898

Postmaster at Lady Grey, Division of Aliwal North, 1 September 1907

GARISCH, CJ, Postmaster at Mostert's Hoek, Division of Stellenbosch, 16 November 1846

GARLAKE, J, Postmaster at Middelburg, 24 March 1874
Postmaster at Swellendam, 1 April 1875

GARNER, DG, Postmaster at South End, Port Elizabeth, 1 September 1902

GARNER, Henry Colburn Schultz, Postmaster at Mount Frere, 10 February 1890
Postmaster at Herschel, 1 June 1894
Transferred to Chief Magistrate's Office at Kokstad, 17 May 1897

GARNER, JC, Clerk to the Chief Magistrate and postmaster at Umzimkulu, 8 February 1879

GARNER, T, Postmaster at Fort Brown, 1 September 1861

GARRATT, Frank, Telegraphist at Birmingham, England in 1892, emigrated to the Cape in 1895
Telegraphist at Barkly East, 1895
Postmaster at Bree Street, Cape Town, 1 March 1904
Postmaster at Barkly East, 1 May 1904

GATES, G Snr, Postmaster at Paarde Poort, 1 April 1867

GATES, G Jnr, Postmaster at Blue Cliff, 1 July 1864
Postmaster at Paarde Poort, 1 April 1868

GATES, H, Postmaster at Blue Cliff, 1 July 1875

GATES, SM, Postmaster at Blue Cliff, 1 June 1872

GATLAND, Frank, Acting postmaster at Caledon Street, Cape Town, 1909
Postmaster at Aberdeen, Division of Aberdeen, 1 October 1909

GATT, JB, Postmaster at Kalk Bay, 1 May 1871

GEARD, Jesse. In 1861 a Receiving Office was established in the shop of Mr Jesse Geard, in Queeen Street, Port Elizabeth

GEARY, John Henry, Station master at Plumstead, 24 August 1908, salary £226 pa

GEDYE, RM, Postmaster and station master at Kraaifontein Station, 1 December 1876

GEERING, John Jas, Postmaster at Robertson, 1 August 1872

GEERINGH, JJ, Postmaster at Jamestown, 1 January 1896

GEERINGH, SJ, Postmaster at Porterville, 1 April 1895
Postmaster at Hopefield, 1 September 1896
Postmaster at Darling, 1 February 1900
Postmaster at Peddie, 1 June 1903
In about April 1902 Republican forces raided the village of Darling. The postmaster, Mr SJ Geeringh, maintained the telegraphic connection until they were about to enter the village. Thereafter he placed the instrument beyond observation and, at great personal risk, renewed communications while they were still in the vicinity (POC 246, 1 May 1902)

GEERINGH, William Martin, Postmaster at Gordon's Bay, 1 February 1904
Postmaster at Napier, 1 April 1905
Postmaster at Vredenburg, 1 April 1906

GELDENHUYS, Postmaster at Roodewal, Division of Robertson, 1881

GELDENHUYS, EH, Postmaster at Robertson, 1881

GELDENHUYS, MW, Postmaster at Nieuwoudtville, 1 March 1903

GENIS, E, Police constable and postmaster at Springbokfontein, 24 March 1860, dismissed from service

GENIS, G, Postmaster at Bowesdorp, 1 May 1877

GEOGHEGAN, John, Postmaster at Ceres, 28 September 1854

GERCHENS, CW, Postmaster at De Rust, 10 November 1860

GERNETZKY, Frederick William, Postmaster at North End, Port Elizabeth, 1 April 1903
Postmaster at Steynsburg, 1 June 1903
Postmaster at Steynsburg, in about 1906
Postmaster at Grahamstown Station, 1 November 1906. Salary £250

GERS, Adolph, Postmaster at Papkuil, 27 October 1905

GEYER, GC, Postmaster and station master at Touws River, 1 December 1877
The village of Montagu Road was established on the farm De Draai, or "*the bend*", on 7 November 1877, when the railway line from Worcester to Matjesfontein was opened to traffic. At about the same time, on 1 December 1877, a post office was added to its facilities. The station was located at a point where the line crossed the Touws River, and was named in honour of the Colonial Secretary, Sir John Montagu. However this was quite misleading, as the village of Montagu was located in a different direction, on the road to Swellendam, and on 1 January 1883 the station was renamed Touws River. In its early days passengers travelling on the Western line frequently had to make an enforced stop at the village, sometimes for more than one night. As a result many of them stayed at the Frere Hotel, an establishment built by the Cape Government Railways for the purpose of accommodating their clients. This monopoly persisted until 1921 when the village's residential area was finally laid out

GEYER, Gustav Edward, Postmaster at Marydale, 1910

GEYER, JC, Postmaster and station master at Kalabas Kraal, 7 August 1879

GEYER, JW, Postmaster and station master at Rosebank, 1 May 1877
Postmaster at Claremont Station, 1881

GHISLIN, A, Postmaster at Grabouw, 1 November 1874

GHISLIN, CW, Postmaster at Sir Lowry's Pass, 1880

GHISLIN, JW, Postmaster at Sir Lowry's Pass 1 May 1869

GIBBS, Mary Anne, Postmaster at Klaarstroom, 1 April 1868
Postmaster at Plettenberg's Bay, 1 October 1876

GIBSON, Robert Kenloch, Postmaster at Balfour, 1 January 1897
Postmaster at Great Brak River, 1 July 1905
Postmaster at Nqamakwe, 1 June 1910

GIE, Sebastina C, Postmaster at Darling, 7 April 1867

GIE, SV, Postmaster at Darling, in about 1867, deceased while in office

GIEMRE, J, Postmaster and station master at Coerney, 1 March 1876
Postmaster and station master at Alicedale, 1 September 1877

GIEMRIE, G, Postmaster at Imvani, 1880

GIESSLER, H, Postmaster at Gamtoos River Ferry, 1 August 1892

GIFFORD, Mr, Postmaster at Spectakel, in about 1866

GILBERT, H, Postmaster at Taungs, 15 August 1896

GILDENHUYS, Burgert Wynand, Postmaster at Hout Kraal, 1 April 1907

Postmaster at Orchard Siding, 1 August 1909

Postmaster at Vredenburg, 1 January 1910

GILFILLAN, CC, Postmaster at Kentani, 1 November 1894

GILLETT, AR, Postmaster at Nieuwoudtville, 1 October 1902

GILLMAN, W, Postmaster at Springbokfontein 1 February 1868

Postmaster at Springbokfontein, 1 September 1874

Postmaster at Spectakel, 1 January 1877

GILLMORE, G, Postmaster at Kendrew Station, 29 September 1879

GIRD, SJC, Deputy-Sheriff and postmaster at George, 1 May 1872

GIRLING, HW, born in about 1853

Postmaster at Colesberg, 1 November 1892

Postmaster at Montagu, 1 August 1898

Postmaster at Robertson, 1 August 1900

Postmaster at Prince Albert, date of appointment not known

The Pension Lists of 30 November 1909 recorded that in 1910 Mr Girling, age 56, was retired on an annual pension of £176.3.4

GLAHOLM, John, also listed as T. Postmaster at Thomas River Station, 1 June 1896

Postmaster at Tylden, 1 October 1899

Station master at Molteno, 14 September 1903, salary £270 pa

GLANVILLE, T, Postmaster at Kuruman, 1 July 1897

GLEESON, P, Postmaster at Berlin Station, 1 April 1869

Postmaster at North End, Port Elizabeth, 1 April 1878

GLENHEAREY, E, Postmaster at Egoso, 1881

GLOSTER, C, Postmaster at Caledon Street, Cape Town, 1 December 1900

GLUCKSTEIN, H, Postmaster at Waterford, Division of Jansenville, in about 1879

GLUECK, Mrs S, Postal assistant at Lady Grey, Division of Aliwal North, 6 May 1897

Postmaster at Lady Grey, Division of Aliwal North, 1 February 1899. On 14 November 1899 a small group of Dutch irregulars from the OFS, together with some local sympathizers, attempted to affix a Proclamation of Annexation to the Lady Grey post office notice board, and demanded its keys from the postmaster, Mrs Sarah Glueck. She not only refused to oblige, but replaced the proclamation with a notice of her own, reminding Cape citizens of their loyalty to the British Crown. On 19th November the Republican forces returned in greater numbers, and despite her vigorous protestations, they took over her offices. Following their withdrawal from the village in March 1900 the postal and communication infrastructure of the north-eastern districts of the Cape was only re-established with difficulty. Owing to a shortage of qualified personnel in this region the postmaster at Herschel was delegated to travel with the military to Barkly East to re-open its telegraph office. In his absence, his work was undertaken by Mrs Glueck and, for a time, she travelled the distance between the two villages on horseback on a daily basis, and served the postal and telegraphic needs of both communities. Her efforts did not go unnoticed, and in his report to Parliament for 1899 the Postmaster General singled her out for her work and made special mention of the manner in which she safeguarded official property during the course of the Republican invasion. Most importantly, the actions of Sarah Glueck at the start of the war seized the imagination of the public, and once the story reached the British press, her courage was given international coverage: poems were written about her, and pictures of her were sold in their thousands throughout the Empire

GLYNN, J, Postmaster at Woodstock Station, 17 March 1865

GODDEN, B, Postmaster at St Marks, 1 November 1896

GODDEN, Bertram Harold Frederick, Postmaster at Lady Frere, 1 February 1904
Postmaster at Hopetown, 1 June 1907

GODFREY, Ernest Fitzroy, Postmaster at Willowvale, 15 July 1900

GODFREY, J, Postmaster at Serjeant's River, 6 January 1858

GODFREY, JA, Postmaster at Touws River, 1 December 1888. For further details see also under GC Geyer, station master at Montagu Road and Touws River

GODFREY, James H, Postmaster at Balfour, 1 August 1885
Postmaster at Seymour, 1 October 1886

GODFREY, RE, Postmaster at Qunu, 1 June 1898

GODFREY, RS, Postmaster at Qunu, 6 September 1904

GOETS, Miss BAM, Postmaster at Stanford, 1 May 1906

GOETS, JA, Postmaster at Stanford, 1 May 1867

GOLDSBURY, Samuel, Postmaster at George, 22 August 1850

GOLDSCHMIDT, Bernard Isaac, Clerk, Postmaster General's Department, GPO, Cape Town, September 1895
Postmaster at Krakeel River, 1 April 1896
Clerk, Postmaster General's Department, GPO, Cape Town, February 1899

GOLDSMITH, N, Postmaster and field-cornet at Riebeek East, 1 April 1875

GONGWANE, P, Postmaster at Emgwali, 1881

GOOD, Mr. Mail transport driver. On 14 March 1901 the driver of the cart conveying mails from Matatiele to Kokstad, Mr Good, was thrown out of his vehicle and sustained a fractured skull. He died of his injuries the following day (PMG 1901)

GOODMAN, J, Postmaster at Glenconnor, 1881

GOODMAN, SJ, Postmaster at Rosmead, March 1883

GOODRICH, C, Postmaster at Britstown, 1 July 1902

GOOSEN, Jan C, Postmaster at Prince Alfred's Hamlet, 1 April 1866, service provided for free in 1867-68. In 1861 Jan Goosen established the village of Prince Alfred's Hamlet, and when a post office was opened there in 1866 he was appointed its first postmaster.

GOODWIN, Albert, Station master Indwe, 13 March 1905, salary £223 plus £48 house allowance

GOODWIN, JF, Postmaster at Simonstown, 19 March 1823

GORDON, AE, Postmaster at Mossel Bay, 1 November 1892

GOULD, R, Postmaster at Blanco, 4 December 1851

GOUS, Gert, Postmaster at Hanover, 6 November 1852. On 6 November 1852 a postal agency was established on the farm Petrusvlei, in the division of Graaff-Reinet, with its owner, Gert Gous, as its first postmaster. The site was proclaimed a village in 1854, and on 6 September 1855 it was officially named Hanover, in honour of its namesake in Germany

GRACE, G, Postmaster at Hondeklip Bay, 1 October 1862

GRADY, GP, Postmaster at Tafelberg, 1 December 1889

GRAHAM, C, Postmaster at Draghoender, 1 April 1904

GRAHAM, Miss Catherin Snow, Postmaster at Mill Street, Gardens, 17 Jan 1901, salary £120 pa

GRAHAM, CJ, Postmaster at Bizana, 1 DE 1907

GRAHAM, Mrs Jessie, Postmaster at Salt River, 1 September 1884. The Pension Lists of 30 November 1909 recorded that in 1910 Mrs Graham was retired on an annual pension of £74.0.5

GRAHAM, JD, Postmaster at Wagenbooms River, 21 April 1855

GRAHAM, JL, Postmaster at Willowmore, 1 August 1883

GRAHAM, JP, Postmaster at Moshesh's Ford, 1 June 1897

Postmaster at Bell, 1 February 1898

Postmaster at Palmietfontein, 1 December 1898

GRAHAM, W, Postmaster at Laingsburg, 1 June 1900

Postmaster at Matjesfontein, Division of Worcester, 1 April 1903

Postmaster at Hanover, 1 October 1903

GRANDEVELD, J, Postmaster at Philipstown, 1 March 1867

GRASSE, Rev H, Postmaster at Enon 1 December 1873, service provided for free

GRASSIE, P, Postmaster and station master at Glenconnor, 1 September 1878

Postmaster and station master at Middleton, 1 October 1879

GRAY, Miss Alice, Postmaster at Elliott, 1 July 1895

Postmaster at Ugie, 1 September 1902

Postmaster at Tsolo, 1 April 1906

Postmaster at Ugie, 1 November 1906

GRAY, HW, Postmaster at Philipstown, 1 March 1887

GRAY, J, Postmaster at Somerset Strand, 21 January 1874

GRAY, J, Postmaster at Fort Beaufort, 1 January 1844

Military Postmaster at Fort Beaufort, 1847-1848

GRAY, SC, Postmaster at Blue Cliff, 1 April 1868

GREATHEAD, HB, Postmaster and station master at Coerney, 1 July 1878

GREEF, SC, Assistant field-cornet, date of appointment not known

Postmaster at Zoute Kloof, 1 September 1864

Postmaster at Zoute Kloof, 1 June 1876

GREEN, Mr, Postmaster at Uitenhage, in about 1848

GREEN, A, Postmaster at Balfour, 1 December 1868

GREEN, AE, Postmaster at Middledrift, probable date 1 April 1902
Postmaster at Tsomo, 1 October 1902

GREEN, C, Postmaster at De Aar, 1 November 1884
Postmaster at Rosmead, 1 November 1892

GREEN, H, Postmaster at Port St John, 1880

GREEN, J, Postmaster at Blue Cliff, 23 January 1857

GREEN, JW, Postmaster at Balfou,r 1 October 1871

GREEN, W, Postmaster and station master at Blue Cliff, in about 1879

GREENAN, Joseph Patrick, Station master at Wellington, 20 July 1908, salary £310 pa

GREENTREE, Mr, Postmaster at Breede River Station, in about 1877

GREENTREE, JFC, Postmaster at Kraaifontein Station, 1881

GREENTREE, JTG, Postmaster at Hex River, 1 November 1877

GREENWAY, T, Postmaster at Burghersdorp, 8 June 1878
Postmaster at Burghersdorp, 1 October 1879
Postmaster at Richmond, 1 January 1899. On 30 November 1909 his widow, HM Greenway, was receiving an annual pension of £21.8.2

GREGAN, T, Postmaster at Van Wyk's Vlei, 1 February 1896

GRELLERT, H, Acting postmaster at Rhodes, 1 August 1906

GREY, E, Postmaster at Laingsburg, 1 January 1896

GRIERSON, James, Station master at Pokwani, 15 September 1909, salary £180 pa

GRIFFIN, WH, Postmaster at Umtata, 1 August 1874.
In 1875 WH Griffin, postal agent for Umtata, recorded that during the year, the outgoing mail traffic from this office included 1140 Official Free letters, 6000 stamped letters, 13 registered letters, 251 books, and 3793 newspapers (Blue Book on Native Affairs 1876:32)

GRIFFITHS, G, Postmaster at Karroo Poort, in about 1877

GRIFFITHS, W, Postmaster at Richmond Road, 1 March 1898

GRIMISH, Baron Victor, Postmaster at Kenilworth, Kimberley, 1 September 1909

GRIMM, WCH, Postmaster at Herschel, 1 February 1890
Postmaster at Ladismith, 1 June 1893

GRISOLD, R, Postmaster at Van Putten's Vlei, 9 February 1859, service provided for free
Postmaster at Elands Bay, 1 July 1873, service provided for free

GRIST, B, Postmaster at Fraserburg Road, 1 April 1899

GRIST, P, Postmaster at Woodstock Station, 1880

GRIST, Peter, Postmaster at Hoetjes Bay, 16 November 1897
Acting postmaster at Philipstown, 1 March 1907, subsequently confirmed
Acting postmaster at Taungs, 1908
Postmaster at Orange River, 1909

GROBBELAAR, C, Postmaster and field-cornet at Zwart Kei, Division of Cradock, 25 Oct 1858

GROBBELAAR, CA, Postmaster and field-cornet at Riebeek West, 1 July 1877

GROBBELAAR, Miss M, also listed as Miss J
  Postmaster at Riebeek Kasteel, 1 October 1896
  Postmaster at Groot Drakenstein, 1 April 1903
  Postmaster at Vredenburg, 1 July 1903
  Postmaster at French Hoek, 1 February 1904

GROENEWALD, HC, Assistant postmaster, Malmesbyry, May 1891, salary £120 pa
  Postmaster at Nieuwe Rust, 1 February 1910

GRUNWALD, J, Postmaster at Philipstown, 20 February 1864

GRYFFENBERG, DP, Postmaster at Porterville, 1 October 1897

GUEST, WC Snr, Postmaster at Hazenjacht, 6 March 1856, service provided for free in 1856-59

GUEST, WC Jnr, Postmaster at Hazenjacht, 1 July 1871

GUNN, RE, Postmaster at Hutchinson, 1 April 1903
  Postmaster at Modder River, Division of Kimberley, 1 February 1904
  Postmaster at Hopetown, 1 November 1906

GUNNING, B, Postmaster at Bathurst, 1 April 1845

GUTHRIE, FH, Resident Magistrate and postmaster at Walfish Bay, 1897. This may be Frank Edward Huntington Guthrie, who entered the Cape Civil Service on 21 January 1888 as a Clerk in the Railway Department. Kilpin (1910) records that he became Resident Magistrate at Walfish Bay, but only on 26 May 1901

GUZERMANN, W, Postmaster at Laingsburg, 1 April 1874

H

HAAK, KD, Postmaster at Prince Albert, 1 July 1861, deceased while in office

HAARHOFF, J, Acting postmaster at Longlands, 1907
  Postmaster at Longlands, 1 July 1907

HACKER, E, Postmaster at Lynedoch, 1883

HAESE, Rev Gustav, Postmaster at Amalienstein, 1 May 1860

HAESE, GT, Postmaster at Avontuur, 1 October 1868

HALFORD, J, Postmaster at Bellville, 18 November 1862

HALL, AG, Postmaster at Elliotdale, 1 November 1903
  Postmaster at Bizana, 1 August 1905

HALL, CC, Postmaster at Qumbu, 1 March 1898

HALL, E, Postmaster at Farm No 219, July 1862, service provided for free in 1867

HALL, FR, Postmaster at Clarkebury, 1 December 1905

HALL, HJ, Clerk, Money Order and Stamp Branch, GPO, Cape Town, 1 December 1869, deceased in 1872

HALL, J, Postmaster at Malagas, in about 1878
  Postmaster at Mount Stewart, 1880

Postmaster at Centlivres, 1881

HALL, JC, Postmaster and station master at North End, Port Elizabeth, 1 July 1879

HALL, P, Postmaster at Nieuwoudtville, 1 June 1905

Postmaster at Steinkopf 1 November 1907

HALL, W, Postmaster at Groen River, 1 January 1867

HALL, William Herbert, Clerk, Telegraph Department, 1876.
Saw active military service in wars against the Gaika, Gcaleka, Mpondo, Zulu, Transvaal Dutch and the Basotho. During the latter conflict he served as Captain in the Basotho Contingent, and was placed in charge of loyal refugees located at Maseru, until 16 November 1881, when he was appointed Magistrate's Clerk and postmaster at Mohaleshoek. Soon thereafter, on 1 February 1882, he was appointed postmaster at Maseru, and in due course moved to Inspector of Native Locations, initially at Bathurst in 1883, then Alexandria in 1888, and finally Barkly West in 1889

HALLIDAY, Miss C, Postmaster at Breakfast Vlei, 1 December 1872

HALLIDAY, H, Postmaster at Cookhouse, 10 May 1858

HALLIDAY, John, Postmaster at Uitenhage, 1 September 1908

HALLOCK, J, Postmaster at King William's Town, 1 May 1885

Postmaster at Grahamstown, 1 January 1892

Postmaster at Port Elizabeth, 1 May 1892

Postmaster at King William's Town, 1 November 1892

Postmaster at Grahamstown, 18 October 1900

HALLS, CH, Postmaster at Barkly West, 1881

HALSE, Henry Basil, Postmaster at Klipplaat, 1 July 1909, Salary £175 pa

HALSE, TE, Clerk to the Civil Commissioner and postmaster at Herschel, 1 January 1874

HAMERSLEY, A, Postmaster at Klipheuvel, 1880

HAMERSLEY, J, Postmaster at Matjesfontein, Division of Worcester, 1 November 1878

HAMILL, Miss T, Postmaster at at The Beach, East London, 1 January 1903

Postmaster at Quigney, East London, 1 July 1903

Postmaster at The Beach, East London, 1 July 1903

HAMILTON, G, Assistant Postmaster at Aliwal North, date not known
The Pension Lists of 30 November 1909 recorded that in 1910 Mr Hamilton, age 56, was retired on an annual pension of £227.18.4

HAMILTON, GD, Postmaster at Graaff-Reinet, 1 July 1883

HAMILTON, SD, Postmaster at Fraserburg Road, 1 January 1890

Postmaster at Stutterheim, 1 November 1894

Postmaster at Sterkstroom, 1 November 1896

Assistant Postmaster at Queenstown, date not known.

The Pension Lists of 30 November 1909 recorded that in 1910 Mr Hamilton, age 45, was retired on an annual pension of £128.7.11

HAMMAN, Mr, Postmaster at Hamman's Hof, October 1882

HAMMAN, EC, Postmaster and field-cornet at Groenberg, 23 Feb 1856, service provided free

HAMMAN, JL, Postmaster and field-cornet at Paardeberg, Division of Malmesbury, 1 January 1866, deceased while in office

HAMMAN, JN Snr, Postmaster at and field-cornet Paardeberg, Division of Malmesbury, 13 December 1859

HAMMAN, JN Jnr, Postmaster and field-cornet at Zwartland and Zout Rivier, 29 May 1858, service provided for free in 1867-73
   Postmaster and field-cornet at Middel Zwartland, 1 February 1863

HAMMOND, JH, also listed as HAMMAN, JS
   Postmaster and station master at Mowbray Station, 1 May 1873
   Postmaster and station master at Newlands, 1 May 1877

HAMPSON, Frederick William, born in about 1856
   United Kingdom Telegraph Service, Southport, date of appointment not known
   Telegraphist, Fort Beaufort, 3 January 1882
   Telegraphist, Port Elizabeth, 1883
   Telegraphist, Cape Town, 1885
   Superintendent of Telegraphs, Kimberley, 1897
   Superintendent of Telegraphs, Cape Town, 1898
   Acting postmaster at Wynberg, 1 December 1907
   Retired from service in about 1908
   The Pension Lists of 30 November 1909 recorded that in 1910 Mr Hampson, age 53, was retired on an annual pension of £243.10.10

HAMSWORTH, AC, Postmaster at Tylden, 1880

HANNELL, William Avenil Attfield, Acting postmaster at Postmasburg, 1 January 1904

HANN, Alfred Henry, Postmaster at Addo, 19 July 1899
   Station master at Bedford, 1 June 1903, salary £249 pa

HANSCOMBE, A, Postmaster at Barkly East, 1 October 1876

HANSEN, Arel Hartoig, Postmaster at Commadagga, 1 November 1891
   Station master at Simonstown, 30 April 1909, salary £295 pa

HANSEN, H, Postmaster and field-cornet at Achter Piquetberg, 13 May 1867

HANSEN, M, Postmaster at Alfred Docks, Cape Town, 1 January 1877

HANSEN, W, Postmaster at Calitzdorp, 26 January 1860
   Postmaster at Gamka's Vlakte, 26 January 1860

HARBOTTEL, J, Postmaster at Indwe, 1 May 1896

HARDIMANN, Miss ST, Postmaster at Emjanyana, 1 January 1903

HARDING, S, Postmaster at Leeuwfontein, Division of Bedford, 10 May 1858

HARDING, WA, Postmaster at Beaufort West, in about 1828

HARDING, WW, Postmaster at Plettenberg's Bay, 17 December 1824

HARDS, RE, Postmaster at Blinkwater, 1881

HARDY, JE, Postmaster at Lawrence Street, Port Elizabeth, 1 September 1897
   Postmaster at Clanwilliam, 1 May 1902

HARE, HA, Postmaster at Hopetown, 1 July 1885
  Postmaster at Ceres Road, 1 October 1885
HARE, HW, Postmaster at Knysna, 1883
HARE, WL, Postmaster at Knysna, 1 October 1880
HAREBOTTLE, CV, Postmaster and field-cornet at Stanley, 1 January 1879
HARGREAVES, Rev P, Postmaster at Clarkebury, 1 January 1874
  Postmaster at Clarkebury, 25 July 1879
  Postmaster at Emgwali, 1880
HARGREAVES, T, Postmaster at Emfundisweni, 1 May 1897
HARISON, C, Conservator of Crown Forests and postmaster at Witte Els Bosch, 7 January 1858, service provided for free
HARKER, RC, Postmaster at Plettenberg's Bay, 15 November 1826
HARRHY, Ernest Edward, Entered the Imperial Postal Service, 1886
  Joined the Cape Telegraph Service, 1889, and was posted to Cradock
  Secretary's Office, GPO, Cape Town, 1891
  Seconded for service to British Central Africa in 1893, travelled with Sir Harry Johnston to Nyasaland, where he organized its postal service; and was appointed PMG for Nyasaland 1893
  Returned to the Cape as Clerk to the PMG, Cape Town, 1895
  Inland Mails Branch, 1900
  Principal Clark, Foreign Mails Branch, 1908
  Elected a Fellow of the Royal Geographical Society, 1902
HARRIS. Postmaster at Claremont 22 May 1846.
  No further details known. At the outset the post office at Claremont was located at the home of its first postmaster, Mr Harris. After his resignation, on or about 15 July 1846, its establishment was transferred to the house of his successor, Mr Thomas Watson
HARRIS, A, Postmaster at Gamtoos River Ferry, 20 August 1849
HARRIS, A, Postmaster at Jagersbosch, 1880
HARRIS, CJ, also listed as JH, Postmaster at Jamestown, 1 March 1897
  Postmaster at Aberdeen, Division of Aberdeen, 1 May 1899
  Postmaster at Pearston, 1 February 1901
  Postmaster at Kuruman, 1 March 1904
  Postmaster at Griquatown, 1 April 1906
HARRIS, HJ, Postmaster at Smith's Mine, 1 July 1903
HARRIS, JH Snr, Postmaster at Lady Grey, Division of Aliwal North, 19 July 1864
  Postmaster at Lady Grey, Division of Aliwal North, 22 May 1877
HARRIS, JL, Postmaster at Tylden, 1 September 1894
  Postmaster at Middleton, 1 March 1895
HARRIS, M, Postmaster at Lady Grey, Division of Aliwal North, 1 April 1871
HARRIS, SC, Postmaster at Sea Point, Cape Town, 1 May 1871
HARRIS, W, Sorter, GPO, Cape Town, 8 November 1866

Registrar of Letters, GPO, Cape Town, 8 August 1873

Clerk, Registered Letter Section, GPO, Cape Town, 1879

HARRIS, W, Postmaster at Somerset Road, 11 November 1863

HARRIS, WO, Postmaster at Deelfontein Station, 1 July 1903

Postmaster at Richmond Road, 1 February 1904

HARRISON, C, Postmaster at Petrusville, 1 May 1896

HARRISON, J, Postmaster at Van Staden's River Hoogte, 14 January 1860

HARROD, BG, Postmaster at Spring Valley, 1 March 1900

HARROWER, R, Postmaster at Paarl Station, 15 January 1868

HARTLEY, TH, Postmaster at Blaauw Krantz, Division of Cradock, 1 June 1876

HARTMAN, JP, Postmaster and field-cornet at Aberdeen, Division of Victoria East, 10 May 1858, service provided for free

HARTMAN, LB, Postmaster at Baroe Kraal, 1 January 1873

HARVEY, Sergeant and Military Postmaster at Post Victoria, in about 1844. Salary £6 pa

HARVEY, AJ, Postmaster at Richmond Hill, 15 June 1896

HARVEY, M, Postmaster and station master at Addo, in about 1876

HARVEY, T, Postmaster at Porterville Road, 1883

HASSELL, A, Postmaster at Ngqeleni, 7 May 1897

HASSENJAGER, C, Postmaster at Cambridge, 1 July 1873

HASSES, S, Postmaster at Great Brak River, 1 November 1908. Salary £150

HATCHARD, AEG, Postmaster at Advance Post, 1 July 1878

Postmaster at Advance Post, in about 1880

Postmaster at Maseru, 1 May 1881

HATELIE, G, Postmaster at Barkly West, 1 April 1897

HAUPT, AP, Postmaster at Paarl, 1 December 1866

HAUPTFLEISCH, WF, Postmaster at Nieuwe Rust, 1 May 1908

HAVENGA, JJ, Postmaster at Van Wyk's Vlei, 1 May 1896

Postmaster at Douglas, 1 June 1897

HAW, C, Postmaster at Somerset East, 1 May 1843

HAWKINS, Annie, Postmaster at Humansdorp, 1 February 1865

HAWKINS, G, Postmaster at Humansdorp, 11 March 1852

HAWKINS, Mrs Martha, Postmaster at Humansdorp, 23 February 1859, deceased while in office

HAWTHORNE, W, Postmaster and clerk and storekeeper at the Michell's Pass Convict Station, 31 December 1852

Between 1852 and 1854 the clerk and storekeeper on the Breede River Convict Station, Mr W Hawthorne, was also employed as its postmaster. On 23 January 1854 the convict station was transferred to Michell's Pass, Mr Hawthorne remained at Breede River for an additional week, and was only transferred to the new camp on 30 January. Before he left, however, he wrote to the Postmaster General, requesting clarification whether his duties as postmaster were to continue at Michell's Pass. It seems probable that his appointment was renewed until 23 December

1855 when his postal establishment was abolished

HAYBITTEL, RH, Postmaster at Mill Street, Gardens, Cape Town, 1 December 1899
    Postmaster at Alfred Docks, Cape Town, 1 July 1900
    Postmaster at Clanwilliam, 1906
    Postmaster at Somerset Strand, 1 August 1908

HAYES, S, Postmaster at Bathurst 1 April 1870, deceased while in office

HAYES, Mrs SG, Postmaster at Bathurst, 1 August 1875

HAYLETT, Mrs Catherine, Postmaster at Villiersdorp, 27 January 1864

HAYLETT, C Smith, Postmaster at Villiersdorp, 3 February 1853
    Postmaster at Villiersdorp, 1 July 1867

HAZLETON, HR, Postmaster at Yellow Wood Trees, 1881

HEAD, S, Postmaster at Komgha, 24 July 1900
    Postmaster at Cathcart, 1 March 1902

HEALEY, P, Postmaster at Murraysburg, 1 September 1869

HEARD, Henry Richard, Station master at Schoombie, 1 October 1907, salary £220 pa

HEASE, GT, Postmaster and field-cornet at Uniondale, 30 October 1871

HEATH, J, Postmaster at Hangman's Bush, 1 January 1875

HEATH, William, Station master at St James, 9 January 1906, salary £235 pa

HEATH, William Samuel Jonathan, Station master at Thebus, 16 January 1903, salary £235 pa

HEFFER, Mrs A, Postmaster at Bredasdorp, 1 May 1888

HELDZINGEN, WF, Postmaster at Worcester, 1 April 1874

HELGESON, JL, Postmaster at Upper Wynberg, 1 August 1903

HELLIER, JH, Postmaster at Berlin Station, in about 1873

HELM, H, Postmaster at De Rust, 1 February 1910

HELM, JE, Postmaster and field-cornet at Oudtshoorn, 1 May 1869

HELM, JSW, Postmaster at De Rust, 1 November 1891

HELM, W, Postmaster at Bredasdorp, 25 April 1846

HELM, W, Postmaster at De Rust, 1 January 1883

HELM, WB, Postmaster at Modderfontein, Division of Clanwilliam, 1 November 1903
    Postmaster at Eendekuil, 1 August 1909

HELMY, Mrs Emily Agnes, Superintendent of Telephone Exchange, GPO, Cape Town, 10 January 1898, salary £224 pa

HEMMING, Alfred William, Station master at Mortimer, 15 May 1906, salary £223 pa

HEMMING, H, Postmaster at Williston, 1 April 1892

HEMMING, RC, Postmaster at Fraserburg, 16 June 1857

HENDERSON, A, Clerk to the Civil Commissioner and postmaster at Alice, 1 December 1850

HENDERSON, Rev James H, (1867-1930), Postmaster at Lovedale, 1 July 1906. After working as a Prebyterian missionary in central Africa, Henderson relocated to the Eastern Cape, where he played a major role in the establishment of the South African Native College at Fort Hare, subsequently known as Lovedale University College

HENDERSON, Matthew, Station master at Tylden, 22 April 1907, salary £195 pa

HENDERSON, R, Postmaster at Riversdale, 1881
    Postmaster at Oudtshoorn, 11 June 1882
    Accountant, at GPO, Cape Town, date not known
    The Pension Lists of 30 November 1909 recorded that in 1910 Mr Henderson, age 56, was retired on an annual pension of £433.6.8

HENDLE, J, Postmaster at Sir Lowry's Pass, 1 October 1863

HENDLEY, Mr, Assistant to the Resident Magistrate, Griqualand East, 1880
    On 23 October 1880 the amaMpondomise, under the leadership of their Chief Umhlonhlo, rose in protest against the annexation of their lands to the Cape Colony. At the time the Resident Magistrate, Mr Hamilton Hope, was travelling to Maclear together with his assistants Messrs Hendley and Warren as well as his clerk, Mr AE Davies. Near the Sulenkama mission station the group was ambushed by a party of Mpondomise and, with the exception of Davies, who was the postmaster at Qumbu as well as the brother of the Wesleyan Missionary to Chief Umhlonhlo, all were killed

HENDRIKSE, F, Postmaster at Groote Vlakte, 22 May 1855, service provided free in 1855-59

HENLEY, JS, Postmaster at Butterworth, 1880

HENLEY, SJ, Postmaster at Fort Beaufort, 1 April 1877

HENRY, J, GPO, Cape Town, date of appointment not known
    Acting postmaster at Kimberley, 8 August 1889
    Postmaster at Kimberley, 1 February 1890. On 30 November 1909 his widow, JM Henry, was receiving an annual pension of £50

HENRY, RD, Postmaster at Fort Beaufort, 1881

HENRY, T, Postmaster at Grabouw, 1 July 1873

HENSHALL, Thomas, born in about 1856
    British and Irish Magnetic Telegraph Company, 1868
    Imperial Post Office, 1870
    Telegraphist, Colonial Service, 1881
    Telegraphist, Port Elizabeth, 1881
    Telegraphist, Fauresmith, OFS, April 1883
    Telegraphist, Queenstown, March 1886
    Postmaster at Kokstad, 1 November 1886
    Telegraphist, Grahamstown, 1887
    Postmaster at Queenstown, 16 October 1891
    Assistant postmaster at, Port Elizabeth, 1895
    Postmaster at Port Elizabeth, 1 July 1898
    The Pension Lists of 30 November 1909 recorded that in 1910 Mr Henshall, age 53, was retired on an annual pension of £400.

HERBERT, Mrs SE, Postmaster at Cookhouse, 1883

HERBERT, W, Postmaster at Mount Stewart, 1881

Postmaster at Sandflats, 1880

HERBST, CR, Acting postmaster at Springbokfontein, 1 April 1906, confirmed 1 May 1906
Postmaster at Porterville Road, 1 April 1908

HERBST, JF, Postmaster at Williston, 1 November 1896

HERD, HM, also listed as WM, Postmaster at Schmidt's Drift, 16 April 1898
Postmaster at Warrenton, 1 March 1899

HERMAN, Mr, Postmaster at Durbanville, 1865

HERMAN, Maria BV, Postmaster at Durbanville, 5 September 1865

HERNING, WJ, Postmaster at Molteno, 1 April 1908
Postmaster at De Aar, 1 November 1909

HEROLD, John, Postmaster at Bredasdorp, 1 February 1886
Postmaster at Carnarvon, 1 February 1887

HEROLD, TJ, Postmaster at Malagas, 26 April 1859
Postmaster at Port Beaufort, 1 July 1874

HERRING, AF, Postmaster at Middelburg, 1 July 1900. On 30 November 1909 his widow, AK Herring, was receiving an annual pension of £16.8.7

HERRING, WP, Postmaster at Somerset East, 1 November 1887
GPO, Cape Town, probable date 15 April 1892

HEUGH, Postmaster at Aberdeen, Division of Aberdeen, in about 1867

HEUGH, CF, Postmaster at Aberdeen, Division of Aberdeen, 10 August 1857

HEUGH, MC, Postmaster at Aberdeen, Division of Aberdeen, 1 January 1860

HEURTLEY, Mrs RF, Postmaster at Sir Lowry's Pass, 10 November 1852

HEURTLEY, RF, Postmaster at Grabouw, 6 March 1860

HEWITT, W, Postmaster at Spectakel, 1 July 1873, service provided for free

HEWSON, J, Postmaster at Falloden, 9 August 1866

HEYDENRYCH, EJ, Postmaster at St Helena Bay, 1880

HEYDENRICH, GF, Postmaster at Jansenville, 17 December 1857, deceased while in office

HICKEN, T, Postmaster at Vlugt, 1881

HICKS, FA, Postmaster at Walfish Bay, 1 September 1863, service provided for free

HIDDINGH, Dr JM, Medical doctor, and postmaster at Platteklip, 13 August 1853, service provided for free

HIGGINS, AW, Postmaster at Port St John, 1 October 1899

HIGGS, Rupert Stanley, Station master at Conway, 24 January 1908, salary £216 pa

HIGGS, TC, Postmaster at Prince Albert, 1 May 1897
Postmaster at Matjesfontein, Division of Worcester, 1 May 1900
Postmaster at Green Point, Cape Town, 1902
Postmaster at Sir Lowry Road, 1 September 1903
The Pension Lists of 30 November 1909 recorded that in 1910 Mr Higgs, age 52, was retired on an annual pension of £129.6.1

HILL, Miss, Postmaster at Salem, 1 June 1895

HILL, M, Postmaster at Salem, 1 May 1892
   Postmaster at Hopefield, 1 June 1895
   Postmaster at Hoetjes Bay, 1 January 1896
   Postmaster at Hopefield, 1 March 1896
HILL, TB, Postmaster at Adendorp, 1881
HILLARD, Postmaster at Barkly West, 1881
HILLS, James Lyttle, Postmaster at Fraserburg Road, 1 October 1903
   Postmaster at Cookhouse, 1 October 1908. Salary £245
HINCHCLIFFE, Mr, Postmaster at Prince Albert Road, 6 April 1898
HINDES, William Duncan, also listed as HINDS, Postmaster at Balfour, 1 February 1888
   Postmaster at Herschel, 1 January 1892
   Postmaster at Klipdam, 1 August 1895
   Postmaster at Barkly West, 1 August 1896
   Postmaster at Kei Road, 15 September 1896
   Postmaster at Colesberg, 1 January 1907, Salary £320 pa
HINDS, G, Postmaster at Eland's Drift, 1880
HINDS, GD, Postmaster at Whittlesea, 15 December 1857
HINDS, TC, Postmaster at Upper Zwart Kei, 7 January 1860
HINSCH, Mrs W, see under HIRSCH, Mrs W
HINWOOD, H, Postmaster at Blaauw Krantz, Division of Cradock, 1 November 1872
HIRSCH, J, Postmaster at Diep River, 1 April 1879
HIRSCH, Mrs W, also listed as HINSCH, Postmaster at Longlands, 1 October 1905
HIRSDELCH, J, Postmaster at Muizenberg, Cape Town, 1881
HISLOP, W, Postmaster at Pont, 1880
HOAL, Arthur, Telegraphist King William's Town, 8 June 1879
   Telegraphist Fort Beaufort, 1 August 1879
   Telegraphist Colesberg, 1 March 1881
   Postmaster at Uitenhage, 1 March 1886
   Postmaster at Knysna, 1 October 1893
   Postmaster at Oudtshoorn, 1 December 1893
   Assistant postmaster at King William's Town, 1 November 1901
   Postmaster at Cathcart, 12 March 1903
   Postmaster at Somerset East, 1 July 1904
   Postmaster at Stellenbosch, July 1908
HOAL, E, Postmaster at Whittlesea, 1 November 1892
HOAL, P, Postmaster at Indwe, 9 April 1896
   Station master at Somerset West, 29 April 1909, salary £238 pa
HOAL, William Thomas, was born at Fowley, Cornwall, the eldest son of William Stribley Hoal. After completing his education at Exeter, in Devon, he emigrated to the Cape in 1872, and in 1880 married Harriet Elizabeth Garner, daughter of Capt Thomas Garner, who bore him nine

children. On 1 June 1872 he joined the Cape of Good Hope Telegraph Co in Port Elizabeth as a telegraphic clerk. He passed into government employment on 1 July 1873 when the Company was taken over by the Cape Post Office, and for the next 35 years his career followed a steady, if unspectacular, upward path. In September 1875 he was promoted to Chief Telegraph Operator at Graaff-Reinet; Chief Telegraph Operator at Kimberley in January 1876; postmaster at Fort Beaufort on 1 May 1878; Supervisor of the Central Telegraph Transmitting Office at Fort Beaufort on 1 July 1881; postmaster at Kimberley on 1 March 1886; and postmaster at Port Elizabeth on 17 August 1889. These peregrinations finally came to an end on 1 April 1892 when he was appointed Accountant and Controller of the Money Order Branch, at the GPO in Cape Town. He rose to Assistant Secretary on 1 July 1894; Secretary on 1 January 1905; and finally Postmaster General on 1 February 1908. When the Union of South Africa was proclaimed on 31 May 1910, he became its first Postmaster General, but died soon after. Given his brief tenure in office, it is difficult to assess Hoal's contribution to the development of the postal system in southern Africa. Most of his work at the GPO in Cape Town was conducted under the management of Somerset French, whose powerful personality and dominant leadership would have overshadowed the achievements of all but the most brilliant of subordinates. Consequently there are few major projects which can be attributed directly to Hoal, and at best we can only assume that French would not have suffered for long the company of an incompetent deputy

HOARE, Frederick Augustus, Chief Constable and postmaster at Seymour, 26 September 1859

HOARE, HG, Acting postmaster at Steynsburg, in about 1905

Postmaster at Stormberg Junction, 1 November 1905

On 30 November 1909 his widow, AJ Hoare, was receiving an annual pension of £16.12.7

HOBERN, C, Postmaster and field-cornet at Jansenville, 1 October 1866

HOBERN, FN, also listed as FH, Postmaster at Ladismith, 1 August 1883

Postmaster at Clanwilliam, 1 June 1889

Postmaster at Somerset West, 1 March 1890

Postmaster at Ceres Road, 1 February 1892

Postmaster at Philipstown, 1 February 1894

Postmaster at Matjesfontein, Division of Worcester, 1 September 1894

HOBSON, Mrs AE, Postmaster at Steytlerville, 1 March 1899

HOCKEY, PE, Assistant Postmaster, King William's Town, date not known

The Pension Lists of 30 November 1909 recorded that in 1910 Mr Hockey, age 48, was retired on an annual pension of £156.14.10

HOCKLEY, B, Postmaster at Port Alfred, 10 May 1858, service provided for free

HOCKLEY, DT, Postmaster at Kowie East, 1 February 1861

Postmaster at Port Alfred, 1 February 1861

HOCKLEY, WH, Postmaster at Kowie East, 16 March 1860

HODDER, Mr, Postmaster at Bailey, 1 July 1895

HODGSON, H, Postmaster at Tulbagh, 1828, possibly acting

HOETS, FK, Postmaster at Mowbray Station, 1 September 1882

Postmaster at Hanover Street, Cape Town, 1 October 1902, Salary £340

Postmaster at Stal Street, Cape Town, 1 June 1910

HOFFMAN, C, Postmaster at Port Beaufort, 1 April 1878

HOFFMAN, CH, Postmaster at Bredasdorp, 1 April 1866

Secretary of the Divisional Council, 1875, deceased while in office

HOFMEYR, JC, Postmaster at Burghersdorp, 8 April 1857

HOGAN, Daniel, Chief Constable and postmaster at Murraysburg, 1 August 1870

HOGAN, J, Postmaster at Pearston, 1 September 1887

HOGARTH, A, Assistant Postmaster at Port Elizabeth

The Pension Lists of 30 November 1909 recorded that in 1910 Mr Hogarth, age 33, was retired on an annual pension of £53.5.11

HOHNE, CG, Postmaster General, Cape Town, 1804. The Cape was returned to Dutch administration on 21 February 1803, and in 1804 the direction of the Cape Post Office was given to Mr CG Hohne. Unfortunately nothing more is known of this official

HOHNE, CG, Clerk to the Civil Commissioner and postmaster at Malmesbury, 1 May 1848

HOHNE, FJ, Controller, Savings Bank, GPO, Cape Town, 1898. FJ Hohne joined the Audit Department in 1871, and after 27 years service, he transferred to the Post Office's Savings Bank. He retired on pension in 1905

HOHNE, JA, Postmaster at Fort Beaufort, 21 September 1850

HOITSEMA, CB, Postmaster at Somerset Strand, 1880

HOLBOROW, JI, Postmaster at St Marks, 1905

Postmaster at Qumbu, 1 October 1908

HOLDER, JB, Postmaster at Ngqeleni, 1 March 1900

Postmaster at Willowvale, 1 July 1902

Postmaster at Elliot, 1 October 1903

HOLDER, W, Postmaster at Aliwal North, 21 June 1850

HOLLAND, F, Postmaster at Komgha, 1 November 1877

HOLLAND, John, Postmaster General, Cape Town, 5 March 1801, retired in 1802. In January 1797 the British Government created a Court of the Vice-Admiralty at the Cape, with a single judge to run its affairs. John Holland was sent out from England to fill this position and, together with his wife, arrived at the Cape on 3 February 1798. A month later, on 3 March, he was also appointed Postmaster General for the Cape, with an office in the Castle. By all accounts Holland was a good humored and agreeable person. Lady Anne Barnard met him soon after his arrival and found him to be "a man who was pleasant, almost handsome, though somewhat of the old Beau, rather clever but *of a spirit too encroaching and eager for influence.*" (Barnard 1994: 287). Holland was not in good health and his stay at the Cape was not destined to be a long one. In addition, the Peace of Amiens, signed in March 1802, made it clear that the Cape was to be returned to the Batavian Republic. As a result on 6 August 1802 Holland sold his house at 47 Bree Street, together with its contents, and on 11 September he finally left the Colony (Philip, 1981: 185). The impact that he had upon the running of the Post Office at the Cape does not appear to have been unduly high. Following his departure, the position of Postmaster General was left vacant, and on 21 February 1802, the administration of the Cape was formally returned to the Dutch

HOLLAND, T, Postmaster at Campbell, 16 April 1898

HOLLIS, GC, Postmaster at Libodi, 1 March 1900
  Postmaster at Ugie, 1 April 1900

HOLLIDAY, H, Postmaster at Somerset East, 1 December 1853

HOLLIDAY, Norman Nathaniel Charles, Postmaster at Umzimkulu, 1 February 1901
  Postmaster at Flagstaff, 1 July 1904
  Postmaster at Willowvale, 1907

HOLLIDAY, RH, Postmaster at Bethulie Bridge, 1 December 1896

HOLLOWAY, EE, Postmaster at Kuils River, 20 February 1864

HOLLOWAY, G, Postmaster at Kuils River, 1 March 1846

HOLLOWAY, Geo, Lighthouse keeper and postmaster at Cape l'Agulhas, 7 July 1853, service provided for free

HOLLOWAY, Mrs G, Postmaster at Sir Lowry's Pass, 31 December 1850

HOLLOWAY, G, Postmaster at Woodstock Station, 1 March 1867, deceased while in office

HOLM, A, Postmaster at Bethulie Bridge, 1881

HOLMES, EL, Postmaster at Elliotdale, 1 August 1905

HOLSCAMP, Postmaster at Plettenberg's Bay, in about 1854

HOLTZHAUSEN, Marthinus, Postmaster at Great Brak River, 1 August 1907
  Postmaster at Great Brak River, 1 July 1908

HOLTZKAMPF, AE, Postmaster at Blanco, 1 September 1887
  Postmaster at De Rust, Meirings Poort, 1 November 1888
  Postmaster at Mount Frere, 1 April 1889
  Postmaster at Rosmead, 1 April 1890
  Postmaster at Steynsburg, 1 July 1891
  Postmaster at Laingsburg, 1 May 1892
  Postmaster at Belmont, 1 August 1892
  Postmaster at Hanover, 1 January 1897
  Postmaster at Warrenton, 15 May 1897
  Postmaster at Griquatown, 1 November 1898

HONEYBOURNE, BS, Postmaster at Prince Albert, 9 March 1866, became insolvent while in office

HONEYBOURNE, Mary Anne, Postmaster at Prince Albert, 31 January 1857

HONIBALL, J, Postmaster and field-cornet at South Middelveld, 1 January 1869

HONIBALL, JF, Postmaster at Uniondale, 1 July 1881
  Postmaster at Orange River, 17 August 1888
  Postmaster at Britstown, 1 February 1895
  Postmaster at North End, Port Elizabeth, 16 April 1900

Postmaster at Willowmore, 1 April 1902
Postmaster at Hopetown, 1 August 1903
Postmaster at Prieska, 1 November 1906

HOOD, Ronald Dennis, Postmaster at Daniel's Kuil, 1 December 1900
Postmaster at Philipstown, 2 September 1902
Postmaster at Klipdam, 1 April 1903
Postmaster at Philipstown, 1 October 1905
Assistant Postmaster at Lawrence Street, Port Elizabeth, salary £235 pa

HOOD, Rev TS, Postmaster at Uniondale, 31 March 1857, service provided for free in 1857

HOOLE, WV, Postmaster at Sterkspruit, 1 January 1903

HOOPER, J, Postmaster at Ruigte Vlei, 1880

HOOPER, Henry, Postmaster at Blanco, 7 February 1853

HOOPER, W, Postmaster at De Rust, 1 April 1877

HOPE, Hamilton, Resident Magistrate, Griqualand East, 1880
On 23 October 1880 the amaMpondomise, under the leadership of their Chief Umhlonhlo, rose in protest against the annexation of their lands to the Cape Colony. At the time the Resident Magistrate, Mr Hamilton Hope, was travelling to Maclear together with his assistants Messrs Hendley and Warren as well as his clerk, Mr AE Davies. Near the Sulenkama mission station the group was ambushed by a party of Mpondomise and, with the exception of Davies, who was the postmaster at Qumbu as well as the brother of the Wesleyan Missionary to Chief Umhlonhlo, all were killed

HOPKINS, Annie, Postmaster at Paardekop, in about 1868

HOPKINS, J, Postmaster and station master at Grootfontein, 11 October 1879
Postmaster at Laingsburg, 1881

HOPKINS, William George, Station master at Mochudi, Bechuanaland Protectorate, 19 September 1909, salary £238 pa

HORNEMAN, Mrs, Postmaster at Port Nolloth, before 1874

HORNER, E, Postmaster at Lady Frere, 1883

HORNIBROOK, Francis Mitchell, Postmaster at Woodstock Station, 1902
Postmaster at Woodstock, 1 December 1902

HORSFFALL, AG, Postmaster and station master at Porterville Road, in about 1877
Postmaster at Bellville, 1 November 1877

HORTON, WH, Postmaster at Kowie West, 1 September 1872, service provided for free in 1872

HOSKINS, PW, Postmaster at George, 17 June 1857

HOSMER, L, Postmaster at Palmietfontein, 1883

HOUGH, Mrs Lydia, Postmaster at Eland's Vlei, in about 1871
Although the GPO only recorded the opening of a post office at Eland's Vlei in May 1884, research by local historians has indicated that this establishment was already open by November 1871, with Mrs Lydia Hough as its first postmaster. She continued in this position until 1913, when she retired and handed the running of the agency over to another member of the Hough

family

HOUGHTON, Thos, Postmaster at Umzimkulu, 1882

HOW, J, Postmaster at Lily Vale, Harts, 1881

HOWARD, C, Postmaster and field-cornet at Bedford, 12 April 1870

HOWARD, JG, Postmaster at Adelaide, 1 November 1875

HOWAT, JV, Assistant, second class, Mafeking, January 1898
- Postmaster at Britstown, 1 May 1889
- Postmaster at Clanwilliam, 1 September 1900
- Postmaster at Matjesfontein, Division of Worcester, 1902
- Postmaster at Paarl, 1 October 1902

HOWE-BROWN, Frederick, Clerk, GPO, Cape Town, February 1882
- Clerk to the Civil Commissioner and Resident Magistrate, Hay, September 1883
- Once he had transferred to the Civil Commissioner's Office, Howe-Brown's career in the Civil Service followed a steady upward path. Moving to Graaff-Reinett on 1 Febrary 1886, he was promoted to Alexandria on 1 May 1890, Aberdeen on 1 October 1892, Assistant Magistrate, Malmesbury, on 28 September 1896, Special Duties in Mafeking in 1897, Williston on 20 May 1898, Wynberg on 1 October 1898, and Acting Magistrate for Cape Town in November 1900. Soon after the outbreak of the South African War in October 1899, he must then have returned to the GPO in Cape Town where, in 1901-1902 he worked in the new Post Office building as Press Censor and Deputy Commandant for Namaqualand. Upon the end of hostilities he then acted in a number of senior positions, including Collector of Customs, Port Officer and Receiver of Revenue for Port Nollith from 1901-1904, as well as Civil Commissioner and Resident Magistrate in such diverse divisions as Alexandra, Aberdeen, Malmesbury, Hopetown and Hopefield

HOWITSON, J, Postmaster at Blanco, 10 September 1857. See also RICHARDSON, PB

HOWSE, Miss AI, Postmaster at Kamastone, 1 January 1907

HUBBE, RC, Postmaster at De Rust, Meirings Poort, 1 January 1903
- Postmaster at Groot Drakenstein, 1 March 1904

HUBNER, David, Postmaster at Constable, 1880
- Postmaster at Hex River, 1881
- Postmaster at Claremont Station, 1 September 1882
- Postmaster at Rosebank, 20 June 1899
- The Pension Lists of 30 November 1909 recorded that in 1910 Mr Hubner, age 55, was retired on an annual pension of £151.1.5

HUDSON, H, Postmaster at Graaff-Reinet, 20 May 1823

HUDSON, Mrs Sarah A, Postmaster and field-cornet at Jagersbosch, 16 September 1863

HUGGETT, AC, Postmaster at Lady Frere, 1 February 1909, Salary £220 pa

HUGHES, E, Postmaster and field-cornet at Waterford, Division of King Williams Town, 1 November 1872, service provided for free

HUGHES, RB, Postmaster at Port St John, 1 April 1879

HUGHES, Thomas, Acting postmaster at Ladismith, in about 1901. The Post Office Circular (No 240 of 1 November 1901) recorded that Mr Thomas Hughes, acting postmaster at Ladismith, repaired the telegraph link between Calitzdorp and Ladismith at great personal risk. While engaged upon this work he was fired upon and captured by Republican forces. Thereafter they relieved him of his coat, watch and horse, and forced him to walk to Calitzdorp.

HUGO, JJ, Postmaster at French Hoek, 17 February 1851

HUGO, Ms MM, Postmaster at French Hoek, 1 July 1872

HUGO, P, Postmaster at Loxton, 1910

HUGO, PJ, Postmaster at Gydouw Pass, 1 April 1866

HUGO, TR, Postmaster at Garies, 1 March 1909

HULLEY, OR, Postmaster at Ugie, 1 August 1897

HULLEY, WB, Postmaster at Maclear, 1 April 1887

Postmaster at Maclear, 1 June 1891

HULTZER, W, Postmaster at Witteklip, 1 July 1902

Postmaster at Sandflats, 1 August 1905

HUMAN, Ebenezer, Postmaster at French Hoek, 26 May 1890

Postmaster at French Hoek, 1 May 1891

Postmaster at Vanrhynsdorp, 1 December 1892

Postmaster at Hopefield, 1 November 1894

Postmaster at Pearston, 1 March 1895

Postmaster at Komgha, 1 January 1896

Postmaster at Mount Fletcher, 1 July 1896

Postmaster at Philipstown, 1 August 1897

Postmaster at Prieska, 1 December 1898

Postmaster at Fraserburg, 22 April 1900

Acting postmaster at Eendekuil, 1 June 1906

HUMAN, LJ, Postmaster at and field-cornet Krombeck's Rivier, 31 August 1859, service provided for free in 1866-72

Postmaster at Malagas, 1 July 1876

HUMPHREY, JR, Postmaster at Paarde Poort, 19 November 1860

HUMPHREYS, John, Postmaster at Fort Brown, 1 August 1872

HUMPHREYS, WH, Postmaster at Ladismith, 1 April 1890

Postmaster at Porterville Road, 1 June 1892

HUMPHRIS, WB, Born in about 1856, Postmaster at Queenstown, 1 April 1883

Postmaster at Graaff-Reinet, 1 August 1891, initially acting

Postmaster at Uitenhage, 1 July 1906

The Pension Lists of 30 November 1909 recorded that in 1910 Mr Humphris, age 53, was retired on an annual pension of £223.13.4

HUNT, Miss ME, Postmaster at Sterkspruit, 1 February 1898

Postmaster at Sterkspruit, 1 September 1900

HUNTER, Mrs L, Postmaster at Millwood, Goldfields, 1 November 1892

HURDLE, J, Postmaster at Spectakel, 1 January 1876

HURDUS, Thomas, Born in about 1869, Postmaster at Touws River, 1 August 1908
Postmaster at Willowmore, 1 February 1909
The Pension Lists of 30 November 1909 recorded that in 1910 Mr Hurdus, age 40, was retired on an annual pension of £97.0.9. For further details see also under GC Geyer, station master at Montagu Road and Touws River

HURFORD, GFP, Postmaster at Graaff-Reinet, 26 May 1853
Postmaster at Grahamstown, 1 July 1883

HURTER, G, Postmaster at Middelburg, 1 December 1869
Postmaster at Cypress Grove, 1 November 1878

HURWORTH, J, Postmaster at Baviaans Drift, 1880

HUSSEY, Martin, Station master at Palapye Road, Bechuanaland Protectorate, 29 May 1906, salary £278 pa

HUTCHENS, WC, was appointed Deputy Sheriff and postmaster of Port Elizabeth on 1 September 1852, with offices on the eastern side of Market Square. Unfortunately his salary proved to be insufficient and in 1854 he resigned his post. It is possible that he was declared insolvent at about the same time

HUTCHINGS, JP, Postmaster at Muizenberg, 1907

HUTCHINSON, Miss E, also listed as N, Postmaster at Simondium, 20 December 1897

HUTCHINSON, FW, Resident Magistrate and postmaster at Walfish Bay, 1908
In the early hours of 23 June 1909 the timber structure housing the post office was destroyed by fire, together with the adjoining police offices and armory buildings. For a number of practical reasons public rescue efforts concentrated upon the evacuation of the armory and, barring the contents of its safe, which was also badly damaged, the entire post office establishment was reduced to embers (PMG 1909)

HUTCHINSON, GL, Postmaster and station master at Hermon, 16 June 1876
Postmaster and station master at Kraaifontein Station, 1 March 1877

HUTCHINSON, GP, Postmaster at Simondium, 1 February 1866

HUTCHINSON, GH, School teacher and postmaster at Simondium, 1 March 1878

HUTCHINSON, H, Postmaster at Strydenburg, 1 April 1906

HUTCHINSON, W, Postmaster at Villiersdorp, 1 October 1878

HUTCHINSON, WIP, Postmaster at Villiersdorp, 15 August 1890

HUTCHONS, H, Postmaster at Dordrecht, 3 July 1862

HUTCHONS, Mrs Jane, Postmaster at Dordrecht, 23 January 1865

HUTTON, AF, Postmaster at Bedford, 7 February 1857

HUTTON, H, Postmaster at Katberg, 25 March 1862
Postmaster at Lemoen Kraal, 1 January 1876

HUTTON, JC, School teacher, postmaster and field-cornet at Post Retief, 30 May 1854

HYMAN, G, Postmaster at Jansenville, in about 1879

Reappointed postmaster at Jansenville, 1 November 1882

HYSLOP, H, Postmaster at Kariega Station, 1881

HYSLOP, R, Postmaster at Klipplaat, 1882
Postmaster at Klein Poort, 1883

I

IMPEY, FW, born in about 1865
Postmaster at Naauwpoort, 1 January 1885
Postmaster at Alexandria, 1 April 1888
Postmaster at Aberdeen, Division of Aberdeen, 1 October 1893
Postmaster at Alexandria 1 August, 1896
Postmaster at Pearston, 1 April 1905
Assistant postmaster at Uitenhage, 1909
The Pension Lists of 30 November 1909 recorded that in 1910 Mr Impey, age 45, was retired on an annual pension of £149.8.7

INCH, J, Principal Clerk at the GPO, Cape Town, date not known
The Pension Lists of 30 November 1909 recorded that in 1910 Mr Inch, age 54, was retired on an annual pension of £276.19.2

INGLETHORPE, Miss, Postmaster at Balfour, 1 February 1901

INGGS, CF, Postmaster at Papkuil, 1 May 1903
Postmaster at Draghoender, 1 April 1905
Postmaster at Marydale, July 1906
Postmaster at Kuruman, 1 November 1906

INGLESBY, WT, Postmaster at Queenstown, 1 December 1879. On 13 May 1884 the *Queenstown Free Press* reported that the body of WT Inglesby, former Postmaster at Queenstown and more recently attached to the Circulation Branch of the General Post Office in Cape Town, had been discovered at his home in Sir Lowry's Road. He appeared to have committed suicide. At the time Ingelsby had been employed at the Post Office Savings' Bank where he was responsible for the handling of postal and money orders. He was reported to have gone home the previous evening looking very pale and *"in a disturbed state of mind."* Once there he had gone to the room of his two children and fallen asleep next to them still wearing his office clothes. A servant saw them like that at about 23.15 but decided not to disturb them. Shortly after 06.00 next day the same servant saw blood flowing from beneath the door of a shed and reported this to her mistress. Mrs Inglesby immediately went to check and found her husband in a sitting position with one leg doubled under his body and the other covered with blood and gore. A Martini-Henri carbine lay at his side and his nose and part of his face had been blown away. Inglesby was a member of Prince Alfred's Own Cape Volunteer Artillery and the carbine had only recently been issued to him. The coroner, JM Crosby, later stated that a bullet had passed through the face, and the crown of the head, finally exiting through the galvanised roof of the shed, a trajectory that indicated that the stock of the weapon must have been resting on the ground when the shot was discharged. A burned out candle indicated he must have committed suicide in the early hours of the morning. The newspaper stated that Ingesby was a steady, but sensitive and nervous man who never drank. Close examination of Post Office accounts revealed that no money was missing, and that therefore no aspersions could be cast upon his integrity

INGRAM, J, Postmaster at Paarde Poort, 30 September 1861

INNES, SF, Clerk to the Civil Commissioner and postmaster at Peddie, 12 May 1852

IRVIN, Henry, Station master at Southernwood. 20 December 1907, salary £220 pa

IRWIN, W, Postmaster at Wynberg, 8 January 1849

ISBELL, Mrs EA, Postmaster at Uitenhage, 1 February 1874

ISBELL, J, Postmaster at Uitenhage, 1 November 1862, deceased while in office

ISEMONGER, James Smith, Postmaster at Naauwpoort, 1 April 1888

    Postmaster at Newlands, Cape Town, 1 May 1899

    Postmaster at Touws River, 1906

    Postmaster at Caledon, 1 August 1908

    For further details see also under GC Geyer, station master at Montagu Road and Touws River

ISEMONGER, W, Postmaster at Mill Street, Gardens, Cape Town, 1 June 1889

J

JACKLIN, James Leonard, Station master at Orange River, 29 January 1909, salary £232 pa

JACKSON, C, Postmaster at Brakfontein, Division of Victoria West, 1 January 1874

JACKSON, S, Postmaster at Brakfontein, Victoria West, 5 May 1866, service provided free

JACOBS, SJ Snr, Postmaster and field-cornet at Phisantfontein, 30 June 1860, service provided for free in 1860-73

JAMES, EH, Postmaster at Darling, 1 August 1869

JAMES, F, Postmaster at Modder River, Division of Kimberley, 1881

JAMES, H, Postmaster at Darling, 1 March 1868, deceased while in office

JAMES, TH, Postmaster at Committees Drift, 17 August 1875

JAMIESON, RL, Postmaster at Ugie, 1 September 1894

    Postmaster at Cala, 1 October 1908

JANCOWITZ, C, Postmaster at Fraserburg, 22 October 1855

JANNASCH, AH, Postmaster and field-cornet at Mamre, 25 June 1860, service provided for free in 1867-70

JANSEN, JH, Postmaster at Hopefield, 22 November 1854

JANUARY, Th, Postmaster at Amalienstein, 3 November 1853

JAQUET, JP, Sorter, GPO, Cape Town, 15 January 1869

    Clerk, GPO, Cape Town, 1 May 1873

    Moved to Port Elizabeth in 1874

JARDINE, George, Postmaster at Ceres Road, 1 August 1889

    Postmaster at Britstown, 1 March 1891

    Postmaster at Matjesfontein, Division of Worcester, 1 October 1891

Postmaster at Somerset Strand, 1 February 1892

Caretaker of public buildings and postmaster at Somerset West, 1 April 1892

JARDINE, G, Postmaster at Umtata, 1909

JARDINE, GV, Postmaster at Cedarville, 1 June 1908

JARDINE, William Wauchope, Postmaster at Klipdam, 1906, Salary £245 pa

JARVIS, Charles Somerville, Station master at Norval's Pont, 1 December 1902, salary £328 pa

JAY, CE, Postmaster at Upington, 1 July 1894

JEFFERIES, Miss, Postmaster at Clarkebury, 1 June 1897

JEFFREY, Albert, Postmaster at Tulbagh, 1 January 1899

Postmaster at Victoria West, 1 October 1908

JEFFREY, CF, Postmaster at Kamastone, 1881

JEFFREY, WE, Postmaster at Lady Frere, 1881

JENCKEN, HD, Postmaster at Sir Lowry's Pass, 27 December 1847

JENKINS, Albert, Station master at Matjesfontein, 13 May 1909, salary £210 pa

JENKINS, W, Postmaster at Spectakel, 1 December 1863, service provided for free, dismissed from service, date not known

JENNINGS, AH, Postmaster at Mount Frere, 15 June 1878

JENNINGS, J, Postmaster at Qunu, 1 May 1879

Postmaster at Qunu, 1882

JENNINGS, WE, Postmaster at King William's Town, 1 September 1908

JENNET, JP, Postmaster at Orange River Bridge, 1881

JENNET, Robert Henry, Station master at Barroe, 9 August 1903, salary £186 pa

JENVEY, William Edward, Station master at Sterkstroom, 8 February 1907, salary £232 pa

JEPPE, H, Postmaster at Swellendam, 4 December 1851

JERVEY, WE, Postmaster at Landing Place, East London, 26 August 1879

Postmaster at Thomas River Station, 14 July 1900

Postmaster at Tylden, 1904

JERVIS, FP, Postmaster at Leribe, 1 July 1877

JESSUP, EA, Postmaster at Gras Kraal, 1 May 1879

JESSUP, W, Postmaster at Durbanville, 1 March 1862

JEVON, G, Postmaster at Somerset Road, 16 April 1865

JOHANNES, W, Postmaster at Butterworth, 1 December 1876

JOHNSON, C, Postmaster at Mount Ayliff, 1883

JOHNSON, D, Postmaster at Salt River, 13 August 1863

Postmaster and station master at Stellenbosch Station, 13 January 1868, service provided for free 1868-1877

JOHNSON, J, Postmaster at Seven Fountains, 1 January 1870

Postmaster at Mount Ayliff, 31 October 1879

JOHNSON, J, Postmaster at Laingsburg, 11 November 1879

JOHNSON, JM Snr, Postmaster at George, 14 February 1859

Postmaster at George, 11 August 1863, deceased while in office

JOHNSON, S, Postmaster at Seven Fountains, 11 March 1865

JOHNSON, WAE, Postmaster at Walmer, 1 December 1905

JOHNSTON, J, Postmaster at Lawrence Street, Port Elizabeth, 1 January 1903

JOHNSTON, W, Postmaster at Elliotdale, 1 October 1902

JOHNSTON, WR, Born in about 1866

Postmaster at Wellington Station, 1 February 1898

Assistant postmaster at Beaufort West, 1 February 1900

The Pension Lists of 30 November 1909 recorded that in 1910 Mr Johnston, age 43, was retired on an annual pension of £124.6.6

JOHNSTONE, Henry Stanley, Station master Storrnberg Junction, 14 Sept 1903, salary £268 pa

JOHNSTONE, VH, Postmaster at Richmond Road, 26 May 1900

JONES, AJ, Postmaster at Trappes Valley, 1 March 1901

JONES, ATD, Postmaster at Walmer, 1 February 1903

JONES, Mrs C, Postmaster at Beenleegte, 1 December 1876

JONES, D, Postmaster at Beenleegte, 1 January 1874

JONES, E, King William's Town, post office agent at Alice, 11 June 1857

JONES, E, Postmaster at Stellenbosch, 1 September 1884

Postmaster at Knysna, 1 April 1890

Postmaster at Uitenhage, 1 October 1893

Postmaster at De Aar, in about January 1902

Acting postmaster at Grahamstown, 1 December 1902

Postmaster at Middelburg, 1 March 1903

Postmaster at Wynberg, 1906

The Pension Lists of 30 November 1909 recorded that in 1910 Mr Jones, age 54, was retired on an annual pension of £204.2.2

JONES, G, Postmaster at Bailey, 1 August 1895

JONES, Horatio Edgar, Station master at Amabele, 5 September 1904, salary £242 pa

JONES, HM, Postmaster at Calitzdorp, 1 September 1887

Postmaster at Britstown, 1 March 1890

JONES, J, Postmaster at Plettenberg's Bay, in about 1866

Postmaster at Plettenberg's Bay, 1 April 1868

JONES, LL, Postmaster at Kenilworth, Kimberley, 1 July 1896

Postmaster at Norval's Pont, 1 May 1902

JONES, P, Postmaster at Kariega Station, 1880

Postmaster at Wolvefontein Station, appointed by 10 May 1880

JONES, RB, Postmaster at Tabankulu, before 1906

JONES, RM, Acting postmaster at Belmont, before 1906

Postmaster at Belmont, 1 April 1906

JONES, W, Postmaster at Aberdeen Road, 1882

JONES, W, Postmaster at Plettenberg's Bay, 1 July 1867

JONES, W, Postmaster at Plettenberg's Bay, 1 May 1896

JONES, WO, Postmaster at Avontuur, 1 February 1891
- Postmaster at St Marks, 1 December 1895
- Postmaster at Maraisburg, 1 March 1895

JOOSTE, Johannes Fredericus Gerhardus, Postmaster at Villiersdorp, 1 November 1898
- Postmaster at Vosburg, 1 May 1899
- Postmaster at Taungs, April 1903
- Postmaster at Marydale, 1 December 1907
- Postmaster at Upington, 1909, salary £205 pa

JORDAAN, A, Postmaster at Willowmore, 1 June 1879

JORDAN, HG, Postmaster at Jamestown, 1 March 1894
- Postmaster at Port Alfred, 1 August 1895
- Postmaster at Aberdeen, Division of Aberdeen, date of appointment not known
- Postmaster at Port Alfred, 1 December 1896
- Postmaster at Lawrence Street, Port Elizabeth, 1 August 1900
- Postmaster at Hopetown, 1 December 1900
- Postmaster at Daniel's Kuil, 1 August 1902
- Postmaster at Clanwilliam, 1 August 1908

JORSSEN, Peter Johannes, Postmaster at Pearston, 18 May 1886
- Postmaster at Alicedale, 1 April 1889
- Postmaster at Cookhouse, 1 February 1891
- Postmaster at Humansdorp, 1 May 1904

JOSS, A, Postmaster at Kloud's Kraal, 1880

JOUBERT, GH, Postmaster and field-cornet at Klein Drakenstein, 28 May 1866, service provide for free

JOUBERT, JG, Postmaster at Campbell, 1 July 1897
- Postmaster at Papkuil, 1 June 1898

JOUBERT, JJ, Postmaster at Lower Paarl, 11 April 1879

JOUBERT, PF, Postmaster at Murraysburg, 1 August 1866

JOURDAIN, C, Postmaster at Patatas River, 1 February 1869, service provided for free

JOURDAIN, WFL, Postmaster at Belmont, 1 October 1891
- Postmaster at Sandflats, 1 December 1893

JUBBER, DC, Postmaster at Piquetberg, 1 October 1907

JUDD, G, Postmaster at Upper Zwart Kei, 1 October 1862

JUDD, WS, Postmaster and station master at Addo, 1 October 1875
- Postmaster and station master at Sandflats, in about April 1876.
- In 1876 Mr WS Judd, postmaster at Sandflats, applied for the position of Inspector of Roads at Uitenhage, claiming he had previously filled a similar situation in the state of Illinois, USA. Having prevailed over 20 other applicants he then disappeared without further trace or explanation,

to the mystification of friends, employers and local residents

JUDSON, Major Dan, Postmaster at Bellville, 1883
   Postmaster at Colesberg, 1 May 1892
   Major Dan Judson went on to become Inspector of Telegraphs for Rhodesia

JULLEMAN, WP, Postmaster at Waverley Siding, 1881

JUNIUS, J, Postmaster at Letjesbosch, 1 February 1864, service provided for free

JUSTELIUS, VJ, Postmaster at Koopmansfontein, 1 July 1903
   Postmaster at Daniel's Kuil, 1 September 1903

K

KAKEWICH, Edmund B, also listed as KEKEWICH, Postmaster at Middelburg, 1883
   Postmaster at Beaufort West, 1 April 1885
   Clerk in charge of telegraphs, Fauresmith, OFS, 1 March 1886
   Postmaster at Mossel Bay, 1 October 1891
   Postmaster at Oudtshoorn, 1 November 1892
   Postmaster at Knysna, 1 December 1893
   The Pension Lists of 30 November 1909 recorded that in 1910 Mr Kakewich, age 56, was retired on an annual pension of £151.5.8

KANNEMEYER, H, Postmaster at Montagu, 1 February 1875

KANNEMEYER, Miss JM, Postmaster at Herbertsdale, 1 May 1903
   Postmaster at Kuils River, 1906

KARG, EA, Postmaster at Cedarville, 1 October 1907

KAVANAGH, WF, Postmaster at Idutywa, 1 December 1879

KAVANAGH, WH, Postmaster at Idutywa, in about 1878

KAY, RC, Postmaster at Philipstown, 1 November 1909
   Postmaster at Taungs, 1 July 1910

KAYE-BROOKE, H, also listed as BROOK
   Postmaster and station master at North End, Port Elizabeth, 1 September 1877
   Postmaster and station master at Coega, 1 April 1878
   Postmaster and station master at Atherstone Station, 3 March 1879

KEARNEY, T, Postmaster at Touws River, 1 February 1909. For further details see also under GC Geyer, station master at Montagu Road and Touws River

KEATING, John Michael, Station master at Hanover Road, 21 November 1901, salary £250 pa

KEENAN, D, also listed as J, Postmaster at Alicedale, 1 February 1896
   Postmaster at Belmont, 16 December 1897
   Postmaster at Douglas, 1902
   Postmaster at Lawrence Street, Port Elizabeth, 1 April 1904
   Assistant Postmaster, Port Elizabeth, date not given
   The Pension Lists of 30 November 1909 recorded that in 1910 Mr Keenan, age 37, took early retirement with an annual pension of £65.15.11

KEENE, R, Postmaster at Worcester, in about 1878

KEET, BJ, Postmaster at Montagu, 15 June 1854

KEHRMANN, CB, Postmaster at Darling, 1 August 1885

KEIGHTLEY, HT, Postmaster at Keightley, 4 September 1874.
>The post office at Farm 335 was opened on 4 September 1874 with Mr HT Keightley its first postmaster. In 1875 its name was officially changed to Keightley

KEKEWICH, EB, see under KAKEWICH

KELLAND, FR, Postmaster at West Bank, East London, 1 November 1909

KELLY, Mrs CJ, Postmaster at Douglas, 1 September 1886

KELLY, D, Postmaster at Douglas, 1 May 1889

KELLY, DJ, Postmaster at Sterkstroom, 1 July 1898
>Postmaster at Postmasburg, 1 January 1899
>
>Postmaster at Strydenburg, 1 April 1900
>
>During the South African War of 1899-1902 a number of Cape postal officials contributed actively to the British war effort, often acquitting themselves with distinction. One such was Mr DJ Kelly, postmaster of Postmasburg, who, having been caught up in the siege of Kimberley, performed duty there as a dispatch rider. This small group of men kept the besieged garrison in contact with the Colonial forces and, if caught by the Dutch, ran the risk of being executed. Kelly was captured but, having been interned for six weeks, was fortunate to be released on the Transvaal-Mocambique border

KELLY, Edward J Snr, Postmaster at Lady Frere, 1 March 1887

KELLY, PJ, Born in about 1867, Postmaster at Lawrence Street, Port Elizabeth, 1 December 1905
>The Pension Lists of 30 November 1909 recorded that in 1910 Mr Kelly, age 42, was retired on an annual pension of £128.19.5

KEMSLEY, GE, Postmaster at Gamtoos River Ferry, 1 February 1891
>Postmaster at Maraisburg, 1 August 1892
>
>Postmaster at Fraserburg Road, 1 April 1896

KENMACK, Mr, Postmaster at Nelspoort, 1 June 1896

KENNEDY, JNF, Postmaster at Achter Zwartland, 1880

KENNEDY, JS, Postmaster at Hanover, 1 April 1856

KENNEDY, Miss M, see under O'KENNEDY, Miss M

KENNEDY, W, Postmaster at Carnarvon, 14 March 1881
>Postmaster at Bredasdorp, 1 February 1887

KENNY, T, Postmaster at Klipplaat, 1880

KENT, C, Jailer and postmaster at Springbokfontein, 10 December 1856, dismissed from service

KENWARD, FE, Postmaster at Porterville Road, 1 January 1898
>Postmaster at Laingsburg, 1 July 1899
>
>Postmaster at Bellville, 1 March 1900

KEOWN, William Martin, Postmaster at Klaarstroom, 1 January 1895
>Postmaster at Avontuur, 1 April 1895

Postmaster at Avontuur, 1 October 1902

Postmaster at Calitzdorp, 1 December 1905

KERNICK, H, Postmaster at Elim, 1 July 1872

KERNSLEY, RW, Postmaster at Seven Fountains, 1881

KEWNEY, FJ, Postmaster and station master at Observatory Road, 1 February 1876

Postmaster at Tulbagh Road Station, 1881

Postmaster at Kalabas Kraal, 1880

Postmaster at Prince Albert Road, 1883

Station master at Newlands, date not given

The Pension Lists of 30 November 1909 recorded that in 1910 Mr Kewney, age 58, was retired on an annual pension of £189.5.7

KEYS, Mrs Ann Margaret, also listed as MA, born in about 1860, Postmaster at Seymour, 9 December 1887

Postmaster at West Bank, East London, 1 October 1895

Postmaster at Palmietfontein, 20 August 1897

Postmaster at Bell, 1 December 1898

Postmaster at Bayville, 1 July 1900

Postmaster at Cambridge, 1 August 1902

Postmaster at Park Avenue, East London, 1 April 1903

Postmaster at West Bank, East London, date of appointment not known

KEYS, Mrs MA, Postmaster at East London, date not given

The Pension Lists of 30 November 1909 recorded that in 1910 Mrs Keys, age 49, was retired on an annual pension of £34.16.0

KEYS, W, Postmaster at Lower Tyumie, in about 1860, service provided for free

KEYTER, BJ, Postmaster at De Rust, 16 March 1861

KEYTER, GC, Postmaster and field-cornet at De Rust, 1 January 1866

KIDD, RD, Postmaster at Warrenton, 1 September 1891

Postmaster at Butterworth, 1 February 1896

Postmaster at Philipstown, 1 December 1898

Postmaster at Upington, 1 February 1899

Postmaster at Aberdeen, Division of Aberdeen, 1 September 1900

Postmaster at Vryburg, 1 March 1902

Postmaster at Hopetown, 1 March 1902

Acting postmaster at Mossel Bay, 1 July 1902

Postmaster at Dordrecht, 1 December 1902

Postmaster at Britstown, 1 February 1903

Postmaster at Komgha, 1 April 1905

Postmaster at Burghersdorp, 1 October 1908

Postmaster at Komgha, 1 January 1910

KIDSON, AJ, Postmaster at Klipspruit Nek, 28 June 1868, service provided for free

KIDSON, GR, Postmaster at Cookhouse, 1 August 1861

KIDSON, R, Postmaster at Emgwali, 1 September 1879

KIESEWETTER, B, Postmaster at Alfred Docks, Cape Town, 16 November 1878

KIFT, M, Postmaster at Klaarstroom, 1 February 1896
- Postmaster at Hoetjes Bay, 1 February 1899
- Postmaster at Hermanus, 1 June 1902

KILBY, R, Jailer, Chief Constable and postmaster at Bathurst, 2 June 1853, dismissed from office

KILBY, WF, Acting postmaster at Umzimkulu, 1910

KILGOUR, H, Postmaster at Ceres, 22 April 1856

KILPATRICK, J, Postmaster at Orange Grove, Division of Victoria East, 1 January 1862

KILPATRICK, WB, Postmaster at Willowmore, 1 December 1896

KILROE, AJ, Postmaster at Port St John, 1 August 1889

KINASS, M, Postmaster at Mount Ayliff, 1 November 1889

KING, C, Postmaster at Mowbray Station, 1 June 1868
- Postmaster at Bellville, 1 November 1870
- Postmaster at Wellington Station, 1 January 1871
- Postmaster at Kalk Bay, 1 January 1874

KING, Charles Ault, Clerk to the Superintendent of Mfengu, and postmaster at Kamastone, January 1880; served in the Basotho War of 1881 as Quartermaster, Landrey's Light Horse

KING, CD, Postmaster at Bizana, in about 1910

KING, Mrs H, Postmaster at Clarkebury, 1883

KING, J, Postmaster at Rockford, 1881

KING, PJ, Postmaster at Upper Paarl, 1 November 1895
- Postmaster at Carnarvon, 1 February 1902
- GPO, Cape Town, date of appointment not known
- Postmaster at Richmond Road, 1 November 1903
- Postmaster at Bolotwa, 1 February 1904
- Postmaster at Stormberg Junction in about 1905
- Postmaster at Upper Paarl, date of appointment not known
- Postmaster at Fraserburg Road, 1 June 1908

KING, TA, Postmaster and field-cornet at Funah's Kloof, 11 Dec 1863, service provided free

KINGWELL, Arthur Darby, Station master at Mount Stewart, 13 May 1906, salary £195 pa

KINNEBURGH, RJ, Postmaster at Bellville, 1886
- Postmaster at Alicedale, 1 May 1886

KIRKHAM, WC, Postmaster at Colesberg, 30 October 1854

KIRKLAND, AE, Postmaster at Willowvale, 1 February 1898
- Postmaster at Qumbu, 1 July 1899
- Postmaster at Mount Frere, 1 August 1902
- Postmaster at Matatiele 1 April, 1904
- Postmaster at Mount Fletcher 1 April, 1905

KIRKPATRICK, WB, Postmaster at Clanwilliam, 1 May 1892
    Postmaster at Woodstock Station, 1 April 1894
    Postmaster at Willowmore, 1 January 1897
KIRBY, G, Letter Carrier, GPO, Cape Town, 12 October 1852. Salary £45 pa
KIRBY, GJ, Surveyor and postmaster at Port Elizabeth, 1 March 1886
    Reappointed postmaster at Port Elizabeth, 1 November 1892
KIRSTEN, AG, Postmaster at Worcester, 1 April 1828. Salary £20 pa
KIRSTEN, PAJ, Additional clerk, GPO, Cape Town, 2 January 1849. Salary £130 pa
    Clerk, fourth class, GPO, Cape Town, 1853
    Clerk, third class, GPO, Cape Town, 1855
KISCH, B, Postmaster at Colesberg, 1839
KISSER, HAC, Postmaster at Kenhardt, 1 September 1875, service provided for free
KISTOW, A, Postmaster at Frankfort, 1881
KITLEY, Edward, Station master at Hopefield, 3 June 1908, salary £220 pa
KITSON, HA, Postmaster at Libodi, 15 August 1896
KLAASEN, JC, see under CLAASEN, JG
KLARES, GP, Postmaster at Strydenburg, 29 February 1896
    Postmaster at Porterville Road, 1 March 1905
    Postmaster at Springbokfontein, 1 April 1908
KLEINSCHMIDT, CP, also listed as KLEYNSCHMIDT and KLYNSCHMIDT
    Postmaster and station master at Porterville Road, in about 1877
    Postmaster and station master at Ceres Road, 1 September 1877
    Postmaster at Porterville Road, in about 1879
    Postmaster and station master at Fraserburg Road, 1 November 1879
    Postmaster and station master at De Doorns, 1881
KLERCK, JRG, Postmaster at Paarl, 16 December 1870
KLERCK, R, Postmaster and assistant field-cornet at Sutherland, 30 March 1870
KLETTE, HJ, Postmaster at Bolotwa, 1 February 1900
    Postmaster at Waverley Siding, before 1902
    Postmaster at Riebeek East, 1 December 1902
KLEYN, W, Postmaster at Caledon, 1817
KLEYN, WH, Postmaster at Caledon, 19 September 1855
KNAAP, J, Postmaster at Wolve Kraal, 1 October 1867
KNIGHT, C, Postmaster at Bloemfontein, Division of Bredasdorp, 10 May 1858
KNIGHT, H, Registrar, GPO, Cape Town, 11 July 1881
    Clerk, third class, GPO, Cape Town, date of appointment not known
KNIGHT, J, Postmaster and field-cornet at Knight's Farm, 1 January 1879. The post office at Knight's Farm, in the division of East London, was opened on 1 January 1879 under the name of Farm No 83. In 1882 it was renamed Knight's Farm, probably because its first postmaster Mr J Knight, field-cornet, was the owner of the property

KNIGHT, JSW, Postmaster at Whittlesea, 27 August 1856

KNIGHTS, J, Postmaster and lighthouse keeper at Cape l'Agulhas 1 August 1871

KNIPE, CB, Postmaster at Wellington Station, 1 October 1887
  Postmaster at Muizenberg, 1 December 1888
  Postmaster at Ceres Road, 1 August 1890
  Postmaster at Eerste River Station, 1 March 1891

KNOBEL, JS, Postmaster at Colesberg, 2 June 1853

KNOESEN, TJ, Postmaster at Salem, 1 March 1902
  Postmaster at Glen Lynden, 1 June 1902
  Postmaster at Witteklip, 1 April 1904

KNOTT, Mr. Actimg postmaster at Setlagoli. In 1892 Mr JH Symons, then acting postmaster at Mafeking, wrote that:"*Setlagoli was originally an out-station during the expedition under Sir Charles Warren; it boasts now a post and telegraph office combined, a store, a house, and a hut, the remains of a fort, and a couple of members of the Bechuanaland Border Police. The acting Postmaster, Mr Knott, sorted his mail - a few minutes work - and retired again to rest.*" (Symons 1997)

KNOTT, Arthur James, Station master at Zwartkops Junction, 1 November 1898, salary £255 pa
  Postmaster at Aberdeen Road, 6 March 1901

KNOTT, Ferguson John, Station master at Paarl, 1 July 1908, salary £279 pa

KNOX, TM, Postmaster at Richmond, 1 October 1908

KOCH, Amelia S, Postmaster at Port Alfred, 1 March 1863

KOCH & NIEMOLLER. Postal Agency at Olyvenhout's Drift, c1888. Messers Koch and Niemoller owned a General Dealership near Olyvenhout's Drift, a mission station which had previously been established by the Rhinish Missionary Society in 1877. Given their location they probably specialised in staple goods serving a rural clientele such as farmers, hunters and passing travellers. They conducted their business from a building which in their wisdom, and not knowing the area very well, they had located in a dry river bed. This did not prove a wise choice as on 1 February 1898 the structure was swept away in a flash flood (PMG 1898)

KOCK, L, Postmaster at Walfish Bay, 1880

KOCKS, JS, Postmaster at Kalk Bay, 1 August 1889

KOENIG, FW, Postmaster at Ladismith, 1 March 1853

KOLVER, AT, Postmaster and jailer at Swellendam, 1 June 1836

KOOPMANS, JC, Clerk, fifth class, GPO, Cape Town, 24 September 1857
  Clerk, fourth class, GPO, Cape Town, 1858
  Clerk, third class, GPO, Cape Town, 1863
  Clerk, fourth class, GPO, Cape Town, 1865
  Clerk, third class, GPO, Cape Town, 1866

KOORTZ, BJ, Postmaster and field-cornet at Blood River, 1 April 1867, deceased while in office

KOORTZ, JAC, Postmaster and field-cornet at Blood River, 1 January 1861

KORSTEN, CM, Postmaster at Somerset Road, 2 June 1846

KORSTEN, H, Postmaster at Calvinia, in about 1879

KORSTEN, J, Postmaster at Willowmore, 30 November 1865

KORSTEN, P, Postmaster at Calvinia, in about 1880

KORSTEN, V, Postmaster at Salt River, 1 July 1865

KOTTICH, Wilhelm Herman Dietrich, Postmaster at Williston, 1 May 1908

KOTZE, JJ, Postmaster at Lange Riet Vlei, 4 February 1873, service provided for free

KRIEL, HH, Postmaster at Malagas, 1 April 1879

KRIEL, HJ, Postmaster at Nieuwoudtville, 1 November 1907

KRIGE, PD, Postmaster and field-cornet at Wittedrift, Division of Piquetberg, 1 July 1872, service provided for free

KRIGE, PJR, Postmaster at Prince Albert, 1 April 1869, removed from office

KROG, PJ, Postmaster and field-cornet at Wolvefontein Station, 11 November 1856

KRUGER, FJ, Postmaster at Pramberg, 30 June 1860

KRUGER, JG, Postmaster at Hottentot's Kloof, 1 January 1877

KRUGER, PH, Postmaster at Balfour, 1 October 1903

KRUMM, C, also listed as KRUNN, Postmaster at Mowbray Station, 1 November 1870

KRUMMECK, WE, Postmaster at Ugie, 15 April 1896

KRYNAUW, Miss Adriana, also listed as B, possibly in error for her sister Bella. See below.
  Postmaster at Doorn River, 1 February 1898
  Postmaster at Riebeek Kasteel, 1 December 1899
  Postmaster at Schoemanshoek, 1 June 1903
  Postmaster at Zuurbraak, 1 October 1903
  Postmaster at River Zonder End, 1905
  Postmaster at Gordon's Bay, 1 April 1905
  Postmaster at Houw Hoek, 1 November 1905
  Postmaster at Schoemanshoek, 1 August 1908
  Postmaster at Gordon's Bay, 1908, salary £100 pa

KRYNAUW, Bella, Postmaster at Schoeman's Hoek, 25 April 1903, salary of £75 pa

KRYNAUW, Miss Frederika Isabella, Postmaster at Philadelphia, before 1903
  Postmaster at Napier, 1 June 1903
  Postmaster at Houw Hoek, 1 April 1905
  Postmaster at River Zonder End, 1 November 1905
  Postmaster at Parow, 1 September 1906
  Postmaster at Schoemanshoek, 1 March 1907
  Postmaster at Grabouw, 1 August 1908, salary £84

KUHL, FC, Assistant Postmaster at Idutywa, no date given
  The Pension Lists of 30 November 1909 recorded that in 1910 Mr Kuhl, age 25, was retired on an annual pension of £35.18.6

KUMM, Angus Wilhelm, Postmaster at Kentani, 1 June 1898
  Postmaster at Flagstaff, 1 December 1905, salary £220 pa

KUYS, Alexander Dale, Clerk, GPO, Cape Town, 23 January 1893

Appointed Third Class Examiner in the Accounts, Control and Audit Office, 1 October 1893

KUYS, CJ, Postmaster at Stanford, 10 December 1859

KUYS, DJ Jnr, Acting postmaster at Burghersdorp, 1861
Postmaster at Burghersdorp 1 November 1863, deceased while in office

KUYS, JB, Postmaster at Bredasdorp, in about 1851

KUYS, WC, Postmaster at Swellendam, 1817

KUYS, William Napier, Clerk, GPO, Cape Town, 20 May 1887, moved to Treasury 25 June 1888

L

LACY, see DE LACY

LAING, JR, Resident Magistrate and postmaster at Tulbagh, 22 July 1852

LAKE, Anna, nee MEYER. Postmaster at Sidbury, 1 January 1869. See LAKE, Nicholas

LAKE, Miss H, Postmaster at Salem, 16 June 1900

LAKE, Nicholas, Postmaster and police constable at Sidbury. 16 December 1852, deceased while in office. Nicholas Lake was born in Sussex in 1801, served his apprenticeship as a coach-builder, and emigrated to the Cape in 1819. During the voyage he met Anna Meyer, the orphaned daughter of a Dutch sea captain who had been placed in the care of a Huguenot couple. Anna was only ten years old at the time but, despite the disparity in their ages, the two appear to have established an immediate bond. Anna and her guardians alighted at Table Bay while Nicholas continued with his journey to Port Natal. According to family tradition, he worked there as a wagon-builder until a few years later when he received a message from Cape Town informing him that Anna had fallen ill. Acting on impulse, he left his now-prosperous business in the hands of a partner, and returned to Cape Town, travelling overland in the company of a Zulu retainer. Nicholas and Anna were married in Cape Town in 1826, and by 1832 they had moved to the district of Sidbury where they raised a family of thirteen children. Nicholas not only plied his trade in the village as a blacksmith and wagon builder, but also found time to serve the community as both police constable and postmaster (Slater 1982). Following his death in 1869, his position as postmaster was taken over by Anna, who died in 1887

LAKE, Miss VE, Postmaster at Salem, first appointment 1 January 1896

LAMBERT, WS, Postmaster at Douglas, 1 September 1890

LANDMAN, KJ, Postmaster and station master at Huguenot, 1 July 1878
Postmaster at Hex River, 1883

LANDRY, J, Postmaster at Frankfort, 1 April 1878

LANDSBERG, S, Postmaster at Pampoenpoort, 1 July 1870, service provided for free

LANGLEY, JH, Postmaster and station master at Coega, in about 1876
Postmaster and station master at Sandflats, 1 November 1876
Postmaster and station master at Uitenhage Station, 1 February 1877
Postmaster and station master at East London East Bank, 24 December 1878

LANGSCHMIDT, EC, Postmaster at Somerset West, 27 February 1850, deceased while in office

LANGSCHMIDT, Wilhelm H, Postmaster at Grabouw, 3 October 1856, service provided for free. In 1856 a trader, Wilhelm Langschmidt, purchased the farm Palmiet River, adjacent to a ford over the Palmiet River, and laid out a village on the site. He named it Grabow, after his home-town in Germany

LANHAM, Charles Arthur, Postmaster at Windsorton, 1 November 1909

LANIGAN, JG, Postmaster at Two Streams, 1 March 1877

LANKSHEAR, HS, Postmaster at Herschel, 1880
   Postmaster at Port Alfred, 1881

LARGESEN, C, Postmaster at Hondeklip Bay, 1 February 1877

LARKIN, Mr, Postmaster at Nelspoort, 1 March 1898

LARKINS, JT, Postmaster and station master at Stellenbosch Station, 1 September 1877

LATALL, Mr, Postmaster at Langverwacht, Division of Oudtshoorn, 1881

LATEGAN, BG, Postmaster and field-cornet at Honingberg, 17 January 1865

LATER, Samuel, Postmaster at Leeuwenbosch, September 1855

LATHOM, Mr, Postmaster at Walfish Bay, 13 December 1861, service provided for free

LAUBMEYER, PL, Postmaster at Steytlerville, 1 September 1889

LAUBSCHER, JA, Postmaster at Achter Riebeek's Kasteel, 29 May 1858, service provided for free

LAUTENBACH, Benjamin Henry, Postmaster at Ceres Road, 1 October 1896
   Postmaster at Bellville, 1 May 1897
   Assistant Postmaster at Wynberg, 13 December 1899, Salary £235 pa

LAVIN, Sophia Mrs, see under ORREN

LAWRENCE, Thomas Henry, Station master at Bailey, 1 June 1908, salary £335 pa

LAWRENCE, William, Postmaster at Upper Maitland, 1 November 1909
   Postmaster at Bowesdorp, 1 April 1910

LAXTON W, Postmaster at Rosebank, 1 May 1898

LEACH, Miss E, Postmaster at Poplar Grove, 1 January 1906

LEACH, WO, Postmaster at St Marks, 1882

LEAHY, JW, Postmaster at Philipstown, 1882

LEARY, JG, Postmaster at Port St John, 1882

LEARY, William Power, Acting Magistrate's Clerk at Tsolo, October 1876; posted to Umtata, October 1877; Clerk to the Resident Magistrate at Mount Frere, 31 July 1878, and postmaster at Mount Frere, 15 March 1879; Resident Magistrate at Mount Fletcher (1882), Mount Ayliff (1883), Umzicaba (1894), Mount Frere (1895), Mount Currie (1908) and Kokstad (1900-1902). Served as Lieutenant in the Mthembu Levies, December 1877, and in the Tsolo Native Levies, April 1878; served with the Baca Contingent as Captain Commanding, 1879; Sub-Commandant and Officer Commanding Qumbu District, 1880-1; served with Native Contingent in the South African War, with rank of Lieut-Colonel

LEDGER, Miss F, Postmaster at Cedarville, 1 August 1901
   Postmaster at Nqamakwe, 1 July 1902
   Postmaster at Ndabakazi, 1 October 1902

LEDGER, JH, Postmaster at Ndabakazi, 1879
  Postmaster at Ndabakazi, 15 July 1896
LEESON, A, Postmaster at Ngqeleni, 7 May 1898
LEEUWNER, Mrs JB, Postmaster at Brand Vlei, 1 July 1878
LEGG, HA, Postmaster at Glenconnor, 1 August 1896
LE GRANGE, A, Postmaster at Seven Weeks Poort, 1881
LE GRANGE, M, Postmaster and field-cornet at Kafir Kuils Rivier, 31 August 1859
LEHMAN, GH, Junior Clerk at the GPO, Cape Town, 16 June 1828
  Chief Clerk, first class at the GPO, Cape Town, 22 June 1837. Salary £250 pa
  Accountant at the GPO, Cape Town, 1848
  Retired on pension, 31 March 1856
LEHMKHUL, F, Postmaster at Willowmore, 6 January 1860
LEIBBRANDT, PU, Postmaster at Koopman's Rivier, 4 July 1849
LEIPOLDT, Johan Gottlieb, Postmaster at Wupperthal, 24 July 1860, service provided for free. Wupperthal was established on 4 January 1830 on the farm Rietmond as a station of the Rhenish Missionary Society. The property was purchased for £225 on behalf of the society by the missionaries Johan Leipoldt, Theobald von Wurmb, GA Zahn and PD Luckhoff, and was named after the Wupper River valley, in Germany, where the Rhenish Mission Institute was located. In 1838 the station became a centre for the settlement of slaves freed from surrounding areas and, in an effort to make them economically self-sufficient, its mission began to focus increasingly upon the training of artisans. Within a relatively short time its graduates had become known as excellent tanners, shoe makers, carpenters, thatchers, and builders (SESA 1972)
LEIPOLDT, JP, Postmaster at Wupperthal, 1880
LEIST, B, Postmaster at Jansenville, 1 July 1864
LEITH, G, Postmaster at Port Beaufort, 25 April 1846
LE LEEUW, RJ, Postmaster and field-cornet at Paardeberg, Division of Paarl, 28 May 1866, service provided for free
LE MESSURIER, JH, Postmaster and station master at Kalabas Kraal, 1 November 1878
  Postmaster and station master at Klapmuts, 1 March 1879
LEMMER, SF, Postmaster at Dikkop Vlaakte, 1 January 1873, service provided for free
  Postmaster at Naauwpoort, 1 January 1873, service provided for free
LEMMERZ, CA, Postmaster at Mamre, 1 July 1871, service provided for free
LENNOX, Mrs, Postmaster at Villiersdorp, 1 March 1899
LENNOX, B, Postmaster at Klipheuvel, 1881
LENNOX, N, Postmaster and station master at Klipheuvel, in about 1879
LENNOX, TJ, Postmaster at Prince Albert Road, 15 September 1890
LENTZ, R, Postmaster at Stutterheim, December 1866
LEONARD, HB, Postmaster at Engcobo, 1 April 1886
LEPPAN, T, Postmaster and field-cornet at Stanley, 1 January 1863
LE ROOS, JL, Postmaster at Ceres Road, 1 November 1875

LE ROUX, EH, Postmaster at Hutchinson, 1 January 1895

LE ROUX, G, Postmaster at Klaarstroom, 1881

LE ROUX, GJ, Postmaster at Kenhardt, 1 April 1894

LE ROUX, HB, Postmaster at Sutherland, 15 April 1896

    Postmaster at Vanrhynsdorp, 14 November 1897

LE ROUX, HJ, Postmaster at Sarah's River, 26 September 1859

LE ROUX, J, Postmaster at Cango, 1 March 1869, service provided for free

LE ROUX, L, Postmaster at De Rust, 1880

LE ROUX, Petrus Malherbe, Postmaster at Belmont, 1 August 1907

    Postmaster at Modder River, Division of Kimberley, 1 December 1907

LE ROUX, T, Postmaster at Jamestown, 1 April 1899

LE ROUX, TF, Postmaster at Jamestown, 1 April 1900

    Postmaster at Komgha, 1 December 1902

    Postmaster at West Bank, East London, 1 January 1903

    Postmaster at Stormberg Junction, 1 September 1907

    Postmaster at Jamestown, 1 December 1909

LE SUEUR, Johannes Adriaan. JA le Sueur was a career bureaucrat who joined the Cape Civil Service on 1 July 1818, and only entered its Post Office on 7 June 1849 when he was appointed postmaster at Mossel Bay. On 4 December 1851 Governor Sir Harry Smith promoted him to the position of Postmaster General, with a fixed salary of £600 per annum. Under his direction during the next thirteen years the Colony's postal income was more than trebled while its Establishment was expanded to include 396 post offices. Unfortunately this growth was not accompanied by a concomitant revision of management structures within the GPO. In some instances reporting lines were allowed to blur and even lapse, thus allowing some members of staff to act without proper authority or supervision. As a result in February 1859 Mr J Armstrong, a clerk who was subsequently shown to have a propensity for gambling and female companionship, was placed in charge of the sale of postage stamps. This action was not authorized by Le Sueur, but was taken by a fellow clerk who wished to rid himself of this responsibility. By the time this move was detected in August 1864, Armstrong had managed to embezzle the sum of £1899.17s.1d from his funds. As a result three members of staff at the GPO were discharged from service and Armstrong was arrested and subsequently convicted of defrauding the Post Office. Despite his past achievements, and the fact that he was not personally responsible, Le Sueur was found to have been in derelict of his duties, and in 1865 he was dismissed from his post and ordered to repay the shortfall to the Post Office. After repeated representations to the Cape Parliament, this sum was initially halved, and then waived in its entirety. From 16 October 1866 he was placed on an annual pension of £315 per annum, but by the time he died, on 26 June 1876, the unfairness of his dismissal had been quietly recognized and he was retired on full pension

LE SUEUR, Jacobus J. Transferred to the Post Office on 24 September 1855 taking up the position of Clerk, fifth class, considered to be a junior clerical position at the GPO in Cape Town.

Initially his duties were not onerous and involved answering the Postmaster's-General correspondence, the examination of way-bills, and monitoring the performance of mail contractors. Within a week of his appointment, he was promoted to Clerk, third Class with a salary of £90 pa and an additional £15 for extra hours. At this stage he was placed in charge of postage stamps but must have been unhappy with this work for he soon requested a transfer to another Department. After some discussion, he was persuaded to remain at the Post Office subject to a promotion to Clerk, second class, and the position of Receiving Clerk. As such he remained in control of the lucrative office of stamp distribution which, at that time, allowed him to pocked a 2½% commission on all stamp sales, but was also in charge of the processing of mails. At this time the use of prepaid postal adhesives was optional and the majority of the letters were handed in unstamped. His duty then was to either attach a stamp to the letters or mark the postage upon them, and forward the mail on to the Inland Department for sorting. In February 1859 he was promoted to Clerk, first class, and his former duties as receiving clerk were handed over to Mr Armstrong, who was newly appointed to this position. Some time later, when it had become obvious to him that his former position was being mismanaged, it was Mr JJ le Sueur who reported Mr Armstrong to his superior. Four years later, on 1 January 1863, he was appointed Chief Clerk, in the GPO, in Cape Town

LEVINE, M, Postmaster at Draghoender, 1 December 1894

LEVY, M, Postmaster at Waterford, Division of Jansenville, 1880

LEWIS, AJ, Postmaster at Rhodes, 1 December 1902

LEWIS, CH, Postmaster at Touws River, 1880. For further details see also under GC Geyer, station master at Montagu Road and Touws River

LEWIS, CW, Postmaster and station master at Klapmuts, 10 August 1875

Postmaster and station master at Paarl Station, 23 January 1879

Postmaster and station master at Beaufort West Station, 1881

LEWIS, Edward, Station master at Alice, 29 April 1904, salary £201 pa

LEWIS, EJ, Postmaster at Sterkspruit, 1 September 1902

LEWIS, John, also listed as H, Postmaster at Kariega Station, in about 1877

Postmaster at Rondebosch, 1 September 1882

Postmaster at Fraserburg Road 1 August 1887

Postmaster at Montagu, 1 February 1888

Postmaster at Caledon, 1 January 1893

Postmaster at Richmond, 1 February 1893

Postmaster at Mowbray, 1 August 1896

LEWIS, JS, Postmaster and field-cornet at Robertson, 1 April 1868

LEY, O, Postmaster and field-cornet at Greyton, 15 November 1862

LIBBEY, John Ernest, Postmaster at Belmont, 1 April 1904

Postmaster at Belmont, 1 December 1907

LIEBENBERG, CR, Postmaster at Kemfontein, 1 July 1873

LIEPOLDT, Rev J, Postmaster at Saron, 29 October 1874, service provided for free

LIESCHING, CF, Postmaster and police constable at Stellenbosch, 2 June 1853

LIESCHING, Elizabeth, Postmaster at Stellenbosch, 1 October 1863

LIND, CM, Jnr, Clerk to the Civil Commissioner and postmaster at Clanwilliam, 1 March 1846

LINDE, GAF, Station master at Rosrnead Junction, 27 May 1906, salary £250 pa

LINDEN, C, Postmaster at Windvogelberg, 1 November 1861

LINDENBERG, JG, Postmaster at Stellenbosch, 1807

LINKS, Barnabas, Postmaster and field-cornet at Lily Fountain, 4 December 1854

LININGTON, Alfred John, Postmaster at Kenilworth, Cape Town, 1 March 1897

LINTON, C, Postmaster at Gretna, 29 September 1858

LINTON, L, Postmaster at Witmoss Station, 1881

LITTLE, AH, Postmaster at Butterworth, 1881

LITTLE, RH, Born in about 1857, postmaster at Adelaide, 1 June 1885

    Postmaster at Dordrecht, 15 November 1895

    Postmaster at Burghersdorp, 1 September 1899

    Postmaster at Beaconsfield, 1 April 1903

    Postmaster at Kokstad, 1 July 1907

    The Pension Lists of 30 November 1909 recorded that in 1910 Mr Little, age 52, was retired on an annual pension of £245.6.3

LITTLE, TJ, Postmaster at Ceres, 11 January 1855

LLOYD, Francis, Postmaster at Griquatown, 1 June 1910

LLOYD, H, Postmaster at Wolvefontein Station, 1881

LLOYD, John, Postmaster at Tylden, 1903

LOADER, AG, Postmaster at Ceres Road, 1 January 1904

    Postmaster at Ceres Road, 1 October 1908

LOCK, BW, Postmaster at Smith's Mine, 1 February 1903

    Acting postmaster at Griquatown, 1 December 1903

    Acting postmaster at Prieska, 1906

    Postmaster at Sutherland, 1 August 1906

LOCKE, RN, Postmaster at Koonap, 1 September 1904

LOCKINGTON, Geo, Postmaster and Chief Constable at Calvinia, 16 November 1856

    Dismissed from the Civil Service, date not known

LOCKWOOD, EE, Postmaster at De Rust, 1881

LOEFFLER, EW, Postmaster at Calvinia, 1 March 1879

LOGAN, J, Postmaster and station master at Touws River, 5 August 1879. For further details see also under GC Geyer, station master at Montagu Road and Touws River

LOGIE, GR, Postmaster at Dordrecht, 1880

    Postmaster at Cookhouse Station, 1882

LOGIE, JA, Postmaster at Claremont Station, 31 July 1851

LOGIE, Miss WE, Postmaster at Caledon Street, Cape Town, 1 September 1897

LOMBARD, HJ, Field-cornet at Fish River Randt, listed in 1886

LOMBARD, J, Postmaster and field-cornet at Klaas Smits River, 1 January 1865

LOMBERG, Charles, Postmaster at Kalk Bay, 1 November 1885

LOMBERG, Charles Thomas, Postmaster at Malmesbury, 1 August 1908

LONG, JB, Postmaster at Prince Albert Road, 1 June 1897

LONG, James Barry Munnik, Station master at Rondebosch, 8 July 1908, salary £280 pa

LONG, W, Postmaster at Simonstown, 1 March 1846

LONG, W, Postmaster and field-cornet at Aberdeen, Division of Victoria East, 8 August 1867, service provided for free

LONGBOTTOM, Ms Ina, Station master at Commadagga, 23 June 1903, salary £188 pa

LONGMORE, Alexander, Postmaster at Prieska, 1 November 1896
    Postmaster at Stormberg Junction, 1 April 1904
    Postmaster at Komgha, before 1905
    Postmaster at Calvinia, 1 April 1905

LONSADA, Mr, Postmaster at Komgha, in about 1878

LONSADA, St L, Postmaster at Ndabakazi, in about 1878

LOOTS, PJ, Postmaster and field-cornet at Voor Sneeuwberg, 30 November 1858

LOTZ, GW, Postmaster at Hooi Kraal 15 June 1846

LOURENS, JH, Postmaster at Krakeel River, 1 January 1893

LOURENS, Jacobus Ryno, Postmaster at Porterville, 1 April 1903

LOUW, AJ, Postmaster at Sterkwater, 14 March 1866, service provided for free in 1867-69

LOUW, FJ, Postmaster at Adelaide, 28 April 1862

LOUW, JH, Postmaster at Hottentot's Kloof, 1 March 1879

LOUW, JMA, Postmaster and field-cornet at Middelzwartland, 29 May 1858

LOUW, PH, Deputy Sheriff and postmaster at Prince Albert, 1 September 1871

LOWE, W, Postmaster at Zeekoegat, Division of Caledon, 17 April 1855

LOVEMORE, RH, Postmaster at Turvey's Post, 1880

LOXTON, AE, Postmaster at Kenhardt, 1 August 1876

LOYNES, J, Postmaster at McGregor, 12 December 1860

LUCKHOFF, PA, Postmaster at Somerset West, 1 May 1843
    Postmaster at Eikenboom, 14 March 1849

LUDWIG, Albert Joseph, Postmaster at Ugie, 1 November 1894
    Postmaster at Whittlesea, 1 May 1896
    Postmaster at Vosburg, 1 September 1906
    Postmaster at Kei Road, 1 October 1908

LUDWIG, Harry Charles Ferdinand Julius, Postmaster at Moshesh's Ford, 1 June 1907
    Postmaster at East London Jetty, 1 January 1910

LUING, Wilfred, Postmaster at Cambridge, 1 February 1906
    Postmaster at Lady Grey, Division of Aliwal North, 1 April 1908, salary £230 pa

LUNNON, Walter Charles, Postmaster at Kalk Bay, 1 July 1906

LUSH, WL, Born in about 1872, postmaster at Klipdam, 1 December 1900

Postmaster at Philipstown, 1 April 1903

Postmaster at Britstown, 1 April 1905

The Pension Lists of 30 November 1909 recorded that in 1910 Mr Lush, age 37, was retired on an annual pension of £59.7.6

LUTTIG, JH, Postmaster at Uitkyk, 1880

LUTTIG, SPS, Postmaster at Uitkyk, 11 September 1862, service provided for free in 1862-64

Postmaster at Uitkyk, 1 April 1869, service provided for free in 1869-72

LUTZ, JH, Postmaster at Williston, 8 August 1859, service provided for free

LUTZ, JH, Postmaster at Upington, 1 February 1890

LYELL, AC, Postmaster at Porterville, 4 August 1885

LYNAR, EA, Postmaster at Atherstone Station, 1880

Postmaster at Oatlands, 1883

LYNCH, C, Postmaster at Hondeklip Bay, 1 January 1864

LYNCH, Mary Mrs, Postmaster at Breakfast Vlei, 1 June 1860

LYNE, Michael John, Junior Assistant, Postal Service, at Port Elizabeth, 12 February 1884

Appointed Clerk to the Civil Commissioner at Uitenhage, December 1889

LYNN, Harry Edward, Postmaster at Lady Grey, Division of Aliwal North, 1 August 1907

M

MABILLE, Florence, Postmaster at Morija, date of appointment not known

Adolphe Mabille was a Swiss missionary who directed the Morija mission station from 1859 until his death in 1894. He established the Morija Missionary Book Depot, which produced and distributed religious books and pamphlets throughout southern Africa. The post office at Morija was established in September 1884 to facilitate the posting of literature by the Depot, and for many years was run by his daughter Florence. The new building was a picturesque example of Edwardian architecture, and was constructed in sandstone quarried and cut by local masons under the supervision of Joseph Andrews. Florence Mabille retired from this position in 1907 (Gill 1995)

MacAULAY, JH, Postmaster at Spectakel, in about 1865

MacDONALD, FW, see under McDONALD, FW

MacDONALD, JM, see under McDONALD, JM

MacINTYRE, Donald Arderne, Born in about 1856

Junior Telegraph Clerk, Swellendam, 1875

Acting Clerk-in-Charge, CTO, Cape Town, 1876

Clerk-in-Charge, Riversdale, 1877

Acting Clerk-in-Charge, George, October 1877

First Clerk, King William's Town, December 1877

Clerk-in-Charge and Postmaster at Burghersdorp, February 1878

Clerk-in-Charge, Kimberley, June 1878

Postmaster at George, 1 March 1886

Retired from service, July 1908

The Pension Lists of 30 November 1909 recorded that in 1910 Mr MacIntyre, age 53, was retired on an annual pension of £308.2.2

MacKAY, D, see under McKAY, D

MacKAY, David, see under McKAY, David

MacKAY, RS, Postmaster at Aberdeen Road, 1882

MacKAY, William, Postmaster and field-cornet at Hankey, 1 October 1867, service provided for free 1870-75

MacKENZIE, Alexander, Telegraphist, Imperial Post Office, 24 December 1876

Tranferred to Colonial Service as Telegraphist at Port Elizabeth, 7 July 1882

Telegraphist at Fort Beaufort, 1 October 1882

Telegraphist at Kimberley, 29 December 1882

Telegraphist at Barkly West, 1 February 1884, postmaster I July 1885

Postmaster at Worcester, 1 February 1893

Postmaster at Worcester, 1 September 1895

Postmaster at Queenstown, 1 September 1908

MACKIE, D, see under McKAY, David

MACKIE, WJ, Postmaster at Windvogelberg, 19 July 1860

MacKINTOSH, Donald, Telegraphist, Imperial Post Office, 25 June 1876

Tranferred to Colonial Service as Telegraphist at Fort Beaufort, 10 June 1881

Telegraphist at King William's Town, 1 December 1891

Moved to Acting Assistant Surveyor, Eastern District, 1 July 1894, confirmed 1 September 1896

Surveyor and District Engineer, Eastern District, 1 July 1897, Midland District 1 July 1898

MacKINTOSH, WGT, Assistant Superintendent at Port Elizabeth, date not given

The Pension Lists of 30 November 1909 recorded that in 1910 Mr MacKintosh, age 47, was retired on an annual pension of £147.11.1

MacLEAN, RM, Station master at Francistown, Bechuanaland Protectorate, 15 July 1908, salary £274 pa

MacPHERSON, R, also given as McPHERSON, Postmaster at Hoetjes Bay, 1 June 1895

Postmaster at Steytlerville, 1 January 1896

Postmaster at Port Nolloth, 1 November 1897

Postmaster at Kenhardt, 1 January 1902

Postmaster at Kenhardt, 1 June 1905

MADER, JA, Clerk to the Civil Commissioner and postmaster at Stellenbosch, 1 March 1846

MADGE, S, Sergeant, 2nd Queen's Regiment, and postmaster at Breakfast Vlei, 20 May 1858, removed from office

MAGEE, CP, Postmaster at Beaconsfield, 1 September 1882

Possibly may have been transferred to the post office at Du Toits Pan. On 30 November 1909 his widow, NCE Magee, was receiving an annual pension of £17.8.10

MAGXABA, J, Labourer at Cookhouse, date not given

The Pension Lists of 30 November 1909 recorded that in 1910 Mr Magxaba was retired on an annual pension of £15

MAITEN, CJ, Postmaster at Quthing, 1 July 1877
    Postmaster at Mafeteng, in about 1879

MAKIN, JL, Postmaster at Diep River, 1882
    Postmaster at Huguenot, 1883

MALAN, Ms SW, Postmaster at Wellington, 1 August 1878

MALLETT, Michael James, Postmaster at Hermanus, 1 January 1903
    Postmaster at Petrusville, 1 March 1903

MALLOCH, D, Postmaster at Kuils River, 1905
    Postmaster at Springbokfontein, 1 October 1905

MALONEY, Mr, Postmaster at Maclear, 1 November 1886

MAMPERS, Mrs, Postmaster at Roodewal, Division of Robertson, in about 1878

MANDY, Arthur Lawrence, Postmaster at De Doorns, 1 April 1905

MANDY, G, Postmaster at Farm No 13, on 1 October 1872

MANDY, GE, Postmaster at Palmietfontein, 1 May 1899

MANER, CF, Postmaster at Koonap, 1 March 1903

MANLEY, W, Postmaster at Daggaboersnek, 15 August 1867

MANN, Alexander, Telegraphist with the Postal Telegraphs Department, Aberdeen, 18 May 1879
    Telegraphist at Cape Town, 1 June 1882
    Telegraphist at Port Elizabeth, 10 September 1886
    Central Telegraph Department, GPO, Cape Town, 1 March 1893
    Inland Mails Branch Department, GPO, Cape Town, 1 July 1894
    Clerk-in-Charge, Returned Letter Office, GPO, Cape Town, 1 July 1896
    Superintendent, Telegraph Message Audit Branch, GPO, Cape Town, 1 July 1902
    Controller of Stores, GPO, Cape Town, 1 July 1908

MANNING, Benjamin, Station master at Mowbray, 26 June 1895, salary £290 pa

MANSFIELD, Miss EH, Postmaster at Doorn River, 1 January 1901

MANSFIELD, HC, Assistant Postmaster at King William's Town, date not given
    The Pension Lists of 30 November 1909 recorded that in 1910 Mr Mansfield, age 53, was retired on an annual pension of £236.13.4

MANSFIELD, Vivian Gordon Clifford, Acting postmaster at Waverley Siding, 1 December 1903

MARAIS, C, Postmaster and field-cornet at Petersburg, 1 November 1873

MARAIS, D, Postmaster at Amoskuil, 1881

MARAIS, DF, Postmaster at Maraisburg, 1 April 1890

MARAIS, J, Postmaster and station master at Breede River Station, in about 1879

MARAIS, PSP, Postmaster and station master at Stellenbosch Station, 26 September 1879

MARCHANT, W, Colour Sergeant, HM's 6th Regiment, and postmaster at Breakfast Vlei, 26 May 1857

MARCHIANO, G, Postmaster at Sea Point, Cape Town, 1881

MARCHIANO, Miss Leonora, Postmaster at Sea Point, Cape Town, 28 August 1883
    Postmaster at Sir Lowry Road, 1 September 1899
    Postmaster at Mill Street, Gardens, Cape Town, before 1902
    Postmaster at Stal Street, Cape Town, 1 August 1902
    Postmaster at Green Point, Cape Town, 1 January 1906, salary £165 pa
MARCUS, CH, Postmaster at Barrydale, 1881
MAREE, Burgert Daniel, Postmaster at Kenhardt, 1 January 1903
MARKS, KJ, Postmaster at Sutherland, 1882
MARILLIER, PR, Postmaster at Somerset East, 1 March 1855
MARITZ, Miss J, Postmaster at Dam's Laagte, 1 March 1898
MARITZ, Peter Johannes, Postmaster at Williston, 1 January 1900
    Postmaster at Hoetjes Bay, 1 April 1905
MARQUARD, L, Postmaster at Clanwilliam, 15 December 1826
MARREN, J, Postmaster at Ceres, 1 March 1861, deceased while in office
MARREN, Maria, Postmaster at Ceres, 11 September 1869
MARSH, Edward Henry, Postmaster at Koopmansfontein, 8 January 1898
    Postmaster at Porterville, 1 September 1900
    Postmaster at Koopmansfontein, 1 September 1903
    Postmaster at Griquatown, 1 August 1905
    Postmaster at Huguenot, 1 September 1906
MARSH, F, Postmaster at Spectakel, 1 July 1874
MARSHALL, David, Acting postmaster at Laingsburg, 1 December 1903
    Postmaster at Norvals Pont, 1 January 1907
    Postmaster at Orange River, 1 February 1908
    Postmaster at Britstown, 1909
MARSHALL, WN, Mail Guard between Cape Town and Sir Lowry's Pass, 12 October 1852, salary £80 pa
MARTELL, C, Postmaster at Ceres, 30 October 1871
MARTIN, B, Postmaster at Struis Bay, 21 October 1861, service provided for free
MARTIN, AB, Postmaster at Wellington Station, 1 November 1872
MARTIN, CJ, Postmaster at Garcia's Pass, 1880
MARTIN, JL, Postmaster at Tarka North, 25 October 1858
MARTIN, JS, Postmaster at Somerset East, 1 April 1886
MARTIN, Matthew Galbraith, Station master at Middelburg, 21 May 1906, salary £246 pa
MARTIN, PJ, Postmaster at Beaufort West Station, 1 March 1897
MARTYN, William Hotten, Station master at French Hoek, 1 July 1907, salary £235 pa
MASAKOWITZ, Wilhelm Karl, Postmaster at East London Jetty, 1 May 1908
MASKREY, W, Postmaster at Barville Park, 1 January 1866
    Postmaster at Dordrecht, 1 January 1873, dismissed from office
MASKELL, DW, Postmaster at Dordrecht, 7 May 1864

MASKELL, EJ, Postmaster at Klopper's Fontein, 1 January 1860

MASKELL, J, Postmaster at Klopper's Fontein, 24 September 1858

MASON, HB, Postmaster at Port Nolloth, 1 April 1878

MASON, J, Postmaster at Kinkelbosch, 14 March 1874, service provided for free

MASON, JT, Assistant Postmaster at the GPO, Cape Town
   The Pension Lists of 30 November 1909 recorded that in 1910 Mr Mason, age 53, was retired on an annual pension of £140.15.5

MASSYN, BJ, Postmaster at Doorn River, 1 March 1867

MASSYN, Jan F, Postmaster at Doorn River, 31 July 1854, service provided for free

MASTERS, Edwin, Postmaster at Schmidt's Drift, 1 May 1909

MATHESON, F, Postmaster at Draghoender, 1 February 1904

MATTHEW, C, Postmaster at Adelaide, 21 December 1873

MATTHEWS, C, Postmaster at Klipkraal, 31 May 1865

MATTHEWS, E, Postmaster at Burghersdorp, 1 August 1874

MATTHEWS, GT, Postmaster at Sterkstroom, 1 January 1892

MATTHEWS, J, Postmaster at Blue Cliff, 1 January 1877

MATTHEWS, J, Postmaster at Boontjes River, 1 February 1865

MATTHEWS, John Richard Benjamin, Postmaster at Norval's Pont, 1 March 1902
   Postmaster at Prieska, 1 May 1902
   Postmaster at Darling, 1 September 1903

MATTHEWS, Steven Thomas, Station master at Glenconnor, 1 October 1907, salary £220 pa

MATTHEWS, W, Postmaster at Commadagga, 1 February 1889

MATTHEWS, William M, Postmaster at Salem, 29 September 1858, service provided for free.
   William Matthews was Salem's first teacher, as well as its first postmaster

MAURER, R, Postmaster at Boontjes River, 21 March 1850

MAYNARD, J, Postmaster at Hondeklip Bay, 1 October 1870

MAYNE, Albert Edward, Postmaster at Draghoender, 1 September 1896
   Postmaster at Orange River, 1 January 1898
   Postmaster at Taungs, 16 June 1900
   Postmaster at Green Point, 1 April 1905
   Postmaster at Heidelberg, 1 February 1906

MAYNE, J, Postmaster at Darling, 1 January 1896

MAYNIER, Mrs A, Postmaster at Jagersbosch, 1 June 1871

MAYNIER, H, Postmaster at and field-cornet Jagersbosch, 8 February 1859

MAYNIER, Martha, Postmaster at Jagersbosch, 1 August 1866

MAYOR, CW, Postmaster at Whittlesea, 1 July 1890

MAYS, Miss CMG, Postmaster at Greyton, 13 January 1902

MAYTHAM, Wilfred Gordon, Postmaster at Bolotwa, 1 February 1903
   Postmaster at Qumbu, 1 May 1910

McADAM, Alexander, Station master at Hermon, 21 October 1907, salary £247 pa

McDERMID, J, Postmaster at Prince Albert, 8 May 1851
   Postmaster at Uitkyk, 1 April 1879

McDIARMID, AR, Clerk to Magistrate with Umditshwa and postmaster at Tsolo, 21 Nov 1876

McDONALD, AC, Postmaster and field-cornet at Upper Zwart Kei, 10 October 1866

McDONALD, FW, Born in about 1858, postmaster at Alicedale, 1 June 1886
   Postmaster at Ceres Road, 1 October 1887
   Postmaster at Touws River, 1 May 1888
   Postmaster at Cookhouse, 1 December 1888
   Postmaster at Woodstock Station, 1 September 1895
   Assistant, first class at Cradock, 1908
   The Pension Lists of 30 November 1909 recorded that in 1910 Mr McDonald, age 51, was retired on an annual pension of £159.8.7. For further details see also under GC Geyer, station master at Montagu Road and Touws River

McDONALD, GRC, Postmaster at Stutterheim, 1 November 1869

McDONALD, H, Garrison Sergeant-Major and postmaster at King William's Town, 1 October 1870, deceased while in office

McDONALD, J, Postmaster and field-cornet at Fort Wiltshire, 18 November 1868, service provided for free

McDONALD, J, Postmaster at Draaibosch, 1880

McDONALD, JM, Postmaster at Steynsburg, 1 August 1876

McDONALD, M, Postmaster at Adelaide, 1 April 1876

McDONALD, Mrs MA, Postmaster at Komgha, 1 January 1879

McDONALD, Robert Francis Levison, Postmaster at Cathcart, 1 September 1904

McDOUGALL, Alexander, Station master at Kraaifontein, 1 August 1905, salary £180 pa

McDOWELL, A, Postmaster at Nqamakwe, 1 January 1907

McENVOY, J, Postmaster at Steinkopf, 1 January 1908

McFARLANE, D, Postmaster at Karnmelk's River, 23 October 1869, service provided for free

McGIBBON, JH, Postmaster at East London, October 1865

McGILLEWIE, AM, Postmaster at Alice, 2 June 1853

McGRATH, J, Postmaster at Ceres Road, 1 December 1879

McGREGOR, A, Postmaster at Modderfontein, Division of Clanwilliam, 26 September 1867

McGREGOR, GR, Postmaster at Stutterheim, 1 November 1869

McGREGOR, J, Postmaster at Salt River, 15 August 1853

McGREGOR, JG, Postmaster at Modderfontein, Division of Clanwilliam, 1 May 1879

McGREGOR, JW, Postmaster at Malagas, 1 February 1867

McGREGOR, Miss M, Postmaster at Modderfontein, Division of Clanwilliam, 1 March 1899

McGUIRE, JF, Postmaster at Prince Albert Road, 1 May 1896
   Postmaster at Middleton, 8 February 1897

McINTYRE, Alex Frame, Postmaster at Nababeep, 1 February 1909, salary £140 pa

McINTYRE, DA, see under MACINTYRE, Donald Arderne

McINTYRE, DJ, Postmaster at Mount Frere, 1 May 1895
   Postmaster at Mount Ayliff, 1 May 1896
   Postmaster at Matatiele, 16 August 1897
McINTYRE, J, Schoolmaster and postmaster at Avontuur, 1 January 1867
McINTYRE, Malcolm Searle, Born in about 1858, entered service as a telegraph learner at Cape Town, January 1876
   Postmaster at Somerset West, 9 August 1876
   Postmaster at Ceres, 1 February 1877
   Clerk in charge of telegraphs at Jacobsdal, 1 July 1879
   Counter Clerk, Telegraphs, at Kimberley, 1 May 1880
   Clerk in charge of telegraphs at Du Toit's Pan, 16 March 1881
   Postmaster at Beaconsfield, Kimberley, 2 August 1883
   Postmaster at Colesberg, 1 March 1886
   Postmaster at Somerset East, 15 April 1892
   Postmaster and telegraphist at Bedford, 1 September 1899
   The Pension Lists of 30 November 1909 recorded that in 1910 Mr McIntyre, age 51, was retired on an annual pension of £220.10.6
McINTYRE, NM, Born in about 1848
   Postmaster at Avontuur, 1 May 1874
   Postmaster at Uniondale, 1 March 1890
   The Pension Lists of 30 November 1909 recorded that in 1910 Mr McIntyre, age 61, was retired on an annual pension of £160.6.10
McINTYRE, R, Postmaster at Nieuwe Rust, 1 May 1907
McINTYRE, W, Postmaster at Avontuur, in about 1880, possibly acting
McKAY, D, Lighthouse keeper and postmaster Cape l'Agulhas, 5 Aug 1854, service provided free
McKAY, D, Postmaster at Blinkwater, 10 September 1859
McKAY, David, Postmaster at Laingsburg, 1 March 1890
   Postmaster at Fraserburg, 1 February 1891
   Postmaster at Muizenberg, 1 February 1892
   Postmaster at Matjesfontein, Division of Worcester, 1 January 1896
   Postmaster at Mowbray, 1 October 1896
McKAY, J, Postmaster and field-cornet at Hankey, 27 December 1858
McKAY, JE, Postmaster at Glenconnor, 1 July 1897
McKAY, Mrs Mary E, nee McCALL, Postmaster at Alexandria, 1 December 1864
McKAY, William, see under MACKAY, William
McKAY, William, Postmaster at Hankey, 1 May 1886
McKENZIE, A, see under MACKENZIE, A
McKENZIE, D, Surveyor of Roads and postmaster at Paarde Poort, 1 December 1863
McKENZIE, JW, Assistant Postmaster at Kimberley, date not available
   The Pension Lists of 30 November 1909 recorded that in 1910 Mr McKenzie, age 44, was re-

tired on an annual pension of £190.12.6

McKINNON, Donald, Station master at Witmoss, 27 June 1901, salary £238 pa

McKINNON, Miss F, Postmaster at Villiersdorp, 1 May 1895
Postmaster at Hermanus, 1 September 1898

McLAGHTON, C, Postmaster at Komgha, possible date 1 October 1898, service provided for free in 1862-67

McLAUGHLIN, E, Postmaster at Colchester, 14 March 1864

McLEAN, RM, Station master at Francistown, Bechuanaland Protectorate, 15 July 1908, salary £274 pa

McLENNAN, GK, Assistant Postmaster at Port Elizabeth, date not available
The Pension Lists of 30 November 1909 recorded that in 1910 Mr McLennan, age 44, was retired on an annual pension of £147.12.0

McLEOD, CA, Postmaster at Cedarville, 1 May 1910

McLEOD, P, Clerk to the Civil Commissioner and postmaster at Bathurst, 16 December 1848

McLUCKIE, PH, Postmaster at Southwell, 6 June 1906

McMILLAN, J, Postmaster at Barkly West, 1 May 1899

McMURRAY, A, Postmaster at Daggaboersnek, in about 1866

McMURRAY, William Alexander, Station master at Ceres Road 27 Feb 1905, salary £236 pa

McNAMARA, Mrs J, nee COFFE, Postmaster at Pearston, 1 April 1870, married in 1874

McNAMARA, P, Postmaster at Somerset Road, 1 November 1861

McNISH, Thomas, Station master at Worcester, 18 August 1906, salary £300 pa

McPHERSON, CG, Postmaster at Douglas, 1883

McPHERSON, R, Assistant Postmaster at the GPO, Cape Town,, date not available
The Pension Lists of 30 November 1909 recorded that in 1910 Mr McPherson, age 44, was retired on an annual pension of £88.14.3

McROBERT, A, Postmaster at Wagenaar's Kraal, 1 June 1908

McROBERT, GF, Postmaster at Wagenaar's Kraal, 15 August 1890

McTAGGART, J, Postmaster at Idutywa, 1878

MEADEN, Rev W, Postmaster at Post Retief, 28 August 1871

MEADWAY, W, Postmaster at Aberdeen, Division of Aberdeen, 1 April 1867

MEDCALF, JF, Postmaster and station master Goudini Road, 16 June 1876, date in some doubt
Postmaster and station master at Kraaifontein Station, 16 June 1876
Postmaster and station master at Paarl Station, 1 December 1876, dismissed from office
Postmaster at Paarl Station 1880

MEDCALF, TF, Postmaster at Bellville, 23 January 1879

MEEDING, HP, Postmaster at Jagersbosch, 1 January 1845, salary £10 pa

MEESER, CH, Postmaster at Doorn River, 16 April 1900

MEESER, F, Postmaster at Heidelberg, 15 March 1856

MEESER, Rev N, Postmaster at Willowmore, 16 March 1873

MEEZER, Johannes Nicolaas, Postmaster at Cape Town, 1816

MEHLISS, O, Postmaster and Chief Constable at Dordrecht, 1 February 1871

MEINTJES, A, Postmaster and field-cornet at Petersburg, 1 July 1877

MEINTJES, JJ, Postmaster at Graaff-Reinet, 1820

MEIRING, DH, Postmaster at Murraysburg, 10 November 1867

MEIRING, GL, Postmaster at Victoria West, 1 April 1846

MEIRING, J, Postmaster at Laingsburg, in about 1879

MEIRING, JSN, Postmaster at Philipstown, 11 April 1876

MEIRING, PF, Postmaster at Lower Olifants River, 10 May 1858

MEIRING, PG, Postmaster at Worcester, 1 July 1873

MEIRING, Petrus Johannes Snr, Postmaster at De Rust, 3 September 1858.
The village of De Rust was established in 1900, on the farm De Rust, which was originally owned by Petrus Johannes Meiring Snr, after whom Meiring's Poort was named

MEIRING, PJ, Postmaster at De Rust, 1 April 1865

MEIRING, R, Postmaster at Britstown, in about 1878

MEIRING, RW, Postmaster at Moshesh's Ford, 1 November 1902

MELCK, Martin, Postmaster at Kersfontein, 1 January 1866, service provided for free. The farm Kersefontein was located on the lower reaches of the Berg River, and was originally granted in 1744 to Johannes Cruywagen. Its name was derived from the Dutch, and was given to a species of wild cherry which grew there. On 13 August 1770 the widow Cruywagen sold it to Martin Melck, a Prussian soldier who had emigrated to the Cape. Barring a short period when it was sold to an outsider, the property has been farmed by the Melck family ever since. On 1 January 1866 Martin Melck was appointed postmaster at Kersefontein and rendered this service gratis. It seems probable, therefore, that this post office was a farm agency run by the Melck family for the benefit of their workers and neighbours

MELVILLE, J, Postmaster at Kalk Bay, 1 April 1868

MELVILLE, S du T, Postmaster and field-cornet at Paardekop, 1 Oct 1868, service provided free

MERRINGTON, EC, Postmaster at Hottentot's Kloof, 1 April 1878

MERRIT, WR, Postmaster at Zwarte Koppen, 11 August 1854

MESHAM, LE, Postmaster at Somerset East, 1 June 1836

METCALF, Miss EH, Postmaster at Millwood, Goldfields, 1 November 1888

METCALFE, FJ, Postmaster at Millwood, Goldfields, 1 December 1887

METELERKAMP, FA, Postmaster at Stanley, 7 September 1859

METELERKAMP, FJA, Postmaster at Stanley, 10 May 1858

METELERKAMP, PC, Postmaster at Bedford, 22 May 1858

METELERKAMP, RW, Ferry keeper at Sunday's River Drift, 1869
In 1869 the lessees of the ferry at Sunday's River Drift became insolvent, and the "*lease of the waterway*", as it was called, went out to public tender. In due course this was awarded to a Mr RW Metelerkamp for an annual rental of £300. However the former lessees refused to give up possession and, after a prolonged legal dispute, the Supreme Court granted an order forcing them to surrender the waterway to the new tenants. The old owners opposed the change-over at

every step of the way and the new punt was only installed after the paid intervention of some very large men. This mode of conveying passengers and vehicles across the river continued until 1895 when a new road bridge was opened-up to traffic (Sellick 1904: 109)

METELERKAMP, W, Postmaster at Zuurbron, 23 October 1852, service provided for free

METELERKAMP, WSG, Postmaster and field-cornet at Zuurbron, 23 October 1852, service provided for free. Reappointed postmaster at Zuurbron, 18 January 1859. Mr WSG Metelerkamp acted as honorary postmaster with no salary, but received £1 per annum for stationery.

MEURANT, LH Jnr, Magistrate's Clerk, Distributor of Stamps and postmaster at Seymour, 15 July 1853

MEYER, Mr, Postmaster at Burghersdorp, 1855

MEYER, AM, Postmaster at WolveKraal, 1 October 1869

MEYER, EJ, Postmaster and field-cornet at Geelbek's Vlei, 16 October 1873

MEYER, ES, Postmaster at Geelbek's Vlei, 1880

MEYER, F, Postmaster at Great Brak River, 3 May 1864, service provided for free

MEYER, F, Post office agent and, subsequently, postmaster at Clifford, 1 June 1906

MEYER, G, Postmaster at Mossel Bay, 1830

MEYER, N, Postmaster at Hartenbosch, 15 February 1846

Postmaster at Mossel Bay, 4 December 1851

Postmaster and field-cornet at Geelbek's Vlei, 10 May 1858, deceased while in office. In the early days of the Cape Post Office, many of its postal agencies were attached to other business concerns, such as hotels and small country trading stores. It seems probable that, in this particular case, the Meyer family ran a number of commercial enterprises in the region; that after starting parallel concerns in 1858, they rationalized their postal operations in about 1860 and located them at Brak River; and that in about 1879 they transferred them to Geelbeks Vlei

MEYER, OC, Postmaster at Mossel Bay, 4 December 1851

MEYER, WJ, Postmaster at Geelbek's Vlei, 16 October 1858

MIDDLECOTT, Thomas, Postmaster, clerk and storekeeper, Berg River Convict Station, 12 April 1853

Postmaster, clerk and storekeeper at the Lichtenburg Convict Station, 24 February 1854

Postmaster, clerk and storekeeper at the Boontjes River Convict Station, 9 July 1856

MIDDLEDITCH, Francis James, Postmaster at De Doorns, 1 July 1903

MIDDLETON, F, Postmaster at Napier, 1 January 1849

MIDDLETON, John E, Assistant postmaster at Kokstad, 1 August 1885

Postmaster at Stutterheim, 1 August 1889

MIDDLETON, JS, also listed as IS, Postmaster at Maclear, 1 September 1892

Postmaster at Ceres Road, 1 September 1894

Postmaster at Worcester Station, date of appointment not known

Postmaster at Laingsburg, 1 March 1896

Postmaster at Worcester Station, 1 May 1896

Postmaster at Tulbagh, 1 October 1907

MIDDLEWICK, W, Postmaster at Blaauw Krantz, Division of Cradock, 6 October 1862

MILES, Henry Edmund, Postmaster at Willowmore, 1 March 1904

Postmaster at Bedford, 1 February 1909

Henry Edmund Miles emigrated to South Africa in May 1896, having sailed from England on the *Drummond Castle*, on the last voyage that this ship made to Cape Town prior to sinking off the coast of France on 16 June 1896. Soon after his arrival he entered the Cape postal service and was seconded to Mafeking as a telegrapher. In June 1899 he returned to England on leave, and by the time he had come back, the South African War had broken out. Unable to return to Mafeking, he volunteered to work as a telegraphist at Orange River which, at that stage, was on the front lines of battle. His duties there were to report on troop movements and casualty lists, and he remained at this position throughout the Battle of Belmont, which took place less than 50km to the north. After the relief of Mafeking on 17 May 1900, he returned to his old post until the end of the war. In June 1902 his fiancée, Rosalind Wilson, arrived in Cape Town. They were married in Rosebank and left immediately for Mafeking. In 1903 he was transferred to George, and when a consignment of gold went missing later that year, Miles became a suspect. As a result the young couple was subjected to repeated harassment and investigations. After the gold was recovered in Mossel Bay, and it was shown that it had been accidentally placed into the wrong mailbag, on 1 March 1904 the young clerk was appointed postmaster at Willowmore, to compensate him for all the unpleasantness that he and his wife had suffered (Emms 1977)

MILFORD, A, Postmaster at Kei Road, 1883

Postmaster at Cathcart, 1 October 1885

MILFORD, C, Postmaster at Tylden, 1881

MILLARD, A, Postmaster at Nelspoort, 12 October 1900

Postmaster at Nelspoort, 1902

MILLER, A, Postmaster at Hops River, 1881

MILLER, J, Postmaster at Delport's Hope, 1 January 1909

MILLER, John, Lighthouse keeper and postmaster at Cape L'Agulhas, 14 June 1856, service provided for free

MILLER, RR, Assistant Postmaster at East London, date not given

The Pension Lists of 30 November 1909 recorded that in 1910 Mr Miller, age 43, was retired on an annual pension of £48.15.10

MILLS, Miss AK, Postmaster at Post Retief, 1 December 1907

MILLS, D, Postmaster at Post Retief, 1 June 1876

MILLS, Mrs EJ, Postmaster at Post Retief, 1 March 1899

MILLS, ES, Postmaster at Douglas, 1 May 1892

MILLS, JD, Postmaster at Zwart River, Division of Knysna, 1 August 1879

MILLS, Miss MA, Postmaster at Balfour, 1 September 1902

Postmaster at Post Retief, 1 October 1903

MILNER, H, Postmaster at Wellington Station, 1 December 1879

MILNER, JW, Postmaster at Napier, 1 September 1909

MILTON, Edward Shirley, Postmaster at Deelfontein Station, 1 February 1901
  Acting postmaster at Postmasburg, before 1904
  Postmaster at Postmasburg, 1 June 1904
  Postmaster at West Bank, 1 June 1910
MILTON, PC, Postmaster at Qumbu, 1 August 1902
MIMMACK, Mrs H, Postmaster at Aliwal North, 16 October 1858
MINNAAR, A, Postmaster at Hermanus, 1 January 1901
MINNAAR, Stephanus Isaack, Station master at Aloes, 17 September 1909, salary £252 pa
MIRYLEES, Leonard, Acting postmaster at Garies, 1907
  Postmaster at Garies, 1 July 1907
MISSELBROOK, William, Station master at Newlands, 12 August 1905, salary £265 pa
MITCHELL, J, Postmaster at Coerney, 1880
MITCHELL, Samuel Frederick, Postmaster at Burghersdorp, 1 January 1910
MITCHELL, TL, Born in about 1845, postmaster at Idutywa, 1 December 1885
  Postmaster at Idutywa, 1 July 1890. Following his retirement on pension, in 1909 Mr Mitchell was receiving an annual pension of £127.10.4, by which stage he was 64 years old
MITCHELL, Thomas, Postmaster at Whittlesea, 1 March 1891
  Postmaster at Sterkstroom, 1 November 1892
  Postmaster at Norval's Pont, 1 April 1895
MOFFETT, Mrs Bertha Jane, Postmaster at Ngqeleni, 1 July 1902
MOGLIA, Augustus Fiorenzo, Postmaster at Richmond, 1 August 1902
MOLL, JC, Clerk to the Civil Commissioner and postmaster at Swellendam, 22 October 1828
  Postmaster at Swellendam, 1 March 1846
MOLLER, CE, Postmaster at Somerset East, 1 January 1828
MOLTENO, JC, Clerk to the Civil Commissioner and postmaster at Nelspoort, 21 June 1849, service provided for free
MONDAY, AE, see under MUNDAY, AE
MONKMAN, J, Postmaster and station master at Wolvefontein Station, 1 August 1878
MONTGOMERY, J, Telegraphist at Manchester, England, 1871
  Postmaster at Middelburg, 1 December 1894
  Postmaster at Beaconsfield, 1 January 1896
  Postmaster at Paarl, 1 January 1899
  Postmaster at Beaufort West, 1 October 1902
  The Pension Lists of 30 November 1909 recorded that in 1910 Mr Montgomery, age 54, was retired on an annual pension of £250.11.8
MONTGOMERY, W, Postmaster and field-cornet at Trumpeter's Drift, 1 January 1861
  Postmaster and field-cornet at Trumpeter's Drift, 1 October 1863, service provided for free in 1867-73
MOODIE, T, Postmaster at Wellington Station, 1 November 1897
MOONEY, Francis E, Postmaster at Mohales Hoek, 1 February 1882

MOORBY, John, Postmaster at Modder River, Division of Kimberley, before1889
    Postmaster at Belmont, 1 October 1889
    Postmaster at Britstown, 1 November 1891
    Postmaster at Laingsburg, 1 May 1893
    Postmaster at Montagu, probable date 1 January 1896
    Postmaster at Somerset Strand, 1 July 1898
MOORBY, Miss L, Postmaster at Sir Lowry Road, 1 May 1895
MOORBY, W, Sorter, GPO, Cape Town, 24 March 1871
    Assistant Clerk, Money Order and Stamp Branch, GPO, Cape Town, 17 August 1876
    Clerk, Money Order Branch, GPO, Cape Town, date of appointment not known
    Chief Counter Clerk, GPO, Cape Town, 1 July 1879. By the time of his retirement on pension Mr Moorby had achieved the position of Cashier at the GPO in Cape Town. In 1909, at the age on 77 he was receiving an annual pension of £127.10.4
MOORE, ET, Postmaster at Klaarstroom, 1 March 1887
    Postmaster at Calitzdorp, 1 February 1892. On 30 November 1909 his widow, MS Moore, was receiving an annual pension of £14.5.6
MOORE, M, Postmaster at Wynberg, 12 March 1846
    Postmaster at Wynberg, in about 1848
MOORE, W, Postmaster at Wynberg, 23 December 1852
MOORE, William, Station master at Salt River, 1 November 1897, salary £330 pa
MORGAN, E, Postmaster at Grootfontein, in about 1879
MORGAN, JF, Postmaster at Grootfontein, 1880
MORGENROOD, George WS, Postmaster at Belmont, 1 May 1890
    Postmaster at Molteno, 1 October 1891
    Postmaster at Butterworth, 1 May 1905. On 30 November 1909 his widow, MJ Morgenrood, was receiving an annual pension of £27.4.9
MORGENROOD, JT, Postmaster at Hazenjacht, 1 June 1877
MORGENROOD, JW, Clerk to the Secretary and Accountant, GPO, Cape Town, 1 Oct 1866
    Acting Secretary and Accountant, GPO, Cape Town, 1871
    Clerk to the Secretary and Accountant, GPO, Cape Town, 1872
    Secretary and Accountant, GPO, Cape Town, 18 October 1875
MORGENROOD, WE, Postmaster at Molen River, 1882
MORKEL, HA, Clerk to the Civil Commissioner and postmaster at Nelspoort, 26 March 1856, service provided for free in 1856-59
    Postmaster at Nelspoort, 7 March 1857
MORKEL, HJ, Postmaster at Millwood, Goldfields, 1 January 1896
MORKEL, MWD, Postmaster at Stanford, 1 August 1865
MORKEL, William, Postmaster at Klaarstroom, 1 December 1886
    Postmaster at Peddie, 1 March 1887
    Postmaster at Vanrhynsdorp, 13 June 1891

    Postmaster at Clanwilliam, 1 February 1892
    Postmaster at Porterville Road, 1 May 1892
    Postmaster at Carnarvon, 1 November 1892
    Postmaster at Alice, 1 April 1895
    Postmaster at Kei Road, 1 June 1895
    Postmaster at Matjesfontein, Division of Worcester, 1 October 1896
    Postmaster at Rosmead, 1 May 1897
MORONEY, J, Postmaster at Fraserburg Road, 1 January 1896
MORRELL, James Frederick Peter, Postmaster at Eerste River Station, 1 May 1893
    Postmaster at Belmont, 1 January 1897
    Acting postmaster at Cradock Station, before 1906
    Postmaster at Cradock Station, 1 September 1906
    Assistant postmaster at Stellenbosch, salary £280 pa
MORRIS, C, Postmaster at Fransche Kraal, 7 April 1856, service provided for free
MORRIS, Mrs Eliza, nee BRIMACOMBE, Postmaster at Faure Siding, 1 June 1858
MORRIS, Ernest Alfred, Postmaster at Seymour, 1 August 1885
    Postmaster at Mount Frere, 1 October 1886
    Postmaster at Maraisburg, 1 January 1892
    Postmaster at Norval's Pont, 1 April 1893
    Postmaster at Sterkstroom, 7 August 1898
    Postmaster at Dordrecht, 1 September 1899
    Postmaster at Upington, 1 December 1902
    Postmaster at Port Alfred, 1 July 1904
    Postmaster at Steynsburg, 1 November 1906
MORRIS, GW, Postmaster and field-cornet at Lower Tyumie, 6 Feb 1863, service provided free
MORRIS, HL, Postmaster at Jan de Boers, 16 March 1877
    Postmaster at Laingsburg, 1 April 1878
MORRIS, JH, Postmaster at Constable, 1 July 1879
MORRIS, JW, Clerk to Magistrate and postmaster at Maclear, 21 November 1871
    Clerk to Magistrate with Dalasili and postmaster at Engcobo, 1 August 1878
MORRIS, S, Postmaster at Bellville, 5 February 1866
MORRIS, S, Postmaster and station master at Coega, 1 September 1875
MORRIS, Th, Postmaster at Faure Siding, 27 December 1850
MORRIS, W, Postmaster at Cuyler Manor, 1 October 1879
MORRIS, W, Postmaster at Wynberg, 15 August 1849
MORRIS, WF, Postmaster at Pietermeintjesfontein, 1 January 1877
MORRISH, GSH, Postmaster at French Hoek, 1 March 1891
MORRISON, A, Postmaster at Wagenaar's Kraal, 1 January 1909
MORRISON, MWJ, Postmaster at Nelspoort, 1882
MORRISON, R, Postmaster and station master at Oatlands, 1881

Postmaster at Klein Poort, 1883

MORRISON, RH, Postmaster at Wolvefontein Station, 1880

MORTON, W, Postmaster at Ceres Road, 1 May 1888

MOSENTHAL, H, Postmaster at Murraysburg, 24 December 1856

MOSENTHAL, J, Postmaster at Murraysburg, 16 July 1858

MOSS, S, Postmaster at Zoutpans Drift, 24 June 1865

MOSTERD, JR, Postmaster at Richmond, March 1846

MOSTERT, JJ, Postmaster at Achter Zwartland, 29 May 1858

MOUTON, Johannes Augustus, Postmaster at Tulbagh Road Station, 1 January 1909

MOYLE, Mr, Postmaster at Malmesbury, 1852

MOYLE, Daniel Ferdinand Thomas, Postmaster at Eerste River Station, 1 January 1897
  Postmaster at Eerste River Station, 1 February 1903
  Postmaster at French Hoek, 1 May 1908

MOYLE, Matthew Albert Henry, Postmaster at Delport's Hope, 1 December 1900

MOYLE, Richard, Postmaster at Claremont Station, 9 October 1854
  The position of postmaster at Claremont appears to have been somewhat precarious as, for reasons that are not known, between 1848 and 1854 it was filled by no less than five officials. Moyle appears to have been made of sterner stuff and for the next fifteen years he managed the postal affairs of the village, probably from his home. The railway line from Salt River reached Claremont on about 19 December 1864 and in about May 1869 the Post Office terminated the services of Mr Moyle. At about the same time the local post office was relocated to the railway station

MOYLE, WHD, Postmaster and station master at Claremont Station, 21 February 1872
  Postmaster and station master at Porterville Road, 20 September 1875

MUGGLESTON, Miss, Postmaster at Ugie, 28 August 1892

MUGGLESTON, Miss Alice D, Postmaster at Ugie, 1 November 1886. The Mugglestons were one of the founding families of Ugie, and Alice, who had been educated at the Convent in King William's Town, in 1885 was appointed the village's first Postmaster. She subsequently married Fred Wilson, and their second daughter, Inez, was the first child to be born in the village.

MUGGLESTON, William James, Postmaster at St Marks, 1909

MUHLENBEEK, FA, Postmaster at Burghersdorp, 1 July 1868

MULDER, Hendrik Frederick, Postmaster at Armoed, 1 July 1909

MULDER, HJ, Postmaster and field-cornet Wynand's River, 14 Nov 1872, service provided free

MULDER, HP, Postmaster at Armoed, 1881

MULLER, AH, Postmaster at Goedemoet, 1880

MULLER, ARG, Postmaster at Graaff-Reinet, 1 October 1821

MULLER, CF, Postmaster at Patatas River, 22 April 1857

MULLER, CJ, Postmaster at Somerset East, 29 August 1840

MULLER, E, Postmaster at Houses of Parliament, 1 April 1904

MULLER, FC, Postmaster at Zwarte Koppen, 1 May 1864

MULLER, H, Postmaster at Voor Attaquas Kloof, 1 January 1861
MULLER, HB, Postmaster at Hermanus, 1 September 1897
    Postmaster at Villiersdorp, 1 September 1898
    Postmaster at Bellville, 1 November 1898
    Postmaster at Mill Street, Gardens, Cape Town, 1 March 1900
    Postmaster at Fraserburg Road, 1 December 1900
MULLER, Ignaas, Postmaster at Witteklip, 11 August 1854
MULLER, JF, Postmaster at Aberdeen, Division of Aberdeen, 1 October 1889
    Postmaster at Alexandria, 1 October 1893
    Postmaster at Jansenville, 1 April 1895
MULLER, John Henry, Postmaster at Herbertsdale, 1905
    Postmaster at Doorn River, 1 May 1905
    Postmaster at Schoemanshoek, 1 May 1906
    Postmaster at Parow, 1 March 1907
MULLER, JJ, Postmaster at Elim, 18 December 1856
    Postmaster and field-cornet at Wynand's River, 3 September 1858
MULLER, JJ, also listed as MULDER, Postmaster at Armoed, 1 August 1899
MULLER, Mrs Mary, nee WOOD, Miss Mary, Postmaster at Kalk Bay, 9 February 1862
MULLER, TNG, Postmaster at Cradock, in about 1820
MULLER, ZJ, Postmaster at Prince Albert, 4 September 1856
MULQUEENY, Miss, Postmaster at Mill Street, Gardens, Cape Town, 1 August 1892
MUNDAY, AE, Postmaster at Porterville Road, 1 July 1890
MUNDAY, CH, Postmaster at Coerney, 1 August 1889
MUNDAY, R, Postmaster at Redhouse, 12 February 1878
MUNNIK, JWA, also listed as JAW, Postmaster at Riet Kuil, Division of Colesberg, 17 June 1854
    Postmaster at Grabouw, 1 June 1861
MUNRO, TD, Postmaster at Brandwacht, 1 January 1907
MURDOCH, JA, Telegraphist in the Imperial Service, 1887
    Telegraphist at Cape Town, 1889, where he was placed in charge of the Instrument Room
MURDOCH, JC, Postmaster at North End, Port Elizabeth, 1 July 1896
    Postmaster at Britstown, 16 April 1900. May have been promoted Assistant Postmaster in East London. On 30 November 1909 his widow, Elsie Murdoch, was receiving an annual pension of £22.16.4
MURPHY, E, Postmaster at Mount Ayliff, 1 March 1894
    Postmaster at Butterworth, 1 December 1898
    Postmaster at Molteno, 1 April 1903
MURPHY, Harold Hazlett, Postmaster at Orchard Siding, 1 April 1907
MURPHY, Thomas, Station master at Touws River, 21 July 1908, salary £290 pa
MURRAY, C, Postmaster at Tarkastad, 1 April 1875
MURRAY, EJ, Postmaster at Norval's Pont, 1 July 1900

Postmaster at Norval's Pont, 1 November 1903

MURRAY, EK, Postmaster at Koonap, 1 July 1903

MURRAY, G, Postmaster at Daggaboersnek, 28 December 1857, service provided for free in 1859

MURRAY, J, Postmaster at Calitzdorp, 1 August 1886

MUSSMANN, C, Postmaster at Keurbooms River, 21 October 1865, service provided for free in 1867-69

MUSSMANN, CM, Postmaster at Kruis River, 8 September 1853, service provided for free
Postmaster at Kruis River, 1 July 1861

MYBURGH, D, Postmaster and field-cornet at Drooge Vlei, 1 September 1870

MYBURGH, PA, Postmaster and field-cornet at Vogelgezang, 12 January 1859, service provided for free in 1867-69

N

NAYLOR, J, Controller Money Order Office, at the GPO, Cape Town, date not available
The Pension Lists of 30 November 1909 recorded that in 1910 Mr Naylor, age 52, was retired on an annual pension of £415.0.6

NANNUCCI, O, Postmaster at Somerset Strand, 1882

NASH, GL, Postmaster at Henley, 18 September 1878

NASH, H, Postmaster at Witteklip, 1 January 1907

NASH, WM, Postmaster at Glen Lynden, 1 April 1876
Postmaster at Eland's Drift, 1881

NATHAN, C, Postmaster at Hanover, 1 August 1879

NATHAN, Isodore Jacob, Postmaster at Williston, 1 April 1905

NAUDE, BJ, Postmaster at Fourteen Streams, 1 July 1891
Postmaster at Middelberg Road, 1 May 1892
Postmaster at Porterville Road, 1 January 1893

NAUDE, CF, Postmaster at Warrenton, 1 April 1896
Postmaster at Hanover, 15 May 1897

NAUDE, JF, Postmaster at Britstown, 1 July 1877

NAUDE, JSD, Postmaster and field-cornet at Achter Op Sneeuwberg, 30 November 1858

NAUDE, PA, also given as PE, Postmaster at Kenilworth, Kimberley, 1 April 1896
Postmaster at Douglas, 1 July 1896

NAUDE, SF, Postmaster at Over Hex River, 10 May 1858

NAUHAUS, Rev CA. The post office at Elim was first opened on 20 December 1853 with the Rev CA Nauhaus as its first postmaster. A short time thereafter, on 26 January 1854, Nauhaus wrote to his superiors in Cape Town, informing them that the number of letters originating from his office hardly warranted its existence. Furthermore, he stated, his business was not faring at all well, and he could not afford to take the time off to visit the nearest Justice of the Peace to render account of the meagre number of postage stamps he had managed to sell that month. As a result he had decided to resign from the postal service and gave his office equipment, together with his stock of stamps, to the local people to do with them as they wished. The GPO in Cape Town appears to have given up all hope of recovering its property. (Cape Archives)

NAUTA, A, Postmaster at Riebeek East, 29 October 1862

NAYLOR, J, Born in about 1857, postmaster at Queenstown, 1 November 1895
Controller, Money Order Branch, GPO, Cape Town, 27 January 1897

NAYLOR, TJ, Postmaster at Eerste River Station, 1 February 1891

NAYLOR, Thos, Postmaster at Wagenaar's Kraal, 4 November 1853, service provided for free

NEALE, Mary, Postmaster at Westford, 1 January 1867, service provided for free

NEEDHAM, Joseph William, Postmaster at Prince Albert Road, 1 March 1893
Station master at Cradock, 18 September 1902, salary £360 pa

NEESER, Ch, A Postmaster at Middelburg, 11 July 1854

NEESER, D, Postmaster at Klipvallei, Koeberg, 18 April 1853, service provided for free

NEETHLING, Mr. It appears that the post office at Neethling's, in the division of Bredasdorp, was opened in about 1891. It was probably either a small wayside inn, or a farm stall which supplied the staple needs of a small rural community

NEETHLING, A van B, Postmaster and field-cornet at Kars River, 10 May 1858

NEETHLING, ML, Postmaster at Bloemfontein, Division of Bredasdorp, 7 May 1865

NEETHLING, PKG, Postmaster at Klaarstroom, in about 1873

NEFDT, JA, Postmaster at Winkel Plaats, 4 July 1861, service provided for free

NEL, JEP, Postmaster and field-cornet at Roggeveld, 4 October 1858

NEL, JEP, Postmaster at Roggeveld, 1 January 1876

NEL, JH, Postmaster and field-cornet at Lemoen Kraal, 1 July 1862

NEL, JJ, Postmaster at Springfontein, 31 August 1859

NELSON, George Cawood, Station master at Somerset East, 5 July 1905, salary £256 pa

NELSON, JB, Postmaster at Nelson's, Ward 1, on 1 February 1878.
The post office at Nelson's, Ward 1, was probably a farm agency located in a trading store, and was run by its owner as a service to a rural clientele

NELSON, WF, Postmaster at Mount Fletcher, 1 February 1896

NESEMANN, WF, Postmaster at Steynsburg, 1 August 1884

NETTLETON, RTL, Postmaster at Aliwal North, 1882

NEUMEYER, O, Postmaster at Balmoral, Division of Knysna, 1 April 1899

NEVILE, PS, Postmaster at Rhodes, 1 November 1903

NEVIN, Thomas, Postmaster at Nieuwoudtville, 1905
Postmaster at Steinkopf, 1 June 1905
Postmaster at Bowesdorp, 1 October 1906
Postmaster at Vredenburg, 1 March 1907
Postmaster at Eerste River Station, 1 January 1910

NEWBY, JE, Postmaster at Port Alfred, 4 May 1876
Postmaster at Bedford, 1 August 1877

NEWDIGATE, W, Postmaster at Forest Hall, 1881

NEWHAM, GJ, Postmaster at Salt River, July 1866

NEWMAN, H, Postmaster at Kimberley, 1 December 1882
   Postmaster at Queenstown, 1 March 1886

NEWTON, JC, Postmaster, Field-cornet and Chief Constable at Witteklip, 1 July 1874

NICHOLSON, JG, Postmaster at Hondeklip Bay, 24 February 1855, service provided for free

NICHOLSON, TD, Telegraphist at Bellville, 1885
   Postmaster at Kalk Bay, 1 September 1887
   Postmaster at Alfred Docks, Cape Town, 1 July 1888
   Postmaster at Knysna, 1 July 1900
   Postmaster at Bellville, 1 February 1905

NIEKERK, J, Postmaster at Misgund, 1 July 1871, service provided for free

NIEKERK, MH, Postmaster at Dam's Laagte, 1880

NIEUWENHUYS, Henry Joseph, Postmaster at the Houses of Parliament, 1 July 1903
   Postmaster at Moorreesburg, 1 August 1907, salary £245 pa

NIEUWOUDT, IA, Postmaster and field-cornet at Willem's River, 1 September 1858. In 1893 the NGK purchased a portion of the farm Groenrivier for £2100, and on 3 May 1897 established a *kerkplaats* upon it. The new village and congregation were named Nieuwoudtville, in honour of the Nieuwoudt family, who owned the farm, and were prominent in local community affairs

NIGHTINGALE, LG, Postmaster on Robben Island, 1 April 1888. It seems probable that LG and WM Nightingale were related, and that both came from a Methodist missionary background

NIGHTINGALE, WM, Postmaster at Middle Post, 1 March 1879

NISBET, Robert Lockwood, Acting postmaster at De Doorns, before 1908
   Postmaster at De Doorns, 1 February 1908
   Postmaster at Springbokfontein, 1 January 1909

NOKES, Frederick H, Postmaster at Lower Paarl, 1883
   Postmaster, Receiver of Revenue and Sub-Distributor of Stamps at Calitzdorp, 1 April 1885
   Postmaster at Prince Albert, 1 August 1886
   Postmaster at De Aar, 1 March 1887
   Postmaster at Touws River, 1 March 1891
   For further details see also under GC Geyer, station master at Montagu Road and Touws River

NOLTE, M, Postmaster at Eerste River Station, 1902

NORMAN, R, Postmaster at Simonstown, 25 March 1830

NORRIS, GH, Postmaster at Clarkebury, 1 April 1908

NORRIS, JH, Postmaster at Fraserburg Road, 1882

NORTON, C, Postmaster at Letjesbosch, 25 March 1861, service provided for free

NORTON, W, Postmaster at Schmidt's Drift, 1 September 1899
   The Postmaster General's report (PMG, 1899) made special mention of the postmaster of Schmidt's Drift, and the manner in which he safeguarded official property in the face of the

Republican invasion

NORWELL, James Henry Burnside, Postmaster at Orchard Siding, 1 January 1910

NOWERS, Miss EMA, Postmaster at Modderfontein, Division of Clanwilliam, 1 June 1902
    Postmaster at Barrydale, 1 February 1903
    Postmaster at Napier, 1 February 1906

NUNAN, DP, Postmaster at Witteklip, 1 March 1909

NUNS, FH, Postmaster at Mount Frere, 1 August 1888

NUNS, LA, Postmaster at Qumbu, 1 October 1893
    Postmaster at Port St John, 1 December 1894
    Postmaster at Umzimkulu, 1 February 1896
    Postmaster at Laingsburg, 1 April 1900

NUTT, WJ, Postmaster at Ceres, 1 September 1882

NXUSANI, S, Messenger at Kimberley, date not given
    The Pension Lists of 30 November 1909 recorded that in 1910 Mr Nxusani, age 43, was retired on an annual pension of £25.13.11

O

OAKENDEN, J, Postmaster at Ibeka, 5 April 1879

OAKLEY, Ernest, Postmaster at Alicedale, 1 April 1899
    Postmaster at Barkly West, 1 June 1909

OBERMEYER, PC, Postmaster at Sutherland, 1880

O'BRIEN, JV, Postmaster at Palmietfontein, 1 July 1896

OCHSE, Andrew, Postmaster at Van Wyk's Vlei, 1 June 1897
    Postmaster at Strydenburg, 1 February 1899
    Postmaster at Strydenburg, 1 June 1900
    Postmaster at Bredasdorp, 1 May 1905

OCHSE, FJ, Postmaster at Fraserburg Road, 1880

O'CONNELL, HEW, Postmaster at Jansenville, 1 August 1863

O'DEA, J, Postmaster at Vanrhynsdorp, 1 March 1903

O'DEA, J George, Postmaster at Millwood, Goldfields, 1 January 1897

O'DELL, WL. In 1861 a Receiving Office was located in the shop of Mr WL O'Dell, in South Union Street, Port Elizabeth

ODENDAAL, CJ, Postmaster and field-cornet at Over Duivenhoks Rivier, 31 August 1859

ODENDAAL, WJ, Postmaster and field-cornet at South Middelveld, 16 October 1858

ODENDAL, Alexander Wingrove, also listed as HW, Junior Assistant at Fraserburg Road, 15 January 1887
    Postmaster at Fraserburg Road, 1 September 1888
    Postmaster at Philipstown, 1 December 1889
    Postmaster at Britstown, 1 February 1894
    Postmaster at Carnarvon, 1 June 1896

Postmaster at Matjesfontein, Division of Worcester, 1 February 1897

Postmaster at Prince Albert, 1 May 1900

Postmaster at Robertson, 1906

ODENDAL, FG, Postmaster at Calitzdorp, 1 May 1876

ODENDAL, PB, Postmaster at Krombeck's Rivier, 5 February 1872, service provided for free

OERTEL, SF, Postmaster at Graaff-Reinet, 1 April 1828

OGLETHORPE, James John, Postmaster at Kenhardt, 1 October 1905

O'HARE, J Mel, Born in about 1856, postmaster at Burghersdorp, 1 January 1877

Postmaster at Komgha, 1 September 1878

Postmaster at Adelaide, 23 January 1879

Postmaster at Prince Albert, 11 February 1887

Postmaster at Swellendam, 1 May 1897

Postmaster at Montagu, 1 January 1904

The Pension Lists of 30 November 1909 recorded that in 1910 Mr O'HARE, age 53, was retired on an annual pension of £211.1.5

O'HARE, M, Postmaster at De Rust, in about 1876

O'HARE, Thomas Edmund, Postmaster at Plumstead, 1 April 1905

Postmaster at Diep River, 1 March 1908

O'KENNEDY, Miss M, also listed as KENNEDY, Miss M, Postmaster at Barrydale, 1901

Postmaster at Greyton, 1 December 1901

Postmaster at Doorn River, 1 February 1902

Postmaster at Great Brak River, 1 April 1903

Postmaster at Houw Hoek, 1904

OLDFIELD, HG, Postmaster at Imvani, 1 September 1879

O'LEARY, HJ, Postmaster at Rosmead, before 1890

Postmaster at Naauwpoort, 1 June 1890

OLIVIER, Miss AH, Postmaster at Armoed, 25 June 1898

OLIVIER, WH, Postmaster at Attaquas Kloof, 4 May 1872, service provided for free

OLKERS, Miss Catherine Louisa, Postmaster at De Rust, 1 February 1906

O'NEILL, James, Postmaster at Mount Fletcher, 1 November 1908. Not to be confused with another James O'Neill who was employed as the gaoler at Victoria East.

OOSTHUYSEN, W, Postmaster and field-cornet at Gouritz River, 16 October 1858

OOSTHUIZEN, Mrs SS, nee VAN DER MERWE, Mrs M, probably remarried in 1898

Postmaster at Maraisburg, 1 April 1895

ORCHARD, H, Postmaster at Claremont Station, 19 May 1849

ORCHARD, J, Postmaster and lighthouse keeper at Cape l'Agulhas, 17 September 1875

ORCHARD, JWM Jnr, Postmaster at Modder River, Division of Kimberley, 1 February 1893

ORDEMANN, ER, Postmaster at Balfour, 1 December 1903

O'REILLEY, I, Postmaster at Simonstown, 1 July 1826

O'REILLY, James, Postmaster at Somerset East, in about 1827

ORPEN, AF, Postmaster at Jansenville, 1 March 1897

ORPEN, Theodore George Herbert, Clerk in the Department of the PMG, GPO, Cape Town, 1 March 1888, Transferred to Custom's Office, Cape Town, 1 June 1889

ORR, RB, Born in about 1852, postmaster at Somerset West, 1 January 1881
   Postmaster at Hanover, 1 April 1890
   Postmaster at Victoria West, 1 November 1896
   The Pension Lists of 30 November 1909 recorded that in 1910 Mr Orr, age 57, was retired on an annual pension of £199.10.8

ORREN, A, Postmaster at Port Alfred, 1 February 1872

ORREN, Mrs Sophia, nee LAVIN, Mrs Sophia, Postmaster at Port Alfred, 3 June 1854
   Postmaster at Kowie West, 3 June 1854
   Deceased while in office in about 1862

OSBORNE, William CE. No further data available. On 6 November 1884 William CE Osborne, formerly employed as a postal clerk at the Beaconsfield Post Office, was charged in the High Court of Griqualand West with the theft of letters addressed to Du Toit's Pan and Old De Beers. He was found guilty and sentenced to three years imprisonment.

OSMAN, Charles H, Postmaster at Peddie, 1 May 1885
   Postmaster at Komgha, 1 March 1887
   Postmaster at Middelburg, 1 January 1896
   Postmaster at Beaconsfield, 1 April 1897. On 30 November 1909 his widow, ES Osman, was receiving an annual pension of £18.18.2

OSMOND, J, Postmaster at Malagas, 1880

OUTHWAITE, HM, Postmaster at Flagstaff, 1 October 1903

OUTRAM, George Edward, Postmaster at Oatlands, 1 June 1879

OWENS, John Charles, Station master at Warrenton, 21 June 1907, salary £238 pa

OXENHAM, W, Postmaster at Coerney, 1881

P

PACE, R, Postmaster at Uniondale, 4 December 1863

PAGE, Daniel, Postmaster at Grahamstown, 1 July 1822

PAGE, William, Postmaster at Colesberg, 27 October 1837

PAINTER, EJ, Postmaster at Yellow Wood Trees, 24 September 1858
   Postmaster at Yellow Wood Trees, 1 November 1865

PAINTER, FT, Postmaster and field-cornet at Springfontein, 3 August 1861, service provided for free in 1867-73

PAINTER, WF, Postmaster at Yellow Wood Trees, 1 January 1862

PAISLEY, John James, Postmaster at Nelspoort, 1904.
   Station master at Darling, 19 December 1904, salary £216 pa

PALGRAVE, WC, Resident Magistrate and postmaster at Walfish Bay, 1880

PALMER, C, Postmaster at Bushman's Hoek, 1 July 1871, service provided for free

PALMER, CT, Postmaster at Tarkastad, 1881

PALMER, HJ, Postmaster at East London Jetty, 1 July 1910

PALPHRAMAND, George Hall, Postmaster at Koonap, 1 October 1902
Postmaster at Daniel's Kuil, 1 April 1908

PALPHRAMAND, GL, Born in about 1856,
Postmaster at Fort Beaufort, 1 December 1891
Postmaster at Vryburg, 1 December 1902
The Pension Lists of 30 November 1909 recorded that in 1910 Mr Palphramand, age 53, was retired on an annual pension of £250.13.4

PARKER, G, Postmaster at Worcester, 1 December 1821

PARKER, G, Postmaster at Klapmuts, 27 October 1860

PARKER, J, Postmaster at Tulbagh Road Station, in about 1878
Postmaster and station master at Prince Albert Road, 11 August 1879

PARKER, JC, Postmaster at Klaarstroom, 23 May 1872

PARKER, JW, Postmaster and station master at Breede River Station, 26 October 1877

PARKES, J, Postmaster and field-cornet at Wheatlands, 30 November 1858

PARKES, JS, Postmaster and field-cornet at Karreeboschfontein, 1 October 1866
Postmaster and field-cornet at Wheatlands, 1 August 1871

PARKES, T, Postmaster and field-cornet at Wheatlands, 1 October 1864, deceased while in office

PARKINS, T, Postmaster at Dordrecht, 29 December 1870

PARKINSON, RJ, Postmaster at Caledon Street, Cape Town, 1883

PARROTT, GH, Secretary of the Divisional Council and postmaster at Piquetberg, 1 June 1872

PARROTT, W, Postmaster at Fort Beaufort, 1 September 1845

PARTINGTON, W, born in about 1854, Postmaster at Humansdorp, 1881

PARTINGTON, JH, Postmaster at Humansdorp, 1 May 1881
Postmaster at Humansdorp, 1 February 1894
Postmaster at Alice, 1 December 1894
Postmaster at Humansdorp, 1 May 1895
The Pension Lists of 30 November 1909 recorded that in 1910 Mr Partington, age 55, was retired on an annual pension of £157.2.11

PARTRIDGE, AC, Postmaster at Vanrhynsdorp, 1 February 1892

PATON, J, Acting postmaster at Kokstad, 1 August 1886
Assistant Controller, Central Telegraph Office, Johannesburg

PATTISON, Miss, Postmaster at Zuurbraak, 16 July 1896

PATTISON, W, Temporary clerk, GPO, Cape Town, in about 1880
Clerk, third class, GPO, Cape Town, 1 November 1881. On 30 November 1909 his widow, E Pattison, was receiving an annual pension of £10.12.7

PATTRON, J, Postmaster at Carlisle Bridge, 1 August 1873, service provided for free

PAULLI, J, Postmaster at Cape l'Agulhas, 1880
Lighthouse keeper at Cape Receiffe, date not given

The Pension Lists of 30 November 1909 recorded that in 1910 Mr Paulli, age 55, was retired on an annual pension of £35.15.7

PAYNE, A, Acting postmaster at Grey's Pass, 1869, service provided for free

PAYNE, A, Postmaster at Grabouw, 1 April 1879

PEACOCK, G, Postmaster at Camdeboo, 1880

PEARCE, EC, Station master at Sir Lowry's Pass, 28 April 1909, salary £223 pa

PEARCE, EW, Postmaster at Glenconnor, 1 November 1892

PEARCE, Henry, Postmaster at Uniondale, 1 October 1908

PEARCE, T, Postmaster at Lady Grey, Aliwal North, 29 March 1862, dismissed from office

PEARCE, Th, Clerk to the Civil Commissioner and postmaster at Burghersdorp, 21 April 1851

PEARMAN, P, Postmaster at Bensonvale, 1 April 1879

PEARSEY, H, Postmaster at Sunday's River Ferry, 6 October 1863

PEARSON, NV, Born in about 1860, postmaster at Stellenbosch, 1 October 1902
The Pension Lists of 30 November 1909 recorded that in 1910 Mr Pearson, age 49, was retired on an annual pension of £219.11.8

PEATT, T, Postmaster at Stutterheim, 1883

PECK, G, Postmaster at Bridgetown 8 September 1865, service provided for free

PEGGS, W, Postmaster at Riversdale, 15 April 1879

PEISER, GD, Postmaster at Koopman's Rivier, 1 January 1871, service provided for free

PENNINGTON, Charles Arthur, Station master De Aar Junction, 1 July 1908, salary £339 pa

PENNY, C, Postmaster and field-cornet at Southwell, 10 May 1858, service provided for free in 1867-1871

PENNY, J, Postmaster at Clearwater, 1 January 1875

PENNY, RC, Postmaster at Southwell, 1881

PENTZ, Christoffel Frederick, Postmaster at Bowesdorp, 1 June 1905
Postmaster at Glen Lynden, 1 August 1909

PENTZ, NW, Postmaster at Heidelberg, 1 January 1873

PENTZ, PJ, Postmaster at Wellington, 11 December 1851

PEPLER, Miss AM, Postmaster at French Hoek, 31 August 1885

PEPLER, JS, Postmaster at French Hoek, 16 February 1876

PEPPER, F, Postmaster at Darling Bridge, 10 June 1869

PEPPER, Harry Blowen, Station master at Berlin, 22 July 1896, salary £232 pa

PERCIVAL, FB, Postmaster at Middleton, 1880

PERCIVAL, TP, Postmaster at Sandflats, 1881

PERKINS, Herbert Ernest Howe, Joined Imperial Postal Service, 1 August 1882
Clerk, GPO, Cape Town, 14 December 1883
Transferred to Savings Bank, GPO, Cape Town, 12 February 1884
Acting Assistant Controller, Savings Bank Branch, GPO, Cape Town, 1 July 1903
Acting Controller, Savings Bank Branch, GPO, Cape Town, 1 July 1908
Controller, Savings Bank Branch, GPO, Cape Town, 1 September 1908

PERROTT, WH, Postmaster at Kuruman, 1 July 1898
  Acting postmaster at Wellington Station, 1 November 1903
  Postmaster at Wellington Station, 1 January 1904
  On 11 November 1899 a Republican force of 200 men under Commdant JH Visser arrived on the outskirts of Kuruman and cut off its telegraph lines. The following day they delivered a written note demanding its surrender. When the British garrison of 35 Cape Police under Captain A Bates understandably declined this invitation, the Dutch invested the town. The siege lasted until 19 November when, to the surprise of its inhabitants, the Dutch abruptly retired to Vryburg for a rest. They returned on 5 December 1899 with a force of 500 men, and after a series of skirmishes, the British capitulated on 1 January 1900. The postmaster, Mr WH Perrott, was one of those wounded during the fighting and was removed to Pretoria as a prisoner-of-war. The town was relieved on 24 June 1900, when a British force under Lt-General Sir Charles Warren entered Kuruman

PERRY, C, Postmaster at Sefantjies Poort, 25 September 1868, service provided for free
  Postmaster and field-cornet at Porterville, 1 March 1871

PERRY, JA, Postmaster at Glenconnor, 1 May 1898

PETERS, H, Postmaster at Bolo Reserve, 1883

PETERS, J, Postmaster at Kalk Bay, 29 September 1847

PETERS, WD, Postmaster at Alfred Docks, Cape Town, 1881

PETERSEN, HD. Work on the first bridge across the Kei River was started in 1876 under the direction of Joseph Newey, an engineer in the employ of the Cape Colonial Government, but was halted soon thereafter following the outbreak of war in 1877-78. The first permanent settlement of Kei Drift took place in about 1879, after work on the bridge had been completed, when the Cape Mounted Rifles (CMR) established a camp and a control point just above the river, probably in an effort to prevent the smuggling of weapons and liquor into the Transkei. Soon thereafter Mr HD Petersen established the Kei Bridge Hotel and a trading store, and sold the property to the firm of Messrs Atwell and Johnson of Mount Frere. They, in their turn, sold it to Ernest Charles Winsloe when he retired from the CMR in 1888 (Coulter 1988:7-10). The post office of Kei Bridge was probably located in one of these establishments. In 1883 a convict station was built to house some 35 labourers engaged in the construction of the Kei bridge access road (PWD 1884)

PETERSEN, L, Postmaster at New Bethesda, 1 December 1892
  Postmaster at New Bethesda, 1 September 1902

PETRIE, A, Postmaster and policeman at Queenstown, 1 July 1862, dismissed from office

PETRIE, Daniel, Station master at Butterworth, 12 December 1906, salary £256 pa

PETTIFER, Leopold, Station master at Cyphergat, 1 November 1906, salary £174 pa

PETTIT, D, Station master at Glenharry, 20 March 1906, salary £200 pa

PETTIT, R, Postmaster at Roodewal, Division of George, 13 Feb 1865, service provided for free

PETTIT, RW, Postmaster at Hutchinson, 1 November 1888

PETTIT, S, Postmaster at Toise River, 1 June 1893

Station master at Sand Flats, 1 October 1901, salary £281 pa

PEVERITT, Richard Simon William, Postmaster at Indwe, 1 December 1896
Postmaster at Stutterheim, 1 October 1907

PEWRIS, PL, Assistant Postmaster at Graaff-Reinet, date not given
The Pension Lists of 30 November 1909 recorded that in 1910 Mr Pewris, age 42, was retired on an annual pension of £129.6.5

PHELAN, J, also listed as PHEELAN, Postmaster at Woodstock Station, 1 October 1870
Postmaster and station master at Hermon, 20 September 1875
Postmaster and station master at Tulbagh Road Station, 16 June 1876
Postmaster at Goudini Road, 1881

PHILIPS, Benjamin Joseph, Postmaster at Mqanduli, 1 February 1906, salary £162.10.0 pa

PHILIPS, E, Postmaster at Risingham, 1881

PHILLIPS, Cecil Morton Thomas, Postmaster at Qumbu, 1 October 1888
Postmaster at Woodstock Station, 16 January 1899
Postmaster at Kenilworth, Cape Town, 1909

PHILLIPS, J, Postmaster at Aberdeen, Division of Aberdeen, 1 December 1870

PHILLIPS, J, Postmaster at St Marks, 1 January 1896
Postmaster at Palmietfontein, 1 May 1897

PHILLIPS, JB, Postmaster at Delport's Hope, in about 1902
Postmaster at Maitland, 1 February 1902

PHILLIPS, Mrs Jessamine Henrietta, Postmaster at Cambridge, 1 April 1903
Postmaster at Greyton, 1 February 1906. Salary £84.

PICK, CJ, Postmaster at Hout Kraal, 1 November 1906

PIEOT, E, Acting postmaster at Genadendal, 1 March 1895

PIERS, Charles. Following the dismissal of Le Sueur in 1865, the Colonial Government temporarily rusticated Le Sueur's deputy, George Aitchison, to a civil service position at Tulbagh and, on 1 October 1867, appointed Charles Piers as Postmaster General. Piers, who had previously held the position of Superintendent of Convicts for the Colony, had no record of employment in the postal service, and it is probable that he was only charged with the implementation of new and more stringent fiscal procedures in the administration of postal affairs. In 1873 George Aitchison was brought back from rural obscurity, and Piers was returned to his former post. The following year a grateful Colonial Administration promoted him to Resident Magistrate for Wynberg.

PIERS, G, Clerk, provisional appointment, GPO, Cape Town, in about 1874
Clerk, third class, GPO, Cape Town, 1 January 1876
Moved to Malmesbury, in about 1878, deceased October 1878

PIETERSEN, Postmaster at Hex River, 1880

PIETERSEN, FAE, Postmaster at George, 1828

PIETERSEN, FJ, Postmaster and station master at Kraaifontein Station, 1 January 1879

PIETERSEN, FP, Postmaster at Ceres Road, 1881

PIKE, AS, Born in about 1855, postmaster at Mossel Bay, 1 August 1893
   Postmaster at Mossel Bay, 1 December 1902
   The Pension Lists of 30 November 1909 recorded that in 1910 Mr Pike, age 54, was retired on an annual pension of £260
PILKINGTON, CA, Postmaster at Port Nolloth, 1 July 1879
PILKINGTON, H, Postmaster at Hondeklip Bay, 1 February 1874
PILLANS, CE, Clerk, second class, GPO, Cape Town, 8 August 1876
PIRRIE, James, Postmaster at Middleton, 1882
   Station master at Rosebank, 26 March 1898, salary £289 pa
PITCHER, I, Postmaster at Aberdeen Road, 1883
PITCHER, Jonathan, Station master at Caledon, 1 August 1902, salary £289 pa
PITCHER, W, Postmaster at Graaff-Reinet Station, 1881
PITT, AJ, Postmaster at Sterkspruit, 1 August 1903
   Postmaster at Qumbu, 1 February 1906
PITT, Geo, Postmaster at Howison's Poort Convict Station, 31 December 1856
   Postmaster at Buffels River Convict Station, 30 September 1867, service provided for free
PITT, O, Postmaster at Highlands, 1 November 1877
POCOCK, HA, Postmaster at De Rust, 1 August 1876
POLACK, MB, Postmaster at Robertson, 15 June 1854
POLACK, MB, Postmaster at Woodstock Station, 1 July 1894
POLLARD, Thomas, Appointed postmaster at Sidbury, 1 July 1844, and again on 1 Oct 1847
   Thomas Pollard was an innkeeper whose family emigrated to the Cape in 1820 when he was 11 years old, as part of Richard Hayhurst's party. Presumably he ran the post office from his premises. Pollard sold his property in Sidbury on 27 November 1852, and possibly moved out of the village at about the same time
POOK, Geo, Postmaster at Oudtshoorn, 30 June 1856
POOK, Lewis George Hedley, Postmaster at Taungs, 1 July 1896
   Postmaster at Jamestown, 1 October 1896
   Postmaster at Middledrift, 8 February 1897
   Postmaster at Matatiele, 1 April 1902
PORTINGALE, William Robert, Postmaster at Woodstock Station, 1 November 1908
POTGIETER, S, Postmaster at Gamtoos River Ferry, 9 March 1854
POTTER, HH, Postmaster at Malmesbury, 1 July 1863, deceased while in office
POVALL, Miss SAE, Postmaster at Durbanville, 1 August 1885
POWELL, Elizabeth A, Postmaster at Falloden, 1 April 1868
POWELL, GL, Postmaster and station master at Barroe, 1 September 1879
   Postmaster at North End, Port Elizabeth, 1 April 1876
POWELL, John, Postmaster at Cape Town, GPO, 1906
POWELL, John, Joined Imperial Telegraph Service, 8 June 1878
   Transferred to Colonial Service as telegraphist at Cape Town, 30 September 1882

    Telegraphist at Philipstown, 1 August 1883; postmaster 1 July 1885
    Postmaster at Murraysburg, 1 March 1887
    Clerk, Secretarial Branch, GPO, Cape Town, 1 April 1890
    Principal Clerk, Inland Mails Branch, 1 July 1891
    Surveyor and District Engineer, Western District, 1 July 1897
    Assistant Controller, Circulation Branch, GPO, Cape Town, 1 July 1903
    Controller, Central Post and Telegraph Office, GPO, Cape Town, 1906, salary £675 pa

POWELL, JA, Postmaster at Fraserburg, 1883
    Postmaster at Fraserburg Road, 11 January 1885
    Postmaster at Rondebosch, 1 August 1887
    Postmaster at De Aar, 1 April 1891

POWELL, L, Temporary deputy postmaster at Beaufort West Station, 29 June 1896

POWELL, Martha, Postmaster at Falloden, 3 December 1870

POWRIE, E, Postmaster at Mossel Bay, 1 October 1861

POYNTON, John Sinclair, Postmaster at Upington, 1 April 1907
    Postmaster at Philipstown, 1 January 1909

PRAED, Ann, Postmaster at Riebeek East, 9 March 1870

PRATT, GL, Postmaster at Port Beaufort, 12 August 1850

PRATT, TB, Postmaster at Bredasdorp, 6 December 1848

PREIS, JA, Postmaster at Kruis River, 26 June 1860
    Postmaster at Kruis River, 1 July 1864

PRENTICE, B, Postmaster at Prentice Hall, 16 October 1873. In 1868 a toll was established at Prentice Kraal, with Mr W Gibbon as tollmaster. On 16 October 1873 Mr B Prentice was appointed postmaster at Prentice Hall and rendered this service gratis. It seems probable that his establishment was run as an adjunct to a small farm trading store strategically located at a toll post

PRESTON, JJ, Postmaster at Witteklip, 1 December 1903
    In 1904 the post office at Witteklip was refitted and transferred to new premises. On 2 December 1906 a fire broke out on its premises and totally destroyed the building. Suspicion in this matter eventually fell upon the postmaster who, after a preliminary examination, was committed for trial on charges of arson and theft. As the result of these events the post office was refitted and provided with new premises (PMG 1904, 1906)

PRESTON, JR, Postmaster at Matatiele, 1 February 1893
    Postmaster at Engcobo, 1 April 1904, retired in 1909

PRETORIUS, IJ, Postmaster and assistant field-cornet at Voor Piquetberg, 1 January 1866, service provided for free

PRETORIUS, IT, Postmaster and assistant field-cornet at Verloren Vallei, 1 January 1866

PRETORIUS, J, Postmaster and assistant field-cornet at Voor Piquetberg, 6 December 1865, service provided for free

PRETORIUS, JL, Postmaster and field-cornet at Brak River North, 15 December 1863

PRETORIUS, JN, Postmaster and field-cornet at Gamka's Vlakte, 18 June 1860
    Postmaster and field-cornet at Calitzdorp, 18 June 1860
    Postmaster at Gamka's Vlakte, 5 January 1868, service provided for free
PRETORIUS, L, Postmaster at Mapassa's Leven, 29 September 1858
PRETORIUS, Z, Postmaster at Klaas Smits River, 25 October 1858
PRICE, Edward, Postmaster-Surveyor at Port Elizabeth, date of first appointment 25 Nov 1879
    Postmaster at Port Elizabeth, 1 September 1908
PRICE, J, Postmaster and station master at Tulbagh Road Station, 1 November 1875
    Postmaster and station master at Ceres Road, 16 June 1876
PRIETSCH, Mrs Elise, Postmaster at Amalienstein, 6 February 1854, service provided for free
PRINCE, Frederick Cardew, Telegraphist at Exeter, England, 1886
    Telegraphist at Cape Town, 1889
    Postmaster at Barkly East, 1 October 1902
    Postmaster at Bree Street, Cape Town, 1 May 1904
    Postmaster at Alfred Docks, Cape Town, 1 August 1908
PRINGLE, RH, Postmaster at Glen Lynden, 31 January 1862
PRINS, D, Postmaster at Vredenburg, 1 January 1902
    Postmaster at Groot Drakenstein, 1 July 1903
PRINS, Dirk Hendrik, Postmaster at Steinkopf, 1 October 1907
    Postmaster at Riebeek East, 1 November 1907
    Postmaster at Witteklip, 1 November 1908
PRINS, Miss J, Postmaster at Vredenburg, 1 March 1896
PRIOR, F, Postmaster at Klipspruit Nek, 1 January 1866
PRITCHETT, William Price, Born in about 1860, postmaster at Hopetown, 16 November 1885
    Postmaster at Aberdeen, Division of Aberdeen, 1 September 1889
    Postmaster at Dordrecht, 1 December 1889
    Postmaster at Colesberg, 1 December 1902
    Postmaster at Malmesbury, 1 April 1906
    Mr Pritchett appears to have taken early retirement soon after, in 1908. In 1909, at the age of 49, he was receiving an annual pension of £179.18.4
PROBART, J, Postmaster at Achter Sneeuwberg, Division of Cradock, 21 August 1868, service provided for free
PROUDFOOT, TR, Postmaster at Prieska, 1882
PRYNN, TC, Postmaster and police constable at Barkly East, 1 July 1878
PUCKLE, JW, Postmaster at Cradock, 1 August 1873
PUGH, Augustus Barnes, Postmaster at Cofimvaba, 1 July 1897
    Postmaster at Lady Frere, 16 August 1900
PUGH, JEP, Telegraphist at Alice, 1887
    Postmaster at Alice, 1 November 1895
    Postmaster at Komgha, 15 December 1897

Postmaster at Alice, 1 February 1903
Postmaster at Upington, 1 November 1906
Postmaster at Hopetown, 1 April 1907
Postmaster at Kimberley, date not given
The Pension Lists of 30 November 1909 recorded that in 1910 Mr Pugh, age 40, was retired on an annual pension of £116.7.3

PUGH, Richard S, Postmaster at Klein Poort, 1881
Postmaster at Fort Jackson, 1883
Postmaster at Molteno, 3 March 1885

PULLEN, JT, Postmaster at Cofimvaba, 23 August 1899

PULLEN, WC, Postmaster and station master at Waku, 1881

PULLEN, WT, Postmaster at Addo Heights, 1 April 1847, service provided for free

PULLEN, WT, Postmaster and station master at Kubusie, in about 1879
Postmaster and station master at Thomas River Station, 1 November 1879

PURCHASE, Herbert Richard, Postmaster at Delport's Hope, 1 January 1910

PYE, John, Postmaster at Leeuwenfontein, 29 January 1855

PYKE, AS, see under PIKE

PYKE, George, Postmaster at Delport's Hope, 1 August 1902

PYLE, WR, Postmaster at Fraserburg Road, 1 February 1888

PYWELL, W, Postmaster at Riversdale, 22 September 1887
Postmaster at Beaufort West, 16 March 1897
Postmaster at Beaconsfield, 1902
Postmaster at Malmesbury, 1 March 1903
Postmaster at Colesberg, 1 April 1906

Q

QUAIL, John Wilson, Postmaster at Trappes Valley, 1 June 1897
Postmaster at Klaarstroom, 1 February 1899
Postmaster at Nqamakwe, 1 September 1907
Postmaster at Stormberg Junction, 1 June 1910

QUINLAN, James, Postmaster at Witmoss Station, 20 May 1891
Station master at Beaconsfield, 15 May 1903, salary £265 pa

QUINN, T, Postmaster and field-cornet at Bedford, 25 March 1859

QUINTON, R, Postmaster at Molen River, 18 November 1856
Postmaster at Roodewal, Division of George, 31 January 1866, service provided for free

QUIRK, J, Postmaster at Winterhoek Convict Establishment, 3 October 1860

R

RAAFF, TW, Postmaster on Robben Island, 1883

RAATH, W, Postmaster at Mount Frere, 16 June 1900

RAATH, WJ, Postmaster at Petrusville, 1 July 1897

RABE, Andries Jacobus, Station master at Piquetberg, 26 May 1909, salary £192 pa

RABE, Andrew, Postmaster and field-cornet at Darling, 23 October 1856, removed from office

RABE, CT, Postmaster at Caledon, 1 August 1820

RABIE, CJ, Postmaster at Beaufort West, 1 February 1826
  Postmaster at Beaufort West, in about 1829

RADEMEYER, JM, Postmaster at Zuur Anys, 1 July 1840

RADEMEYER, PA, Postmaster and field-cornet at East Riet River, February 1872

RADEMEYER, Stephen Martin, Postmaster at Klipplaat, 1 June 1909
  Postmaster at New Bethesda, 1 July 1909

RAHN, F, Postmaster at Frankfort, 1 March 1876

RAINEY, John Gordon, Postmaster at Sterkspruit, 1906
  Postmaster at Lady Frere, 1 May 1908

RALEY, JR, Postmaster at Tulbagh Road Station, 1880

RALEY, TR, Postmaster at Goudini Road, 1880
  Postmaster at Kalabas Kraal, 1881

RAMPF, F, Postmaster at Spring Valley, 1 August 1908

RAMPF, FW, Postmaster at Qumbu, 1 December 1894
  Postmaster at Lady Frere, 1 August 1897

RAMPF, JA, Postmaster at Spring Valley, 1 July 1906

RAMPF, MJ, Postmaster at Tarkastad, 1 October 1877

RAMPF, WA, Postmaster at Spring Valley, 1 September 1903
  Postmaster at Spring Valley, 1 April 1905

RAMSAY, D, Overseer and postmaster at the Katberg Convict Station, 1 August 1866

RAMSAY, Peter McNab, Postmaster at Adelaide, 1 January 1896
  Station master at Cookhouse, 17 September 1901, salary £300 pa
  Postmaster at Middelburg, 1 November 1902
  Postmaster at Beaconsfield, 1 March 1903
  Postmaster at Jamestown, 1 April 1903.
  He was later appointed Special Justice of the Peace, Jamestown. He passed away soon thereafter for the Civil Service Records report that on 30 November 1909 his widow, AMM Ramsay, was receiving an annual pension of £101.2.11

RAND, Frederick William George, Postmaster at Sandflats, 1 March 1891
  Postmaster at Norval's Pont, 1 March 1892
  Postmaster at Stutterheim, 1 January 1899
  Postmaster at Elliot, 1 February 1902

RANDALL, James Andrew, Postmaster at Vanrhynsdorp, 1 August 1902
  Postmaster at Ceres Road, 1 March 1903
  Postmaster at Porterville Road, 1 September 1904

RANDALL, Nathan. On 3 April 1854 Nathaniel Randall, a local shopkeeper, was appointed postmaster at Port Elizabeth, and the post office was moved to his premises on Main Street. Unfortunately, by this time, the state of the town's postal services had become a matter of public concern, and when the Postmaster General, JA le Seuer, visited Port Elizabeth in November 1855, its citizens presented him with a list of necessary reforms. The Cape Parliament had already voted to increase the postmaster's salary to £150 pa but, wishing to appoint a civil servant, had excluded Randall from this position. On 23 February 1856 he was replaced by Edward Altham Cook, a capable administrator who had previously served in India. Despite Cooks' obvious qualifications, the good citizens of Port Elizabeth were outraged. The Eastern Province Herald rose to Randall's defense, pointing out that he had given "*universal satisfaction*" and had been "*careful, diligent and obliging*", going so far as to use his "*paltry salary to engage a diligent clerk and sacrificed his own business and given up the shop in which it was conducted*"

RANDALL, S, Postmaster at Rondebosch, 1 March 1846

It seems likely that, in keeping with Post Office practice of that time, from 1846 to 1879 Mr S Randall ran the postal affairs of Rondebosch from private premises, probably as an extension of other commercial interests, and as an act of goodwill to his customers. The Cape Government Gazette (No 5900 of 8 April 1879) announced that from 5 April 1879 the post office establishment at Rondebosch had been removed to the railway station. This was probably precipitated by Randall's retirement, when his office was transferred to Mr W Butler, who had previously acted as postmaster at Rondebosch Station from 1868 to 1872, and was now employed by the Railway Department as the local station master, The transfer of the post office to the railway station, under the management of a railway official, highlights the staffing crisis which the Cape Post Office was undergoing at the time. By 1882 the GPO had abandoned its policy of using the services of private citizens and had been forced to bring more and more of its staff into the Civil Service Establishment

RATHFELDER, Ms A, Postmaster at Diep River, 1 April 1869, service provided for free

RATHFELDER, Johann Georg, Postmaster at Diep River, 7 September 1854, service provided for free. Johann Georg Rathfelder was born in Stuttgart in 1811 and emigrated to the Cape in 1835. Following his marriage, he inherited a halfway-house near Wynberg, on the Cape Town-Simonstown road. Rathfelder's Inn, as it soon became known, was famous for its hospitality and in the 1840's became the headquarters of the Cape Hunt. It also became a popular destination for Cape Town day-trippers. The site, which was officially known as Halfway House, Simonstown Road, was also a mail-coach halt, and thus became the obvious location for a post office. Consequently when one was opened there on 7 September 1854, Rathfelder was appointed its first postmaster. When the inn was sold to WH Coghill in 1861, these duties were passed on to the new owner

RATTRAY, GF, Postmaster at Swellendam, 20 November 1844

RATTRAY, J Snr, Postmaster at Zandvliet, 18 November 1856

RAUBENHEIMER, HJ. The post office at Heimer's River was opened on 5 August 1867 with Mr HJ Raubenheimer as its first postmaster. He rendered this service gratis. It seems probable that the office was located on premises owned by the Raubenheimer family, and that "*Heimer*"

was an abbreviated form of his family name

RAUBENHEIMER, Peter J, Postmaster and field-cornet at Attaquas Kloof, 10 May 1858

RAWSTONE, Eliza G, Postmaster at Colesberg, 29 July 1859

RAWSTONE, J, Postmaster at Philipstown, 1 April 1866

READ, H, Postmaster at Paarde Poort, 1 May 1862

READ, M, Postmaster at Philipton, 1 April 1879

REARDER, J, Postmaster at Laingsburg, 1880

REDELINGHUYS, JNL, Postmaster and field-cornet at Verloren Vallei, 10 May 1858, dismissed from service in 1870

The farm Wittedrift was located in the Verloren Vlei river valley, and originally lay on the wagon road linking Piquetberg to Eland's Bay. It was owned by Mr JNL Redelinghuys, and when a post office, known as Wittedrift, Verloren's Vlei, was opened there on 10 May 1858, he was appointed its first postmaster. In about June 1895 Redelinghuys donated a portion of the farm to the Dutch Reformed Church for the purpose of establishing a *kerkplaats* upon it, and the village was subsequently named Redelinghuis in his honour

REEBEIN, Johannes Michael, Postmaster at Moorreesburg, 1 October 1897

Junior assistant Laingsburg, 1 January 1898

Postmaster at Laingsburg, 1 April 1899

Postmaster at Porterville Road, 1 July 1899

Postmaster at Porterville Road, 1 January 1901

Postmaster at Eerste River Station, before1903

Postmaster at Porterville Road, 1 February 1903

Postmaster at O'Okiep, 1 September 1904

REED, Henry, Postmaster at Paarde Poort, 1 April 1872

REED, W, Postmaster at Sunday's River Ferry, 7 August 1861

REEDER, A, Postmaster at Schoemansdorp, 22 December 1860

Postmaster at Schoemansdorp, 7 May 1863, service provided for free

REES, GA, Postmaster at Rondebosch 1 November 1892

REESBERG, J, Postmaster at Hondeklip Bay, 1 January 1873

REESBERG, JV, Postmaster at Bowesdorp, 1 December 1902

REGENSTEIN, O, Postmaster at Diep River, 1880

REID, J, Postmaster, clerk, storekeeper and keeper of cows on Robben Island, 20 October 1862, service provided for free in 1862-64

REID, J, Lighthouse keeper and postmaster on Bird Island, 1 May 1872

REID, WJ, Postmaster at Sunday's River Ferry, 8 September 1868, service provided for free

REILLEY, J, Postmaster at Fish River Randt, 15 July 1867, service provided for free

REINDERS, Herman James, Postmaster at Seymour, 1 May 1904

REINHOUD, JF, Letter Carrier, GPO, Cape Town, 9 July 1850. Salary £45 pa

REITZ, G, Secretary to the Divisional Council and postmaster at Riversdale, 1 April 1862

REITZ, J, Postmaster at Wellington Station, in about 1879

Postmaster at Calvinia, 1880

REITZ, Mrs JF, Postmaster at Ladismith, 1881

REITZ, JG, Postmaster at Somerset West, 1 December 1879

RENNICK, Jane, Postmaster at Simonstown, 4 April 1848

RENS, BP, Postmaster at Hankey, 1881

RENSBURG, Mrs M, nee SMITH, married in 1873, postmaster River Zonder End, 20 May 1871

RENSFORD, W, Postmaster at Caledon, 1 January 1867

RESTALL, R, Postmaster at Zuurbron, 1 April 1874

RETIEF, FJ, Postmaster at Karroo Poort, 8 March 1877

RETIEF, J, Postmaster at Van Wyk's Vlei, 1 November 1894

RETIEF, J, Postmaster at Koopman's Rivier, 1 March 1862

REX, G, Postmaster at Knysna, 1830. The village of Knysna was established in about 1830 on the farm Melkhoutkraal. Its owner, George Rex, is reputed to have been the son of a morganatic union in 1759 between George III of England and Hannah Lightfoot, the daughter of a Quaker shoemaker from Wapping. It was said that, after he ascended the throne in 1760, the King was obliged to take a royal consort, and young George, who had been born in 1765, was packed off to the Cape in 1797. There he entered into a liaison with a local widow, Johanna Ungerer, who bore him four children. In 1803 Rex moved to Knysna and resided there until his death in 1839. After a relationship of some eight years, Johanna Ungerer died, and was supplanted in the Rex household by Carolina Ungerer, her daughter by a previous marriage. Carolina made it her business to ensure that Rex was not unduly inconvenienced by the loss of her mother and, in due course, bore him nine children. One of their daughters, Caroline, married Captain Thomas Duthie who established the Belvidere estate nearby. Rex never married either of his mistresses, claiming that his status as *"royalty"* made it impossible for him to ever do so. Nonetheless, recent DNA testing has established that his claims to a connection to the British royal house were based on fiction

REX, G, Postmaster at Knysna, 1 April 1866

REX, John, Postmaster at Knysna, 1 January 1845

REX, John, Postmaster at Plettenberg's Bay, 1 July 1887

REX, JO, Station master at Stellenbosch, 1 July 1908, salary £290 pa

REX, TH, Postmaster at Plettenberg's Bay, 5 March 1850

REYERKERK, MC, Postmaster at Schoemansdorp, 5 July 1861, service provided for free

REYNDERS, J, Postmaster at St Helena Bay, 1 October 1877

Postmaster at St Helena Bay, 1880

REYNEKE, Miss W, Postmaster at River Zonder End, 1 June 1902

REYNOLDS, W, Postmaster at Molen River, 15 September 1874

RFOLL, JI, Postmaster at Daggaboersnek, 1880

RHODES, Ernest Borril, Postmaster at Stutterheim, 1905

Postmaster at West Bank, East London, 1 April 1905

Postmaster at Idutywa, 1 January 1910

Postmaster at Komgha, 1908

RICE, Postmaster at Somerset East. On 30 November 1909 his widow, Jesse Rice, was receiving an annual pension of £29.18.5

RICHARDS, GW, Postmaster at Worcester, 1 July 1878, possibly acting
Postmaster at Simonstown, 1 June 1879

RICHARDS, John Morrow, Clerk, Attorney-General's Office, January 1890. Thereafter served in various administrative capacities at Fort Beaufort (1891), Herschel (1893), Barkly East (1895), Albert (1896), Kimberley (1898), Port Elizabeth (1899), Middelburg (1901), Hopefield (1903), Keiskammahoek (1904),. Finally he was appointed Resident Magistrate, Collector of Customs and postmaster at Walfish Bay, 21 March 1908. He saw active service during the South African War, achieving the ranks of Lieutenant and Captain in the Prince Alfred's Volunteer Guard

RICHARDSON, Caroline, Postmaster at Schoenberg, 1 October 1862, service provided for free in 1867-73. See also RICHARDSON, Peregrine Bertie

RICHARDSON, J, Postmaster at Kowie West, 1862, deceased while in office

RICHARDSON, N, Postmaster at Steytlerville, 1 November 1897

RICHARDSON, Peregrine Albert (Bertie), Postmaster at Schoenberg, 17 August 1859. Schoenberg, also later given as Schoonberg, was a loan farm located in the Upper Langkloof region, near Mossel Bay. In about 1835 or 1836 it was acquired by Peregrine Bertie Richardson, who also owned a whaling station at Mossel Bay. Richardson's farming enterprise evidently flourished, for by the early 1850s it was reported that about 70 workers were employed on his estate. Initially their need for a postal service was met by a postal agency nearby at Woodville, which may have been opened as early as 1852. However this proved insufficient for local services and by the end of 1856 or the beginning of 1857 an office known as Schoenberg was opened by the Colonial Post Office, probably to meet the needs of the Richardson estate and its immediate neighbours. Peregrine Richardson was appointed the local postmaster, a service which he initially rendered for free. However, the work involved must have proved too onerous for Richardson to handle and after representations were made to the Postmaster General in Cape Town, he was promoted to Deputy Postmaster with a salary of £6 per annum. At the time this was the standard minimum annual salary accorded to a country postmaster.

Because of the low standing that this accorded a postmaster in the hierarchy of the Colonial postal service, Richardson was obviously of the opinion that his work at Schoenberg warranted a higher standard of remuneration, and this led to a certain amount of correspondence with his employers at the GPO in Cape Town. In one letter Richardson complained that the mail contractor on his route was in the habit of leaving the mail bag destined for his office hanging from a pole at the side of the road, which he then had to collect at his own expense six times a week, involving a distance of more than a mile each way. At about the same time, the postmaster for nearby Blanco, Mr Howitson, also commented that this practice left the mail to the mercy of the weather, and that local cattle were in the habit of eating the leather straps used to secure the bags. See also HOWITSON, J.

On 11 October 1862 Peregrine Richardson was elected to the George Divisional Council and had to resign his position at the Post Office. He was succeeded by his daughter Caroline who, for the greater part, rendered this service for free. This reinforces the idea that the Richardsons ran their post office at Schoenberg for the benefit of the neighbouring community and that the Agency was probably attached to a small country store trading in basic staple goods.

By 1875 Richardson appears to have given up his position on the Regional Council and returned to farming. However, despite the fact that he resumed his duties as postmaster, he moved his residence to another farm, Matijes Drift, located about 6.5km from Schoenberg. The latter agency was closed down although it retained its original name at the new location. This arrangement did not meet with local approval, leading a nearby resident of Ezeljacht, JW Groenewald, to complain to the GPO in Cape Town that owing to Richardson's conflicting business interests, local residents now found it difficult to know where to collect their mail, at Schoenberg or at Matijes Drift. On 2 February 1874 six residents of Ezeljacht petitioned the GPO to move the post office premises to the village of Matijes Drift where Richardson now lived but as no local resident could be found willing to undertake this responsibility, matters were left unchanged. As far as the Colonial Post Office was concerned the post office as Schoenberg had been abolished in about 1875 when Caroline Richardson had resigned from this post, but the matter was finally laid to rest on 1 May 1882 when Peregrine Richardson died on his farm at Matijes Drift

RICHARDSON, W, Postmaster at Warrenton, 1 November 1898

RICHTER, B, Postmaster at Riet Kuil, Division of Colesberg, 1 April 1846

RICHTER, Matthias Lotter, Postmaster at Ndabakazi, 1 January 1902

   Postmaster at Nqamakwe, 1 October 1902

RICE, A, Postmaster and policeman at Cradock, 1 February 1877

RICE, A, Postmaster at Somerset East, 1 January 1904.

RICE, Adam A Jnr, Postmaster at Graaff-Reinet, 1 October 1886

RICKARD, A, Postmaster at Mount Frere, 1881

RIDDIFORD, Miss EJ, Postmaster at 44 Adderley Street, Cape Town, 1 December 1905

RIDGARD, Benjamin, Postmaster at Toise River, 1 March 1897

   Station master at Toise River, 1 April 1897, salary £255 pa

RIDGILL, C, Acting postmaster at Spectakel, 1 March 1877

RIDGILL, RF, Postmaster at O'Okiep, 1 November 1888

RIDOUT, George Harry, Station master at Bellville, 7 July 1908, salary £280 pa

RIGBY, Albert, Postmaster at Alfred Docks, Cape Town, 1 July 1903

RILEY, Joseph, Postmaster at Zuurbron, 24 July 1854, service provided for free

RILEY, R, Postmaster at Klaarstroom, 1 May 1891

RINTOUL, HJ, Postmaster at Millwood, Goldfields, 1 October 1895

RIVE, LM, Postmaster at Olifant's Kraal, 28 February 1863, service provided for free in 1867-71

RIVERS, Frederick Charles, Postmaster at Hoetjes Bay, 1 September 1894

   Postmaster at Draghoender, 1 May 1895

   Postmaster at Herschel, 6 March 1898

Postmaster at Elliot, 1 March 1908

ROACH, MW, Postmaster at Graaff-Reinet, 1 May 1885

ROACH, W, Postmaster at King William's Town, 1 February 1876

ROBERTS, Charles Bloom, Postmaster at Klipplaat, 1 December 1903
Postmaster at Taungs, 1 January 1907, initially acting
Postmaster at Hutchinson, 1 March 1909

ROBERTS, Mrs E, Postmaster at Upper Paarl, date of appointment not known

ROBERTS, Ms MA, Postmaster at Durbanville, 6 November 1873

ROBERTS, R, Postmaster at Drooge Vlei, 20 October 1875

ROBERTS, W, Postmaster at Belvidere, 1881
Postmaster at Prince Albert Road, 1881

ROBERTS, WJ, Postmaster at Tulbagh Road Station, 1883

ROBERTSON, Charles Frank, Station master at Aberdeen Road, 1 April 1909, salary £174 pa

ROBERTSON, DD, Postmaster at Middelburg, 17 November 1853

ROBERTSON, F, Postmaster at Centlivres, 1880

ROBERTSON, Mrs F, Postmaster at Gordon's Bay, 1 April 1903

ROBERTSON, T, Postmaster at Schietfontein, Division of Graaff-Reinet, 3 October 1878
Postmaster at Commadagga, 22 November 1879
Postmaster at Coega, 1881
Postmaster at Kendrew Station, before 1888
Postmaster at Coerney, 1 September 1888

ROBERTSON, W, Ranger of Crown Forests and postmaster at Hooge Kraal, 1 January 1875

ROBEY, J, Postmaster at Manly's Flats, 30 April 1860, service provided for free in 1860-73 and in 1874-75

ROBEY, W, Postmaster at Manly's Flats, 1 July 1876

ROBINSON, Thomas Henry, Postmaster at Porterville Road, 1 December 1900

ROBINSON, W, Postmaster at Bailey, 1 December 1895

ROCHER, GA, Postmaster at Achter Piquetberg, 10 March 1857
Postmaster at St Helena Fontein, 1 January 1866

ROCHER, Pierre, Postmaster at St Helena Fontein, 16 December 1871, service provided for free

RODGER, Mrs, Postmaster at Green Point, 2 August 1881

RODGERS, Miss D, Postmaster at River Zonder End, 26 May 1904

ROENTGEN, Mrs, Postmaster at Calvinia, 15 July 1854

ROESKY, A, Postmaster at Katberg, 1 January 1863

ROGERS, Edmund, Postmaster at Great Brak River, 1 September 1902
Postmaster at Nieuwoudtville, 1 February 1903

ROGERS, Miss Ellen, Postmaster at Zuurbraak, 1906

ROGERS, J, Postmaster at Little Brak River, 1 May 1879

ROGERS, Mrs MA, Postmaster at Kalk Bay, 23 July 1853

ROGERS, W, Postmaster at Hutchinson, 1 October 1895

Postmaster at Wellington Station, 1 December 1896

Postmaster at Heidelberg, 1 January 1902

ROGERS, William Francis Joseph, Postmaster at George, 1 August 1908

ROGERSON, JW, Postmaster at Bellville, 1 May 1871

Postmaster at Eerste River Station, 1 April 1873

Postmaster and station master at Paarl Station, 18 February 1874

Postmaster and station master at Klipheuvel, 1 May 1877

ROLLAND, Mrs M, Postmaster at Mafeteng, 1 September 1874

ROODT, Frederick C, Station master at Mochudi, Bechuanaland Protectorate, 22 March 1906, salary £267 pa

ROODT, FD, Postmaster at Dordrecht, 14 January 1859

ROOKE, RDL, Postmaster at the Hex River Railway Works, 16 August 1876

ROOS, Simon Stephen, Postmaster at Vanrhynsdorp, 1 November 1895

Postmaster at Fraserburg, 15 September 1896

Postmaster at Fraserburg, 1 October 1902

Postmaster at Moorreesburg, 1 November 1905

Postmaster at Prince Albert, 1 October 1908

Postmaster at Wellington Station, 1 February 1909

ROPER, J, Postmaster and station master at Observatory Road, 1 April 1874

Postmaster at Kalabas Kraal, 22 November 1877

Postmaster and station master at Tulbagh Road Station, 8 November 1878

Postmaster at Porterville Road, in about 1879

ROPER, R, Postmaster at Springbokfontein, 3 December 1855

RORKE, CF, Postmaster at Seymour, 1882

RORKE, TJ, Postmaster at Queenstown, 5 July 1854, resigned on 20 December 1854.

Postmaster at East London, 1 August 1868

On 20 December 1854 TJ Rorke, postmaster at Queenstown, communicated to the PMG in Cape Town that: *"Sir, In answer to your letter of the 14th December I have the honour to inform you that there is no stamp in the office for stamping letters with the date of their receipt, the only one in the office being the one Stamped in the margin and which is the only one that has ever been supplied to this office."* (Cape Archives, letter 1566, GPO 1/46). Mr Rorke then went on to tender his resignation

ROSCOE, GE, Postmaster at Vlugt, 18 May 1859

ROSELT, ACM, Postmaster at Tarkastad, 1882

ROSENSTRAUCH, Johann Carel Ferdinand, Postmaster at Upper Paarl, 1 May 1904

ROSKOSCH, F, Postmaster at Bell, 1 January 1864

ROSS, CR, Clerk, Post Office Savings Bank, GPO, Cape Town, 1 April 1890

Transferred to Department of Agriculture, 19 July 1894

ROSS, Francis B, Postmaster on Robben Island, 16 December 1885. Francis Ross also published a broadsheet called *The Robben Island Times*, popular among the residents of the island, and was probably related to Dr William Ross, Surgeon Superintendent of the Infirmary on Robben

Island
ROSS, Rev R, Postmaster at Cunningham, 12 May 1874
ROSS, W, Postmaster at Kowie East, 1 July 1865
ROTH, J, Postmaster at Daljosaphat, 7 December 1860
ROTH, JWF, Postmaster at Zaaiplaats, 1 March 1862
ROTH, JFW, Postmaster at Durbanville, 24 December 1856
ROTHKUGEL, R, Postmaster at Darling Bridge, 10 June 1865
ROTHMAN, Hendrik Binnenhof, Postmaster at Uniondale, 1 November 1886
  Postmaster at Calvinia, 1 March 1890
  Postmaster at Clanwilliam, 1 April 1890
  Postmaster at Port Nolloth, 1 November 1895
  Postmaster at Carnarvon, 1 September 1897
  Postmaster at Peddie, 18 March 1900
ROTHWELL, A, Postmaster at Tylden, 1 October 1895
ROUS, GR, Postmaster at Lady Frere, 1 January 1895
  Postmaster at Laingsburg, 1 March 1897
  Postmaster at Piquetberg, 1 February 1903
  Postmaster at Cambridge, 1 September 1907
  Postmaster at Elliot, 1 March 1909
ROUS, S, Postmaster at Daniel's Kuil, 1 November 1898
ROUS, SR, Postmaster at Tsomo, 1 October 1894
ROUSSOUW, D, Postmaster at Krakeel River, 1 December 1872
ROUX, Rev Dr A, Minister, Dutch Reformed Church, and postmaster at Riebeek East, 29 September 1858, service provided for free
ROUX, CA, Postmaster at Riebeek East, 1 August 1877
ROUX, DGJ, Postmaster at Prince Alfred's Hamlet, 1 September 1871, service provided for free
ROUX, Paul, Postmaster at Wellington, 20 April 1854
ROWAN, S, Postmaster at Witteklip, 19 April 1855
ROWE, E Valentine, also listed as V, Telegraphist at Bolotwa, 1901
  Postmaster at East London Jetty, 1 November 1902
  Postmaster at East London Jetty, 1 May 1903
  Postmaster at St Marks, 1 October 1903
  Postmaster at Bolotwa, 1906
  Postmaster at Herschel, 1 November 1906
ROWE, J, Postmaster at Sunday's River Ferry, 1 March 1846
ROWE, S, Postmaster at Sunday's River Ferry, in about 1839
ROWING, T, Postmaster at Barville Park, 31 January 1861
ROWLANDS, JE, Station master at Klein Poort, 1 April 1909, salary £215 pa
ROWLEY, John Augustine, Postmaster at Prince Albert Road, 1909
RUDDOCK, Alfred Nat, Postmaster at Witteklip, 1 May 1908

RUGEN, John, Station master at Plumtree, Southern Rhodesia, 1 June 1909, salary £75 pa
RUSHFORTH, J, Postmaster at Bayville, 1 March 1898
RUSSEL, Mr, Postmaster at Boontjes River, in about 1858
RUSSEL, A, Postmaster at Bathurst, 1 January 1896
    Postmaster at Whittlesea, 1 March 1897
RUSSELL, F, Postmaster at Malmesbury, 1 April 1897
    Postmaster at Observatory Road, 1 March 1899
RUSSELL, FR, Telegraphist at the Central Telegraph Office, Cape Town, date not available
    The Pension Lists of 30 November 1909 recorded that in 1910 Mr Russell, age 44, was retired on an annual pension of £132.14.8
RUSSELL, George Read, Special Justice of the Peace and postmaster at Steytlerville, 1 Oct 1902
    Postmaster at Hankey, 1 June 1903
    Postmaster at Stormberg Junction, 1 December 1909
RUSSELL, Samuel Griffith, Acting postmaster at Cambridge, 1910
RUSSELL, WA, Postmaster at Petrusville, 1881
RUSSOUW, G, Postmaster at Serjeant's River, 1 July 1871
RUSSOUW, JN, Postmaster at Schoongezicht, 1 July 1872
RUTHERFOORD, Mr, Postmaster at Richmond, 1854
RUTLEDGE, F, Postmaster at Springbokfontein, 1856
RYAN, J, Postmaster at Dohne, 1881

S
SAGAR, W, Acting postmaster at Montagu, 15 July 1873
SALTER, Herbert William, Postmaster at Hutchinson, 1 January 1904
    Postmaster at Cambridge, 1 March 1909
SALVAGE, R, Postmaster at Lynedoch, 1882
SAMMONS, WL, Postmaster at Somerset Road, 23 November 1860
SAMPHIRE, E, Postmaster at Mortimer, 1881
SAMPSON, C, Postmaster and field-cornet at Cuylerville, 1 September 1864, service provided free
SAMPSON, JH, Postmaster at Abbotsdale, 1 January 1879
SANDERS, JJ, Postmaster and field-cornet at Achter Sneeuwberg, Division of Cradock, 25 October 1858, service provided for free
SANDERS, William, Postmaster at Cradock, 1 March 1846
SANDERSON, J, Postmaster and station master at Zwartkops Station, 1 September 1875
SANSOM, Arthur Edward, Station master at Krankuil, 15 September 1905, salary £200 pa
SARGENT, Vinton Evelyn, Postmaster at Flagstaff, 1 November 1902
    Postmaster at Willowvale, 1 October 1903
    Postmaster at East London Jetty, 1 July 1909
SAUNDERS, Mrs Anne, Postmaster at Uitenhage, 19 May 1843
SAUNDERS, A, Postmaster at Adelaide, in about 1876

SAUNDERS, E, Postmaster at Petersburg, in about 1877

SAUNDERS, J, Postmaster at Coega, 1880

SAUNDERS, M, Postmaster at Durbanville, 12 December 1853

SAVAGE, GF, Postmaster at Langbaken, 1881

SAVAGE, WF, Postmaster at Wagenaar's Kraal, 1 January 1879

SAWYER, W, Postmaster at Observatory Road, 8 August 1870
   Postmaster and station master at Rosebank, 1 August 1874
   Postmaster and station master at Mowbray Station, 1 May 1877
   Postmaster and station master at Breede River Station, 23 September 1879
   Postmaster and station master at Hermon, 1880, dismissed from office

SAWYER, WH, Postmaster at Venterstad, 28 March 1889

SAYERS, WS, Postmaster at Worcester, 1 July 1879

SAYLE, T, Postmaster at De Doorns, in about 1879

SCARBROW, H, Postmaster at Bridgetown, 3 November 1866, service provided for free. The settlement of Bridgetown was established on the farm Vledermuisdrift, a site which included a crossing over the Berg River. Its owner, Mr IJ van der Merwe, sold it for £850 on 27 January 1847 to William Edmund Scarbrow, a Master Mariner. Sensing its potential, Scarbrow immediately renamed the farm Bridgetown and set about developing the land, including an irrigation scheme and the erection of a new farmhouse, a smithy, stables, a mill and a store. He also motivated for the construction of a bridge over the river in the belief that this would serve as a focus for the new town. When the bridge did not materialize and his project ran into financial difficulties, Scarbrow left for England in an attempt to raise investments overseas. Unfortunately his ship was wrecked en route and he was lost at sea. The project never fully recovered and Bridgetown eventually vanished in the 1950s

SCHAEFER, Emil Calvin, Station master at Knapdaar, 14 September 1903, salary £270 pa

SCHAEFER, JF, Postmaster at Darling, 3 April 1874

SCHEEPERS, IM, Postmaster at Clarkebury, 1 April 1903

SCHENCK, FAW, Postmaster at St Helena Bay, 1 April 1862

SHEWRING, Thomas Biggleston, Station master at Woodstock, 1 Oct 1902, salary £244 pa

SCHICKERLING, H, Postmaster at Langebaan, 26 March 1858, service provided for free

SCHICKERLING, H, Postmaster at Langebaan, 14 March 1874, service provided for free

SCHIERHOUT, MJ, Postmaster at Bellville, 5 November 1863

SCHIERHOUT, PA, Postmaster at Sutherland, 10 April 1865

SCHIERHOUT, WH, Postmaster at Hopefield, 17 November 1880

SCHLEMMER, JG, Postmaster at Daggaboersnek, 1 September 1864

SCHMIDT, E, Postmaster at Amalienstein, 1883
   Postmaster at Grahamstown Station, 1 February 1898

SCHMIDT, FA, Postmaster at Amalienstein, in about 1860

SCHMIDT, FW, Postmaster at Port Nolloth, 1 September 1897

SCHNEIDER, JC, Postmaster at Highlands, in about 1879

SCHNEIDER, JWC, Postmaster at Addo, 1880
Postmaster at Toise River, 1883
SCHNEIDER, NG, Postmaster at Petrusville, 20 August 1890
SCHOENEGEVEL, ET, Postmaster at Wellington Station, 1 September 1890
Postmaster at Bellville, 1 May 1894
SCHOLEFIELD, Francis Henry, Postmaster at Flagstaff, 25 November 1895
Postmaster at Lusikisiki, 1 September 1902
SCHOLTZ, C, Postmaster at Tulbagh, 1 April 1822
Postmaster at Worcester, 1 October 1822
SCHOLTZ, CF, Clerk to the Civil Commissioner and postmaster at Worcester, 1 March 1846
SCHOLTZ, Maria L, Postmaster at Napier, 1 May 1866
SCHOLTZ, MCV, Secretary to the Divisional Council and postmaster at Oudtshoorn, 2 Feb 1859
SCHOLTZ, PW, Postmaster at Worcester, 3 June 1853
SCHOLTZ, R, Postmaster at Bathurst, 1881
SCHOMBIE, J, Postmaster at Vriesfontein, 30 May 1861, service provided for free in 1861-62
SCHONKEN, AG, Postmaster at Hazenjacht, 1 December 1878
SCHONKEN, Daniel J, Postmaster at Aberdeen, Division of Aberdeen, 1 May 1885
Postmaster at Alicedale, 1 September 1887
In 1889 Daniel Jacobus Schonken, formerly postmaster of Alicedale, was convicted in the Eastern Districts Court, Grahamstown, of embezzling a portion of the official moneys entrusted to him. As a result he was sentenced to eighteen months imprisonment, with hard labour (POC 90, 1 June 1889)
SCHONKEN, M, Postmaster at Greyton, 1 July 1879
SCHONKIN, DJ, Postmaster at Lower Paarl, 1882
SCHORN, John, Postmaster at Queen Street, Port Elizabeth, 1 May 1885
SCHROEDER, JPD, Postmaster at Worcester Station, 1882
On 4 February 1884 JPD Schroeder, former postmaster of Worcester Station, was charged in the Magistrate's Court, Worcester, with the theft of three letters. He was found guilty and sentenced to a fine of £15, or three months imprisonment with hard labour
SCHULE, Mrs A van Buren, Postmaster at Riebeek East, 1 May 1871, service provided for free in 1873
SCHULTZ, AR, Postmaster at Somerset Strand, 1 February 1879
SCHULTZE, RH, Postmaster at Bathurst, 1883
SCHUMAN, Mrs, Postmaster at Britstown, 1 January 1889, possibly acting
SCHUMANN, Mrs E, Postmaster at Willowmore, 1882
SCHUMANN, Mrs, Postmaster at Balfour, 1 July 1893
Postmaster at Moorreesburg, 1 November 1895
SCHUMANN, Miss M, Postmaster at Barrydale, 1 January 1902
Postmaster at Modderfontein, Division of Clanwilliam, 1 February 1903
SCHUR, J, Postmaster at Bowesdorp, 1 October 1896

SCHUURMANN, WGVE, Postmaster at Somerset Strand, 1 May 1891

SCOTT, Miss, Postmaster at Libodi, 7 March 1900

SCOTT, Miss, Postmaster at Seymour, 1 February 1902

SCOTT, Mr, Postmaster at Umzimkulu, 1 May 1878

SCOTT, Mrs, also listed as Mrs BIRT from 1873. Postmaster at Peelton, July 1862. Mrs Scott was the daughter of Robert Hart of Glen Avon, England, and a wealthy widow in her own right. She emigrated to South Africa in about 1862, probably as a volunteer worker for the London Missionary Society, and soon thereafter joined the Rev Richard Birt at his mission station at Peelton, near King William's Town. In July 1862 she took on the position of postmaster, and continued to fulfill these duties for free until 1878. In the meantime in 1873 she also married the Rev Burt who, by this stage had become a respected patriarch of his church. Burt had been born in May 1810 at Bromsberrow, in Glouchestershire, and had been ordained at the Weigh House Chapel in June 1838. Following his marriage to his first wife, Eliza Hansen Budden, the family emigrated to the Cape in 1838 where Mrs Birt died as the result of a tragic wagon accident on 21 January 1842

SCOTT, Miss Catherine, Postmaster at Springbokfontein, 1 October 1893

Postmaster at Moorreesburg, 1 August 1897

SCOTT, Miss EA, Postmaster at Upington, 1885

SCOTT, H, Postmaster at Heidelberg, 1880

Postmaster at Clanwilliam, 1881

SCOTT, J, Postmaster at Peelton, 1 September 1878

SCOTT, JH, Resident Magistrate and postmaster at Walfish Bay, 1904

SCOTT, W, Postmaster at Hondeklip Bay, in about 1869

SCOTT, WA, Postmaster at Qumbu, 1 March 1908. On 30 November 1909 his widow, EB Scott, was receiving an annual pension of £15.2.9

SCULLY, William Charles, Clerk at Tarkastad, June 1876

Postmaster, 13 December 1876.

Thereafter served in a variety of administrative positions until 1 July 1906 when he was appointed Civil Commissioner and Resident Magistrate at Caledon. In 1881 he served as Lieutenant and Paymaster in Nesbitt's Light Horse

SEARLE, Mrs A, Postmaster at Great Brak River, 1 October 1872

SEARLE, Charles, Postmaster at Great Brak River, 17 January 1865, service provided for free. The village of Great Brak River was founded by Charles Searle, an English paper-mill hand who, together with his wife and four children, emigrated to the Cape in 1859. They landed at Mossel Bay following a sea voyage of 68 days. After a few months he was awarded the tender for Keeper of the Toll Bridge at Great Brak River which, at that stage, consisted of a tollhouse, a small boarding house called Ferreira's and a farmhouse on the Mossel Bay side of the river. There he began making boots as a part-time occupation but, as these found a ready market among travellers passing through his toll, he soon found he had more work than he could handle and employed his first full-time boot-maker. In 1864 he lost the tender for the toll but, being reluctant to move, he purchased land behind the toll-house and started up a general store. In 1865 he again won the tender for the toll and became the village's postmaster, a position the Searle family was to monopolize for the next 34 years. During that time the postal and telegraphic business of Great Brak River was conducted from the Searles' store, a portion of which was set aside for this purpose. The Searle family continued to prosper and soon expanded their business interests by erecting a boarding house known as the Temperance Hotel. The Searles were staunch abstainers and expected everyone else in the village to follow suit. From the outset, therefore, they opposed the sale of liquor and, in time, Great Brak River became known in the neighbourhood as "*Prohibition Village*". In 1886 a new boot factory was erected there, and the following year its business was extended by the addition of a tannery. In 1893 a mule-drawn cart service was started to deliver groceries to holiday makers as well as to carry mail from Oudtshoorn and Mossel Bay to Great Brak River (Nattrass 1999)

SEARLE, J, Postmaster at Blanco, 1 April 1866

SEARLE, J, Management, Department of Telegraphs, 1880

SEARLE, PR, Postmaster at Kuils River, 1910

SEARLE, R, Postmaster at Claremont Station, 17 January 1848

SEARLE, Thomas, Postmaster at Great Brak River, 1 August 1890

SEARLE, T, Management, Department of Telegraphs, 1880

SEARLE, W, Postmaster at Great Brak River, 1883

SEDGWICK, C, Postmaster at Spectakel, 8 June 1865

SEEBER, CL, Postmaster at Surbiton, 1881

SELLICK, WEW, Postmaster at Pearston, 1 April 1890

SELZER, Conrad, Postmaster at Cambridge, 1 July 1862

SENNETT, JP, Postmaster at Woodstock Station, 1880
Postmaster and station master at Observatory Road, 1881

SEPHTON, AW, Postmaster at Wartrail, 15 June 1890

SETTEN, J, Postmaster at Carnarvon, 1 December 1872

SEWELL, JF, Postmaster at Plettenberg's Bay, 1 November 1851

SEWELL, WD, Sorter, GPO, Cape Town, 6 November 1866
Assistant clerk, Money Order and Stamp Branch, GPO, Cape Town, 1 January 1875
Clerk, GPO, Cape Town, 17 August 1876
Clerk, second class, GPO, Cape Town, in about 1880
Superintendent, Newspaper Branch, GPO, Cape Town, 1 January 1881

SHACKLETON, HWR, born in about 1856
Postmaster at Port Alfred, 23 June 1882
Postmaster at Uitenhage, 1 October 1907
The Pension Lists of 30 November 1909 recorded that in 1910 Mr Shackleton, age 53, was retired on an annual pension of £290.17.9

SHAKESPERE, WA, Postmaster at Adelaide, 1 October 1864

SHAND, G, Postmaster at Retreat, 1 October 1903

Postmaster at Postmasburg, 1 June 1910

SHAND, Miss Winifred Agnes, Postmaster at Emjanyana, 1 July 1905
    Postmaster at Ndabakazi, 1 July 1906
    Postmaster at Bayville, 1 June 1907

SHARP, J, Telegraphist at Philippolis, date not available
    The Pension Lists of 30 November 1909 recorded that in 1910 Mr Sharp, age 49, was retired on an annual pension of £48.12.3

SHARP, W, Additional Clerk, GPO, Cape Town, 6 July 1852, Salary £90 pa

SHARPE, E, Additional clerk, GPO, Cape Town, 6 July 1852
    Clerk, sixth class, GPO, Cape Town, 1853
    Resigned on 15 February 1854

SHAW, Rev B, Postmaster at Salem, 1 May 1860

SHAW, Miss EM, Postmaster at Woodstock Station, 20 July 1886

SHAW, Geo. Postmaster at Salem, 1882

SHAW, GH, Postmaster at Glenconnor, 1883

SHAW, John M, Postmaster at Woodstock Station, 1 May 1885

SHAW, K, Temporary clerk, GPO, Cape Town, 18 November 1866
    Clerk, GPO, Cape Town, 1868
    Assistant clerk, Money Order and Stamp Branch, GPO, Cape Town, 1 January 1870

SHAW, SB, Clerk to the Civil Commissioner and postmaster at Tulbagh, 8 March 1848

SHAW, SB, Postmaster at Salem, 1 July 1865

SHAW, Sidney, Postmaster at Petrusville, 1 July 1893
    Postmaster at Philipstown, 1 May 1896
    Postmaster at Hopefield, 1896
    Postmaster at Porterville, 1 September 1896
    Postmaster at Postmasburg, 1 September 1898
    Postmaster at Petrusville, 1 December 1898
    Postmaster at Steytlerville, 1903, possibly acting
    Postmaster at Hermanus, 1 March 1903

SHAW, W, Postmaster at Teleur Gate, 29 September 1858, service provided for free

SHAW, WB, Postmaster and station master at Coega, 1876
    Postmaster and station master at Blaney Junction, 18 December 1876
    Postmaster and station master at Kei Road, 1 May 1877
    Postmaster at King William's Town Station, 1878
    Postmaster and station master at Dohne Toll, 1 September 1878

SHAWE, GJ, Postmaster at Herschel, 1883

SHAWE, S, Postmaster at Van Putten's Vlei, 21 September 1866, service provided for free

SHEARD, AO, Postmaster and station master at Coerney, 1 September 1877

SHEARD, B, Postmaster at Eerste River Station, 1 January 1901

SHEARD, Oswald Francis, Postmaster at Postmasburg, 1 July 1897

Postmaster at Koopmansfontein, 1 November 1899

Postmaster at Daniels Kuil, 1 August 1900

SHEPPARD, CA, Postmaster at Koonap, 1 May 1902

SHEPPARD, Mrs M, Schoolmistress and postmaster at Simonstown, 25 April 1838

SHEPPERSON, JF, Acting Tide Waiter at Port Alfred, and postmaster and field-cornet at Kowie West, 1 September 1863

SHERWIN, HG, Postmaster at Herschel, 1 October 1897

SHIEL, O, Postmaster at Ceres Road, 1 February 1894

SHIPWAY, Joseph, Postmaster at Laingsburg, 1 April 1903

Postmaster at Windsorton, 1 May 1904

SHIRLEY, Stephen Henry, Postmaster at Rondebosch, Cape Town, 1 March 1891

Postmaster at Newlands, Cape Town, 1 February 1898

Postmaster at Alicedale, 1 May 1899

Postmaster at Kloof Street, Gardens, Cape Town, 1 January 1904

Postmaster at St George's Street, Cape Town, 1 October 1907

SHROSHBREE, S, Postmaster at Sandflats, September 1870, service provided for free

SIEBERT, MW, Postmaster at Humansdorp, 1 January 1875

SIEBRITZ, Miss HM, also listed as HW, Postmaster at French Hoek, 16 February 1899

Ladies' Branch, GPO, Cape Town, date of appointment not known

Postmaster at French Hoek, 1 November 1902

SIEBRITZ, Miss Jacoba Johanna, Postmaster at Riebeek Kasteel, 8 May 1905

SIEVERS, F, Postmaster and field-cornet at Glen Lynden, 1 June 1867

SILBERBAUER, CG, Postmaster at Doorn Kloof, Division of Victoria West, 15 November 1861, service provided for free

SIMONIS, JF, Postmaster at Rawsonville, 1 May 1897

SIMPKINS, H, Postmaster at St Marks, 1 August 1895

SIMPKINS, HW, Postmaster at Murraysburg, 28 November 1896

SIMPSON, Charles Henry, Postmaster at Woodstock Station, 1 August 1908

SIMPSON, CH, Postmaster at Kalk Bay, 1 August 1893

SIMPSON, H, Postmaster at Vanrhynsdorp, 1 October 1896

SIMPSON, John, Postmaster at Griquatown, 1 November 1893

Postmaster at French Hoek, 1 May 1894

Postmaster at Sutherland, 29 May 1894

Postmaster at Hanover, 1 November 1896

Postmaster at Modder River, Division of Kimberley, 1 December 1896

Postmaster at Carnarvon, 1 November 1898

Postmaster at Victoria West Road, 1 September 1900

SIMPSON, JA, Assistant Postmaster at the GPO, in Cape Town, date not available

The Pension Lists of 30 November 1909 recorded that in 1910 Mr Simpson, age 45, was retired on an annual pension of £88.1.2

SIMPSON, JF, Postmaster at Cradock Station, 1 January 1907

SIMPSON, JG, Clerk of Magistrate with Umhlonhlo and postmaster at Qumbu, 8 February 1877

SIMPSON, JS, Postmaster at East London, September 1867

SIMPSON, William Brown, Postmaster at Jansenville, 1 March 1899
    Postmaster at Upington, 27 September 1900
    Postmaster at Port Alfred, 1 December 1902

SIMPSON, WJ, Acting postmaster at Kalk Bay, 1 January 1904

SISSISON, Frederick Joseph, Clerk, GM Telegraph Office, GPO, Cape Town, 10 Nov 1881
    Clerk, Telegraph Branch, GPO, Cape Town, 18 May 1885
    Relieving Officer, Metropolitan District, 1 May 1897
    Assistant Engineer for the Cape Town and suburban telephone construction, 1 April 1903
    Outdoor Telephone Engineer, date not available

SISSISON, John William Faulding, Telegraphist at Alicedale, 1886
    Postmaster at Alicedale, 1 July 1891
    Postmaster at Steynsburg, 1 February 1895
    Postmaster at Cookhouse, 1 February 1896
    Postmaster at Somerset East, 1 January 1902
    Special Justice of the Peace and postmaster at Alicedale, 1 January 1904

SIVEWRIGHT, James, Born in Fochabers, Scotland, in 1848
    Educated at the University of Aberdeen, MA 1866
    Worked in India as a telegraph engineer
    Superintendent, Engineering Branch, British Telegraph Service
    In 1877 Sivewright travelled to the Cape as a consultant at the behest of the then General Manager, Mr Den, to inspect and report upon the telegraph plant of the Cape Department. Through an unfortunate set of circumstances, Mr Den passed away and the Colonial Government invited Sivewright to stay on in his stead. He was thus appointed Acting General Manager, Telegraphs, in 1877
    Manager CTO, Cape Town, 1877
    Served in the Anglo-Zulu War of 1879, awarded the Companion of the Order of St Michael and St George
    Left the Civil Service in 1890 to enter into politics and won election to Parliament, representing Griqualand West. He was appointed Commissioner of Crown Lands and Public Works in the first Rhodes Cabinet. The railway link from the Cape to Johannesburg was completed during his first term in charge of the Railways portfolio. In the General Election of 1898 he stood for the Progressive Party in Stellenbosch but was defeated. He was in Scotland at the time and never returned to this country
    Knighted, date before 1908
    The Pension Lists of 30 November 1909 recorded that in 1910 Sir James Sivewright, age 64, was retired on an annual pension of £370
    Sivewright was not reputed to be a man of fiew words where many others would do, and upon

the outbreak of hostilities in Mpondoland in 1880, he congratulated his staff stating that *"I should be wanting in my duty towards a body of public servants if I failed to place on record my appreciation of the manner in which the telegraph officials of this Colony have worked during the trying period passed through with a cheerfulness which I have rarely seen equaled, even upon isolated occasions. They have from the first sacrificed every possible consideration to that of duty and this, I feel assured, they will continue to to the last"* (Bennett, 1908: 9)

SKEA, J, Postmaster at Lawrence Street, Port Elizabeth, 1883

SKEADE, JC, Postmaster at French Hoek, 9 July 1847

SKEEN, A, Postmaster and field-cornet at Bland's Drift, 1 July 1873

SKEEN, Miss F, Postmaster at Tygersfontein, 1 January 1901

SKEEN, Miss MI, Postmaster at Tygersfontein, 1 November 1903

Postmaster at Albertinia, 1 April 1904

SKINNER, WB, Postmaster at Breede River Station, 1881

SKINNER, WE, Postmaster and station master at Mulder's Vlei, 17 January 1877

Postmaster and station master at De Doorns, 1 January 1879

SKORBINSKI, H, Jailer and postmaster at Uniondale, 1 April 1877

SLABBER, Miss HB, Postmaster at Moorreesburg, 1 July 1898

Postmaster at Napier, 1 September 1902

Postmaster at Moorreesburg, 1 February 1903

SLABBERT, JF, Postmaster at Jansenville, 1 September 1879

SLABBERT, MJ, Postmaster at Middledrift, 1 April 1896

Postmaster at Krakeel River, 1 October 1896

Postmaster at Pearston, 1 July 1900

Postmaster at Krakeel River, 1 February 1901

SLATER, A, Postmaster at Balfour, 1 January 1892

SLATER, George, Postmaster at Quagga's Flats, 23 October 1851

SLATER, J, Postmaster at Willow Park, 13 July 1868

SLOGROVE, Charles Henry, Station master at Komgha, 9 September 1904, salary £174 pa

SMALBERGER, HB, Postmaster and field-cornet at Buffels Kraal, 1 January 1864, service provided for free

SMALBERGER, JJW, Postmaster and field-cornet at Valsch River, 31 Aug 1859, service provided for free

The post office at Valsch River was opened on 31 August 1859 with Mr JJW Smalberger, field-cornet, as its postmaster. He rendered this service gratis until 1867 when the post office was abolished. In 1870 Mr Smalberger reappeared in the Civil Establishment Listing, this time as the postmaster of The Grove. Significantly though, his date of appointment remained 31 August 1859. This seems to indicate two things: that the establishment at Valsch River was probably not abolished in 1867 as given; and that sometime between 1867 and 1870 its name was changed to The Grove. In 1874 its name was omitted from the Civil Establishment Blue Books, and it was probably abolished soon thereafter

SMALL, CJ, Postmaster at Riet Huis, 15 August 1866, service provided for free

SMART, Joseph, born in about 1853
 Assistant Superintendent and Travelling Inspector, GPO, Cape Town, 4 January 1883
 Postmaster at Peddie, 1 August 1887

SMART, Miss M, Postmaster at Rhodes, 1 August 1897
 Postmaster at Tabankulu, 1 March 1900

SMIT, DA, Postmaster and field-cornet at Achter Piquetberg, 1 September 1861
 Acting postmaster at Achter Piquetberg, 1869
 Postmaster at Achter Piquetberg, 22 August 1871, service provided for free

SMIT, CH, Assistant Postmaster at Graaff-Reinet, date not available
 The Pension Lists of 30 November 1909 recorded that in 1910 Mr Smit, age 45, was retired on an annual pension of £109.13.1

SMIT, HF, Postmaster at Komgha, 1902
 Postmaster at Jamestown, 1 December 1902

SMIT, Miss H, Postmaster at Dams Laagte, 1 February 1899
 Postmaster at Philadelphia, 1 January 1901

SMIT, HF, Postmaster at Seymour, 1 June 1903

SMIT, James, Postmaster at Wellington Station, 1 March 1887

SMIT, NJ, Postmaster and field-cornet at Karreeboschfontein, 30 November 1858

SMITH, Postmaster at Zaaiplaats, 1881

SMITH, AE, Postmaster at Maitland, 1 December 1899

SMITH, B, Postmaster at Paardeberg, Division of Malmesbury, 18 December 1873

SMITH, Charles A, Postmaster at Wynberg, in about 1847

SMITH, Miss CC, Postmaster at Napier, 1 February 1894
 Postmaster at Great Brak River, 1 July 1899

SMITH, CH, Postmaster at Aberdeen, Division of Aberdeen, 1 August 1899

SMITH, Miss CM, Postmaster at Dam's Laagte, 1 May 1894

SMITH, Miss EH, Postmaster at River Zonder End, 1 September 1898

SMITH, ER, Postmaster and field-cornet at Fraserburg, 1 April 1879

SMITH, F, Postmaster at Winkel Plaats, 16 June 1874, service provided for free

SMITH, G, Postmaster at Gamtoos River Ferry, 1 December 1870

SMITH, Godfrey Cannon, Postmaster at Port St John, 1 February 1896
 Postmaster at Herschel, 1 September 1900
 Postmaster at Alice, 1 November 1906

SMITH, GD, Postmaster at Gamtoos River Ferry, 1 January 1868

SMITH, H, Postmaster at Commadagga, 1 April 1885
 Postmaster at Nelspoort, 1 November 1896

SMITH, H, Postmaster at Prince Albert Road, in about 1889
 Postmaster at Porterville Road, 1 May 1889

SMITH, HG, Postmaster at Qumbu, 1883

SMITH, James, Postmaster at Gamtoos River Ferry, 1 April 1846
SMITH, J, Postmaster at Gamtoos River Ferry, 6 January 1855
SMITH, J, not the same person as the postmaster at at Klipplaat
    Postmaster at Orange River, 16 May 1899
    Postmaster at De Aar, 1 March 1903
    Postmaster at Naauwpoort, 1 July 1906
SMITH, J, not the same person as the postmaster at at Orange River
    Postmaster at Klipplaat, 1 August 1896
SMITH, J, Postmaster at Kenilworth, Cape Town, 1 July 1905
SMITH, J, Acting postmaster at Bree Street, Cape Town, 1 August 1908
    Postmaster at Rosebank, 1 October 1908
SMITH, J, Postmaster at River Zonder End, 1 October 1874
SMITH, J, Postmaster at Aliwal North, 1909
SMITH, John, Station master at Despatch, 9 March 1906, salary £238 pa
SMITH, John Albert, Circulation Branch, GPO, Cape Town, 29 October 1880
    Clerk, Money Order Branch, 16 February 1882
    Correspondence Clerk to the Accountant, 1885
    Seconded for service to the British South Africa Company as Private Secretary to the Superintendent of Telegraphs and Paymaster, northward extension of telegraph lines from Mafeking, 1 April 1889
    Clerk, Saving Bank, GPO, Cape Town, 1890
    Money Order Office, GPO, Cape Town, 1 June 1896
    Acting Assistant Controller, MOO, Postal Order and Draft Branch, 1 July 1903
    Controller, GPO, Cape Town, 1 September 1908
SMITH, J de Wilton, Postmaster at Butterworth, 1882
SMITH, JF, Postmaster at Alexandria, 7 September 1857
SMITH, JF, Postmaster at East London, 1 September 1870
    Postmaster at Fort Beaufort, 24 June 1874
SMITH, JW, Postmaster at Klipplaat, 1881
SMITH, Mrs M, Postmaster at River Zonder End, 20 May 1871
SMITH, R, Garrison Sergeant-Major and post office agent at Alice, King William's Town, 1 September 1860
    Postmaster at King William's Town, 1 July 1862
SMITH, Rebecca, Postmaster at Gamtoos River Ferry, 13 August 1861
SMITH, Miss SH, Postmaster at Blanco, 1 January 1888. Miss SH Smith was probably the daughter of WK Smith, who was the keeper of the toll at Montagu Pass
SMITH, SW, Postmaster at Griquatown, 16 September 1881
SMITH, W, Postmaster at Debe Nek, 1 January 1867, service provided for free
SMITH, W, Postmaster at Mulder's Vlei, 1881
SMITH, Walter H, Postmaster at Engcobo, 1 October 1885

Postmaster at Engcobo, 1 DE 1886

SMITH, WH, Postmaster at River Zonder End, 31 July 1850, deceased while in office

SMITHERS, JB, Postmaster at Cape l'Agulhas, 1881

SMYTH, W, Postmaster at Fairfield, 8 January 1856, service provided for free

SMYTH, H, Postmaster at Wynberg, in about 1848

Letter Carrier, GPO, Cape Town, 5 January 1852. Salary £45 pa

SMYTHE, JE, Postmaster at Idutywa, 1881

Postmaster at Mount Frere, 1 May 1882

SNAILES, W, Postmaster at Shaw Park, 1880

SNEDDON, WD, Postmaster at Matatiele, 1 April 1905

SNELL, Charles Ernest, Assistant, Engineering Division, GPO, Cape Town, 13 July 1901. Salary £215 pa

Postmaster at Vanrhynsdorp, 1 September 1904

SNELL, Edward Walter, Clerk, 2nd Class, Accounting Division, GPO, Cape Town, 31 March 1900. Salary £280 pa

SNELL, Peter Adolphus, Assistant in the GPO, Cape Town, 3 October 1903. Salary £175 pa

SNIDER, JWE, Postmaster and station master at Centlivres, 1 December 1879

SNOOKE, S de la C, Postmaster at St Marks, 15 January 1886

SNOW, BJ, Postmaster at Muizenburg, 1906

SNYDERS, PC, Postmaster and field-cornet at Gouph No 5, on 29 September 1858, service provided for free in 1859

SODERLAND, Carl Abraham, Postmaster at Nelspoort, 17 July 1899

Station master at Muizenberg, 8 July 1908, salary £253 pa

SOLOMON, E, Postmaster at Caledon Street, Cape Town, 1 July 1897. On 30 November 1909 his widow, BJ Solomon, was receiving an annual pension of £15.7.4

SOLOMON, M, Postmaster at Modderfontein, Division of Victoria West, 1 July 1873

SOMERSET W, Postmaster at Schmidt's Drift, 1 March 1910

SOMERVILLE, J, Postmaster at Middelburg, 1 March 1877

SOUTHEY, WR, Postmaster at Varkenskop, 1 August 1873, service provided for free

SOWDEN, R, Postmaster at Sidbury, 1 October 1845

SPALDING, R, Postmaster at Spitzkop, Division of Barkly West, 1881

SPARKE, Robert David, Station master at Barkly Bridge, 1 April 1909, salary £208 pa

SPARKES, FW, Postmaster at Fraserburg Road, 1 June 1888

SPENCE, J, Postmaster and field-cornet at Klipplaat, 1 July 1864

SPENCELY, Alfred Burton, Postmaster at Nelspoort, 1905

Station master at Dohne, 22 November 1907, salary £230 pa

SPENCELY, Geo, Postmaster and station master at Fort Jackson, 1 May 1877

Postmaster at Cathcart, 1883

Postmaster at Kei Road, 7 August 1885

SPENCELEY, J, Postmaster at Toise River, 1880

SPENCELEY, W, Postmaster at Bailey, 18 February 1899

SPENCELY, JJ, Postmaster at Prince Albert Road, 17 December 1890

SPENCER, CJ, Postmaster at Kenilworth, Kimberley, 1 September 1900

SPENCER, George Robert, Postmaster at Lawrence Street, Port Elizabeth, 1 August 1905

SPENCER, Miss LA, Postmaster at Daniel's Kuil, 1 June 1904

SPENCER, W, Postmaster at Blue Cliff, in about 1877

SPENGLAR, Miss E, Postmaster at Philadelphia, 1 May 1897

SPENGLER, A, Postmaster at Philadelphia, 1880

SPREETH, N, Postmaster at Kookfontein, 22 April 1865, service provided for free

SPEIRS, E, Postmaster at Maitland, 1 August 1908

SPRENGER, EA, Postmaster at Maclean Town, 1 August 1900

SPRIGG, Miss EH, Postmaster at Bizana, 1 August 1899

Assistant, Telephone Exchange, GPO, Cape Town, 1 August 1905, salary £120 pa

SPRING, GW, Postmaster at Mqanduli, 1 January 1903

SPRING, HG, also listed as GH, Postmaster at Flagstaff, 1 March 1900

Postmaster at Engcobo, 1 June 1909

SPRING, HL, Postmaster at Keiskammahoek, 1 April 1870

SPRING, Mrs HL, Postmaster at Keiskammahoek, 7 November 1881

SPRING, SW, Postmaster at Mount Frere, 1 April 1904

SPYRON, J, Postmaster at Komgha, 1 December 1869, service provided for free in 1869-72

SQUIRES, J, Postmaster at Bushman's Hoek, 1 January 1872, service provided for free

STAEDAL, FH, Postmaster at Grahamstown, 1820

STAFFORD, GP, Clerk to the Magistrate and postmaster at Umzimkulu, 1 October 1877, deceased while in office

STAMPER, WF, Postmaster at Hanover, 1 September 1869

STANFORD, Arthur Henry Bell, Clerk to British Resident with Gangelizwe, 15 February 1875. Clerk to Chief Magistrate, Tembuland, 1 July 1876, and postmaster at Emjanyana, 15 October 1876. Thereafter he served as Resident Magistrate at Umtata (1878), Engcobo (1885), Libode (1894), Umtata (1897), and eventually rose to Chief Magistrate, Transkeian Territories, 1 June 1907. Saw active service as Lieutenant and Assistant Staff Officer in the Gcaleka uprising of 1877, served as Captain in 1878, and commanded the Umtata Native Contingent in 1881

STANFORD, W, Assistant Engineer at the GPO, in Cape Town, 1880

The Pension Lists of 30 November 1909 recorded that in 1910 Mr Stanford, age 5355, was retired on an annual pension of £399.0.7

STANLEY, Miss AM, Postmaster at Lawrence Street, Port Elizabeth, 1 May 1899

Postmaster at Jansenville, 1 August 1900

STANTON, WH, Postmaster at Katberg, 1 January 1879

STAPLETON, HW, Postmaster at Alfred Docks, Cape Town, 1 April 1888

Postmaster at Worcester Station, 15 May 1889

STAPLETON, WC, Clerk, Money Order and Stamp Branch, GPO, Cape Town, 1 Nov 1872

STARK, JF, Postmaster at Aberdeen Road, 1881

STARKE, J, Postmaster and station master at King William's Town Station, 1877
    Postmaster and station master at Cambridge, in about 1879
    Postmaster and station master at Toise River, 16 September 1879

STARKE, JE, Postmaster at Briedbach, 18 December 1876
    Postmaster and station master at Blaney Junction, 1 November 1877
    Postmaster at Kubusie, 1880

STEBBING, J, Postmaster at Blaauw Krantz, Division of Cradock, 1 October 1866

STEBBING, JF, Storekeeper and postmaster at the Boontjes River Convict Station, 28 April 1859

STEBBING, Maria Mrs, Postmaster at Boontjes River, 7 January 1864

STEEL, William, Postmaster at Hout Kraal, 1 August 1894

STEENKAMP, W Jnr, Postmaster at De Hoop, 1883

STEGMAN, JF, Postmaster at Normandie, 18 November 1863

STEGMANN, G, Postmaster at Houw Hoek, 14 May 1849

STEGMANN, the Rev GW, Dutch Reformed Church Minister and postmaster at Adelaide, 5 May 1859, service provided for free

STEGMANN, P, Junior assistant Murraysburg, 1 July 1897
    Postmaster at Omdraai's Vlei, 1 February 1899

STEGMANN, PW, Postmaster at Genadendal, 1 September 1904

STEINBACH, J, Postmaster at Bredasdorp, 12 March 1849

STEINMAN, E, Postmaster at Humansdorp, 1 January 1869

STEMMET, J, Postmaster at Roodewal, Division of Robertson, 16 October 1878

STEPHEN, Robert, Postmaster at Stal Street, Cape Town, 1 May 1890

STEPHEN, William Watson, Postmaster at Naauwpoort, 1909

STEPHENS, CE, Postmaster at Uitvlugtfontein, Division of Victoria West, January 1866

STEPHENS, W, Postmaster at Izer Nek, 14 August 1863

STEPHENSON, GF, Postmaster at Klipspruit Nek, 4 September 1862

STEPHENSON, J, Postmaster at Kuils River, 11 February 1858

STERNDORFF, W, Postmaster at Hooge Kraal, 1 August 1878

STERRENGBURGH, P, Postmaster at Carnarvon, 15 August 1871

STEVEN, JC, Postmaster at Barkly West, 1 October 1896

STEVEN, John Forbes, Postmaster at Claremont Station, 1902
    Postmaster at Worcester, 1 August 1908
    Postmaster at Grahamstown, 1 November 1909

STEVENS, CFWM, Born in about 1871, postmaster at Jansenville, 1 December 1891
    Postmaster at Alexandria, 1 April 1895
    Postmaster at Richmond, 1 August 1896
    Postmaster at Clanwilliam, 1 November 1897
    Principal Clerk, Registry, GPO, Cape Town, 1907
    The Pension Lists of 30 November 1909 recorded that in 1910 Mr Stevens, age 38, was retired

on an annual pension of £94.2.7

STEVENS, JC, Postmaster at Modder River, Division of Kimberley, 1 November 1906

STEVENS, JH, Postmaster at Fraserburg Road, 1 September 1902
Postmaster at Lower Paarl, 1 October 1903

STEVENS, M, Postmaster at Greystone, 1 August 1873

STEWART, A, Postmaster at Aberdeen Road, 1880
Postmaster at Cookhouse Station, 1881

STEWART, GC, Postmaster at Lower Tyumie, 10 May 1858, service provided for free

STEWART, GE, Postmaster at Mount Coke, 1 January 1879

STEWART, GM, Postmaster at Ceres, 7 February 1853

STEWART, Dr James (1831-1905), Postmaster at Lovedale, 1 January 1898. James Stewart studied divinity at Edinburgh, traveled widely in central Africa, qualified as a medical doctor, and eventually relocated to Lovedale in 1867. In 1870 he was elected Principal of Lovedale College, a post he held until his death in 1905. He founded and edited *The Christian Express* and *Isigidimi samaXhosa*, and wrote a number of books and pamphlets

STEWART, J, Postmaster at Uniondale, 25 May 1863

STEWART, M, Postmaster at Prieska, 1 July 1877

STEWART, Mrs M, Postmaster at Cookhouse, 1882

STEYN, D, Postmaster at Vosburg, 1 May 1897

STEYN, DJ, Postmaster at Attaquas Kloof, 10 May 1858
Postmaster at Safraan River, 3 September 1858

STEYN, J, Postmaster at Belmont, 1 April 1902

STEYN, H, Postmaster at Sutherland, 1 November 1895
Postmaster at Eerste River Station, 1 May 1896

STEYN, JM, Postmaster at Delport's Hope, 1 July 1897
Postmaster at Modder River, Division of Kimberley, 1 December 1900
Assistant Postmaster at the GPO in Cape Town, date not available
The Pension Lists of 30 November 1909 recorded that in 1910 Mr Steyn, age 30, was retired on an annual pension of £33.17.0. Given his retirement at such an early age, and the nature of his posting at a time when Modder River was one of the centers of fighting during the early stages of the South African War of 1899-1902, it is possible to surmise that Mr Steyn may have been a civilian victim of this conflict

STEYN, P, Postmaster and field-cornet at Buffels Kraal, 31 August 1859

STEYN, P, Postmaster at Fraserburg Road, 1 October 1899

STEYN, PH, Postmaster at Villiersdorp, 1 June 1893
Postmaster at Hoetjes Bay, 1 May 1895
Postmaster at Hutchinson, 1 July 1895

STEYN, PHL, Postmaster at Carnarvon, 1 May 1903

STEYN, PG, Postmaster at Heidelberg, 1 November 1862

STEYN, WD, Postmaster at Stellenbosch, 1829, possibly acting

STILL, T, Postmaster and station master at Coega, in about 1877
    Postmaster and station master at Kariega Station, 1 September 1877
    Postmaster and station master at Addo, 1 April 1878
STOCK, A, Postmaster at Maclean Town, 1881
STOCKENSTROM, E, Postmaster at Graaff-Reinet, 1 May 1826
STOCKENSTROM, PEF, Postmaster at Graaff-Reinet, 1817
STOCKENSTROOM, JJ, Postmaster at Klaarstroom, 1 January 1894
STODDART, G, Assistant third class, GPO, Cape Town, 21 January 1897
    Postmaster at Modder River, Division of Kimberley, 16 October 1898
    Postmaster at Vryburg, 1 March 1902
    Postmaster at Matjesfontein, Division of Worcester, 1 December 1902
    Postmaster at Butterworth, 1 April 1903
    Assistant Postmaster at Queenstown, date not available
    The Pension Lists of 30 November 1909 recorded that in 1910 Mr Stoddard, age 36, was retired on an annual pension of £85.11.4
STOFFELS, GE, Postmaster at Port St John, 1880
STOKES, Harry Vernon, Postmaster at Newlands, 1 December 1908
STONE, Gilbert Percival, Postmaster at Avontuur, 1 December 1905
STONE, M, Postmaster at Bowesdorp, 1 February 1902
STONIER, CS, Postmaster at Maclear, 1882
STOREY, John Horne, Station master at Cambridge, 11 September 1903, salary £233 pa
STOREY, William, Station master at Lobatsi, Bechuanaland Protectorate, 21 March 1906, salary £234 pa
STORM, WT, Postmaster at Delport's Hope, 1 April 1904
STORR, HB, In 1909 Mr Storr, then employed as a post and telegraph assistant in King William's Town, was awarded first prize in the telephony examinations of the City and Guilds of London Institute of Telegraphy
STORRIER, JWA, Postmaster at Diep River, 1883
    Postmaster at Retreat, 1 October 1895
    Postmaster at Richmond Road, 1 October 1895
STOW, J, Postmaster at Tarkastad, 1 September 1867
STOYLE, W, Postmaster at Idutywa, 1 December 1876
STRACHAN, Miss AM, Postmaster at Libodi, 1 December 1900
STRACHAN, Robert Adamson, Postmaster on Robben Island, 1 February 1909
STRATFORD, Postmaster at Mount Coke, 1881
STRATHAM, CW, Telegraphist at Beaufort West Station, 1901
STRETCH, RA, Postmaster at Somerset East, 1 August 1854
STRETTON, WH, Postmaster at Buffelsfontein, 1 November 1877
STRINGER, J, Postmaster at Jansenville, 1 September 1878
STROBOS, A, Postmaster at Prince Alfred's Hamlet, in about 1869, service provided for free

STROUD, CH, Assistant Postmaster at Grahamstown, date not available

The Pension Lists of 30 November 1909 recorded that in 1910 Mr Stroud, age 49, was retired on an annual pension of £106.2.2

STRYDOM, CJ, Postmaster at Vinke Nest, Wynand's River, 3 September 1858

STRYDOM, CJ Snr, Postmaster and field-cornet at Kruis River, Cango, 3 September 1858

Postmaster and field-cornet at Kruis River, Cango, 1 March 1869, service provided for free

STUART, F, Postmaster at Lusikisiki, 13 March 1898

STUBBINS, Arthur Bertram, Telegraphist at Barkly West, 1897

Postmaster at Windsorton, 1 October 1905

Postmaster at Barkly West, 1 February 1906

STUBBS, GM, Postmaster and station master at Eerste River Station, 26 August 1875, deceased while in office

STUMPKIE, A, Postmaster at Greystone, 1 October 1874

STURM, W, Postmaster at Hazenjacht, 1 June 1876

STURMAN, Edward Albert, Imperial Service Central Telegraph Office, 19 April 1879. Transferred to the Engineering Branch, London, 1885

Cape Telegraph Office, 22 February 1889

Telegraph Construction, April 1891

Clerk, Inland Mails Branch, GPO, Cape Town, 1 December 1891

Foreign Mails Branch, GPO, Cape Town, 1 October 1892

Principal Clerk, Appointments Branch, GPO, Cape Town, 1 July 1897

Temporarily attached to Agent-General's Office, March 1901

Pricipal Clerk, Telegraph Branch, 1 May 1902

Chief Clark, GPO, Cape Town, 1 February 1908

Acting Assistant Secretary, GPO, Cape Town, 18 January 1910

STYLE, JB, Postmaster and field-cornet at Kowie West, 1 March 1867

SURMUN, Edward, also listed as A, Born about 1857, United Kingdom Telegraph Service, 1874

Cape Government Telegraphs, Cape Town, 1879

Telegraphist, King William's Town, 1880

Postmaster at Umtata, 1 January 1881

Postmaster at De Aar, 1902

Acting postmaster at Grahamstown, January 1903

Postmaster at Queenstown, October 1903

Retired from service in August 1908

The Pension Lists of 30 November 1909 recorded that in 1910 Mr Surmun, age 52, was retired on an annual pension of £318.8.8

SURMUN, JC, Postmaster at Quthing, 1883

SURMUN, JE, Postmaster at Mohales Hoek, 1 July 1877

Postmaster at Advance Post, 1 July 1879

Postmaster at Mafeteng, 1 March 1880

SURMUN, Louisa, Postmaster at Driver's Bush, 18 August 1860, service provided for free
SUSSENS, R, Postmaster at Barville Park, 1 July 1859
SUSSMAN, J, Postmaster at Nieuwe Rust, 1 March 1907
SUTHERLAND, J, Postmaster at Klein Zwartberg, 1 January 1861
SUTHERLAND, J, Postmaster at Sandflats, 1 July 1893
SUTHERLAND, RH, also listed as RW, Postmaster at Ladismith, 1 June 1889
    Postmaster at Avontuur, 1 April 1890
    Postmaster at Norval's Pont, 14 September 1891
    Postmaster at Sandflats, 1 March 1892
SUTTON, BC, Postmaster at O'Okiep, 1 February 1876
SUTTON, S, Postmaster at Stoney Drift, 1 February 1863, service provided for free
SUTTON, W, Postmaster at Clarkebury, 1881
SWAIN, J, Postmaster at Mostert's Hoek, Division of Stellenbosch, in about 1847
    Postmaster at Bain's Kloof, 1 June 1847
SWAN, Abraham Haddon, Postmaster at Upper Paarl, 1 June 1908
SWAN, R, Postmaster at Seven Fountains, 12 December 1864, deceased while in office
SWANSEN, D, Assistant Postmaster at East London, date not available
    The Pension Lists of 30 November 1909 recorded that in 1910 Mr Swansen, age 38, was retired on an annual pension of £34.8.8
SWANEFELDER, J, Postmaster at Zoute Kloof, 22 April 1858
SWANEPOEL, WJ, Postmaster and field-cornet at Klein Zwartberg, 6 October 1863
SWART, DA, Postmaster and field-cornet at Buffels Klip, 3 September 1858
    Postmaster at Buffels Klip, 15 January 1868
SWART, DA Jnr, Postmaster at Buffels Klip, 1 March 1879
SWART, JL, Postmaster at Serjeant's River, 1 January 1863, deceased while in office
SWARTS, JJ, Postmaster and field-cornet at Uitvlugtfontein, Victoria West, 30 June 1860
SWEENEY, Christopher John, Clerk to the Mthembu Agent, 7 February 1876
    Postmaster at Cofimvaba, 1 February 1877
    Thereafter filled a number of administrative posts in the Transkei, rising to Special Commissioner under the Glen Grey Act, in 1895. Served as Captain of Volunteers during the Mpondo uprising of 1880, and commanded, with the rank of Major, the Glen Grey Native Levies raised for the defence of the district during the South African War of 1899-1902. Both times he was decorated
SWEMMER, Benjamin, Born in about 1858, postmaster at Mossel Bay, 1 June 1885
    Postmaster at Paarl, 22 September 1887
    Postmaster at Middelburg, 1 August 1894
    Postmaster at Humansdorp, 1 December 1894
    Postmaster at Barkly East, 1 June 1895
    Postmaster at Alice, 1 April 1896
    Postmaster at Aberdeen, Division of Aberdeen, 1 August 1896

The Pension Lists of 30 November 1909 recorded that in 1910 Mr Swemmer, age 51, was retired on an annual pension of £124.14.3

SWEMMER, JP, Postmaster at Cape Town, 1827

SWIFT, D, Postmaster at Qunu, 1 June 1878
Postmaster at Kokstad, in about 1879

SYLVESTER, Louis George, Postmaster at Plumstead, 17 January 1898, initially acting
Postmaster at Maitland, 1 October 1902
Postmaster at De Rust, Meirings Poort, 1905
Postmaster at Retreat, 1 June 1905

SYMES, HJC, Postmaster at Williston, 1 May 1876

SYMONS, A, Postmaster at Kei Road, 1 January 1891

SYMONS, JE, Postmaster at Mafeking, in about September 1890
Postmaster at Macloutsi early in 1892
Postmaster at Vryburg, late in 1892
JE Symons was probably employed by the Cape Post Office as a locum postmaster, and was posted to Mafeking on 16 September 1890. Early in 1892 he was transferred to Macloutsi, in the Bechuanaland Protectorate, where he conducted his postal business out of a mud hut whose roof had a tendency to collapse in the rain. At this stage he began to submit short poems and articles about his work in Macloutsi to the *St Martin-le-Grand Post Office Magazine*, published in London and, for the next few months, his letters and contributions to the journal were published regularly, to the warm acclaim and obvious delight of its editor. In September 1892 he was appointed postmaster of Vryburg, which he described as "*the capital of British Bechuanaland, and, comparatively speaking, it is but a village. Some people consider it a dull hole, but some people are never satisfied. In my opinion villages are preferable to great cities, and Vryburg is a dear little village.*" Symons was during the South African war siege a first-class assistant in the Post Office at Kimberley and again wrote about his experiences to the Post Office Magazine. In September 1900 he testified to a select committee appointed by the Cape Assembly to inquire into the alleged grievances of the employees of the Postal and Telegraph Department. At that point he was already lobbying to get permission to join the Transvaal telegraph service as inspector. It is possible that he got this permission and ended up in the Transvaal abruptly bring a stop to his correspondences with the Post Office Magazine (Symons 1997).

SYMONS, S, Postmaster at Butterworth, 1885
Postmaster at Qumbu, 15 July 1886

T

TAINTON, GFB, Postmaster at Herschel, 22 August 1879

TAIT, BB, Postmaster at Hopefield, 1 March 1898
Postmaster at Schmidt's Drift, 1 April 1899
Postmaster at Philipstown, 1 September 1899

TANCRED, P, Postmaster at Nieuwe Rust, 26 May 1899

TARBETT, James, Postmaster at North End, Port Elizabeth, 1 August 1908

TASKER, J, Controller, Central Telegraph Office at Cape Town, date not available
  The Pension Lists of 30 November 1909 recorded that in 1910 Mr Tasker, age 53, was retired on an annual pension of £450

TAUBER AND CARSTENS, Postmaster at Pearston, 16 November 1858. This was probably a commercial firm

TAUKE, G, Postmaster at Beaufort West, 1 December 1818

TAUTE, J, Postmaster at Molen River, 1883

TAUTE, JF, Postmaster at Molen River, 20 April 1852

TAYLOR, Bertram Latimer, Postmaster at Plumstead, 1 October 1902
  Postmaster at Groot Drakenstein, 1 May 1905
  Acting postmaster at Prince Albert Road, 1 July 1906
  Postmaster at Prince Albert Road, 1 October 1906
  Postmaster at Vanrhynsdorp, 1 July 1908

TAYLOR, CH, Postmaster at Phisantfontein, 1880

TAYLOR, CJ, Postmaster at Addo, 26 February 1848

TAYLOR, Charles Thomas, Junior Assistant, CTO, Cape Town, 7 February 1879
  Telegraphist at Malmesbury, 1 December 1883
  Postmaster at Clanwilliam, 11 October 1883
  Postmaster at Richmond, 1 May 1889
  Postmaster at Caledon, 1 January 1893
  Postmaster at Kokstad, 1 September 1908

TAYLOR, EH, Born in about 1855, postmaster and station master at East London East Bank, 1 May 1877
  Postmaster and station master at Kei Road, 1 July 1878
  Postmaster at Mulder's Vlei, 1880
  Postmaster at Newlands, Cape Town, 1 September 1882
  The Pension Lists of 30 November 1909 recorded that in 1910 Mr Taylor, age 54, was retired on an annual pension of £62.8.4

TAYLOR, GH, Postmaster and station master at Berlin Station, 7 April 1878

TAYLOR, HR, Clerk to the Civil Commissioner and Postmaster at Riversdale, 8 March 1848

TAYLOR, Harry R, Postmaster at Klaarstroom, 13 October 1884
  Postmaster at Calitzdorp, 1 December 1886

TAYLOR, Hugh, Postmaster at Maclear, 1 June 1891

TAYLOR, J, Postmaster at Riversdale, 20 September 1849

TAYLOR, JT, Postmaster on Robben Island, 13 October 1888

TAYLOR, Margaret, Postmaster at Salem, 1 September 1863

TAYLOR, R, Clerk to the Civil Commissioner and Postmaster King William's Town, 11 Jan 1849

TAYLOR, R, Postmaster at Komgha, 26 April 1875

TAYLOR, WR, Postmaster at Maraisburg, 1 June 1881

TEGGIN, Frederick Wilson, Postmaster at Philipstown, 1 June 1904

TEITJE, CFW, Postmaster at Sutherland, 1 January 1875

TELFORD, Alexander, Postmaster at Mount Fletcher, October 1908

TEMLETT, Arthur Peter William, Postmaster at Bolotwa, 9 September 1898
Postmaster at Peddie, 1 November 1903

TEMLETT, Mrs S, Postmaster at Bolotwa, 1 October 1895

TEMPLAR, T, School teacher and postmaster at Barville Park, 1 January 1865

TEMPLEMAN, James George Sorey, Clerk, Telegraph Department, 1 September 1894
Postmaster at Porterville, 1 April 1897
Postmaster at O'Okiep, 15 December 1897
Clerk to the Civil Commissioner and Resident Magistrate at Hay, 1 February 1903

TENNANT, A, Postmaster and field-cornet at Richmond, 1 August 1870
Postmaster at Richmond, 10 February 1874

TENNANT, CW, Postmaster at Observatory Road, 1 July 1897
Postmaster at Malmesbury, 1 February 1899

TENNANT, JH, Postmaster at Uitenhage, 14 February 1850

TENNANT, JT, Postmaster at Observatory Road, 1 January 1868

TERBLANCHE, PM, Postmaster and field-cornet at Hops River, 1 March 1873, service provided for free in 1867-73
Postmaster at Hops River, 1 March 1878, assumed to be a reappointment

TERBURGH, DP, Schoolmaster and postmaster at Krakeel River, 26 April 1856, service provided for free in 1856-61 and 1870-72

TERRELL, Miss LE, Postmaster at Steinkopf, 1 September 1904

TERRINGTON, W, Postmaster at Somerset West, in about 1845, possibly acting

TESSELAAR, JGB, Assistant Registered Letter Clerk, GPO, Cape Town, 15 October 1879
Sorter, second class, GPO, Cape Town, 1 January 1881
Assistant Postmaster at the GPO in Cape Town, date not available
The Pension Lists of 30 November 1909 recorded that in 1910 Mr Tesselaar, age 52, was retired on an annual pension of £118.18.4

THACKER, S, Postmaster at Muizenberg, 1882

THACKHAM, William, Postmaster at South End, Port Elizabeth, 1 August 1903

THACKWELL, Arthur William, Postmaster at Orchard Siding, 1906
Postmaster at Bowesdorp, 1 April 1907

THERON, William Adolph Vogel, Postmaster at Rhodes, 1 February 1903
Postmaster at Lady Grey, Division of Aliwal North, 1 November 1903
Postmaster at Moshesh's Ford, 1 March 1908

THEUNISSEN, Miss E, Postmaster at Somerset West, 25 May 1871

THEUNISSEN, M, Postmaster and field-cornet at Voor Attaquas Kloof, 10 May 1858
Postmaster at Somerset West, 20 November 1866, deceased while in office

THEUNISSEN, Martin William, Postmaster at Adelaide, 1 November 1902

Postmaster at Port Alfred, 1910

THIEL, O, Postmaster at Fraserburg, 1 January 1896

THOM, G, Acting postmaster at Middelburg, in about 1874

THOM, Miss Hester, see under VAN RENSBURG, Mrs Hester

THOM, W, Postmaster and Field-Cornet at De Keur, 31 March 1857, deceased while in office

THOMAS, J Snr, Postmaster at Riet Vlei, Division of Uitenhage, 1 October 1865

THOMAS, J Jnr, Postmaster at Riet Vlei, Division of Uitenhage, 1 January 1866

THOMAS, JL, Postmaster and field-cornet at Whittlesea, 1 March 1867

THOMAS, RD, Postmaster at Riet Vlei, Division of Uitenhage, 1 Oct 1868, service provided free

THOMAS, WB, Sergeant, 10th Regiment and postmaster at Falloden, 8 May 1860

THOMAS, WE, Postmaster at Richmond, 1 May 1873

THOMAS, WE, Sorter, GPO, Cape Town, 7 November 1866
  Clerk, GPO, Cape Town, 24 March 1871
  Clerk, GPO, Cape Town, 10 February 1874
  Clerk, first class, GPO, Cape Town, in about 1880
  Superintendent, Letter Branch, GPO, Cape Town, 1 January 1881
  Chief Clerk, Circulation Branch, GPO, Cape Town, date not available
  The Pension Lists of 30 November 1909 recorded that in 1910 Mr Thomas, age 65, was retired on an annual pension of £333.4.7.

THOMAS, WH, Postmaster at Cookhouse Station, in about 1879

THOMAS, William John Watts, Postmaster at Murraysburg, 21 March 1899
  Postmaster at Clanwilliam, 1 February 1902
  Postmaster at Murraysburg, 1 August 1902
  Postmaster at Tarkastad, 1 October 1908

THOMPSON, AD, Postmaster and field-cornet at Farm No 27, in 1868

THOMPSON, Donald, Postmaster at Pearston, 1 November 1907

THOMPSON, Mrs L, Postmaster at Thompson's Farm, 1 January 1875

THOMPSON, NO, Postmaster at Nqamakwe, 1 October 1878

THOMPSON, Thomas William, Postmaster at Kimberley Station, 1 December 1897
  Postmaster at Swellendam, 1 August 1908

THOMPSON, W, Postmaster at Maclear, in about 1878

THOMPSON, William, Postmaster at Swellendam, 1 October 1819

THOMPSON, WJG, Postmaster at Port St John, 1 July 1885

THOMPSON, WR, Postmaster and field-cornet at Nieuwveld No 1, on 29 September 1858, service provided for free in 1867-1872

THOMSON, JR, Postmaster at Port St John, 1 June 1894

THOMSON, SE, Postmaster at Britstown, 1 February 1887

THOMSON, WR, Dutch Reformed Church Minister and postmaster at Hertzog, 1 January 1867

THORN, S, Postmaster at Steynsburg, in about 1878

THORNE, G, Postmaster at North Paarl, 1 January 1865

THORNE, JT, Postmaster at Touws River, 1882. For further details see also under GC Geyer, station master at Montagu Road and Touws River

THORNE, WT, Postmaster at Fourteen Streams, 1 April 1891

THURSBY, F, Postmaster at Grootfontein, 22 November 1878

THWAITS, WT, Assistant, Money Order and Stamp Branch, GPO, Cape Town, 1 August 1867

TIDBURY, G, Postmaster at Blinkwater, 1883

TIFFANY, William Henry, Telegraphist at Leeds, 5 November 1875
 Transferred to Colonial Service in Cape Town, 7 December 1880
 Clerk and shorthand writer to the General Manager, 1 January 1881
 Clerk and shorthand writer to the Telegraph Branch, GPO, Cape Town, 16 May 1885
 Pricipal Clerk, General Correspondence Branch, GPO, Cape Town, 1 November 1889
 Provincial Post Offices, Buildings and Equipment Branch, GPO, Cape Town, 1 September 1908. Salary £625
 Tiffany was placed on etirement on 31 May 1910 when the Union of South Africa was proclaimed, and the four colonial Post Offices were united under a single management based in Pretoria

TILBURY, JL, Postmaster at Alexandria, 22 June 1854

TILLEMAN, AJ, Postmaster at Panmure, 1 April 1875

TIMM, P, Postmaster at Bell, 1 June 1863

TIMMELMAN, CJ, Postmaster at New Bethesda, 1881

TINNENY, Mr, Postmaster at Colesberg, 1854

TINNENY, Hugh, Postmaster at Hopetown, 1 September 1856

TINNENY, P, Postmaster at Hopetown, 1 September 1857

TODD, D, Postmaster at Two Streams, 1881

TODD, JSB, Clerk, Money Order and Stamp Branch, GPO, Cape Town, 1 April 1875
 Moved to Colonial Secretary's Office, 1876

TOMKINS, R, Postmaster at Wellington Station, 1881

TOPLIS, A, Postmaster at Plettenberg's Bay, 25 January 1860
 Postmaster at Plettenberg's Bay, 1 October 1864

TORBETT, W, Postmaster at Riet Huis, 22 October 1864, service provided for free

TOUCH, PHJ, Assistant Postmaster, GPO, Cape Town, date not available
 The Pension Lists of 30 November 1909 recorded that in 1910 Mr Touch, age 42, was retired on an annual pension of £147.17.1

TOUGH, RA, Postmaster at Ceres Road, 1 January 1890
 Postmaster at Mill Street, Gardens, Cape Town, 1 August 1890

TOWNSEND, Mrs, Postmaster at Port Nolloth, 1 September 1874

TOWNSEND, C, Postmaster at Cathcart, 1880

TOWNSEND, G, Postmaster at O'Okiep, 1 October 1880

TOWNSEND, J, Postmaster at Malagas, 29 September 1853
 Postmaster at Spectakel, 17 April 1862, service provided for free

TOWNSEND, W, Postmaster at Glen Lynden, 25 August 1859

TRACEY, Richard Elliott, Postmaster at Huguenot, 1882
  Station master at Uitenhage, 27 September 1905, salary £314 pa

TRANTER, J, Postmaster and Police Constable at Groote Vlakte, 27 January 1860, service provided for free

TREADWAY, GC, Postmaster at Greytown, 1 May 1874

TREDOUX, JG, Postmaster at Groot Berg River, 10 May 1858
  Postmaster at Melkplaats, 1 January 1866, service provided for free

TREGARTHEN, Abraham, Imperial Telegraph Service, 29 May 1879
  Transferred to the Colonial Service as Telegraphist at King Willim's Town, 2 December 1880
  Telegraphist at Aliwal North, 1 March 1882
  Telegraphist at Mossel Bay, 1 August 1884
  Telegraphist at Cape Town, 1 May 1885
  Superintendent of Telegraphs at Kimberley, 1 February 1889
  Assistant Controller, Telegraphs, Cape Town, 1 November 1895
  Postmaster at East London, 1 September 1908, salary £550 pa

TRENAM, P, Assistant Postmaster at King William's Town, date not available
  The Pension Lists of 30 November 1909 recorded that in 1910 Mr Trenam, age 47, was retired on an annual pension of £113.19.1

TRENAN, PE, Postmaster at Barkly East, 1 August 1883
  Postmaster at Malmesbury, 1 October 1887

TREVETHICK, Richard Thomas, Postmaster at De Doorns, 14 July 1899
  Station master at Fraserburg Road, 9 October 1905, salary £226 pa

TREVOR, C, Postmaster at Herschel, 1881

TROLLIP, J, Postmaster at Berlin Station, 20 October 1875

TROWER, J, Postmaster and field-cornet at Trappes Valley, 13 February 1860, service provided for free in 1867-73

TRUTER, HA, Additional clerk, GPO, Cape Town, 22 July 1848. Salary £150 pa
  Clerk, third class, GPO, Cape Town, 1853

TRUTER, JC, Postmaster at Doorn River, 1881

TRUTER, JL, Clerk to the Civil Commissioner and postmaster at Paarl, 8 March 1848

TRUTER, PI, and Son, Postmaster at Clanwilliam, 1 October 1829

TRUTER, PJ, Clerk to the Civil Commissioner and postmaster at George, 1 March 1846

TRUTER, Mrs PJ, Postmaster at Piquetberg, 2 June 1853

TRUTER, PJS, Postmaster at Piquetberg, 26 April 1849

TUBB, W, Postmaster at Faure Siding, 9 March 1846

TUBB, WE, Postmaster at Darling Bridge, 1 April 1870

TUCK, Mary, Postmaster at Somerset East, 1 September 1863

TUCK, M, Postmaster at Blood River, 1 December 1878

TUCK, W, Postmaster at Somerset East, 31 May 1860

TUNBRIDGE, C, Postmaster at Cradock, 1 June 1872

TUNBRIDGE, Edward, Postmaster and field-cornet at Addo Drift, 7 August 1855
> In 1848 Edward Tunbridge purchased *"The Elephant and Castle,"* a wayside inn located near Addo Drift, a crossing of the Sunday's River frequently used by visitors travelling from the coast into the South African interior. When a post office was opened there on 7 August 1855 he was appointed its first postmaster, and was succeeded to this position by his younger brother Tilden on 1 June 1870. In time the inn became known as *"Tunbridge's,"* and between 1856 and 1862 it was also listed as such in postal records

TUNBRIDGE, Tilden, Postmaster and field-cornet at Addo Drift, 1 June 1870

TURNER, Frederick John, Postmaster at Port Nolloth, 1 May 1902

TWEED, A, Acting Secretary and Accountant, GPO, Cape Town, in about 1868
> Secretary and Accountant, GPO, Cape Town, 1 January 1869
> Master of the High Court of Griqualand West, 1871
> Returned to GPO, Cape Town, 1872
> Audit Office, GPO, Cape Town, 1875

TWENTYMAN, William, Postmaster at Storm's Vlei, 1 August 1868, service provided for free.
> In 1818 Lawrence Twentyman emigrated to the Cape and, working as a silversmith, established himself in Cape Town. His business prospered, and in 1841 the firm of Twentyman & Co purchased land in the district of Swellendam. It established the village of Storm's Vlei upon the farm Avontuur, and probably named it in honour of its previous owner, Christiaan Andreas Storm. In 1844 Lawrence's nephew, William Twentyman, arrived from England to assist his uncle, and was placed in charge of developments at Storm's Vlei. At that stage the village began to play an important role in the postal affairs of the region, and when a twice-weekly post to the eastern frontier was established in 1849, it became a stop for the post-cart. William was awarded the contract to change post horses, and also established a well-appointed smithy to conduct repairs. In 1864 he married a young widow, Annie Sarah McIntyre, nee Arderne, who had already been twice married, and had borne four children. Somewhat suspiciously, both her previous husbands had died by the knife, the first allegedly having cut his own throat. The family then left for England, but when Lawrence Twentyman died soon thereafter in 1868, William returned and purchased Storm's Vlei from his uncle's deceased estate. On 1 August 1868 William was appointed postmaster for Storm's Vlei, and in 1869 he was granted a liquor license and opened up an inn to cater for the overnight needs of passengers travelling to Grahamstown. It seems probable therefore, that he ran his post office from the inn, for the benefit of his guests. On 13 May 1871, at the age of 48, Twentyman was stabbed to death outside his inn, and although he managed to crawl inside, he bled to death. The identity of his assailants was never discovered, but the motive was thought to be *"interference with local women."* His wife, reportedly *"a tiny woman of great personality"* continued to run the inn

TWYCROSS, Henry William Stephen, Junior Assistant, Telegraph Department, 1 Dec 1876
> First Class Clerk, Secretarial Branch, GPO, Cape Town, 28 August 1893
> Principal Clerk, Inland Mails Branch, GPO, Cape Town, 1 July 1897

Acting Chief Clark, GPO, Cape Town, 15 August 1901
Attached to Agent-General's Office on special duty, 22 April 1902
Acting Surveyor and District Engineer, Western Postal District, 7 December 1902
Acting Chief Clark, GPO, Cape Town, 1 October 1903
Chief Clark, GPO, Cape Town, 1 January 1905
Assistant Secretary, GPO, Cape Town, 1 February 1908, salary £700 pa

TYNDALL, William Henry, Postmaster at Sea Point, Cape Town, 1902
Postmaster at Three Anchor Bay, Cape Town, 1 April 1902

U

UBSIDELL, George, was born in England, and travelled to South Africa on the ship *Nautilus*, as part of a party of settlers from Surrey led by George Scott. He, together with his wife Betsy and their three children, landed in Algoa Bay on 14 April 1820. He was appointed postmaster at Port Elizabeth on 1 January 1828, but eventually resigned his position in 1840 because of the poor pay on offer. He went on to become a highly successful chemist, with premises in Main Street.

ULLYETT, Albert George, Postmaster at Wellington Station, 1 April 1897
Postmaster at Queen Street, Port Elizabeth, 1 December 1903

UNSWORTH, J, Sorter, GPO, Cape Town, 24 February 1875

UPHAM, Joseph George, Station master at Carnarvon, 28 March 1906, salary £180 pa

URIE, Mrs, Postmaster at Steynsburg, in about 1878

URIE, J, Postmaster at Steynsburg, 1 November 1878

URRY, Herbert Charles, Postmaster at Krakeel River, 1 October 1909

USHER, Charlotte L, Postmaster at Falloden, 1 July 1862

UYS, H, Postmaster at Barrydale, 1 March 1879

UYS, W, Postmaster at Hoornbosch, 19 April 1855

V

VAILLANT, JB, Letter carrier, GPO, Cape Town, 16 November 1873
Moved to Port Elizabeth in 1874
Junior sorter, GPO, Cape Town, in about 1881

VAN AARDE, JW, Postmaster at Paardeberg, Division of Malmesbury, 29 May 1858

VAN AS, Ch, Postmaster at Ladismith, 17 February 1852

VAN BART, H, Acting postmaster at Prieska, 1 July 1892

VAN BLERK, JPJ, Postmaster at Lower Paarl, 1 December 1876

VAN BLOMMESTEIN, CA, see under VON BLOMMESTEIN

VAN BREDA, A, Postmaster and field-cornet at Geelbeck, 29 May 1858

VAN BREDA, DG, Postmaster at Ratel River, 13 September 1866, service provided for free

VAN BREDA, H, Postmaster at Zeekoegat, Division of Caledon, 21 December 1853

VAN BREDA, HJ de W, Clerk, GPO, Cape Town, 1 April 1867
Clerk, Bredasdorp, date of appointment not known

VAN BREDA, MA, Postmaster at Ratel River, 5 October 1863, service provided for free

VAN BREDA, MJ, Postmaster at Zoetendal's Vlei, Division of Bredasdorp, 21 December 1853, service provided for free

Zoetendal's Valley was a farm in the vicinity of Caledon, in the southern Cape, credited to have conducted the earliest experiments in Merino stud. It was named after the Dutch East Indiaman *Zoetendal*, which was wrecked in 1673 off Cape Agulhas, near the farm. It was sold in 1830 to the firm of Reitz, Breda, Joubert & Co, who continued with the Merino project until it was closed down in 1851, when it was purchased by Mr MJ van Breda and his family. They probably ran its post office for the benefit of his workers

VAN BREDA, P, Postmaster at Hondeklip Bay, 16 May 1859

VAN BUUREN, Mrs PS, Postmaster at Burghersdorp, 25 November 1853

VAN COPPENHAGEN, see under COPENHAGEN

VAN DEN BERGH, DP, Postmaster and field-cornet at Aberdeen, Division of Aberdeen, 15 November 1861

VAN DEN BERGH, J, Postmaster at Petersburg, 16 October 1871, possibly acting

VAN DER BERG, Postmaster at Molen River, 1880

VAN DER BERG, AF, Postmaster and field-cornet at Karreeboschfontein, 1 October 1864

VAN DER BERG, AP, Postmaster and field-cornet at Karreeboschfontein, 1 November 1871

VAN DER BYL, JJ, Postmaster at Van Der Byl's Kraal, 16 May 1896. JJ van der Byl was the owner of the farm Van Der Byl's Kraal, and probably ran a small rural store and post office agency from the site. In 1904 he sold the property to the Dutch Reformed Church at Beaufort West for £4500, who then laid out a village on the site and named it Merweville, in honour of the Rev P van der Merwe, DRC minister at Beaufort West

VAN DER BYL, P, Postmaster at Merweville, 1 March 1904. P van der Byl was probably related to JJ van der Byl, the original owner of and postmaster at Van Der Byl's Kraal

VAN DER BYL, PJ, Postmaster at Langebaan, 1 October 1868, service provided for free

VAN DER HORST, CT, Letter carrier, GPO, Cape Town, in about 1876

VAN DER MERWE, CJ, Postmaster at Patatas River, 13 September 1853

VAN DER MERWE, CJ, Postmaster at Hottentot's Kloof, 13 September 1853

VAN DER MERWE, DS, Postmaster at Willowmore, 1 July 1868

VAN DER MERWE, GWC, Postmaster at Prieska, 1 December 1883

VAN DER MERWE, JE, also listed as IE, Postmaster at Omdraai's Vlei, 1 January 1897

Postmaster at Daniel's Kuil, 1 May 1898

Postmaster at Campbell, 1 November 1898

Postmaster at Campbell, 1 January 1901

Postmaster at Prieska, 1 January 1904

VAN DER MERWE, JJ, Postmaster at Groot Doorn Pan, 1872, service provided for free

Postmaster at Groot Doorn Pan, 1 July 1873, service provided for free

VAN DER MERWE, JR, Postmaster at Hottentot's Kloof, 1 August 1868

VAN DER MERWE, Pieter Johannes, Postmaster Norval's Pont, 1 Feb 1908, salary £185 pa

VAN DER MERWE, P, Postmaster and field-cornet at Porterville, 10 May 1858

VAN DER MERWE, Mrs SS, see OOSTHUIZEN, Mrs SS

VAN DER POEL, SJ, Secretary, Divisional Council, and postmaster at Bredasdorp, 1 Aug 1877

VAN DER RIET, R, Clerk, fifth class, GPO, Cape Town, 7 September 1857

VAN DER RIET, W, Clerk, second class, GPO, Cape Town, 9 April 1856

VAN DER SCHYFF, Henry David, Station master at Hutchinson 5 July 1908, salary £200 pa

VAN DER SPUY, M, Postmaster at Durbanville, 1 May 1861

VAN DER SPUY, Pieter Melt, Clerk to the Civil Commissioner and Resident Magistrate at Riversdale, April 1865

    Postmaster at Oudtshoorn, 1 February 1872, and telegraphist, 1875

    Returned to other administrative duties in the Colonial Service, eventually being appointed Civil Commissioner and Resident Magistrate at Van Rhynsdorp, 2 March 1908

VAN DER VEEN, H, Postmaster at Schoemansdorp, 1 January 1865, service provided for free

VAN DER VLIES, Miss S, Postmaster at Schoemanshoek, 8 May 1898

VAN DER WESTHUIZEN, Postmaster at Kloud's Kraal, 1881

VAN DER WESTHUIZEN, HP, Postmaster at Groot Doorn Pan, 30 June 1860

VAN DER WESTHUIZEN, PM, Postmaster at Armoed, 1 June 1905

VAN DER WESTHUIZEN, W, Postmaster at Willem's River, 1880

VAN DER WETERING, JH, Postmaster at Drooge Vlei, 1 July 1873, service provided for free in 1873

VAN DER WORM, W, Postmaster at Napier, 30 September 1852

VAN DOLDER, JW, Postmaster at Simondium, 1 September 1861

VAN DRUTEN, N, Postmaster at Postmasburg, 1 December 1896

VAN DYK, AJ, Postmaster at Cradock, 28 July 1822

VAN DYK, Bergert Wynand Rossouw, also listed as VAN DYKE, Postmaster at Hankey, 1 March 1900

    Postmaster at Richmond Road, 1 May 1903

    Postmaster at Maraisburg, 1 November 1903. Salary £205 pa

VAN DYK, Mrs CM, Postmaster at Cradock, 23 July 1840

VAN DYK, H, Postmaster at Paardenberg, 28 February 1859, service provided for free in 1859-61

VAN DYK, JE, Postmaster at Springer's Kuil, 8 April 1856, service provided for free in 1856-57

VAN DYKE, BWR, see under VAN DYK, BWR

VAN EDEN, Gert, Postmaster at Storm's Vlei, 1 June 1872, service provided for free

VAN ENTER, J, Postmaster at Uitkyk, 30 December 1864, service provided for free in 1867-8

VAN EYK, JFB, Postmaster at Kariega Station, 1 January 1864

    Postmaster and field-cornet at Kariega Station, 1 April 1875

VAN HEERDEN, LCJ, Postmaster at Eland's River, 1881

VAN HUYSTEEN, DP, Postmaster and field-cornet at Wittedrift, Division of Knysna, 13 October 1863, service provided for free in 1867-72

VAN LEGER, Mrs, Postmaster at Daljosaphat, December 1861

VAN LELYVELD, HJ, Postmaster at Uitenhage, 16 February 1814

VAN LIER, JP, Postmaster at Cape Town, 1813

VAN MANEN, J, Postmaster at Prince Albert, 4 January 1854

VAN NIEKERK, APB, Postmaster at Riet Kuil, Division of Colesberg, 15 October 1855, service provided for free

VAN NIEKERK, Jacs, Postmaster at River Zonder End, 15 May 1846

VAN NIEKERK, JA, Postmaster and field-cornet at Pramberg, 1 May 1864, service provided for free 1867-72

Postmaster at Spytpoort, 1 July 1872

VAN NIEKERK, JA, Postmaster and field-cornet at Wolvefontein Station, 1 April 1867

VAN NIEKERK, JP, either JP or GL, Postmaster at Matjesfontein, Division of Uitenhage, 15 July 1839

VAN NIEKERK, PC, Postmaster at Matjesfontein, Division of Uitenhage, 1 February 1843

VAN NIEKERK, PC, Postmaster at Wolvefontein Station, 1 October 1870

VAN OS, JK, Postmaster at Malmesbury, 1 March 1861

VAN OUDTSHOORN, G, Postmaster at Swellendam, 7 February 1849

VAN PUTTEN, James William, Postmaster at Van Putten's Vlei, 1 February 1897

VAN REENEN, Mr, Postmaster at Lower Paarl, in about 1879

VAN REENEN, A, Postmaster at Quagga's Flats, 7 April 1853

VAN REENEN, E, Postmaster at Riet Vlei, Division of Uitenhage, 17 April 1856

VAN REENEN, F, Postmaster at Seymour, 1 August 1902

VAN REENEN, F, Postmaster at Pella, 1880

VAN REENEN, FA, Postmaster at Rosebank, 1 December 1897

VAN REENEN, I, Postmaster at Kalk Bay, 18 August 1857

VAN REENEN, JP, School teacher and postmaster at McGregor, 15 July 1861

VAN REENEN, JW, Postmaster and field-cornet at Groenekloof, Division of Malmesbury, 29 May 1858, service provided for free

VAN RENSBURG, H, Postmaster at Molen River, 1 July 1875

VAN RENSBURG, Mrs Hester, nee THOM, married in about 1880, Postmaster at De Keur, 1 October 1871

VAN RENSBURG, William DJ, Postmaster at Villiersdorp, 7 January 1901

VAN RHYN, Anna CD, also listed as Mrs PB VAN RHYN, probably wife of Petrus Benjamin van Rhyn. Postmaster at Vanrhynsdorp, 1 October 1868, service provided for free

Postmaster at Vanrhynsdorp, 1 September 1873. Also see Petrus Benjamin van Rhyn

VAN RHYN, Petrus Benjamin, Postmaster and field-cornet at Vanrhynsdorp, 15 January 1859. The settlement of Troe Troe was probably established in 1868 on the farm Troe Troe, in the field-cornetcy of Lower Olifants River, in what was then the division of Clanwilliam. Its name originated from the Khoikhoi and means "*a place of fighting*" (Nienaber 1983). Initially Petrus Benjamin van Rhyn, who was also a field-cornet, was appointed as its first postmaster, but on 1 October 1868 Anna Van Rhyn succeeded her husband to the position and performed this duty free. The post office was abolished in 1871 and when it was reopened on 1 September 1873 Anna van Rhyn was reappointed its postmistress, but with a salary of £6 per annum. In July 1885 it was renamed Vanrhynsdorp

VAN ROOYEN, GJ, Postmaster at Molen River, 1 April 1878

VAN ROOYEN, Mrs H, Postmaster at Blinkwater, 1 December 1878. In 1849 the Rev Arie van Rooyen entered the ministry of the United Congregational Church, the first man of *"colour"* to do so, and in 1850 took charge of Tidmanton, an outstation of Blinkwater which thereafter became known as *"the Hottentot mission"*. Mrs H van Rooyen appears to have been his wife

VAN ROOYEN, RP, Postmaster at Doorn River, 20 March 1858

VAN RYNEVELD, Ann M, Postmaster at Alexandria, 1 December 1869

VAN RYNEVELD, GN, Postmaster at Stootje, 1 December 1871

VAN RYNEVELD, WS, Postmaster at Clanwilliam, 15 April 1861

VAN SANTEN, PJ, Postmaster at Riebeek Kasteel, 1 October 1864, service provided for free

VAN SCHOOR, JC, Postmaster at Eendekuil, 1 March 1905

VAN SCHOOR, WA, Postmaster at Philadelphia, 1883

VAN SELM, Mrs Baatje, Postmaster at Daljosaphat, 1 January 1862

VAN SITTERT, Mrs Emma E, Postmaster at Sutherland, 1 October 1863

VAN URESEN, W, Postmaster at Karree Kop, 1880

VAN WYK, AF, Postmaster at Langeberg, 10 July 1868, service provided for free

VAN WYK, J, Postmaster and field-cornet at Van Putten's Vlei, 1 May 1869, service provided free

VAN WYK, JA, Postmaster and field-cornet at Langeberg, 11 June 1869

VAN WYK, JJ, Postmaster at Bellville, 1 February 1892

VAN WYK, MS, Postmaster at Hertzog, 9 July 1879

VAN ZYL, A, Postmaster and field-cornet at Langeberg, 31 August 1859

VAN ZYL, AJ, Postmaster and field-cornet at Upper Olifants River, 9 February 1859, service provided for free in 1870-74

VAN ZYL, B, Postmaster at Hoetjes Bay, 5 March 1899
  GPO, Cape Town, probable date 1 May 1903
  Postmaster at Eendekuil, 1 July 1904
  Postmaster at Eendekuil, 1 March 1907

VAN ZYL, DB, Postmaster at Millwood, Goldfields, 1 June 1892
  Postmaster at French Hoek, 1 January 1893
  Postmaster at Carnarvon, 1 December 1893
  Postmaster at Calvinia, 1 May 1896
  Postmaster at Ceres Road, 1 June 1900
  Postmaster at Strydenburg, 1 January 1904
  Postmaster at Hopefield, 1 April 1906

VAN ZYL, G, Postmaster at Fonteins Vlei, 31 August 1859, service provided for free in 1867-73

VAN ZYL, G, Postmaster and field-cornet at Berg and Lange Vlei, 19 June 1865, service provided for free in 1870-73

VAN ZYL, GH, Postmaster at Zandvliet, 7 June 1854, service provided for free

VAN ZYL, Miss Lettie Francina Johanna, Postmaster at Albertinia, 1 June 1906
> Postmaster at Barrydale, 1 October 1908
> Postmaster at Houw Hoek, 1 October 1909, salary £72 pa

VAN ZYL, L, Postmaster at Spruitdrift, 1 October 1868, service provided for free

VAN ZYL, P, Postmaster and field-cornet at Berg and Lange Vlei, 15 January 1859

VAN ZYL, PHS, Postmaster at Upper Olifants River, 29 August 1871

VAN ZYL, WJN, Postmaster and field-cornet at Zandvliet, 1 March 1864
> Postmaster and field-cornet at Zandvliet, 1 August 1872
> Postmaster and field-cornet at Zandvliet, 1 July 1874
> Postmaster at Zandvliet, 1 January 1877

VEARY, CR, Postmaster at Nelspoort, 1 January 1895

VEARY, Wallace John Biggerstoff, Station master at Malmesbury, 20 July 1908, salary £280 pa

VEARY, Ernest Edward, Postmaster at Hout Kraal, 1 May 1899

VEARY, W, Postmaster at Imvani, 23 July 1896

VENN, TB, Postmaster at Palmiet River, 1 January 1846

VENN, TB, Postmaster at Grabouw, 1 January 1846

VENTER, J, Postmaster at Tafelberg, 1 December 1875

VENTER, PJ, Postmaster and field-cornet at Vlekpoort, 25 October 1858

VERSCHUUR, Johannes Thomas, Clerk, Postal Department, GPO, Cape Town, February 1889
> Moved to othe administrative positions in the Colonial Service, rising to Resident Magistrate at Elliot, 26 August 1907

VERMAAK, SJ, Postmaster at Moordenaar's Kraal, 11 November 1856

VERMEULEN, CF, Postmaster and field-cornet at Groot Doorn Pan, 1 January 1864, service provided for free in 1867-71

VERMOOTEN, D, Postmaster Venterstad, before 1879
> Postmaster at Burghersdorp, 1879, possibly acting
> Postmaster at Venterstad, 1 October 1881
> Postmaster at Ventersburg, 1883

VERNON, H, Postmaster at Hooge Kraal, in about 1878

VERSCHUUR, W, Postmaster at Calitzdorp, 1 June 1874
> Postmaster at Calitzdorp, 1 June 1877

VERSVELD, M, Postmaster at Platteklip, 8 May 1854, service provided for free

VERSFELD, M, Postmaster at Storm's Vlei, 1 January 1875, service provided for free in 1875-78

VERSVELD, M, Postmaster at Barrydale, 1 July 1890

VERSFELD, WF, Sorter, GPO, Cape Town, 20 April 1854
> Clerk, third class, GPO, Cape Town, 1 January 1856

VERSTER, Mr, Postmaster at Zoute Kloof, in about 1864

VERZYL, A, Postmaster at Malagas, 1 March 1874

VICARY, J, Postmaster at Westford, 1 October 1868

VICE, Miss A, Postmaster at Emjanyana, 1 October 1898

VICE, George, Postmaster at Paarden Kraal, 1 August 1871
    Postmaster at Molteno, 1 January 1877

    George Vice was born in Grahamstown in 1830, the youngest son of John and Elizabeth Vice, who had emigrated to South Africa in 1820. After serving in the colonial militia during the frontier war of 1850-53, Vice joined Cawood Brothers, a firm of general dealers based in Cradock. In 1856 his job took him to Cyphergat where, for a time, he ran the local trading store. Carboniferous deposits had been discovered in the region in 1856, and Vice spent most of his spare time prospecting for the mineral. As a result, in 1865 he purchased the farm Paarden Kraal from Hendrik Willem Lategaan, and began mining operations. Because of a shortage of local labour, Vice sponsored the immigration of miners from Wales and Scotland, housing them in a hostel near the coal pits. Within a short time the community began to expand, and soon included a wool-washery, a mill, a smithy, a grocery store and, from 1 August 1871, a post office with Vice as its first postmaster. Given the above, it appears likely that it was opened to meet the needs of the growing mining community at Paarden Kraal, and that it was run either from the local general store, or from the offices of the Great Stormberg Coal Mining Company. The mining settlement also began to provide the local farming community with a ready market for its produce, and it was understandable, therefore, that in 1873 its representatives should petition Vice to also include, on their behalf, a *nachtmaal plek* on the site. As a result Vice had a formal residential village laid out on Paarden Kraal, and in May 1874 the first erven were sold on auction. The new village was named in honour of John Molteno, who became the first Premier of the Cape in 1872, and who Vice had met during the frontier war of 1850-3. The village plan made provision for the erection of a number of churches, and although Vice was a Methodist, he made sizeable grants to the Dutch Reformed Church which, under the leadership of its pastor, the Rev AJ Peplar, became a dominant force in the community. George Vice died at Molteno on 26 April 1917 (Meintjies 1980).

VICE, S, Postmaster at Middledrift, 1 January 1867, service provided for free in 1867-73

VIGNE, H, Postmaster at Zandfontein, 1 April 1878

VILJOEN, CF, Postmaster at Avontuur, 1 January 1895
    Postmaster at Klaarstroom, 1 April 1895

VILJOEN, DH, Postmaster at Britstown, 1 May 1885

VILJOEN, Daniel Johannes, Postmaster at Springbokfontein, 1 August 1902
    Postmaster at Garies, 1 April 1903

VILJOEN, Mrs Margaretha, Postmaster at Serjeant's River, 1 January 1860

VILLET, CM, Postmaster at Humansdorp, 1 October 1870

VIRGIN, D, Postmaster at Hankey, 1 November 1894

VISSER, J, Postmaster at Gordonfontein, June 1862

VISSER, P, Postmaster at Philadelphia, 5 February 1864

VOGES, GJ, Postmaster at Carnarvon, 1 November 1888

VOGES, W, Postmaster at Groot Drakenstein, 1 November 1903

VOIGT, FCM, Postmaster and field-cornet at French Hoek, 16 December 1852
VOIGT, FC, Postmaster at French Hoek, in about 1875
VOLKWYN, DW, Letter carrier, GPO, Cape Town, 1 August 1873
VON BEULWITZ, Mrs S, Postmaster at Steinkopf, 1 March 1904
VON BEUTWITZ, E, Postmaster at O'Oboop, 1 January 1878
VON BLOMMESTEIN, Christiaan Abraham, also given as VAN BLOMMESTEIN
    Postmaster at Carnarvon, 1 February 1889
    Postmaster at Matatiele, 1 February 1892
    Postmaster at Prieska, 1 August 1896
    Postmaster at Fraserburg, 1 November 1905
    Postmaster at Piquetberg, 1 March 1909, salary £245 pa
VON BRESSENDORFF, A, Postmaster at Kimberley, 1881
VON CURSINGER, J, Postmaster at Potsdam, 1 July 1862
VON GERARD, H, Resident Magistrate and postmaster at Walfish Bay, 1910
VON HIRSCHBERG, C, Postmaster at Jamestown, 1 February 1888
VON HIRSCHBERG, W, Postmaster at Herschel, 1 April 1886
VON LILIENSTEIN, A, Postmaster at Berlin Station, 18 July 1864
VON SCHLICHT, Miss E, Postmaster at Grabouw, 1 October 1898
VON SCHLICHT, E, Postmaster at Somerset Strand, 1 December 1875
VORSTER, J, Postmaster at Aberdeen, Division of Aberdeen, in about 1870
VOS, Miss Dora, Postmaster at Tulbagh, 25 September 1877. The Telegraph Department Circular of September 1882 recorded that *"Miss Dora Vos ... was married at Tulbagh Village on the 10th ultimo to Mr John Adams. We have the strongest objections to our officials being enticed away in this manner, but as the lady was determined to leave us, and as the gentleman is a trifle over six feet, we were compelled to waive them in this case"*
VOS, GG, Postmaster at Beaufort West, 10 October 1823
VOS, Miss L, Postmaster at Tulbagh, 1 October 1882
VOS, NG, Postmaster at Ceres, 7 March 1857
VOS, PP, Postmaster at Beaufort West, 6 August 1824
VOS, RD, Postmaster at Campbell, 1 July 1891
VOSKULE, Julius, Postmaster at Katkop, 15 October 1875
    Postmaster at Kenhardt, 1 November 1886
VOWLES, C, Postmaster and station master at Cambridge, 15 September 1879

W
WADLEY, Walter David, Postmaster at Queen Street, Port Elizabeth, 1 October 1908
WAGENAAR, H, Postmaster at Spring Valley, 1 June 1903
WAGNER, A, Postmaster at Elim, 1881
WAGNER, HH, Postmaster at Helderberg, 6 June 1877
WAGNER, JE, Postmaster at Zuurpoort, Murraysburg, 1 July 1871, service provided for free

WAHL, JC, Clerk, second class, GPO, Cape Town, 22 June 1837

WAITES, GC, Postmaster at Plettenberg's Bay, 3 May 1886

WAKEFORD, BK, Postmaster at Cuylerville, 1 January 1862, deceased while in office

WAKEFORD, J, Postmaster at Lesseyton, 1 July 1871

WAKEFORD, G, Postmaster at Niekerk's Rush, 1881

WALCOTT, J, Postmaster at Malmesbury, 1 November 1845
   Clerk to the Civil Commissioner and postmaster at Piquetberg, 22 April 1848

WALE, AC, Head letter carrier, GPO, Cape Town, in about 1881

WALKER, Miss EY, also listed as ET, Postmaster at Mqanduli, 16 September 1897

WALKER, GF, Postmaster and assistant field-cornet at Steynsburg, 1 March 1879

WALKER, J, Letter carrier, third class, GPO, Cape Town, 9 January 1840

WALKER, J, Postmaster at Calvinia, 17 March 1861

WALKER, James, Clerk to the Civil Commissioner and postmaster at Colesberg, 1 January 1842

WALKER, Mrs LT, Postmaster at Hebron Station, 1883

WALKER, Margaret W, Postmaster at Calvinia, 1 July 1865

WALKER, WJ, Postmaster at Glen Lynden, 6 April 1899
   Postmaster at Lusikisiki, 1 March 1901
   ostmaster at West Bank, East London, 1 September 1902
   Acting postmaster at Lady Frere, 1 April 1903
   Postmaster at Lady Frere, 1 July 1903

WALLACE, AE, Postmaster at Norvals Pont, before 1904
   Postmaster at Springbokfontein, 1 February 1904

WALLER, John Henry, born in about 1856
   United Kingdom Telegraph Service, Southampton, 1872
   Cape Government Telegraphs, Fort Beaufort, 1879
   Clerk-in-Charge of Telegraphs, Fauresmith, OFS, 1881
   Clerk-in-Charge of Telegraphs, East London, 1883
   Clerk-in-Charge of Telegraphs, Grahamstown, 1885
   Postmaster at Beaconsfield, March 1886
   Postmaster at Beaufort West, 1 December 1888
   Postmaster and Chief Telegraph Clerk at East London, 1 April 1894
   Retired on pension in August 1908
   John Henry Waller was born in about 1856, and entered the British Post Office in Southampton in 1872. He emigrated to the Cape and joined the Cape Telegraph Service at Fort Beaufort in 1879. In 1881 he was promoted to clerk-in-charge of telegraphs at Fouriesberg, Orange Free State, which at that time was run by the Cape Post Office. He was then transferred to the telegraph offices at East London in 1883 and Grahamstown in 1885. Finally he served as postmaster at Beaconsfield in 1886 and Beaufort West in 1888 before returning to East London in 1894. He retired from the Service in about August 1908 (Bennett 1908)

WALSH, SE, Postmaster at Ugie, 1 November 1899

WALTER, Lewis Walter, Station master at Goudini Road, 1 July 1907, salary £235 pa

WALTERS, N, Postmaster at Riebeek Kasteel, 1 May 1874, service provided for free
Postmaster at Riebeek Kasteel, 1 October 1875, service provided for free
Postmaster at Riebeek Kasteel, 1 July 1876

WALTERS, SH, Postmaster at Vogel Vlei, Division of Tulbagh, 1 July 1855

WALTON, Miss Johanna C, Postmaster at Van Wyk's Vlei, 1 February 1899
Postmaster at Salt River, 1 August 1902, may not have taken office
Postmaster at Mill Street, Gardens, Cape Town, 1 August 1902
Postmaster at Hoetjes Bay, 1 May 1903
Assistant postmaster at Salt River, date of appointment not known
Despite its isolated location, Republican forces appear to have conceived an irrational antipathy towards the post office at Van Wyk's Vlei, and during the course of the South African War they sacked it on three separate occasions. On 13 March 1900 a group of about 20 Republican sympathizers entered Van Wyk's Vlei and demanded that its postmaster, Miss Johanna Walton, hand over the keys to her establishment. Much to their surprise, she not only refused to do so, but also stood her ground, taunting them with the words "*Shoot, coward, and kill me.*" Despite her bold action, she was forcibly removed from the premises, and her telegraph equipment was stolen. On 12 February 1901 Republican forces, probably under General Barry Hertzog, entered Van Wyk's Vlei and ransacked the post office, inflicting extensive damage upon its premises. On 28 August 1901 Republican commandos looted the post office for a third time and, obviously tiring of this repetitious ritual, for good measure they also burnt down the post office building as well as the village's public offices. In her efforts to safeguard government property, the postmaster, Miss Johanna Walton, once again put up a courageous resistance to the enemy, but she was ultimately forced to abandon her post when fire began to engulf her premises (POC 240, 1 November 1901). Obviously mindful of the courage she had shown under fire, after the war the Cape Post Office seconded Walton to more convenient postings closer to Cape Town, where she continued to work until her retirement on pension in 1908. She may have died soon thereafter

WANCKEL, EAG, Postmaster at Middledrift, 1 September 1889

WANNENBURG, Alfred James, Postmaster at Bellville, 1 June 1894
Postmaster at Laingsburg, 1 February 1897
Postmaster at Somerset Strand, 1 March 1897
Postmaster at Sir Lowry Road, 1 October 1908

WANTENAAR, C, Postmaster and field-cornet at Porterville, 1 May 1867, removed from office

WARD, Mr, In Post Office Circular No 65 of 1 May 1887 the Postmaster General expressed "*his appreciation of the services rendered by Mr Ward, Lighthouse Keeper and Telegraphist at Cape Point, who, on several occasions, has removed faults from the line, re-planted poles, &c.*" This may have been Arthur Thomas Ward who was listed by the Civil Service List of 1910 as a Clerk 2nd Class, Imperial Service, in the Cape Town Telegraph Branch

WARD, AF, Born in about 1853, postmaster at Willowmore, 1 March 1895

Postmaster at Aberdeen, Division of Aberdeen, 1 December 1896

Postmaster at Sterkstroom, 1 May 1899

Postmaster at West Bank, East London, 1 April 1903

Postmaster at Stutterheim, 1 April 1905

Postmaster at Kloof Street, Gardens, 1 October 1907

The Pension Lists of 30 November 1909 recorded that in 1910 Mr Ward, age 56, was retired on an annual pension of £137.9.8

WARD, S, Junior sorter, GPO, Cape Town, in about 1881

WARE, William Henry Norman, Station master at Fish River, 21 March 1909, salary £205 pa

WARREN, Mr, Assistant to the Resident Magistrate, Griqualand East, 1880

On 23 October 1880 the amaMpondomise, under the leadership of their Chief Umhlonhlo, rose in protest against the annexation of their lands to the Cape Colony. At the time the Resident Magistrate, Mr Hamilton Hope, was travelling to Maclear together with his assistants Messrs Hendley and Warren as well as his clerk, Mr AE Davies. Near the Sulenkama mission station the group was ambushed by a party of Mpondomise and, with the exception of Davies, who was the postmaster at Qumbu as well as the brother of the Wesleyan Missionary to Chief Umhlonhlo, all were killed

WARREN, JH, Postmaster at Cedarville, 20 April 1896

WARREN, JW, Postmaster at Warrenton, 1 August 1889

Postmaster at Porterville Road, 1 October 1891

GPO, Cape Town, probable date 1 May 1892

Postmaster at O'Okiep, 1 October 1894

Postmaster at Riversdale, 1 April 1897

Postmaster at Green Point, Cape Town, 1 September 1900

WARREN, Miss M, Postmaster at Cedarville, 1 July 1902

WARREN, Miss MM, Postmaster at Cedarville, 1 October 1899

WARREN, TH, The post office at Nelson's, Ward 1 in the Division of East London, was opened on 1 February 1878 with Mr JB Nelson as its postmaster. On 5 December 1882 the Cape Government Gazette recorded that a postal establishment had been opened at Warrendale to replace the one at Nelson's, Ward 1, with Mr TH Warren as its postal agent. In both these instances the post office was probably a farm agency located in a trading store, and was run by its owner as a service to his clientele. It is interesting to note, however, the ease during the colonial era with which private individuals could seemingly ventilate their egos by having a post office named after them. Other notable examples include Cadle's Hotel, Thompson's Farm and Smith's Mine, to mention but a few

WARRINGTON, James. James Warrington was the son of an American sailor who settled in the Cape following the Anglo-American War of 1812. He worked as a fisherman along the southern Cape coast, but eventually settled in Herries Bay where he met and married Elizabeth Henn. In 1857 the extended Henn and Warrington families migrated to a new fishing spot some 11km further east, and made their camp on the farm Rietfontein, where good drinking water was available from a strong-flowing spring. Although a village had been proclaimed there some time previously, it was as yet uninhabited, and the first houses to be built there were erected by the Henns and the Warringtons. However, as news of its good fishing spread, so then more families were attracted to the settlement. The site was probably given the name of Hermanuspetrusfontein by the Henn children, who knew that Hermanus Pieters, a local shepherd and itinerant teacher, often camped at the spring with his flocks (Tredgold 1986). Its name was contracted to Hermanus in August 1902. In about 1868 Warrington opened a small store attached to his home, and when a post office was opened there in 1881, he became its first postmaster. It seems probable that, for the next sixteen years, the postal affairs of the village were run from Warrington's store

WARWICK, E, Postmaster at Sutherland, 1 November 1893

WASSERFALL, JN, Postmaster at Klaarstroom, 11 March 1865

WATCHAM, H, Postmaster at Committees Drift, 1 September 1878

WATSON, A, Postmaster at Caledon, 1 March 1846

WATSON, AW, Postmaster at Seymour, 1 September 1903

Postmaster at Upington, 1 May 1904

Postmaster at Port Alfred, 1 November 1906

Controller of Mails, Johannesburg, date of appointment not known

WATSON, Mrs Elizabeth, Postmaster at Breakfast Vlei, 1 October 1862

WATSON, Emily, Postmaster at Breakfast Vlei, 12 July 1865

WATSON, Henry Macrae, was appointed President of sorters, at the GPO in Cape Town on 25 February 1853. By all accounts he was a popular personality who had been credited with the introduction of a number of important innovations in the postal system, and when Edward Cook, the recently-appointed postmaster of Port Elizabeth, died prematurely in November 1858, Henry Watson was appointed as his successor. Port Elizabeth was an important position for, at that time, it was the Cape's second-largest settlement, and within ten years would become its busiest point of access into the southern African interior. It was imperative, therefore, that its postal affairs be placed upon a sound professional footing. Watson was seemingly a good choice for the position, but before taking up his new posting, the GPO gave him a brief holiday during which he suddenly died

WATSON, JJ, Sorter, GPO, Cape Town, 28 January 1857

Clerk, sixth class, GPO, Cape Town, 1858

Clerk, fourth class, GPO, Cape Town, 1863

Moved to Prince Albert in 1864

Mr Watson does not appear to have been entirely dedicated to his work at the Post Office and was mentioned a number of times by witnesses giving evidence before a "*Committee on the Petition of the Postmater-General,*" which sat in July 1865. At one stage Mr JJ leSueur, Chief Clerk to the Postmaster-General, pointed out to the Committee that "*Mr Watson was very frequently absent, and that the department was left almost entirely up to boys and sorters.*" His move to Prince Albert in 1864 was listed in the Civil Establishment Listings as a "*promotion,*" but this should be interpreted quite liberally

WATSON, Ms M, Postmaster at Breakfast Vlei, 1 August 1878

WATSON, Thomas, Postmaster at Claremont Station, 15 July 1846. Initially the post office at Claremont was located at the home of its first postmaster, Mr Harris. After his resignation, on or about 15 July 1846, its establishment was transferred to the house of his successor, Mr Thomas Watson. He only remained in office until 1848 and, within the short period of five years, was succeeded in rapid succession by no less than five officials

WATT, GJ, Postmaster at Orange River, before 1903
   Postmaster at Griquatown, 1 April 1903
   Postmaster at Barkly West, 1 July 1904
   Postmaster at Windsorton, 1 February 1906

WATT, J, Postmaster at Venterstad, 1 September 1876

WATT, Mary, Postmaster at Venterstad, 1 April 1878

WATTS, C, Postmaster and station master at Salt River, 1 September 1868
   Postmaster at Salt River, 1 July 1877
   Postmaster at Mowbray Station, 1881

WATTS, CH, Station master at Lyndoch, 1 July 1897, salary £235 pa

WATTS, OP, Postmaster at Middelburg, 1881
   Postmaster at Middelburg, 1883

WATTS, PB, Postmaster at Griquatown, 1 June 1902
   Postmaster at Kuruman, 1 November 1903
   Postmaster at Darling, 1 March 1904
   Postmaster at Porterville, 1 April 1904

WATTS, PR, Postmaster at Tarkastad, 10 April 1883

WAYT, Arthur Edward, Station master at Alicedale Junction, 30 June 1908, salary £355 pa

WEARN, G, Postmaster at Bellville, 6 May 1898

WEBB, E, Postmaster at and field-cornet Fort Wiltshire, 4 December 1862, service provided free

WEBB, J, Postmaster and field-cornet at Farm 211, in 1868, service provided for free

WEBB, J, Office messenger, GPO, Cape Town, 15 May 1877

WEBB, Oliver P, Postmaster at Cala, 1 February 1887

WEBB, OR, Junior assistant, fifth class, Cala, 1 May 1896
   Postmaster at Mount Fletcher, 1 July 1899

WEBB, RG, also listed as RP, Acting postmaster at Ndabakazi, 1 March 1898
   Postmaster at Willowvale, 1 September 1898

WEBB, W, Postmaster at Trumpeter's Drift, 1 September 1897

WEBBER, B, Postmaster at Glen Lynden, 1 December 1874

WEBBER, BWM, Postmaster at Glen Lynden, 1 January 1878

WEBBER, Edmund Arthur, Station master at Dassie Deur 17 February 1909, salary £226 pa

WEBBER, G, Postmaster at Witteklip, 23 February 1856

WEBBER, HB, Postmaster at Poplar Grove, 1 July 1907

WEBBER, O, Postmaster at Salem, 1 April 1889
    Postmaster at Hankey, 1 August 1892
WEBBER, PS, Postmaster at Poplar Grove, 1 January 1909
WEBSTER, AB, Postmaster at Cookhouse Station, 1880
WEBSTER, AC, Postmaster at Dordrecht, 30 May 1861
WEBSTER, Albert James, Postmaster at Daniel's Kuil, 1 January 1904
    Postmaster at Draghoender, 1 June 1904
    Postmaster at Smith's Mine, 1 May 1905
    Postmaster at Orange River, 1 October 1906
WEBSTER, John, born in about 1854, Telegraphist at Aliwal North, 1871
    Postmaster at Aliwal North, 1 May 1885
    The Pension Lists of 30 November 1909 recorded that in 1910 Mr Webster, age 55, was retired on an annual pension of £310
WEBSTER, John. The Zuurberg Inn was a wayside establishment run by the Webster family located on top of the Zuurberg Pass. On 17 May 1859 its owner, John Webster, was appointed postmaster at Zuurberg, and until he retired in February 1874, received no remuneration for this work. The village was sometimes also referred to as "*Webster's, Zuurberg*", although in about 1896 it was renamed Ann's Villa, in honour of his wife, Ann Webster
WEBSTER, S, Postmaster at Ann's Villa, 1 March 1874
    Postmaster at Ann's Villa, 1881
WEBSTER, Samuel Henry, Postmaster at Glen Lynden, 1 March 1901
    Postmaster at Riebeek East, 1 June 1908
WEBSTER, Samuel Wilmot, Station master at Tarkastad, 10 May 1904, salary £198 pa
WEDDERBURN, Miss RW, Postmaster at Mqanduli, 12 March 1903
WEDDERBURN, WRW, born in about 1851
    Postmaster at Kokstad, 1 August 1887
    The Pension Lists of 30 November 1909 recorded that in 1910 Mr Wedderburn, age 58, was retired on an annual pension of £232.16.8
WEGE, D, Postmaster at Fransche Kraal, 1 February 1865, service provided for free
WEHMEYER, BM, Postmaster at WolveKraal, 12 August 1836
WEHMEYER, GWB, Postmaster at WolveKraal, 30 May 1850
WEHMEYER, MJ, Postmaster and field-cornet at WolveKraal, 1 December 1859
WEHMEYER, PH, Postmaster at WolveKraal, 12 March 1855
WEHNEKE, Anna J, Postmaster at Sir Lowry's Pass, 1 July 1867
WEHNEKE, JA, Postmaster at Sir Lowry's Pass, 10 May 1854
WEHNEKE, Sanna A, Postmaster at Sir Lowry's Pass, 1 April 1864, deceased while in office
WEICH, C, Postmaster at Komaggas, 1 July 1878
WEICH, F, Postmaster at Komaggas, 17 April 1862, service provided for free in 1862-63
WEICH, TSD, Postmaster at Upington, 1 September 1890
WEINRICH, Mrs F, Postmaster at Humansdorp, 1 January 1878

WEINRICH, JJ, Postmaster at Humansdorp, 1 March 1868
   Postmaster at Humansdorp, 1 October 1878
WEIR, JG, Postmaster at Rhodes, 1 October 1907, retired in 1909
WEISS, C, Postmaster at Oatlands, 1880
WEISS, CHM, Postmaster at Barroe, 1882
WELCH, CB, Postmaster and Chief Constable at Steynsburg, 1 July 1877
   When the Chief Constable for Steynsburg, Mr CB Welch, resigned from his additional duties as postmaster on 1 September 1877, Mr Henden, Resident Magistrate at Steytlerville, wrote to the Postmaster General in Cape Town suggesting that the postal affairs of the village be put on a more professional standing. The need for such a move became more evident after 1886 when the post office at Steynsburg was raised to the status of a Head Office in the Midland Administrative District
WELDON, J, Postmaster at Leeuwenbosch, 9 August 1856, previously acting
WELGEMOED, DJ, Postmaster and field-cornet at Tarka South, 25 October 1858
WELLS, HH, Postmaster at Lady Frere, 1 June 1885
WELSH, AR, Postmaster at Glen Lynden, 16 February 1856
WENTZEL, H, Additional clerk, GPO, Cape Town, 2 January 1849.
WENTZEL, WA Jnr, Deputy Sheriff, Secretary of the Divisional Council and postmaster at Middelburg, 9 December 1858. In 1869 Mr Wentzel was reported to have absconded from his duties
WENTZEL, WC, Postmaster at Klein Berg River, 1 June 1876, service provided for free
WEPENER, JL, Postmaster at Klipspruit Nek, 10 May 1858
WERNBERG, WAO, Postmaster at Fraserburg, 1 February 1889
   Postmaster at Fraserburg Road, 1 February 1891
   Postmaster at Muizenberg, 1 December 1895
   Postmaster at Muizenberg, date not known, probable reappointment
   The Pension Lists of 30 November 1909 recorded that in 1910 Mr Wernberg, age 53, was retired on an annual pension of £118.7.0.
WERNER, CG, Postmaster at Zuurpoort, Waschbank, 10 February 1858
WERNER, WA, Postmaster at Riet Vlei, Uitenhage, 1 April 1872, service provided for free
WESSHHEIZER, HVD, Postmaster at Hondeklip Bay, 1881
WEST, Alfred William, Postmaster at Rosmead, 16 December 1899
   Postmaster at Newlands, Cape Town, 1 October 1902
   Postmaster at Bree Street, Cape Town, 1909
WEST, G, Postmaster at Genadendal, 1 May 1894
WEST, Mrs M, Postmaster at Genadendal, 16 July 1890
WEST, Robert, Station master at Coega, 20 September 1909, salary £215 pa
WESTAWAY, Lewis William, Postmaster at Stal Street, Cape Town, 1 January 1906
   Postmaster at Hanover Street, Cape Town, 1 June 1910
WETHMAN, PW, Postmaster at Malmesbury, 26 June 1866

WHEELER, F, also listed as H, Postmaster at Kenilworth, Kimberley, 1 December 1897
    Postmaster at Koopmansfontein, 1 January 1901
    Postmaster at Delport's Hope, 1 March 1901
    Acting postmaster at Barkly West, 1 February 1902
    Postmaster at Schmidt's Drift, 1 August 1902
    Postmaster at Steytlerville, 1 December 1903

WHILEY, WD, Postmaster at Steynsburg, 1 June 1869, service provided for free
    On 18 May 1869 Mr WD Whiley was appointed postmaster at Groote Vlei, and two weeks later, on 1 June, the doors of his establishment were opened for business. The post office was located on the farm Groote Vlei, and was probably a farm agency which operated out of a small trading store. The village of Groote Vlei was established on the site in 1872, and in 1873 it was renamed Steynsburg in honour of Douw Gerbrandt Steyn, grandfather of President Paul Kruger (Raper 1987)

WHILEY, E, Postmaster at Katberg, 1 April 1865

WHILEY, Edwin, Postmaster at Faure Siding, 22 May 1854

WHITAKER, JH, Assistant Postmaster at Queenstown, date not available
    The Pension Lists of 30 November 1909 recorded that in 1910 Mr Whitaker, age 33, was retired on an annual pension of £56.2.1

WHITAKER, PH, Postmaster at Richmond Hill, 1 August 1907

WHITBURN, Miss A, Postmaster at Knysna, 1 December 1876

WHITBURN, M, Postmaster at Knysna, 1 March 1870

WHITE, C, Postmaster at Kubusie, 1881
    Postmaster at Tylden, 20 May 1889
    Postmaster at Tylden, 1 November 1891

WHITE, Thomas, Postmaster at Robertson, 1 July 1882
    Postmaster at Mafeking, 13 July 1900
    Postmaster at Mowbray, 1 January 1901
    Postmaster at Rondebosch, 1 February 1902
    Postmaster at Kuruman, 1 July 1905
    Postmaster at Balfour, 1907

WHITE, Victor Thomas Henry, Postmaster at Rhodes, 1 October 1909

WHITEHEAD, GJC, Postmaster at Libodi, 1 October 1898

WHITEHEAD, W, Postmaster at Campbell, 1881

WHITEHORN, H, Postmaster at Market Square, Grahamstown, 1880

WHITTLE, Miss A, Postmaster at Balfour, 1 March 1897
    Postmaster at Whittlesea, 1 February 1901

WHITTLE, Miss D, Postmaster at Riebeek East, 1 June 1903

WHYTE, Andrew, Postmaster at Farm No 13, on 1 March 1866

WHYTE, John William, Postmaster at Griquatown, 1 March 1899
    Postmaster at Dordrecht, 1 February 1903

WIBLIN, H, Postmaster at Redhouse, 1880

WIDDAS, Walter, Postmaster at Mill Street, Gardens, Cape Town, 1 December 1902
    Postmaster at Sea Point, Cape Town, 1 June 1903
    Postmaster at Somerset West, 1 August 1908

WIEGMAN, HP, Postmaster at Paarl, 6 December 1858

WIEGMAN, LFW, Postmaster at Paarl, 1 June 1865

WIESE, JJ, Postmaster and field-cornet at Kruisman's Rivier, 27 April 1867, service provided free

WIESE, Tobias Johannes, Postmaster at Longlands, 1 August 1906

WIGGETT, AC, Postmaster at Laingsburg, 1 July 1891
    Postmaster at Klipdam, 1 November 1892
    Postmaster at Kei Road, 1 November 1894

WIGGETT, S, Postmaster at Wynand's River, 22 July 1867, service provided for free

WIGGILL, Alfred Garnett, Postmaster at Bolotwa, 1 November 1906

WIGGINS, ER, Postmaster at Halfmanshof, 1883

WIGGINS, F, Postmaster at Halfmanshof, 1 July 1897

WIGGINS, HO, Postmaster at Halfmanshof, 1 July 1875

WIGGINS, JP, Postmaster at Koopman's Rivier, 27 January 1852

WIGGLE, TM, Postmaster at Farm No 101, in July 1862

WIGHTMAN, H, Postmaster at Steinkopf, 1 October 1906

WILBRAHAM, Harry Walter, Postmaster at Idutywa, 1 February 1906. Salary £265 pa

WILCOX, G, Letter carrier, GPO, Cape Town, 26 May 1860

WILCOX, G, Postmaster at Klein Berg River, 1 March 1875, service provided for free

WILKIE, DC, Born in about 1868, postmaster at Woodstock Station, 1 January 1903
    Postmaster at Kenilworth, Cape Town, 1 May 1905

WILKENS, Cyril Frank, Postmaster at Moorreesburg, 1 March 1906
    Postmaster at Vredenburg, 1 August 1907
    Postmaster at De Doorns, 1 January 1909

WILKIE, DC, Postmaster at Kenilworth, date not available
    The Pension Lists of 30 November 1909 recorded that in 1910 Mr Wilkie, age 41, was retired on an annual pension of £131.11.3

WILKINS, EW, Postmaster at St Marks, 1 January 1902

WILKINS, JH, Postmaster at Breede River Station, 1880

WILKINS, William Joseph, Station master at Moorreesburg, 1 November 1902, salary £214 pa

WILKINS, WJW, Postmaster and station master at Mulder's Vlei, 1 January 1879
    Postmaster at Constable, 1881
    Postmaster at Grootfontein, 1883
    Postmaster at Commadagga, 1 October 1892

WILKINSON, Robert Watson, Postmaster at Mowbray, 16 July 1898
    Postmaster at Rondebosch, 1 January 1901
    Postmaster at Middelburg, 1906

WILLCOX, G, Postmaster at Somerset Road, 30 May 1862

WILLETT, Mrs, Postmaster at Willowmore, 1882

WILLETT, J, Postmaster at Murraysburg, 5 December 1857
  Postmaster at Zuurpoort, Division of Murraysburg, 20 July 1866, service provided for free

WILLIAMS, A, Postmaster at Mlengana, 16 September 1896

WILLIAMS, C, Letter carrier, GPO, Cape Town, 25 June 1876

WILLIAMS, EV, Postmaster at Gong Gong, 1881

WILLIAMS, G, Postmaster at Papkuil, 1 November 1898

WILLIAMS, GH, Postmaster at Campbell, 1902, in office through to Union

WILLIAMS, George Hoefler, Born in about 1854, postmaster at Umzimkulu, 1 October 1883
  Postmaster at Tarkastad, 1 April 1896
  The Pension Lists of 30 November 1909 recorded that in 1910 Mr Williams, age 55, was retired on an annual pension of £250

WILLIAMS, H, Assistant Postmaster at Kimberley, date not available
  The Pension Lists of 30 November 1909 recorded that in 1910 Mr Williams, age 45, was retired on an annual pension of £148.6.6

WILLIAMS, H, Postmaster at Maitland, 1906
  Postmaster at Mowbray, 1 August 1908

WILLIAMS, James Henry William, Imperial Telegraph Service at Birmingham, 1878
  Telegraphist at Fort Beaufort, 27 February 1889
  Telegraphist at King William's Town, 1 December 1892
  Telegraphist at Port Elizabeth, 1 October 1892
  Telegraphist at the Central Telegraph Office, Cape Town, 1 March 1894
  Assistant Superintendent, 1 July 1900
  Superintendent, Instrument Room, 1 August 1902
  Acting Postmaster at Grahamstown, 1 July 1908, postmaster 1 August 1908
  Postmaster at Kimberley, 1 October 1909
  Saw active service with the Cape Town Highlanders during the South African War of 1899-1902. Subsequently raised and commanded the Somerset Strand Town Guard and a local troop of the Western Province Mounted Rifles with the rank of Lieutenant. He was decorated for these efforts

WILLIAMS, J, Postmaster at Willowmore, 20 February 1874
  Postmaster at Salt River, 1883

WILLIAMS, WFG, Postmaster at Herschel, 1 October 1908

WILLIAMS, WJ, Station master at Klipplaat, 27 September 1909, salary £259 pa

WILLIE, F, Station master at Carnarvon 1 June 1908, salary £335 pa

WILLIE, Frank, Station master at Beaufort West, 1 June 1908, salary £335 pa

WILLIS, I, Clerk, sixth class, GPO, Cape Town, date of appointment not known
  Clerk, fifth class, GPO, Cape Town, 3 December 1864, dismissed in 1866

WILLIS, J, Postmaster at Touws River, 1881. For further details see also under GC Geyer, station master at Montagu Road and Touws River.

WILLIS, JE, Postmaster at Hanover, 12 December 1882
  Postmaster at Stellenbosch, 1 April 1890
WILLMAN, H, Postmaster at Nelspoort, 7 March 1857
  Postmaster at Klaarstroom, 31 July 1858
WILLMER, H, Postmaster at Mount Fletcher, 23 July 1897
  Postmaster at Seymour, 1 March 1899
  Acting postmaster at Sir Lowry Road, 1 April 1903
  Postmaster at Sir Lowry Road, 1 June 1903
  Postmaster at Green Point, Cape Town, 1 September 1903
WILLS, G, Postmaster and station master at Matjesfontein, Division of Worcester, 1 Dec 1879
WILLS, GA, Postmaster at Matatiele, 1 July 1891
WILLS, W, Postmaster at Mill Street, Gardens, Cape Town, 1 October 1889
WILMER, HC, Postmaster at Walfish Bay, 1881
WILMOT, Alex, Clerk, fifth class, GPO, Cape Town, 28 September 1854
  Clerk, fourth class, GPO, Cape Town, 1855
WILMOT, Alexander, was born in Edinburgh on 9 April 1836 and was educated at the Universities of Edinburgh and Glasgow. He immigrated to the Cape in 1853 and in 1860 married Alice Mary Slater, who bore him six sons and seven daughters. He initially joined the Civil Service as Clerk to the Civil Commissioner, but on 28 September 1854 he was transferred to the GPO in Cape Town as Clerk, fifth class. The following year he was promoted to Clerk, fourth class, and on 4 March 1859 he was appointed acting postmaster at Port Elizabeth. He was confirmed in this position the following year, at a salary of £260, plus accommodation and commission on the sale of postage stamps, and filled the post until his retirement in 1886. From 1889 to 1910 he represented the South-Eastern Districts in the Cape Legislature. In addition he gained prominence in a number of other fields, being active as a layman in the Catholic Church, President of the Temperance Society, a Fellow of the Royal Geographical Society, and a prolific writer and amateur historian who collaborated with GM Theal. He gained a number of honours, including the titles of "*the Honorable,*" Honorary Chamberlain to the Pope, Papal Count, Knight of the Holy Sepulchre, and Knight of St Gregory. His name appears on the Civil Service Pension List of 30 November 1909, where it is recorded that in 1910 he was receiving an annual pension of £400. He died in Cape Town on 3 April 1923. The post office of Springvale was located on a farm of the same name owned by the Wilmot family
WILMOT, Cuthbert William Windsor, Postmaster at Glen Lynden, 1 February 1907
WILMOT, H, Postmaster at Phisantfontein, 1 July 1873, service provided for free
WILMOT, HGS, Postmaster at Phisantfontein, 1 July 1876
WILMOT, JC, Postmaster at Bathurst, 1 October 1833. JC Wilmot may have been the Joseph Wilmot who sailed to the Cape in 1820 on the Aurora
WILMOT, JR, Postmaster and field-cornet at Lower Riebeek, 29 September 1859, service provided for free in 1859-73

WILMS, Mrs F, Postmaster at Longlands, 1 March 1906

WILSON, Alfred Lorentz Frederick, Postmaster at Upington, 23 July 1897
    Postmaster at Philipstown, 1 February 1899
    Postmaster at Hanover, 1 August 1903
    Postmaster at Matjesfontein, Division of Worcester, 1 October 1903

WILSON, D, Postmaster and station master at Bellville, 13 February 1874
    Postmaster and station master at Malmesbury Station, 1 November 1877
    Postmaster and station master at Beaufort West Station, 1880
    Postmaster at Tsolo, 1 April 1895
    Postmaster at Seymour, 1 December 1895
    Postmaster at Indwe, 1 August 1897

WILSON, Jeremiah, Imperial Telegraph Service, Newcastle-on-Tyne, 22 May 1876
    Telegraphist at Beaufort West, 2 December 1880
    Telegraphist at Fort Beaufort, 1 March 1882
    Telegraphist at Port Elizabeth, 1 May 1883
    Chief Counter Clark, CTO, Cape Town, 10 September 1886
    Principal Clerk, Foreign Mails Branch, 1 July 1893
    Chief Clark, GPO, Cape Town, 7 February 1898
    Special assignment to England with PMG, 1899
    Secretary, GPO, Cape Town, 1 February 1908

WILSON, John, Postmaster at Bolotwa, 11 June 1872

WILSON, J, Postmaster at Plettenberg's Bay, 1 January 1864

WILSON, JA, Letter carrier, GPO, Cape Town, 1 August 1873, deceased while in office in 1874

WILSON, JA, Postmaster and station master at Observatory Road, 6 December 1875

WILSON, JE, Postmaster at Brandewyn's Kuil, 1881

WILSON, R, Postmaster at Sefantjies Poort, 7 July 1862, service provided for free in 1867

WILSON, Thomas George, Postmaster at Mount Fletcher, 1 July 1904

WILSON, Thomas Weir, Station master at Fort Jackson, 17 October 1904, salary £201 pa

WILSON, WE, Postmaster at Orange River, 1 April 1905
    Postmaster at Smith's Mine, 1 October 1906
    Postmaster at Longlands, 1 April 1910

WILTER, JB, Letter carrier, third class, GPO, Cape Town, 3 August 1845

WILTERS, J, Letter carrier, GPO, Cape Town, 8 December 1874

WINDELL, JH, Postmaster at Balfour, 1 January 1867

WINDERS, E, Postmaster at Breakfast Vlei, 1 June 1861

WINFIELD, Henry, Postmaster at Hopefield, 1 June 1903
    Postmaster at Hopetown, 1 August 1903
    Postmaster at Willowmore, 1 August 1903

WINSLOE, Ernest Charles. See under PETERSEN, HD

WINT, Clement, Postmaster at De Rust, 1 June 1905

Postmaster at Upper Maitland, 1 November 1907

WINTERBACH, JC, Postmaster at Tulbagh, 1817

WINTERBACH, JC, Postmaster at Karroo Poort, 1 August 1873, service provided for free

WISE, G, Postmaster at Mount Stewart, 1883

WISEMAN, G, Postmaster at Philipstown, 1 August 1903. On 30 November 1909 his widow, E Wiseman, was receiving an annual pension of £14.12.0

WITTHUHN, WG, Postmaster at Bolotwa, 1 November 1909

WOCKE, F, Postmaster at Grabouw, 1880

WOEST, B, Postmaster at Upper Tyumie, 10 May 1858, service provided for free

WOEST, HC, Postmaster and field-cornet at Upper Tyumie, 11 Aug 1864, service provided free

WOISTER, Ms SJH, Postmaster at Clanwilliam, 1 July 1876

WOLFE, C Jnr, Clerk, third class, GPO, Cape Town, 1 July 1877

WOLFE, J, Postmaster at Upper Kloof Street, Cape Town, 1 April 1903

WOLHOUTER, JH, Postmaster at Klipdam, 1 December 1892

WOLLASTON, AR, Postmaster at Wagenaar's Kraal, 6 May 1852.
The post office at Van Der Walt's Poort was opened on 6 May 1852 in the, then, division of Beaufort (West). The 1853 Cape Almanac listed a post office called Wagenaar's Kraal (Van Der Walt's Poort), opened in the same division on 4 November 1853. It therefore seems probable that both names refer to the same establishment. This is believed to have been located on a farm in the district of Victoria West, which also served as a stopping-off point for mail-coaches travelling between Wellington and Kimberley

WOLLWARD, T, Letter carrier, GPO, Cape Town, in about 1881

WOOD, A, Postmaster at Kalk Bay, 18 August 1857, deceased while in office

WOOD, Joseph Charles, Postmaster at Balfour, 1 April 1905

WOOD, Miss Mary, see under MULLER, Mrs Mary

WOOD, RH, born in about 1852, Postmaster at Simonstown, 1 August 1881
The Pension Lists of 30 November 1909 recorded that in 1910 Mr Wood, age 57, was retired on an annual pension of £240

WOOD, Reginald William, Postmaster at Elliotdale, 1 March 1910

WOOD, T, Postmaster at Karroo Poort, 30 October 1866, service provided for free

WOOD, TU, Postmaster at King William's Town Station, 1880

WOODALL, Percival Edward, Postmaster at Middledrift, 1 January 1908

WOODEAN, W, Postmaster at Spectakel, 1 July 1866

WOODEN, F, Postmaster at Piquineer's Kloof, 24 June 1857

WOODING, F, Postmaster at New Kloof, 27 December 1858

WOODING, SG, Postmaster, jailer and police constable at Ceres, 1 January 1872

WOODS, RB, Postmaster at Karroo Poort, 30 December 1869, service provided for free

WOOLFREY, A, Assistant Postmaster at Queenstown, date not available
The Pension Lists of 30 November 1909 recorded that in 1910 Mr Woolfrey, age 56, was retired on an annual pension of £125.9.2

WORMINGTON, Mr, Postmaster at Klipplaat, 1 February 1879
WORRALL, RW, Temporary clerk, GPO, Cape Town, in about 1880
WORRALL, SJ, Postmaster at Maclear, 1 November 1890
WOSTENHOLM, JW, Postmaster at Whittlesea, 1 October 1889
WOSTENHOLM, Thomas William, Station master at Elliot 18 March 1905, salary £180 pa
WRANKMORE, Mrs AC, Postmaster at Paarl, 27 September 1816
WREYFORD, William John Edward, Postmaster at Van Wyk's Vlei, 1 June 1895
    Postmaster at Kenhardt, 1 February 1896
    Postmaster at Hutchinson, 15 January 1898
    Postmaster at Modder River, 1 September 1900
WRIGHT, Mr, Postmaster at Somerset East, 1854
WRIGHT, A, Postmaster at Dwingfontein, 1880
WRIGHT, Miss BL, Postmaster at Bowesdorp, 1 January 1907
WRIGHT, Mrs C, Postmaster at Kalk Bay, 1883
WRIGHT, J, Postmaster and station master at Kalabas Kraal, in about 1879
WRIGHT, JM, Postmaster at Kalabas Kraal, 1880
WRIGHT, JS, Boy sorter, GPO, Cape Town, in about 1880
WRIGHT, James S, Postmaster at Somerset East, 17 March 1856
WRIGHT, Joseph S, Postmaster at Somerset East, 22 September 1857, deceased while in office
WRIGHT, P, Postmaster at Achter Zuurberg, 1880
WRIGHT, S, Postmaster and station master at Tulbagh Road Station, 8 August 1879
WYLIE, J, Postmaster at Alfred Docks, Cape Town, 1 September 1884
WYTHUS, A, Postmaster at Eland's River, 1880

Y
YATES, John Edward, Station master at Queenstown, 18 September 1902, salary £325 pa
YEATES, J, Postmaster at Darling, 27 December 1896
YELL, Robert James, Postmaster at Trappes Valley, 16 January 1898
YELLING, W, Postmaster at Zwarte Koppen, 31 October 1859
YOUNG, Charlotte, Postmaster at Peddie, 2 June 1853
YOUNG, Edward William Austin, Postmaster at Hutchinson, 1 October 1896
    Postmaster at Prieska, 1 September 1900
    Postmaster at Prieska, 1 August 1903
YOUNG, GW, Postmaster at Glengarry, 1881
YOUNG, Miss HKC, Postmaster at Riebeek East, 1 January 1907
YOUNG, John, Letter carrier, GPO, Cape Town, 12 October 1853
YOUNG, John Mould, Clerk, GPO, Cape Town, 6 June 1893.
    Transferred to Clerk to the Resident Magistrate at Tsomo, 11 June 1893
YOUNG, W, Letter carrier, GPO, Cape Town, in about 1880
YOUNG, William Charles, Born in about 1867, postmaster at Windsorton, 1 March 1889

Postmaster at Windsorton, 1 October 1893

Acting postmaster at Philipstown, 1 June 1907

The Pension Lists of 30 November 1909 recorded that in 1910 Mr Young, age 42, was retired on an annual pension of £104.19.11

YOUNGMAN, WF, Letter carrier, GPO, Cape Town, 22 May 1855

Z

ZEEMAN, RJ, Letter carrier, GPO, Cape Town, May 1870

Acting stamper, GPO, Cape Town, 1873-1878

Sorter, GPO, Cape Town, 1 May 1879

Sorter, first class, GPO, Cape Town, 11 July 1881

Assistant Postmaster, GPO, Cape Town, date not available

The Pension Lists of 30 November 1909 recorded that in 1910 Mr RJ Zeeman, age 61, was retired on an annual pension of £127.11.0

ZEILER, JF, Postmaster and field-cornet at Bradford, 29 September 1858

ZIERVOGEL, CB, Postmaster at Cradock, in about 1821

ZIERVOGEL, CB, Clerk to the Civil Commissioner and postmaster at Graaff-Reinet, 1 March 1846

ZIERVOGEL, CE, Postmaster at Zoutpans Drift, 1 August 1872

ZIERVOGEL, JP, Postmaster at Pearston, 1 March 1868

ZIERVOGEL, ST, Postmaster at Somerset East, in about 1826

ZIETSMAN, JP, Postmaster and field-cornet at Gouritz River, 1 October 1877

ZINN, HA, Postmaster at Tulbagh, 29 August 1842

Postmaster at Tulbagh, 2 June 1853, suspended from duty

ZONDAG, M, Postmaster at Wolve Kraal, in about 1832

TWO

DIARY OF EARLY VISITORS TO THE CAPE
1530-1646

What follows is a diary of engraved stones left at the Cape during the era immediately prior to the establishment of a permanent settlement by the VOC in 1652. Only some of them are known to have served postal use Visits by ships that might have left stones behind, but of which there is no record, are also listed.

1530: The French vessels *Sacre* and *Pensee* dropped anchor in Table Bay before proceeding home. Unlikely as it sounds, they claim not to have landed, despite having seen people and cattle on the shore (Raven-Hart, 1967: 11).

1591, July 31: The English vessels *Penelope*, *Merchant Royall* and *Edward Bonaventure*, outward bound to Batavia, dropped anchor in Table Bay and traded for provisions with local inhabitants. Their log mistakenly identified their location as *Agoada de Saldanha*, an error that English mariners only began to rectify after 1624. No mention is made in the log of letters having been found or left behind.

1595, August 4: The Dutch vessels *Mauritius*, *Hollandia*, *Duijfken* and *Amsterdam*, outward bound, with at least 50 members of the crew ill with scurvy on one ship alone, dropped anchor in Table Bay and traded for provisions with local inhabitants. No mention was made of letters being either found or left behind.

1601, September 9: The English vessels *Dragon*, *Ascension* and *Susan*, outward bound, anchored in Table Bay. They set sail on 29 October, having lost 107 men to scurvy out of a total complement of 480. Upon their return in 1603 the *Ascension* and *Susan* were sent on ahead, and probably landed at the Cape in January 1603. Capt Hippon, Master of the *Susan*, left behind a batch of letters beneath a flat stone with the following inscription: "*ANTO HIPON MA OF THE HECTOR BOVN HOME JANVARI 1600*". Apart from the fact that the year given was obviously wrong, this is the first recorded use of a stone as a postal marker. The letters were probably intended for the *Dragon* who rounded the Cape on 3 February without making landfall.

1604, July 13: The English vessels *Red Dragon*, *Ascension*, *Hector* and *Susan*, outward bound, anchored in Table Bay, their crews greatly depleted by scurvy, and only set sail for Banten on 20 August 1604. When they departed the Indies in about September 1605 the *Hector* and *Susan* were sent on ahead of the others. The *Dragon* and *Ascension* followed on 6 October, but were soon separated, and on 19 December the *Dragon* caught up with the *Hector* just off the Cape. Through disease it had lost 53 men, and was now limping along with a crew of 14. As a result it had to be assisted into Table Bay by a skeleton crew from the *Dragon*. The Ascension joined them on 27 December, but the *Susan* was never heard of again. They set sail for home on 16 January 1607.

1607, July 16: The English vessel *Consent*, homeward bound, anchored in Table Bay, and, during her stay, her crew left behind a stone engraved with the words "THE FOURE AND TWEN-TIETH OF JULY, 1607, CAPTAIN DAVID MIDDLETON IN THE CONSENT". The *Consent* had been part of an expedition headed by William Keeling, which included the *Dragon* and *Hector*, but had left for home ahead of the others. The stone, which was intended to inform Keeling of its safe arrival at the Cape, was found in December 1607 when the main fleet put into Table Bay. Its discovery was noted by Keeling as follows:

"Then our generall with other sought amongst the stones for to see yf the consent hadd bene heer or not where at length wee found Capt David Middleton in the Consent the 29 July 1607 but no Letter to hee was determined to doe. Wee were all gladd to heare of his arryvall heer in salvetie ..." (Raven-Hart, 1967: 36). The account provided by William Keeling is probably the first recorded use of the word "*Cafares*" in regard to the Khoikhoi residents of Table Bay. The sense in which this noun was used is not known.

1607. December 17: The English vessels *Dragon* and *Hector*, homeward bound under the command of William Keeling, anchored in Table Bay. Before leaving they searched for the engraved stone left behind by Capt David Middleton in the *Consent* on 29 July 1607. This was found but without any letters beneath. Hippon, now Master of the *Dragon*, found the engraved stone he had used six years before, and left behind a batch of letters beneath it, adding the following inscription "ANT HIPON MA OF T-E DRAGON 28 DECEMBER 1607". They set sail on 1 January 1608.

1608, April 1: The Dutch vessel *Oranjie*, homeward bound under Capt Cornelis Matelief, dropped anchor in Table Bay. Shortly before leaving on 22 April, the crew visited Robben Island where they nailed a pewter plate to a whalebone engraved with the words "*Matelief landed twenty sheep her on April 19, 1608*" (Raven-Hart, 1967: 40). This was found by Jourdain's men in July 1608.

1608, July 14: The English vessels *Ascension* and *Union*, outward bound, dropped anchor in Table Bay. They found "*where the shipps that are bound outward or homeward doe use to sett their names, where we found the names of Captain Keeling, Captain Myddleton and divers others*". He also recorded that: "*We found near the watering place many English names of the year 1604 and also some of December 1607*". They set sail on 19 September 1608 (Raven-Hart, 1967: 41).

1609, 10 August: David Middleton arrived in Table Bay, and returned there, homeward bound on 24 July 1610, where he must have had sight of his brother's stone.

1609, December 22: The English vessels *Dragon* and *Hector* sailed into Table Bay homeward bound. The *Consent*, that had been part of the same expedition, had gone ahead before them. At anchor in the bay they found a Dutch ship already there. They purchased from the Dutch some livestock as well as a main topsail for the *Hector*, and together they set sail on 10 January 1610. The *Hector* also left behind a packet of letters *"as others had done before"* (Raven-Hart, 1967: 35).

1610, July 24: The English vessels *Trade's Increase*, *Peppercorn*, *Darling* and *Samuel*, outward bound, dropped anchor in Table Bay, finding three Dutch ships already at anchor. Sir Henry Middleton, captain of the *Trade's Increase*, found out *"the names of Captaine Keeling, and others bound home in January, 1609. And also my brother Davids name bound in August the ninth, 1609"* (Raven-Hart, 1967: 35). He also found a letter buried in the ground which, unfortunately, was so damaged by moisture as to be illegible. They set sail on 13 August.

1611, May 20: The English vessel *Globe*, homeward bound, dropped anchor in Table Bay and left a packet behind beneath an engraved stone. She set sail on 6 June.

1611, August: The English vessels *Clove*, *Hector* and *Thomas*, outward bound, dropped anchor in Table Bay. The crew visited Robben Island to look for any letters left behind.

1612, April 18: The English vessel *Pearl*, outward bound, anchored in Table Bay.

1612, June 8: The English vessels *Dragon*, *Hosiander*, *James* and *Solomon*, outward bound, anchored in Table Bay. The *Dragon* staggered into harbour, with about 50% of its crew down with scurvy. When they set sail on 28 June they left behind an engraved stone.

1613, April 26: The English vessel *Expedition*, outward bound, anchored in Saldanha Bay. Upon a visit to an island they found *"a carved boord"* by which they *"perceived the Hollanders had beene here"*. On 26 April they proceeded to Table Bay where, upon arrival on 28 April, they found the *Hector* and *Thomas*, as well as four other Dutch ships, all homeward bound. They were joined by the *Peppercorn* on 10 May. All set sail out of the bay on 15 May. The *Expedition* returned here on 20 March 1614 on her way home, and left behind an engraved stone.

1614, February 20. The English vessel *Dragon*, homeward bound from Batavia, anchored in Table Bay and left behind a batch of letters beneath an engraved stone. On 28 June 1614 they were discovered by William Edwards, who made a report to this effect to his directors in London.

1614, May 9: The English vessel *Concord*, outward bound, anchored in Table Bay, and left behind an engraved stone.

1614, June 14: The English vessels *New Year's Gift* (or *Gift*), *Hector*, *Merchant's Hope* (or *Hope*), and *Solomon*, outward bound, anchored in Table Bay. Upon their departure on 3 July they left behind a packet of letters beneath an engraved stone.. When they came ashore they discovered: *"engrauen vpon the stones the ariual of the Expedicon homwardes, March the 21 ao 1613, departinge the 31st dito ... Likwise there we founde the ariuall of captaine Best, with the Dragon homwardes, departing from there the third of March 1613: and Richard Petty with the Concord outwarde, May the nynth, and depted Jeune the third 1614"* (Raven-Hart, 1967: 64).

1614, October 3: The English vessels *Samaritan*, *Thomas* and *Thomasine*, outward bound, arrived in Table Bay only to discover that their visit coincided with that of a Dutch ship. During the course of subsequent communication between the two groups, the Dutch handed them a packet of letters they had discovered on top of a hill "*2 miles distant*". Upon reading, these were found to originate from a previous English expedition headed by a Captain Downston. The packet was resealed and returned to its place beneath their own stone slab. The crew also found inscriptions on stones from the *Dragon* on 14 February 1614, the *Expedition* on 31 March 1613, the *Concord* on 9 May 1614, and the *Dragon* on 20 June 1612. The flotilla set sail on 20 October, but before departing they left behind a packet of letters of their own.

1615, June 5: The English vessels *Expedition*, *Lion*, *Peppercorn* and *Dragon*, outward bound, dropped anchor in Table Bay. On 17 June they were joined by the *Hope*, homeward bound, which brought news of an English defeat at Surat at the hands of the Portuguese. Engraved stones from the *Advise*, *Attendance*, *Globe* and *James* were discovered on the shore. They resumed their journey on 20 June. A significant feature of this landfall was the release on shore of ten convicts that had previously been condemned to transportation. Having equipped each of them with a canvas bag, some seed, weapons and basic equipment, they were allowed to leave and do as they wished in their new land. Their subsequent fate was not clear (Raven-Hart, 1967: 73).

1615, August 27: The English vessels *Clove* and *Defence*, outward bound, dropped anchor in Table Bay. The *Clove* returned this way on 22 February 1617.

1616. The VOC decided that, in future, its outward-bound fleets should always make landfall at Table Bay (Theal, 1907: 365).

1616, March 4: The English vessel *Gift*, homeward bound, dropped anchor in Table Bay, and departed eight days later.

1616, May 25: The English vessels *Lion*, homeward bound, dropped anchor in Table Bay.

1616, June 12: The English vessels *Charles*, *Unicorn*, *Globe*, *James* and *Swan*, outward bound, dropped anchor in Table Bay. The *Rose* was part of the same fleet, but only reached Table Bay on 10 July. Upon arrival they found a Dutch ship already in harbour, together with her Portuguese prize, which she abandoned on 20 June.

1617, January 2: The English vessels *Dragon* and *Expedition*, homeward bound from Batavia, anchored in Table Bay and, during their stay, left behind a batch of letters beneath an engraved stone. The Master of the Expedition, William Peyton, proposed in his log that the English should now standardize the practice of leaving mail at the Cape and bring out from England a slab especially made for this purpose, approximately 120cm high, 75cm wide and 15cm deep, and embossed with the British coat of arms (Ravan-Hart, 1967: 76).

1617, February 10: The Dutch vessels *Amsterdam* and *Groot Sonne*, homeward bound, anchored in Table Bay, and during their stay left behind a batch of letters beneath an engraved stone.

1617, June 22: The English vessels *James Royal*, *Anne Royal*, *Gift*, *Bull*, and *Bee*, outward bound, dropped anchor in Table Bay, and found the *Hound* already there. They set sail on 13 July.

1618, June 20: The English vessels *Dragon*, *Samson*, *Expedition* and *Lion*, outward bound, anchored in Table Bay, and upon their departure, they left behind a batch of letters beneath an engraved stone inscribed as follows: "*NNO 1618 JO WDAL MAS O LN ARID THE 23 O DEPD*

FOR SVRRAT TH JVNE & DANIE WRHT GEORE PIKE MARCTS ISAC SEVEN-SON MR MATE ARV JVN E Ye O 3 I LYON 1620".

1618, July: The English vessels *Sun*, *Moon*, *Clove*, *Globe* and *Peppercorn*, outward bound, anchored in Table Bay.

1619: The Dutch vessel *Amsterdam* under Jacob Dedel outward bound, anchored in Table Bay, and left behind an engraved stone.

1619, May 15: The English vessel *Anne*, homeward bound, anchored in Table Bay, and during her stay her crew left behind a batch of letters beneath an engraved stone.

1619, May 20: Soon after the *Anne* departed the Dutch vessels *Dordrecht* and *Amsterdam*, under the command of Frederik de Houtman, *Den Opperkoopman* and *Jacob Dedel*, anchored in Table Bay. When they sailed, on 8 June, *Dedel* left behind a *"carved stone"* recording their visit.

1619, June 24: An English fleet, including the vessels *Charles*, *Elizabeth*, *Diamond* and *Ruby*, outward bound, anchored in Table Bay. There they found a letter left behind but too rotted by damp to be legible. On 8 July they were joined by a Danish fleet of some seven ships, and on 12 July set sail for the Indies.

1619, July 8: A Danish fleet including the vessels *David*, *Elephant*, *Christian*, *Jaeger*, *Fyrmand*, *Patientia* and *Copenhagen*, homeward bound, anchored in Table Bay, and found eight English ships already there. Subsequent correspondence shows this number to be unreliable. When they landed the Danes built an earth redoubt to protect their camp, probably from the English. Relations between the two groups were strained, but outwardly friendly, until the English delivered to them three letters which had obviously been opened and read. Matters were not assisted when one of the Danish ships was accidentally grounded, and the wreck was openly looted by the English. Nonetheless when the English fleet departed on 2 August they took with them a number of Danish letters whose contents had first been vetted by the fleet's Council. The Danes set sail on 5 August having lost more than 200 men through dysentery, with more being expected to die en route.

1619, November 29: The English vessel *Bull*, outward bound, anchored in Table Bay, and during her stay her crew left behind a batch of letters beneath an engraved stone inscribed as follows: "RO ADAMS COM OF THE BVL ARIVED 29 OF NOVEM & DEP THE 12 OF DE 1619 FOR BANTAM JO COCKRAM CAPE MARCH LETTERS VNDER".

1620, January 20: The English vessel *Rose*, homeward bound, anchored in Table Bay, and during her stay her crew left behind a batch of letters beneath an engraved stone. They also found letters from Capt Adams of the *Bull*. They set sail on 2 February, having left behind letters of their own.

1620, February 2: The Dutch vessel *Goude Leeuw*, outward bound, lost her mast off the Cape and had made Table Bay the worse for wear. There she found at anchor the Dutch ship *Goede Fortuijn*, also outward bound, who had lost 60 men through illness and had barely made it into port. Finding no food available there both made for Saldanha Bay where, by some accounts, the *Goede Fortuijn* was abandoned. During their stay the crew of the *Goude Leeuw* left behind a batch of letters beneath an engraved stone, packed in a most thorough and efficient

TWO: Early Visitors

manner.

1620, March 15: A French fleet including three vessels, the *Montmorency, Esperance* and *Hermitage*, outward bound, anchored in Table Bay. Upon coming ashore the crew found: "*a large stone, under which there were two packets of tarred cloth, which made them think that they were letters from Flemings or Englishmen. These I delayed opening until I had assembled the officers of my ship ... and when persons capable of interpreting them had arrived*" (Raven-Hart, 1967: 102). While in the bay they were joined by the English ships *Bull*, outward bound, and the *Rose*, homeward bound. They set sail on 12 April. On the journey back they anchored in Table Bay on 5 May 1622, and over the next week they were joined by the Dutch ships *Livree de Roterdam, Maurice* and *West Frisland*, and on 23 May the *Gouda* arrived in a state of distress. The French estimated that more than 80 Dutch crewmen died there during their stay. They were finally able to set sail on 30 May.

1620, June 24: The English vessels *Roebuck, London, Hart* and *Eagle*, outward bound under the command of Capt Andrew Shilling, anchored in Table Bay. When they arrived they found that the *Lion*, homeward bound, as well as nine other Dutch ships, outward bound, were already there. Soon after their arrival the English were joined by the ships *Exchange* and *Unity*. On 25 June the Dutch fleet, together with the Lion, bearing their letters home, set sail, but later that evening they welcomed the arrival of the Dutch ship *Schidam*. The *Bear* arrived on 10 July. The English flotilla was finally able to set sail on 25 July. During their stay their crew left behind a batch of letters beneath an engraved stone.

1620, June 24: The English vessels *Exchange* and *Unity*, outward bound, anchored in Table Bay.

1620, June 25: The Dutch vessel *Schidam*, outward bound, anchored in Table Bay.

1620, July 3: A party of English officers from Shilling's flotilla, gathered on shore with as many crew as could be mustered, and read a proclamation placing the whole country under the sovereignty of King James I of England. Capt Jan Kunst, of the *Schidam* and some of his officers were also present and reportedly raised no objection. The flag of St George was then raised on the Lion's Rump, recently renamed King James' Mount, and a small copy of the flag was presented to the Khoikhoi residents present. As, at that stage, the English and Dutch East India Companies were seeking to amalgamate, nothing ever came of this declaration.

1620, July 10: The English vessel *Bear*, homeward bound, anchored in Table Bay.

1621, May 24: The English vessel *Lesser James*, homeward bound, dropped anchor in Table Bay, where she found the *Anne Royal* and the *Fortune* already there, together with Dutch ships *Gauda, Black Bear* and *Herring*, all outward bound. Three more Dutch ships sailed in the next day. The English set sail on 28 May.

1622, January 29: The English vessels *Roebuck, London* and *Hart* returned to Table Bay. Prior to setting sail on 3 February they "*buried our letters*", probably beneath another engraved stone.

1622, May 5: The Dutch vessel *Wapen*, outward bound, anchored in Table Bay, having lost 60 men to scurvy, out of a complement of 380. She set sail on 21 May.

1622, May 7: The Dutch vessel *Mauritius*, outward bound, anchored in Table Bay.

1622, May 12: The Dutch vessel *West Friesland*, homeward bound, anchored in Table Bay, fully laden with pepper and cloves, and was joined by the *Gouda* soon thereafter.

1622, June 27: The English vessels *Blessing*, *Discovery* and *Reformation*, outward bound, anchored in Table Bay, and set sail on 8 July.

1622, December 8: The English vessel *Lesser James*, homeward bound, anchored in Table Bay. On !7 December the English ship *Abegail*, outward bound, joined her in the bay. Upon its departure, the crew left behind a batch of letters beneath an engraved stone inscribed as follows: "JOHN ROBERTS COMMAVNDER OF THE LESSER JAMES AR Y 8 DECEM DE Y 26 1622 LOVK WITH THIS LINE FOR LETERES". This stone was added to a few days later by the crew of the *Abegail*. Their inscription reads as follows: "HENRY MANCHES JAMES BVRGES M OF THE ABIGALL AR Y 17 DEPAR Y 26 OF DECEMBAR 1622". The same stone was reused in 1627 by the crew of the *Hart*.

1623, March 10: The English vessels *London*, *Jonas* and *Lion*, homeward bound from Surat, anchored in Table Bay. During her stay her crew left behind an engraved stone with the following inscription: "THE LONDON ARIVED THE 10 OF M HERE FROM SVRAT BOND FOR ENGLAND AND DEPAR THE 20 DICTO RICHARD BLYTH CAPTAINE 1622 HEARE VNDER LOOKE FOR LETTERS". In 1629 the same stone was reused by Dutch sailors. It was discovered on 17 August 1827, during the course of repairs to a sewer on the Heerengracht, but for some reason it was reburied, and was only brought to light again in 1897.

1623, March 19: The Danish East India Company vessels *Christianshaven* and *Flensborg*, outward bound for the Indies, with Icelander Jon Olafsson on board, anchored in Saldanha Bay. His log recorded that, before leaving, the crew had buried the ship's letters in a wooden casket in a very deep hole, and had then marked the position with a wooden post giving the name of the ship. The entry explained, somewhat laconically, that *"those homeward bound take the letters of those outward bound ..."*. They then sailed on to Table Bay where they found four English ships at anchor, the *London*, *Jonas* and *Lion*, homeward bound, and the *Roebuck*, outward bound. The Danes set sail on 23 March, *"after feasts given by the Danes and the English, each to the other"* (Raven-Hart, 1967: 112). It is not known whether Saldanha Bay was frequented often enough by passing vessels to warrant Olafsson's optimism that their mail would be found.

1623, May 29: The English vessel *Hart*, outward bound, anchored in Table Bay and, during her stay, her crew left behind a batch of letters beneath an engraved stone. They also found the letters left behind by the *Jonas*, some three months previously. The ship set sail on 8 June.

1624, April: The Dutch vessels *Hollandia*, *Gouda*, *Dordrecht* and *Leeuwinne*, outward bound, anchored in Table Bay. While in harbour, on 24 April 1624 the Chief Mate of the *Hollandia* died, and his grave was marked with a stone. The fleet set sail on 11 May.

1624, April: The English vessel *Dolphin*, homeward bound, anchored in Table Bay and left behind some letters beneath an engraved stone. While there they met up with the *Charles*, outward bound.

1624, July 17: The English vessels *Royal James*, *Eagle*, *Jonas*, *Star*, *Spy* and *Scout*, outward bound, anchored in Table Bay and, during their stay, discovered an engraved stone left behind by the *Dolphin* four months previously. However no letters were discovered underneath, and it was assumed that they had been taken by a Dutch or Danish ship. Before leaving the crew left behind a batch of letters of their own similarly placed beneath an engraved stone. The fleet set sail on 29 July.

1625, October 14: The English vessel *Star* anchored in Table Bay and, during its stay, the ship's surgeon, Edward Wilson, left behind a batch of letters beneath a stone painted with the words "*Edwa.Wilson ship - Star 1625*".

1625, October 14: The Dutch vessels *Maagd van Dort* (also known as the *Dordrecht*) and *Weesp*, homeward bound, anchored in Table Bay. They set sail with the *Star* on 25 October.

1625, October: The Dutch vessel *Tholen*, outward bound, anchored in Table Bay at the same time as the *Star*, *Maagd van Dort* and *Weesp*. It remained in harbour for 14 days.

1625, December 18: The Dutch vessel *Middelburg*, homeward bound, anchored in Table Bay, and set sail on 28 December. It left behind a packet of letters, which was later found by another Dutch ship.

1626, January 20: The English vessel *Scout*. homeward bound, anchored in Table Bay and found two Dutch ships already at anchor, the *Wapen van Hoorn* and *Eendracht*, both also homeward bound. A search for letters only produced engraved stones from the *Star*, and the Dutch ships *Maagd van Dort* and *Weesp*, that had visited Table Bay on 14-25 October 1625. The three had been under instruction to sail home together. The letters were collected by the Dutch ship *Tholen*, in Table Bay at the same time. On 23 January the Dutch ship *Leyden*, outward bound, came into the bay and an exchange of provisions took place. The *Scout* and its two Dutch companions set sail on 27 January.

1627, January: The Dutch vessel *Wapen van Rotterdam*, homeward bound, anchored in Table Bay. It left behind a packet of letters beneath an inscribed stone, which was later found by another Dutch ship, the *Grotenbroek*.

1627, July 6: A flotilla of Dutch vessels, outward bound, begins to arrive in Table Bay, including the *Wapen van Hoorn*, *Gallias*, *Utrecht*, *Vianen*, *Texel*, *Leeuwin* and *Kamphaen*. On 19 July five English ships joined them, the *Mary*, *Star*, *Hopewell*, *Hart*, *Refuge* and *Scout*. It appears that some unpleasantness may have arisen between the two groups. The English flotilla left port on 30 July, and on 4 August the Dutch vessels *Dobbelen Arend* and *Velsen* arrived in the bay. The last of the Dutch ships set sail on 7 August.

1627, July 7: The English vessel *Hart*, homeward bound, anchored in Table Bay and, during her stay, her crew left behind a batch of letters, reusing the engraved stone originally carved by the crew of the *Lesser James* on 8 December, and by the crew of the *Abegail* on 17 December 1622. Their inscription, which is largely illegible, reads partly as follows: "*M R ARIVED LY DEPARTED DIT FOR SARAT 27*".

1627, July 8: The English vessels *Mary*, *Star*, *Hopewell*, *Hart*, *Refuge* and *Scout*, outward bound, anchored in Table Bay. The fleet set sail on 19 July. Also see above.

1628, January 19: A fleet of some eleven Dutch vessels, including the *Vlissingen*, *De Veer*, *Zeeburgh* and *Delffshaven*, outward bound, anchored in the bay at some time between 19 and 31 January.

1628, May 9: The English vessels *Discovery*, *Palsgrave* and *Dolphin*, homeward bound, anchored in Table Bay. Over the next few days they were joined by the *Dove*, outward bound, and by the Dutch ship *Vianen*, also on its way home. They set sail on 21 May.

1628, September 1: The English vessel *William*, homeward bound, anchored in Table Bay and, during her stay, her crew left behind a batch of letters beneath an engraved stone. She set sail on 18 September.

1629, March 11: The English vessel *Star*, homeward bound, anchored in Table Bay.

1629, September 7: The English vessel *Hopewell*, homeward bound, anchored in Table Bay and found letters left behind by Capt Pynne of the *London*. They buried a packet of letters of their own before setting sail on 21 September (Raven-Hart, 1967: 131).

1630, February 17: The Dutch vessel *Gallias van Hoorn*, homeward bound together with other ships, anchored in Table Bay. After protest from the crew against the incompetence of their captain, they set sail on 26 February. A packet of letters was left on shore, presumably under an engraved stone.

1630, April 12: The English vessel *Star*, outward bound, dropped anchor in Table Bay. When the crew went ashore at Robben Island looking for English letters, they *"could not find any, wee found the dutch packett of letters which we opened, because wee could not find no English letters, supposing they had taken vp our letters, & therein wee founde English letters left here by Mr Alnuts (Master of the Speedwell) &the ships Hart, Expedition and Hopewell, the Coppies wheroff wee send you herewith"* (Raven-Hart, 1967: 134).

1630, October 23: The English vessel *Charles*, homeward bound, dropped anchor in Table Bay. When the crew went ashore they *"found Flemish letters"*, and on 5 November the Dutch vessels *Der Veer* and *Vlissingen* sailed into the bay, outward bound. The latecomers also came on shore to trade for provisions, and obviously outbid the English for *"we could get non afterwards"* (Raven-Hart, 1967: 134).

1631: The Khoikhoi chief *Autshumato*, known subsequently to foreign visitors variously as *Hadah*, *Hada*, *Adda*, *Haddot* and, after 1652, as *Harry*, was befriended by the English and taken on the *London*, under Capt John Pynne, to the Javanese port of Banten, probably in 1629. During his stay he gained a broad knowledge of their language, and after his return to the Cape early in 1632, he and some thirty of his followers were transported, at their own request, to Robben Island. There he was employed by the English as an agent, liaising on their behalf with other Khoi groups on the mainland, and keeping mail in his possession until collected by the next ship. Consequently he must be regarded to be South Africa's first resident postmaster. By 1638 records indicate that a second Khoikhoi, known as Isaac, had also learnt to speak English, and that sometime later he was taken by the Dutch to Batavia. He was returned to the bay in 1642, the Dutch no doubt intending to employ him as their own agent. He probably died in 1646. Autshumato and his people left Robben Island sometime in the early 1640s, and after 1652 he was installed by the Dutch as their chief translator. However on 19 October 1853, while the Dutch were attending church, Autshumato absconded with most of their cattle. Eventually the herd was captured by a rival Khoikhoi group, the Goringhaiqua, and in June 1655 Autshumato returned to the Dutch and managed to persuade them that the theft had been perpetuated by the Goringhaiqua, who now held the cattle. The Dutch believed him and reinstated him as their chief translator. Autshumato then proceeded to amass a large herd of cattle and sheep, largely at the expense of his employers. As a result, in June 1658, he was arrested and banished to Robben Island, while his herds were confiscated. In December 1659 he managed to return back to the mainland, escaping in a leaky rowboat, and went into exile among his own people, where he died in 1663.

1631, May 29: The English vessels *Palsgrave* and *London*, outward bound, anchored in Table Bay and, during their stay, left behind a batch of letters beneath an engraved stone.

1631, June 10. The Dutch vessels *Middelburgh*, *Wassenaaer*, *Egmont*, *Delffshaven*, *Deventer* and *Leeuwinne*, homeward bound, dropped anchor in Table Bay.

1631, July 13: The English vessels *Discovery* and *Reformation*, homeward bound, anchored in Table Bay, discovering the *Palsgrave* and *London*, also outward bound, already there. They all departed together on 2 August and the two groups parted company later that day. During their stay, the crew left behind a batch of letters beneath an engraved stone.

1632, about May: Captain Weddell, probably on the English vessel *Charles*, anchored in Table Bay and, upon his departure, left behind on Robben Island a batch of letters in the keeping of the Khoikhoi chief Autshumato.

1632, April 3: The earliest surviving engraved stone inscribed in Dutch was left behind when the sailing ships *Nassau*, *Nimmegen*, *Wesel* and *Galyas*, homeward bound from Batavia, anchored in Table Bay. It bore the following inscription: "HIER ONDER LEGGEN BRIEVEN VAND COMAND DV LEE EN VICE COMD P.CROOCK MET DE SCHEPEN NASSAU FRE HENDRIK NIMMEGEN WESEL EN DE GALIAS. ALHIER DEN 9 APRIL 1632 VAN BATTAVIA GEARIVEERT VIR OCKEN DEN 15 DITTO". They set sail from there on 20 April, and not on 15 April as they had originally planned.

1632, May 15: English seamen from the vessel *Pearl* landed in St Helena Bay where they discovered "*a certain Ler written in french … in a glasse bottle hangeing vppon a post*", which had apparently been left there by a passing ship twenty days previously. There being no provisions available they moved south to Table Bay, where they were met by the Khoikhoi chief Autshumato. He delivered to them a batch of letters which had been left in his safekeeping by the crew of the "*London*" (Raven-Hart, 1967: 136).

1632, November 12: The English vessel Blessing, homeward bound, anchored in Table Bay and, during her stay, her crew collected the mail which had been left by the *Charles* on Robben Island in the keeping of the Khoikhoi chief Autshumato, in about January 1632.

1634, February 24: The Dutch vessels *Wesel*, *Nassouw* and *Middelburg*, homeward bound, anchored in Table Bay. Having left a batch of letters, presumably under an engraved stone, they left on 3 March (Raven-Hart, 1967: 139).

1634, April 7: The Dutch vessels *Wassenaer*, *Banda* and *Egmont*, outward bound, anchored in Table

Bay and, during their stay, they left behind a batch of letters beneath an engraved stone inscribed as follows: "*BANDA WASSENAER END EGMONT SYN DEN XI APRIL VERTROCKE SOECKT BRIEF*".

1634, May 13: The English vessel *Mary*, homeward bound, anchored in Table Bay and, upon her departure, her crew left behind on the shore a batch of letters beneath an engraved stone. Copies were also entrusted to the Khoikhoi chief Autshumato on Robben Island. He then delivered letters previously entrusted to him by the English vessel *Exchange*, some weeks earlier (Raven-Hart, 1967: 143).

1634, June 4: The English vessel *Coaster*, outward bound, anchored in Table Bay and during her stay her crew collected two batches of mail which had previously been left on Robben Island in the keeping of the Khoikhoi chief Autshumato.

1635, April 8. A flotilla of six ships led by the *Amsterdam* with Commander Wollebrant Geleijnsen de Jong on board left the Dutch port of Texel on 26 December 1634, bound for Batavia. They sailed into Table Bay on 8 April 1835 and stayed until 15 April, reaching Batavia on 14 June 1635. Judging by the speed of their journey their travel route must have taken them south into the roaring forties. They marked their visit with an engraved stone which was discovered during excavations in Adderley Street in 1974 (Schoonees, 1991).

1635, April 26: The English vessel *Jonas*, homeward bound, anchored in Table Bay and, upon her departure, her crew left behind a batch of letters beneath an engraved stone.

1638, February 20: Six Dutch vessels, including the *Wezel*, *Haerlem*, *Middelburg*, *'t Hoff van Holland*, *Hollandia* and *Nassau*, outward bound, anchored in Table Bay. Upon their arrival they collected mail which had previously been left behind on Robben Island, in the keeping of the Khoikhoi chief Autshumato. Having found him to be reliable, upon their departure they left their mail with him. This was collected on 18 March by the Amsterdam. However they also marked their visit with an engraved stone, which they left on the mainland.

1638, March 17: The Dutch vessel *Amsterdam*, homeward bound, anchored in Table Bay. The next day its crew went ashore and were met by a local resident who spoke a little English and was dressed in the Dutch manner. He handed them a packet of letters left two days previously by a Dutch fleet, and an engraved stone inscribed "*On February 20 Governor Gijsels arrived here, and went on to the Fatherland on March 15, 1638, with the ships Wesel, Nassouw, Hof van Holland …*" (Raven-Hart, 1967: 149).

1639, May 6: The English vessel *Mary*, homeward bound, anchored in Table Bay. Travelling on her was Johan von Mandelslo, who reported that "*The Dutch have there a certain place or stone in which they lay latters, so that other Dutch travellers who pass may have news of their journey and all else*" (Raven-Hart, 1967: 151). Another passenger, William Bayley wrote: "*we sent our shallop and Jollywatt ashoare … to looke for lres (letters)*", and when they left five days later "*we sent our shallopp to (Robben) Iland to carry Thomas with whom we lefte our letters with the Rest of his family of watermen there to reside the whole number Consisting of 20 psons men, weomen and Children*" (Raven-Hart, 1967: 146).

1643, February 22: The Dutch vessel *Nassau*, homeward bound together with a fleet of seven other ships, anchored in Table Bay. The ships sailed on 12 March and were joined by others at St Helena.

1643, March 31: The English vessel *Hester*, homeward bound, sailed out of Table Bay, passing on the way the *Crispiana* and *Aleppo Merchant*.

1643, March 31: The English vessels *Crispiana* and *Aleppo Merchant*, homeward bound, anchored in Table Bay.

1643, July 12: The English vessel *Royall Mary*, outward bound, anchored in Table Bay for repairs.

1644, February 7: The *Mauritius Eiland* set sail on 4 October 1643 together with three other ships. The flotilla was dispersed in a storm and set sail individually for the Cape. They arrived off Table Bay on 7 February 1644, but the ship was wrecked close to Mouille Point while attempting to sail into harbour. They were joined two days later by their companion ship, the *Vrede*, who was able to take on most of the cargo as well as 69 men. After a minor mutiny, the remaining 280 men restored the earthworks of a fort previously built by a Danish crew and settled down to wait for rescue. Their ship was eventually beached and abandoned. On 25 May 1644 the *Tijger* was dispatched from Batavia to bring home the survivors as well as any remaining cargo.

1644, February 22: The English vessel *Royall Mary*, homeward bound, anchored in Table Bay in time to witness the plight of the *Mauritius Eiland*. After having traded a case of spirits for a keg of white wine, a barrel of butter and some powder and shot, she left for home on 2 March.

1644, 25 March: The English vessel *Endeavour*, outward bound, anchored in Table Bay and found some 280 castaways of the *Mauritius Eiland* living on shore. Gave them some provisions before sailing out on 29 March.

1645, December 29. The English vessel *Malacca*, outward bound for the Indies, anchored in Table Bay, and set sail on 15 January 1646. It left behind a packet of letters with Isaac, which were handed over a month later to the *Zutphen*.

1646, February 25. The English vessel *Eagle* anchored in Table Bay, and set sail for home on 9 March. During its stay they were met up with a Dutch flotilla from Batavia that arrived two days after them and set sail six days before them. If any mails were left behind by the Captain of the *Eagle*, this would have been given to the care of Isaac.

1646, February 27: Dutch vessels, including, among others, the *Tiger*, *Walvisch*, *Vrede* and *Zutphen*, homeward bound, anchored in Table Bay where they met up with the *Eagle*. Upon their arrival the Chief Mate of the *Zutphen* was sent ashore to make contact with the English and to collect any Dutch mail from Isaac. This is where the story becomes curious. The *Eagle* had been in the bay for five days before the Dutch arrival but, despite all efforts, had failed to make contact with the locals. The Dutch on the other hand, had no such difficulty, and although Isaac was immediately found, he refused to hand over his mails until the next day, when he could make the delivery in person to the Captain of the *Zutphen* aboard his ship. The bulk of this was a packet of letters from Admiral Le Maire, outward bound with a flotilla of six ships, but it also included letters left behind by the English ship *Malacca* six weeks previously. There is no doubt that the Dutch commander opened and read the English mail, otherwise its contents would not have been recorded in the Dutch account, but there is no reference to it being forwarded to its legal recipients. The *Eagle* had already been in the bay for some days and, like the Dutch, was also homeward bound, so one can only conclude that Jacob perceived himself to be serving Dutch interests. This perception was supported later on in the same report when it stated that a separation of the mails had now taken place, with Isaac taking charge of Dutch letters. This, apparently did not prevent him from handing over to his masters any English mail that came his way. Before their departure on 3 March the Dutch left behind with Isaac a consignment of letters, paying him with "*some trifles such as copper rings, tobacco and brandy.*"

THREE

LISTING OF LICENSED STAMP VENDORS

In addition to their local post office, during the 1890s the residents of most major urban centers in the Cape Colony could also purchase stamps from a number of licensed stamp vendors. These were usually private individuals, such as retailers, professional firms and organisations that either used a quantity of postage in their own right, or came into contact with members of the general public as part of their daily business. In exchange the Colonial Post Office paid a commission of 2½% on all sales provided they also allowed a posting box to be erected on their premises. Although the financial returns were relatively small, amounting to 4.8d for every sheet of 120x1d stamps sold, the availability of stamps and a receptacle for posting made a basic postal service available to communities where the use of the post office was not a daily occurrence. Thus Indian and Malay traders such as Mr E Goolam, of No 9 Buitengracht Street, in Cape Town, Mr Ismail Mullah of No 1 Bellevue Street, Cape Town, or Mr Mahomed Ismail, of Malay Street, Uitenhage could provide a service to their communities while also drawing upon their custom. By the same token Black businessmen trading in the segregated residential suburbs, such as Tom Lomdyala, Distributor of Native Letters in Bedford, Thomas Mzozoyana, in Campbell Street, Colesberg, or Nisini Mbambani, in the Strangers' Location, Port Elizabeth, could derive the same benefits. The list provided below is long but is not by any means definitive and, at the very least, demonstrates some of the positive effects of the Cape's relatively progressive constitution introduced in the Colony in 1872. No such arrangements are known to have existed in any of the other three territories in Southern Africa.

Aberdeen	WT Brown, postbox located on the premises
	S Cohen, postbox located on the premises
Adelaide	A Saville, Distributor of Native Letters.
Alfred Docks, Cape Town	J Campbell, 3 Ebenezer Road
	CH Percival, Docks Location Store.
Aliwal North	E Loescher, Branspruit)
	JE Griffiths & Co, Market Square.
Barkly West	Mrs ET Smith, Queen's Hotel.
Beaconsfield	JR Barnsley, Main Street, Du Toit's Pan, postbox located on

	premises
	GT Belding & Co, Main Street
	J Bermingham, Wesselton
	T Bermingham, Wesselton
	Dixon & Co, Old Market Square, postbox located on the premises
	H Feldmann, Old Market Square, postbox located on the premises
	Mrs Kennedy, Matthew Street
	W Leinberger & Co, Old Market Square
	P McFarlane, Cape Town Road, postbox located on the premises
	J Molyneaux, postbox located on the premises
	W Robinson, Bultfontein, postbox located on the premises
	Sagar, Main Street, Du Toit's Pan
	HT Strugnell, Du Toit's Pan Road
	G Summers, Bultfontein
Beaufort West	PJ Alport & Co, Donkin Street, postbox located on the premises
	EC Brown, Bird Street, postbox located on the premises
	GD Brown, Bird Street, postbox located on the premises
	P Crummeck & Co, Meintjes Street
	W Primmer, Upper Donkin Street
Bedford	Tom Lomdyala, Distributor of Native Letters
	H Mbeti, Distributor of Native Letters
	WRH Stent.
Blue Cliff	W Jurgens, Sunday River, Blue Cliff
Bredasdorp	Bennett & Louw.
Bushman's River	RJ Bright, during the 1890s
Butterworth	Edward Blanck
Cala	W Hammond, during the 1890s
Caledon Street, Cape Town	Miss S Aston, 48 Tenant Street
	H Howell, 149/155 Caledon Street
	Mrs F Miller, corner de Villiers and Constitution Streets, post box located on the premises
	JS Mocke, corner Caledon and Tenant Streets, postbox located on the premises
	H Randall, 53 Caledon Street
	Woolff Shames, 64 Caledon Street
Calitzdorp	Sanders Bros & Co, during the 1890s

Cape Town and Suburbs

S Adams, 111 Long Street, postbox located on the premises
F Ballinger, Shepherd Street
J Berghout, corner Napier Street and Somerset Road, postbox located on the premises
L Bernstein, 101c Long Street
W Preston Buchanan, Long Street
Mrs M Buchner, corner Buiten and Buitengracht Streets
S Campbell, Ebenezer Road, postbox located on the premises
Mohedien Camroodien, corner Russell and Pontac Streets
A Candrey, 93 Buitenkant Street
Cohen & Lenson, 186 Loop Street, postbox located on the premises
Dalton & Reid, 217 and 219a Long Street
A Epstein, 89 Loop Street, postbox located on the premises
Fletcher & Co, Merchants, Darling Street
M Gabriel, 2 Jubilee Villas
Goldberg & Levin, 5 Justice Street, postbox located on the premises
JM Golding, Buitenkant Street, postbox located on the premises
E Goolam, 9 Buitengracht Street
A Harder, 69 Rose Street
Hazell and Son, Harrington Street
PE Hickel, Moravian Hill, Ashley Street
I Hoossen, corner Roger and Muir Streets
J Iverson, Buitenkant Street
James & Williams, corner Tennan and Longmarket Streets, postbox located on the premises
JF Johnson, 22 Hyde Street, postbox located on the premises
NL Joseph, 78 Long Street
EA Khan, corner Camden and Hasting Streets
P Kannemeyer, top of Buitengracht Street
J Knoop, corner Loop and Buitencingel Streets
EF Laden, 7 Castle Buildings
DJ Langham, Breakwater Station
CJ Mason, 67 Chiappini Street, postbox located on the premises
N Maleris, 14 Burnside Road, postbox located on the premises
M Melman, 58 Darling Street

THREE: Stamp Vendors

Ismail Mullah, 1 Bellevue Street
JS North, 89 Loop Street, postbox located on the premises
JS North, corner Napier Street and Somerset Road, postbox located on the premises
Pfuhl Bros, corner Pepper and Long Streets, postbox located on the premises
S Posener, Rosebank Place, Upper Orange Street
W Preston & Co, Tram Station, Long Street
Rev F Rauh, Ashley Street, Moravian Hill, postbox located on premises
D Robinson, Tramway Company's Office, Long Street, post box located on the premises
Seconder Rowson, 2 De Villiers Street
FT Secretan, 13 Somerset Road
GG Schreiner, 65 Keerom Street
S Shasskolsky, 226 Loop Street, postbox located on the premises
Shinwold & Co, Constitution Street, postbox located on the premises
S Short, Donald's Buildings, Kloof Road
F Silva, 34 Orange Street
H Smith, corner Park Road and New Church Street
SA Newspaper Co, 23 Church Street, later Keerom Street
A Strates, 93 Buitenkant Street, postbox located on the premises
Geo Toppe, corner Wale and Loop Street
J Torode, corner Loop and Buitencingel Streets, postbox located on the premises
A van Zalingen, 6 Justice Street, Gardens, postbox located on premises
Watson & Co, corner Buiten and Jordaan Streets
R White, Masonic Hotel, Darling Street, postbox located on premises
M Wicks, corner Wale and Loop Street
F Wood, New Somerset Hospital
J Yates, 69 Rose Street
YMCA, 44 Long Street

Cathcart
Malcomess & Co
Smale & Co

Ceres
H&D Home, Main Street

Ceres Road	EL Marais, Market Square, postbox located on the premises
	Waverley Woolwashing Company
Clanwilliam	B Foster,
	Downes and Visser
	Rud Seydell,
	EHN Smit, Onderlange Vley
	DJA van Zy, agency office in the Augsburg Hotel, postbox located on the premises
Claremont	Manager, Attwell Baking Company, postbox located on the premises
	John Bell, St Matthew's Road
	Henry Boyli, Lansdowne Road
	OJ Griffith, Main Road
	TF Lenthall, Main Road
	A Palvie, Lansdowne Road, postbox located on the premises
	E Pape-Skinner, Lansdowne Road
	SG Purchase, Key of the Flats
	Mrs M Scott, Palmyra Road, postbox located on the premises
	J Taylor, corner Vineyard and Protea Roads
	FWC Thomas, Main Road
Colesberg	AJ Greenaway, Church Street
	Thomas Mzozoyana, Campbell Street
	Teengs Brothers, Church Street
Cookhouse	A Weddell, Distributor of Native Letters
Cradock	Butler Bros, Midland House
	A Shrunk, Stockenstrom Street
	JJ Webber, Adderley Street
Diep River	Joseph Kendal, postbox located on the premises
	Penschin and Street
	J Sterner, postbox located on the premises
Dock Road, Cape Town	S Chapman, Dock Road
	FA de Gruchy, 19 Dock Road
	M Goodall, Dock Road, postbox located on the premises
	EC Gorvett, Dock Road
	Nicholas Kutgies, 1a Dock Road
Durban Road, Cape Town	B Cohen, Elsies River Halt
	James Jansen, Kraaifontein
	Mendelsohn Bros & Ellis
Dynamite Factory	Norwitz & Marks, De Beer's Explosive Works
	Shenker & Perel, Block Z, Lochner Hoff Estate

THREE: Stamp Vendors

East London	Abdoola & Co, 64 Buffalo Street
	Abramowitz Bros & Hoffman, corner Buffalo and Hill Streets
	RY Barbour, Oxford Street
	Brown & Co, Currie Street
	C Cassel, North End, postbox located on the premises
	WE Courtney, Oxford Street
	Crouch Bros, corner Oxford and Argyle Streets, postbox located on the premises
	H Davidson, Buffalo Street
	G Egerton, St James' Road
	D Ensor, Park Avenue, postbox located on the premises
	W Estment, Durban Street
	John Forbes, 147 Oxford Street
	Greig & Greig, St Peter's Road
	Grocott & Sherry, Oxford Street, postbox located on the premises
	C Hutchinson, The Beach, postbox located on the premises
	FLA Kurtz, 14 Oxford Street
	J Latinsky, North End, postbox located on the premises
	Lawzeli, Native Location
	HC Luke & Co, Oxford Street
	Joseph Meier, St John's Road
	JG Nelson, 58 St James' Road
	PH Potter, Native Location
	L Rosenstein, Southernwood
	A Sansom, Fleet Street
	Mrs C Stickellis, Southernwood
	Unsworth & Co, 154 Oxford Street
Elsie's River Halt	B Cohen, at Elsie's River Halt
Fort Beaufort	W Estment, Durban Street
Fraserburg	JMF Keller, postbox located on the premises
George	SR Cornish
	AJ Sayers, at the George & Knysna Herald Offices, postbox located on the premises
	Mrs CM Sayers, York Street, postbox located on the premises
	C Searle & Co, corner York and Courtney Streets
	Walter Young, York Street
Gouritz River	F Harries
Graaff-Reinet	J Breger
	MC Dippenaar, Donkin Street

THREE: Stamp Vendors

	W Goldsmith, Latskraal
	AM Grundlingh, Stockenstrom Street
	HF Haarhoff, Cradock Street
	I du P Haarhoff, Caledon Street
	JJ Haarhoff, corner Bird and Cradock Streets
	JP Haarhoff, Caledon Street
	J Kruger, Goedhals Square, Distributor of Native Letters
	J Lichtenstein, Goedhals Square
	HJ Marais, Church Street
	ISJ Marais, Church Street
	John McQuirk, Church Street
	S Rabone, Somerset Street, later Caledon Street
	I Suttner, Goedhals Square, Distributor of Native Letter
	Thorne & Lane, Caledon Street
	RS van der Merwe.
Grahamstown	CH Abbott, African Street
	Barraud & Co, Noah's Ark
	Alfred Britten, Wood Street
	J Dyce, Roberts Street
	H Fichat & Co, Bathurst Street
	JH Grocott, High Street
	TH Grocott, High Street
	Grocott & Sherry, High Street
	T Knowles, Wood Street, later Victoria Road
	J McCarthy, Beaufort Street
	T McCarthy, Beaufort Street
	J Slater & Co, High Street
	Jabez South, Somerset Street
	J Templer, Beaufort Street
	HJS Turner, Lower Beaufort Street
	Mrs MC Turner, Lower Beaufort Street
Green Point	CW Barnes, Boer Prisoners' Camp
	D Cooke, Three Anchor Bay
	Heynes, Mathew & Co, corner Main and Clyde Roads, post box located on the premises
	Mrs M Middleton, Bay Road, Mouille Point
Hackney	South African Trimming
Hankey	Charles Colling of Lower Quagga
Kalk Bay	JS de Villiers, Noordhoek
	GW Lund, Kommetje

Kenilworth, Kimberley
Kimberley

W van Benge, Brakkloof
Station Master, St James' railway station
J Flynn, Kenilworth Club, postbox located on the premises
WN Allen, Green Street Ext
GT Belding & Co, Transvaal Road
RM Blent & Son, 42 Bean Street
Miss Flora Brown, De Beers Road, later De Beers Crossing, postbox located on the premises
SS Brown, 140 Transvaal Road, postbox located on the premises
C Brooks, Barkly Road, postbox located on the premises
RB Browning, De Beer's Crossing, postbox located on the premises
C Burgard, Grand Hotel, postbox located on the premises
JW Cooper, West End, postbox located on the premises
WN Cooper, Tucker Street, later West End, postbox located on the premises
S & A Cotty, De Beers, postbox located on the premises
JP Curran, off Lennox Street
TR English, DBC Mines
AH Fleury, De Beers, postbox located on the premises
Fleury & Brown, De Beers Road, postbox located on the premises
J Freel, De Beers, postbox located on the premises
Godlinton & Co, Du Toit's Pan Road
S Gordon, 74 Jones Street, postbox located on the premises
Graham & Co, Main Street
Handel House Ltd, Du Toit's Pan Road, postbox located on premises
James Bros, 107 Du Toit's Pan Road
CA Jeduld, Selby Street, postbox located on the premises
WA Jones, Selby Street, postbox located on the premises
B Joseph, 48 Old Main Street, postbox located on the premises
AS Levi, Handel House, Du Toit' Pan Road, postbox located on the premises
Librarian, Residents Library, postbox located on the premises
R McNally, Selby Street
A Mosely, Handel House, Du Toit's Pan, postbox located on premises

THREE: Stamp Vendors

	A Peterson, Grand Hotel, postbox located on the premises
	SH Rees, 81 Du Toit's Pan Road
	JW Robinson, De Beers Road
	J Smith, Barkly Road
	Smith & Bosman, Long Street
	P Sullivan, De Beers Road, postbox located on the premises
	ED Weinberg, Grand Hotel
	HA Ziegenbein, Long Street, postbox located on the premises
King William's Town	J Adam, PA Square, later Smith Street, postbox located on the premises
	A Ballack, Louisa Street
	FW Bartlett, Victoria Square, postbox located on the premises
	TJ Blake, Cambridge Road
	CW Bluhm, Market Square, postbox located on the premises
	C Born, Percy Street
	A Crawford, Durban Street
	C Devantier, Brownlee Station, postbox located on the premises
	Federal Supply & Cold Storage Co, Smith Street, postbox located on the premises
	B Gershung, Market Square
	L Goldberg, Cambridge Road, postbox located on the premises
	L Golding, Cambridge Road, postbox located on the premises
	CL Harvey, Ayliff Street, postbox located on the premises
	G Hatch
	James Hyde, Maclean Street
	CA Jay, Maclean Street
	T King, Victoria Square
	W Manthe, Percy Street
	J Newing, Maclean Street, postbox located on the premises
	CE Nixon, Maclean Street, postbox located on the premises
	EB Page, Victoria Square
	WM Seti, Distributor of Native Letters
	CW Winkelman, Victoria Square
	Paul Xiniwe, Market Square
Kloof Street, Cape Town	Mahomed Amein, 1 Brownlow Road, Tamboer's Kloof
	W Gasson, Kloof Street
	WG Haines, 102 Kloof Street
	E Kopelovitz, Upper Kloof Street

locat	Levitus & Lucas, Kloof Street
	N Malerio, Burnside Road, Tamboer's Kloof, postbox located on the premises
	Schneier & London, Burnside Road, Tamboer's Kloof, post box located on the premises
	E Simenhoff, corner Kloof and Camp Streets, postbox located on the premises
	J Stewart, corner Kloof and Camp Streets, Gardens, postbox located on the premises
Knysna	JH Templeman, Main Street
	B Wehrle, Main Street
Kokstad	AH Williams & Co
Kuils River	ST Anderson, postbox located on the premises
	Mr Kets, postbox located on the premises
	JB Norden, postbox located on the premises
Lower Paarl	Bohlmann Bros, Breda Street, postbox located on the premises
	WH Curlewis, postbox located on the premises
	GAW de Villiers, postbox located on the premises
	MS du Toit, postbox located on the premises
	GF King & Co, postbox located on the premises
	P Koster & Co, postbox located on the premises
	L Lurie, postbox located on the premises
	Nelson & Siebert, postbox located on the premises
	TJP Retief, postbox located on the premises
	DG Rossouw, postbox located on the premises
Maitland	Bridges, Main Road, postbox located on the premises
	HP Eckerman, Yzerplaats
	H Fachs, Ndabeni, postbox located on the premises
	DW Morison, Main Road, postbox located on the premises
Malmesbury	HP du Toit, Riebeek Street, postbox located on the premises
	PW Hougaard, corner Riebeek Street and Piquetberg Road, postbox located on the premises
	NA Smit, Piquetberg Road, postbox located on the premises
	J Smith, corner Darling Road and Ludolph Street, postbox located on the premises
	Smith and Kift, postbox located on the premises
Merriman Street	Hancock's
Middelburg	Harbour & Powse
	P Joffe, The Camp

THREE: Stamp Vendors

	W Turpin, Receiver of Native Letters, later Distributor of Native Letters, postbox located on the premises
	WT Whelan, postbox located on the premises
Mill Street, Cape Town	Alfred Aitken, corner Mill and Gordon Street
	Kadir Bawa, 53 Upper Mill Street
	GW Davies, Mill Street, postbox located on the premises
	FW de Wet & Co, Justice Street, Gardens
	Hyman Ginsberg, Mill Street, postbox located on the premises
	PJ Zoutendyk, Mill Street, postbox located on the premises
Molteno	W Parrable, in Smith Street
Montagu	Brink Bros
	J Campion
	L Jordaan, Goedemoed
Mossel Bay	F Harries, Gouritz River
	Dr Francis McIntyre, Marsh Street, postbox located on the premises
	E Powrie
	AC Rensburg, Little Brak River
	JB Weymouth, Marsh Street
Mount Frere	EW Fordham, Glenhope
	SK Fordham, Rockford
	GA Freemantle, Mtshazie
Mowbray	C Clark, corner Victoria and Main Roads, postbox located on premises
	RJ Hamilton
	Cuthbert & Co, Main Road
	A Lawrence, Klipfontein Road
	C Matthews, Durban Road, Bloemendal
	Mr Venner, Main Road, postbox located on the premises
	H van Post, corner Spin and River Streets
Muizenburg	Abelman, Lakeside, postbox located on the premises
	Haworth & Son, St James
	Morris Oblowitz, Lakeside, postbox located on the premises
Naauwpoort	W Pepper
Newlands	WW Allison, Mount Road, postbox located on the premises
	J Cramer, Mount Road
	Alf Erikson, Kildare Road
	JW Jacobs, Kildare Road
	S Short, corner Irene Street and Avenue Road
	Mrs A Wilkinson, Supply Stores, Main Street

THREE: Stamp Vendors

North End, Port Elizabeth	W Armstrong, Distributor of Native Letters.
Observatory Road	Bawa Beppo, corner Station and Victoria Roads
	F Copelard, 29 Scott Road
	E Gillard, Upper Main Road
	J Fairbanks & Co, Scott Road, postbox located on the premises
	W Herapath, Lower Main Road
	John Scott, Islington House, postbox located on the premises
	S Shaskolsky, Bowden Cash Stores, Lower Main Road
	P Williams, Lower Main Road
Oudtshoorn	Jacob Broude, Queen Street
	EW Dicks, Church Street
	J Elion, corner St John and Adderley Streets, postbox located on the premises
	Alfred Gibbs, High Street
	Geo King Snr, Queen Street
	GW King, Queen Street
	Chas Macklin, High Street
	J Matare, Church Street, later High Street, postbox located on premises
	S Phillips, corner St John and Adderley Streets, postbox located on the premises
Paarl	Bohlman Bros, Oude Tuin, corner van der Lingen and Breda Streets, postbox located on the premises
	GAW de Villiers, Upper Paarl, postbox located on the premises
	SG du Toit, The Windmill, Slot van Paarl
	Jas Gribble, Market Square, postbox located on the premises
	NJ Malherbe, Upper Paarl, postbox located on the premises
	HL Minnaar, postbox located on the premises
	Mrs P Wannenburgh
Park Avenue, East London	D Ensor
Plein Street, Cape Town	Miss MA Aschen, 53 Plein Street
	F Riechenbach, 62 Plein Street
Plumstead	RG Darroll & Co
	AM Matz, Main Road
Poplar Grove	JB Leach.
Port Alfred	Jno Bell, Park Terrace
	W Cole, Hill Street
Port Elizabeth	SH Bale, Main Street

SJ Bale, 98 Main Street
JH Barnes, Rufane Lane
Arthur Bright, Main Street
Mrs E Carlesi, Middle Street, St Paul's Hill, postbox located on the premises
F Carlesi, St Paul's Hill, postbox located on the premises
WL Chandler & Co, Main Street
JW Couldridge, 113 Princess Street
EG Driver, Sherlock Street
W Finlay, 71 Rudolph Street
FB Floyd, Burgess Street
Forbes & Caulfield, Cape Road, postbox located on the premises
Ford & Macleod, Cape Road, postbox located on the premises
CW Forley, 12 Victoria Street
Otto Fulton, Russel Road, postbox located on the premises
HC Gibbs, South Union Street, postbox located on the premises
Harper & Younge, 58 Cape Road
H Haslop, Lansdowne Place
Thos Haslop, 3 Lansdowne Place
Impey, Walton & Co, Market Square
C Ingram & Co, Family Grocers, Western Road, postbox located on the premises
C Jurgens, Middle Street
W Jurgens, 4 Middle Street, St Paul's Hill, postbox located on premises
FJ Kemp, Burgess Street
C Linck, Callington Street, postbox located on the premises
Ernest Lloyd & Co, Main Street
Mahalba & Co, Reservoir Location
Howard Mtshutshisa, Vlei Post
M Murray, 8 Prince Street
Nisini Mbambani, Strangers' Location
H Page, Perkin Street
Whiley Pikoli, Reservoir Location
G Poole & Co, 71 Rudolph Street
C Rogers, Burgess Street, later Cooper's Kloof
J Schorn, Adderley Street, postbox located on the premises
EI Siberry, Middle Street

	W Singson, 92 Queen Street, postbox located on the premises
	Smith & Braithwaite, Walmer Road
	J Smollan, 132 Russel Road, postbox located on the premises
	EE Spring, Walmer Road
	C Steers, 113 Princess Stree
	A Stuart , Burgess Street, postbox located on the premises
	G Tesoriere, Victoria Street, postbox located on the premises
	AA Walker, Russel Road, postbox located on the premises
	JO Walker & Co, Queen Street, postbox located on the premises
	A Wishart, Sprigg Street, postbox located on the premises
	James Wynne Jnr, Grocer, Princess Street, postbox located on the premises
Prince Albert	PK Neethling, postbox located on the premises
Queenstown	Edkins Bros, Cathcart Road
	A Govindasamy & Co
	RA Henderson, West End
	Henderson & Co
	SG Temlett, West End
	FJ Houlgate, Calderwood Street
	Mager & March, postbox located on the premises
	E Pearsall, Dugmore Street
	Stern & Gruss
Queen Street, Port Elizabeth	WA Howard, Grocer, Queen Street, postbox located on the premises
	Jos John, 11 Queen Street, postbox located on the premises
	James Naylor, Queen Street, postbox located on the premises
	W Singson, 92 Queen Street, postbox located on the premises
	JO Walker & Co, postbox located on the premises
	E Walsh, postbox located on the premises
Qumbu	WP Wilson, at Culunca
Richmond	Mrs White, Pienaar Street, postbox located on the premises
Richmond Hill, Port Elizabeth	AR Cooke
Riversdale	Messrs Nainkin & Lipschitz, Long Street
Robertson	R Cotto, Church Street, postbox located on the premises
	JE Miller, Church Street, postbox located on the premises
	CW Moller, Keerom Street, postbox located on the premises
	JC Neethling, corner Reitz and Church Streets, postbox located on the premises
	JJ Swanepoel, Keerom Street, postbox located on the premises

	W van Dyk, Barry Street
Rondebosch	LA Davies, Camp Ground
	Mrs J de Souza, Camp Ground
	Mrs M Franck, Rouwkoop Road
	A Fraustaedter, Main Road, postbox located on the premises
	Mrs M Georgala, Camp Ground Road
	Mr Harris, Camp Ground
	M Holbery, Rouwkoop Road, postbox located on the premises
	J Sowden, corner Main and Camp Ground Roads
	W Twine, Eureka Road
Rosebank	H van Post, corner of Spin and River Streets
St George's St, Cape Town	The Cape Argus, St George's Street, later in Longmarket Street
	The Cape Times, St George's Street, later in Church Street
St John's Street, Cape Town	Geo Gibbs, 37 St John's Street, postbox located on the premises
	Mohamed Hosseen, 81 St John's Street, postbox located on premises
	G Kilpatrick, 37 St John's Street
St Mark's	S Mabula, Qombolo
	R Ntlabati, Qombolo.
Salt River	S Alcock, Rutterfield
	JJ Atmore, Albert Road, postbox located on the premises
	C Capralis, Albert Road
	The Co-operative Society, Albert Road
	H Feder, station buildings
	J Holperin, 322 Albert Road
	A Hopkins, corner Great More Street and Victoria Road
	FH Morton, Rochester Road, postbox located on the premises
	D Rittman, corner Pope Street and Fenton Road, postbox located on the premises
	Solomon & Gluck, 143 Cecil Road
	Solomon Stein, 143 Cecil Road
	C Zerbo, 277 Albert Road
Sandflats	Mr Fowler, Patterson.
Sea Point	Bussel & Co, corner Wisbeach and Main Roads
	Mr Halcrow, railway station
	B Klugman, Barkly Road
	Albert Martin, railway station, postbox located on the premises

THREE: Stamp Vendors

	FA Poupard, Main Road, near Milton Road
	KM Webster, Main Road
	J Weigh, Main Road
Seymour	RW Hunt, Curzon Street
Simondium	H Bailey, Pniel
Simonstown	B Arlosoroff, Seaforth
	W Baron, St George's Street
	H Freedberg, Arsenal Road
	E Goldblatt, Main Street, postbox located on the premises
	A Knopf, St George's Street
	H Levy, Green Terrace
	AE Lindley & Co
	A Peimer, Arsenal Road
	H Schroeter, Main Street, postbox located on the premises
	B Wood, stationer
Sir Lowry Road, Cape Town	A Fernandes, 1a Sir Lowry Road
	JW Gird, Sir Lowry Road
	AW Lilliestone, 112 Sir Lowry Road
	AW Ross, corner Buissinne and Hyde Streets, Zonnebloem, postbox located on the premises
Somerset East	Rev BS Dlepu, Distributor of Native Letters
	S du Plessis, Native Location, postbox located on the premises
	GD Farley, Charles Street, West End
	CD Lake, Paulet Street, postbox located on the premises
	J Schutz, Paulet Street, postbox located on the premises
	Webber Bros
Somerset Strand	CS Haylett, postbox located on the premises
Somerset West	C Hopfelt, corner Station Road and Main Street
	TS Martin, Main Street
	Norwitz & Marks, De Beers Explosive Works
	FG Seaborn, De Beer's Bridge
South Union Street	Port Elizabeth DD Blend
	HC Gibb.
Stellenbosch	ST Anderson. Kuils River, postbox located on the premises
	PW Immelman, Plein Street
	AF Joerning, corner Plein and Bird Streets
	Mr Kets, Kuils River, postbox located on the premises
	AE Lewis, Dorp Street, postbox located on the premises
	Lewis & Bloemberg, Dorp Street, postbox located on the premises

	Mrs CJ Lindenbergh, Plein Street
	W Martin, Andrica Street
	JB Norden, Kuils River, postbox located on the premises
	LH Schaffer, Remount Depot
	Miss SM Schroder
	JF Stadler, Dorp Street
Sterkstroom	SS Nadasen, Van Zyl Street
	GA van Broembsen, The Camp
Swellendam	Jas Greathead & Co, Main Street, postbox located on the premises
	J Murray, Main Street, postbox located on the premises
The Beach, East London	C Hutchinson, The Beach
	Mrs C Stickells, The Beach
Three Anchor Bay	HD Cooke
	JJ Nyman, Three Anchor Bay, postbox located on the premises
	AEW Reeler, Three Anchor Bay
	H Strother, Three Anchor Bay
	Van Riet, Three Anchor Bay
	AE Walker, Combrinck's Buildings, Three Anchor Bay
Tsomo	B Phillips, at Tsojana.
Tulbagh	GJ Cellarius
	HA Fagan, Commercial Street
Uitenhage	Assaf & Atta, Caledon Street
	L Brooks, Caledon Street
	M Colling, Durban Street
	J Daly, Bay Road
	Fennell & Austin, Lower Caledon Street
	WT Green, Constitution Road
	JJ Harvey, Constitution Road
	Mahomed Ismail, Malay Street
	H Jones, Caledon Street
	M Kirsnor
	J McQuillan, Cannon Street
	E Nechemoirtz, Oatlands
	JG Nicholl, Caledon Street
	MJ Tarbet, Caledon Street
	T Taylor & Co, Market Street
	C Whitby, Stow Road
Umtata	T Baylis

	WRV Blayney, CMR Camp
	W Hayward, Ncisi
Uniondale	B Bernstein, postbox located on the premises
	GJ Cellarius
	Shear & Ryan, postbox located on the premises
Upper Paarl	NJ Malherbe, postbox located on the premises
Vryburg	OW Trollip, at Doornbult
Vryburg Station	The Station Master.
Wellington	Mrs Jemima Louw, Murray Street
	JJ Malan, Church Street
	JP Verwey, Market Square.
West End, Kimberley	JW Cooper, Tucker Street, West End
	WN Cooper, Tucker Street, West End.
Whittlesea	JB Leach
Woodstock	Allison & Co, 237 Albert Road
	C Anderson, Albert Road, postbox located on the premises
	B Bernstein, 25 Chester Road
	A Brown, corner Victoria Road and Gympie Street
	The Central News Agency
	FE Cheek, 4/6 Palmerston Street, Rodebloem
	B Dogan, corner Devon and Regent Streets
	G Eato, Chester Road, postbox located on the premises
	Mrs M Huckell, Victoria Road
	Humphrey & Martin, 14 Victoria Road, postbox located on the premises
	J Knoll, 206 Albert Road, postbox located on the premises
	EA Kuhnne, 27 Albert Road
	J Laerman, corner Dublin and Regent Streets
	SAR Parker, corner Salisbury Street and Roodebloem Road
	J and G Pitkethly, Albert Road, postbox located on the premises
	GG Pitkethly, Albert Road, postbox located on the premises
	W Rodman, 33 Fairview Avenue
	W Rodman, 203 Victoria Road
	E & L Rose, Albert Road, postbox located on the premises
	JM Shaw, Albert Road, postbox located on the premises
	Walmer Supply Stores, Warwick Street
Worcester	JH Adams, Durban Street
	Paul Anderson, Napier Street, postbox located on the premises

THREE: Stamp Vendors

	Bull & Meiring, Church Street
	HG Fisher, Napier Street, postbox located on the premises
	F Gooding-Field, Porter Street, postbox located on the premises
	V Harris, Stockenstrom Street
	AI Hermann, Remount Camp
	PW Immelman, High Street
	Isaac le Roux, High Street, postbox located on the premises
	Miss M Marais, Philipsdale
	R Menzies & Co, postbox located on the premises
	Mrs Nigrini, Fairbairn Street
	GJ Nigrini, High Street
	Quinn Bros, corner Church and Stockenstrom Streets, postbox located on the premises
	LC Streeter, Porter Street
	H van Biene, Napier Street, postbox located on the premises
Wynberg	Bennett & Baker
	EH Clarke, Main Road
	G Dunkling, corner Wolfe and Riebeek Streets
	M Fig, Ottery Road
	Mrs Genan, corner Alphen Hill and Bower Road, postbox located on the premises
	Mr Heesen, Durban Road
	C Hurlin, Main Road
	TG Kell, Ottery Road
	Mr McCrindle
	HF Miller, Durban Road
	S Rogoff, Gabriel Road
	G Schwabel, Ottery Road, postbox located on the premises
	Shiffman, Ottery Road
	C Vosper, Durban Road
	T Wilson, Market Building, Plumstead
Yzerplaats	HP Eckerman
Zwartkops	E Alcock

THREE: Stamp Vendors

FOUR

RETURN OF POST OFFICE BUILDINGS IN 1899

Alice	Public Offices and Post Office premises
Beaconsfield	Post Office premises and postmaster's quarters
Beaufort West	Public, Postal and Telegraph Office premises
Bizana	Public Offices and Post Office premises
Bolotwa	Court Room, New Post Office and Superintendent Native Quarters
Britstown	Post Office premises
Burghersdorp	Cape Police Office in Post Office premises
	Post and Telegraph Office premises
Butterworth	New Post Office premises
Cala	Public Offices and Post Office premises
Calvinia	Post Office premises
Cathcart	Public Offices, Court House, and Post Office premises
Cofimvaba	Public Offices and Post Office premises
Colesberg	Civil Commissioner and Resident Magistrate's Offices and Post Office
Douglas	Public Offices, Court Room and Post Office premises
	New Post Office premises
East London	Public Offices and Post Office premises
	Post Office premises and Court Room, for East London West Bank
Elliot	New Post Office premises
Engcobo	Post Office premises
Flagstaff	Public Offices and Post Office
	Postal Office Hut
Fort Beaufort	Court Room, Post and Telegraph Office premises
Grahamstown	New Post and Telegraph Office premises
Griquatown	Post Office premises, Court House, Police Offices
Idutywa	Post Office premises and Quarters
Kenhardt	Post Office premises
	Old Post Office premises
Kentani	Public Offices and Post Office premises

Kimberley	Post and Telegraph Office premises and Postmaster's Residence
	Residence of Inspector of Telegraphs
King Williams Town	Public Offices and Post Office premises
Klaarstroom ..	Public Offices and Post Office premises
Klipdam	New Post Office premises
	Old Post Office premises
Knysna Heads	Post Office, New Pilot Station
	Post Office, Rocket Shed
	Post Office, Signal Station
Komgha	Public Offices, Post Office premises, Cape Police
Lady Frere	New Post Office premises
Libode	Public Offices and Post Office premises
Lusikisiki	Public Offices and Post Office premises
	Postal Hut
Maclear	Public Offices and Post Office premises
Matatiele	Public Offices and Post Office premises
Middledrift	Public Offices, Post and Telegraph Offices and Postmaster's Quarters
Molteno	Assistant Resident Magistrate's and Post and Telegraph Offices
Mount Ayliff	Public Offices and Post Office premises
Mount Fletcher	Post Office premises
Mount Frere	Post Office premises
	Public Offices and Post Office premises
Mqanduli	Public Offices and Post Office premises
Murraysburg	Public Offices and Post Office premises
Ngqeleni	Public Offices and Post Office premises
Nqamakwe	Old Public Offices and Post Office premises
Palmietfontein	Post Office premises
Peddie	Public Offices, Post and Telegraph Office premises
	Old Calvary Barracks, Civil Commissioner's Quarters, Postmaster's Quarters, Chief Constable's Quarters, Miss Seymour's Quarters, Scab Inspector's Quarters, Police Horses
Philipstown	Court House and Post Office premises
Port Alfred	Court and Post Office premises
	Postmaster's Quarters
Port Elizabeth	Post Office premises
Port St John's	Public Offices, Post Office and Customs
Queenstown	Public Offices and Post Office premises
Qumbu	Public Offices and Post Office premises
St Mark's	Residence and Post Office premises

Setlagoli	Old Telegraph Office premises
Simonstown	Post Office and Searcher's Office premises
	Post Office Quarters
Sutherland	Public Office, Post Office premises, Jail and Jailer's Quarters
Tabankulu	Public Offices and Post Office premises
Taungs	Old Post Office premises
Tsolo	Public Offices, Post Office premises and Jail
Tsomo	Post Office premises and Quarters
Ugie	Post Office premises
Umtata	Post Office premises
	Post Office Store
Umzimkulu	New Public Offices and Post Office premises
	Old Public Offices and Post Office premises
	Old Post Office premises
Uniondale	Post Office premises
	Postmaster's Quarters
Upington	Post Office premises
Venterstad	Assistant Resident Magistrate's Office, Court, Quarters and Post and Telegraph Office premises
Vryburg	Post Office premises
Willowmore	Public Offices and Post Office premises
Willowvale	Public Offices, Post Office premises and Jail
	New Post Office premises
Woodstock	Telegraph Form Destructor

Two facts can be derived from this listing: the comparatively large investment that the Cape Post Office must have made in the creation a postal infrastructure in the Transkeian territories; and the fact that a relatively large number of post offices shared their premises with other agencies of local government. This underlines the inter-departmental role played by the Post Office in the creation of a colonial administration for the Cape, and perhaps more to the point, the importance of a well-subsidised and efficient system of communication to a developing economy. The postal system was never a profitable service for the Colonial Government, not until it was united with the Telegraph Department anyway, but there was never any discussion about cutting back services to districts that showed poor financial returns (CGH, 1879, CGH, 1881).

FIVE

LIST OF HEAD AND SUSIDIARY POST OFFICES, 1886

All offices given here in capital letters are Head Post Offices, which were normally denoted by the Cape GPO in its listings by the acronym HO. Sub-Post Offices were given the acronym of SO, while all others listed here with no acronyms attached were listed as Post Office Agencies or POAs.

ABERDEEN	Aberdeen Road SO, Doorn Draai and Putfontein
ADELAIDE	Mancazana
ALEXANDRIA	Niekerk's Hope SO
ALICE	Funah's Kloof
ALICEDALE	Coerney SO, Enon and Sandflats SO
ALIWAL NORTH	Patriot's Klip
BALFOUR	none listed
BARKLY EAST	Barkly Pass, Clearwater, Lyndale, Moshesh's Ford and Ravensfell
BARKLY WEST	Boetsap SO, Daniel's Kuil, Delport's Hope, Gong Gong SO, Hebron SO, Klein Boetsap, Longlands, Niekerk's Rush, Spitzkop and Waldeck's Plant
BEACONSFIELD	none listed
BEAUFORT WEST	Brakfontein, Letjesbosch, Nel's Poort SO, Phizantefontein, Slangfontein, Uitkyki and Wagenaarskraal
BEDFORD	Baviaan's Drift, Daggaboer's Nek, East Riet River, Fish River Randt and Glen Lynden
BLANCO	none listed
BREDASDORP	Cape L'Agulhas
BRITSTOWN	Jackhals Kuilen and Walthoorns Kraal
BURGERSDORP	Bethulic Bridge, Brand Spruit, Haaspoort and Klein Plaats
BUTTERWORTH	Entlambe, Ibeka SO, Kentani SO, Nqamakwe SO and Toleni SO
CALA	Bonawe SO, Embokotwa and Minard SO
CALEDON	Fairfield, Genadendal SO, Greyton, Hermanuspetrusfontein, Houw Hoek SO, River Zonder End SO, Stanford SO, Villiersdorp and Zandfontein
CALITZDORP	none listed

CALVINIA	Bloemfontein SO, Boterkloof, Boven Douwnes, Brand Vlei De Drift, Groen River, Kloudskraal, Mariasdal, Middle Post, Onderste Doorns, Spitzkop and Vaalfontein
CARNARVON	Boterleegte, Paarde Vlei and Van Wyk's Vlei
CATHCART	Glencairn, Rockford, Thomas River, Toise River SO and Waku Station
CERES	Bokfontein, De Keur, Groenfontein, Hottentot's Kloof and Prince Alfred's Hamlet
CERES ROAD	Breede River Station SO
CLANWILLIAM	Ebenezer, Eland's Vlei, Lambert's Bay, Modderfontein, Pakhuis, Rondegat, Van Rhynsdorp SO, Vredendal and Wupperthal
CLAREMONT	none listed
COLESBERG	none listed
COMMADAGGA	Middleton SO
COOKHOUSE	none listed
CRADOCK	Achter Sneeuwberg, Dwingfontein, Eland's Drift, Fish River, Mortimer, Northam, Paardekraal and Witmoss
CYPHERGAT	none listed
DARLING	Mamre
DE AAR	Hout Kraal and Potfontein
DORDRECHT	Bankies, Buffelsfontein and Indwe
DOUGLAS	Thornhill
DURBANVILLE	Durban Road SO and Philadelphia
EAST LONDON	Amalinda, Cambridge SO, East London Station, Fort Jackson SO, Knight's Farm, Maclean Town, Thompson's and Warrendale
ENGCOBO	Ncora and Slang River SO
FORT BEAUFORT	Blinkwater SO, Edendale, Koonap Bridge, Orange Grove SO, Post Retief SO and Yellow Wood Trees
FRASERBURG	Grass Kraal , Karee Kop, Riet Vlei, Spioenberg and Steenkamp's Poort
FRASERBURG ROAD	none listed
FRENCH HOEK	none listed
GEORGE	Doorn River, Great Brak River SO, Hooge Kraal, Mill River SO, Sinksa Bridge and Woodville
GRAAFF-REINET	Adendorp, Kendrew Station, Klip Drift, Naudesberg, New Bethesda, Oudeberg, Petersburg and Wheatlands
GRAHAMSTOWN	Atherstone SO, Bowden SO, Carlisle Bridge, Committee's Drift, Fort Brown, Hell Poort, Highlands SO, Lemoen Kraal, Riebeek East SO, Seven Fountains and Sidbury
GRIQUATOWN	Campbell

HANKEY	Andries Kraal SO
HANOVER	Hanover Road SO
HEIDELBERG	none listed
HERSCHEL	Bensonvale and Palmietfontein SO
HOPE FIELD	Hoetjes Bay SO, Langebaan, Lange Riet Vlei, Oliphant's Kraal, St Helena Bay SO and Vredenberg SO
HOPE TOWN	Belmont SO and Witteputs
HUMANSDORP	Assegaai Bush, Cape St Francis, Clarkson, Gamtoos River Ferry, Jagersbosch SO, Witte Els Bosch and Zuurbron
IDUTYWA	Clarkebury SO
JAMESTOWN	none listed
JANSENVILLE	Greystone, Klipplaat SO, Mount Stewart SO, Oatlands SO, Waterford and Volkers River
KALK BAY	none listed
KENHARDT	none listed
KEI ROAD	none listed
KEISKAMMAHOEK	none listed
KIMBERLEY	Charlottesdal, Modder River SO, Riverton, Schmidts Drift and Warrenton
KING WILLIAM'S TOWN	Berlin SO, Blaney Junction, Debe Nek, Frankfort, Green River, Iquibica, King William's Town Station SO, Middle Drift, Mount Coke, Peelton, St Matthew's and Welcome Wood
KNYSNA	Barrington, Belvidere, Kransbosch, Kruis Valley, Millwood SO, Vlugte and Yzerneck
KOKSTAD	Cedarville Drift, Fort Donald, Glengarry, Matatiele, Mount Ayliff SO, Mount Fletcher, New Amalfi and Strydfontein
KOMGHA	Draaibosch, Kei River Mouth, Kuku, Lilyvale (Hart's), Mooiplaats and Silver Vale (Cronk's)
LADISMITH	Amalienstein
LADY FRERE	none listed
LADY GREY	Karnmelkspruit
MACLEAR	none listed
MALMESBURY	Abbotsdale, Kalabas Kraal, Klipheuvel Station SO, Malmesbury Station SO, Middle Swartland, Moorreesberg and Paardeberg
MARAISBURG	none listed
MIDDELBURG	Alandale, Brandt Kraal, Conway, De Kuilen, Middelburg Road SO, Roode Hoogte, Schoongezicht, Tafelberg SO, The Willows and Varkenskop
MOLTENO	none listed

FIVE: Post Offices

MONTAGU	Brakfontein (Onder Wagen Boomberg) and Concordia
MOSSEL BAY	Blands Drift SO, Brandwacht, Geelbeck's Vlei, Hartenbosch, Herbertsdale SO, Ruytersbosch, South Middelveld, Upper Gouritz River, Vogel Vlei and Voor Attaquas Kloof
MOUNT FRERE	none listed
MOWBRAY	none listed
MURRAYSBURG	Groot Plaats and Zuur Poort
NAAUPOORT	none listed
NAPIER	Elim
NEWLANDS	none listed
O'OKIEP	Concordia
ORANGE RIVER	Kranskuil
OUDTSHOORN	Armoed, Groot Kraal, Hazenjacht, Jan Fourie's Kraal, Kruis River, Langeverwacht, Lategaan's Vlei, Matjes River, Meirings Poort SO, Rankins, Schoeman's Hoek, Vlakteplaats and Wynands River SO
PAARL	Klapmuts SO, Lady Grey Bridge SO, Paarl Station SO and Simondium SO
PEARSTON	none listed
PEDDIE	Bell, Breakfast Vlei, Falloden and Wooldridge SO
PHILIPSTOWN	Petrusville SO
PIQUETBERG	Drommel Vlei, Kersefontein, Roode Baai, St Helena Fontein, The Kruis and Verloren Vallei
PIQUETBERG ROAD	Bridgetown, Halfmanshof SO, Hermon Station, Kleinberg River, Riebeek Kasteel SO, Riebeek West SO and Saron
PLETTENBERG'S BAY	Forest Hall, Groot River, Keubooms River and Witte Drift
PORT ALFRED	Bathurst SO, Clumber, Cuylerville, Kowie West and Southwell
PORT ELIZABETH	Addo, Coega, Gedultz River, Green Bushes, Kinkelbosch, Lawrence Street SO, Nanaga, North End Station, Thorn Hill, Witte Klip SO and Zwartkops SO
PORTERVILLE	The Rest
PORT NOLLOTH	none listed
PRIESKA	Brandewyn's Kuil, Draghoender, Grootdoorn Pan, Modderfontein and Omdraais Vlei
PRINCE ALBERT	Grootfontein SO, Klaarstroom SO, Prince Albert Road SO, Seven Weeks Poort and Zeekoegat
QUEENSTOWN	Bailey, Bolotwa SO, Bradford, Glen Grey, Hackney, Imvani SO, Kamastone, Lesseyton Drift Hotel, Mapassa's Leven, Turvey's Post and Tylden SO
QUMBU	Fair Valley and Tsolo SO
RICHMOND	Richmond Road SO and Rietfontein

RIVERDALE	Buffels Kraal, Fontein Vlei, Langeberg and Toll House
ROBBEN ISLAND	none listed
ROBERTSON	Klaas Voogt's River, Lady Grey, Middelbosjesveld and Roodewal
RONDEBOSCH	Rosebank SO
ST JOHN'S RIVER	Egoso, Emfundiswani and Palmerton
ST MARKS	Southeyville
SALEM	none listed
SALT RIVER	Maitland
SEA POINT	none listed
SEYMOUR	Buxton SO, Erf No 17, Hertzog, Katberg, Philipton SO and Upper Blinkwater
SIMONSTOWN	none listed
SOMERSET EAST	Been Leegte, Coetzer's Kloof, Groot Vlakte and Zuurberg SO
SOMERSET WEST	Eerste River SO, Eerste River Station SO, Grabouw, Mosterds Bay (Strand), Raithby and Sir Lowry's Pass
SPRINGBOKFONTEIN	Bitterfontein, Garies, Komaggas SO, Lilyfontein SO, Namroep, Pella, Spectakel SO, Steinkopf and Walle Kraal
STELLENBOSCH	Lynedoch SO, Kuils River, Mulder's Vlei, Stellenbosch Station SO and Vredenberg Station
STERKSTROOM	Sterkstroom Station SO
STEYNSBURG	none listed
STUTTERHEIM	Bolo SO, Dohne Toll SO, Emgwali, Grey Town and Kabousie SO
SUTHERLAND	none listed
SWELLENDAM	Barrydale SO, Malagas, Middel River, Port Beaufort, Storms Vlei and Zuurbrak SO
TARKASTAD	Kleinhaasfontein, Klipkraal, Spring Valley, Upper Zwart Kei and Vogelstruis Nek
TOUWS RIVER	Buffels River Station, Constable and Triangle
TSOMO	Main
TULBAGH	Tulbagh Road SO
UGIE	Longdens
UITENHAGE	Afdak, Barroo Kraal SO Blue Cliff, Centlivres, Despatch, Glen Connor, Kariega Station, Klein Poort, Kromme Poort, Redhouse, The Fountain, Two Waters, Uitenhage Station, Welgevonden, and Wolvefontein
UMTATA	Elliotdale, Mtentu and Old Morley
UMZIMKULU	none listed
UNIONDALE	Avontuur SO, Buffels Klip, Haarlem, Krakeel River, Misgund and Twee Rivieren
UPINGTON	none listed

UPPER PAARL	none listed
VENTERSTAD	none listed
VICTORIA WEST	Liebenberg's Dam, Pampoen Poort, Spytpoort and Victoria West Road SO
WELLINGTON	Wellington Station SO
WEST BANK	none listed
WHITTLESEA	none listed
WILLOMORE	Heuvel Kraal, Steytlerville and Swanepoel's Poort
WOODSTOCK	none listed
WORCESTER	Goudini Road, Hammansdoorn River, Hex River, Hex River East, Matjesfontein SO, Rawsonville and Worcester Station SO
WYNBERG	Diep River SO, Kenilworth, Muizenburg SO, Plumstead SO and Retreat

SIX

LIST OF MAIN POSTS 1903

Aberdeen to Aberdeen Road, mails transported by motor
Alexandria to Grahamstown, mails transported by cart
Adelaide to Bedford, mails transported by cart
Alice to Seymour, mails transported by cart
Aliwal North to Aliwal North Station, mails transported by cart
      to Herschel, mails transported by cart
      to Jamestown, mails transported by cart
Ashton to Montagu, mails transported by cart
Avontuur to Uniondale, mails transported by cart
Barkly East to Dordrecht, mails transported by cart
      to Lady Grey, mails transported by cart
Barkly West to Kimberley, mails transported by cart
Barroe to Steytlerville, mails transported by cart
Barrydale to Buffelsjagts River Bridge, mails transported by cart
Beaconsfield to Kimberley, mails transported by tram
Bedford to Adelaide, mails transported by cart
      to Cookhouse, mails transported by cart
      to Fort Beaufort, mails transported by cart
Belmont to Douglas, mails transported by cart
Berlin to Maclean Town, mails transported by cart
Biesjespoort to Murraysburg, mails transported by cart
Breakfast Vlei to Peddie, mails transported by cart
Bredasdorp to Caledon, mails transported by cart
      to L'Agulhas, mails transported by horse
Britstown to De Aar, mails transported by cart
      to Prieska, mails transported by cart
      to Vosburg, mails transported by cart
Buffelsjagts River Bridge to Barrydale, mails transported by cart
Butterworth to Kei Road, mails transported by cart
      to Tsolo, mails transported by cart

       to Umtata, mails transported by cart
Cala to Indwe, mails transported by cart
       to Maclear, mails transported by cart
       to Umtata, mails transported by cart
Caledon to Bredasdorp, mails transported by cart
       to Caledon Station, mails transported by cart
       to Worcester, mails transported by cart
Calitzdorp to Oudtshoorn, mails transported by cart
Calvinia to Clanwilliam, mails transported by cart
Campbell to Daniel's Kuil, mails transported by cart
Camp's Bay to Sea Point, mails transported by tram
Cape Town to Gardens, mails transported by tram
       to Sea Point, mails transported by tram
       to Sir Lowry Road, mails transported by tram
Carnarvon to Kenhardt, mails transported by cart
       to Victoria West, mails transported by cart
Ceres to Ceres Road, mails transported by cart
Clanwilliam to Calvinia, mails transported by cart
       to Eendekuil, mails transported by cart
       to Vanrhynsdorp, mails transported by cart
Colesberg to Colesberg Junction, mails transported by cart
Constantia to Wynberg, mails transported by cart
Cookhouse to Bedford, mails transported by cart
       to Somerset East, mails transported by cart
Cradock to Maraisburg, mails transported by cart
       to Cradock Station, mails transported by cart
Daniel's Kuil to Campbell, mails transported by cart
Darling to Malmesbury, mails transported by cart
De Aar to Britstown, mails transported by cart
Dordrecht to Barkly East, mails transported by cart
       to Dordrecht Station, mails transported by cart
       to Jamestown, mails transported by cart
Douglas to Belmont, mails transported by cart
       to Griquatown, mails transported by cart
Draghoender to Kenhardt, mails transported by cart
       to Prieska, mails transported by cart
D'Urban Road to Durbanville, mails transported by cart
East London to East London Landing, mails transported by boat
Eendekuil to Clanwilliam, mails transported by cart
Engcobo to Tsomo, mails transported by cart

Fort Beaufort to Bedford, mails transported by cart
    to Grahamstown, mails transported by cart
    to King Williams Town, mails transported by cart
    to Seymour, mails transported by cart
Fraserburg to Fraserburg Road, mails transported by cart
    to Williston, mails transported by cart
French Hoek to Paarl, mails transported by cart
Gardens to Cape Town, mails transported by tram
Garies to O'okiep, mails transported by cart
    to Vanrhynsdorp, mails transported by cart
George to Humansdorp, mails transported by cart
    to Knysna, mails transported by cart
    to Mossel Bay, mails transported by cart
    to Oudtshoorn, mails transported by cart
Gordon's Bay to Sir Lowry's Pass, mails transported by cart
Graaff-Reinet to Graaff-Reinet Station, mails transported by cart
    to Murraysburg, mails transported by cart
    to Pearston, mails transported by cart
Grahamstown to Alexandria, mails transported by cart
    to Fort Beaufort, mails transported by cart
    to Grahamstown Station, mails transported by cart
    to King William's Town, mails transported by cart
Griquatown to Douglas, mails transported by cart
    to Kimberley, mails transported by cart
Hanover to Hanover Road, mails transported by cart
Heidelberg to Riversdale, mails transported by cart
    to Swellendam, mails transported by rail
Hermon to Riebeek West, mails transported by cart
Herschel to Aliwal North, mails transported by cart
Hopefield to Moorreesburg, mails transported by cart
Hope Town to Orange River, mails transported by cart
Hout Bay to Wynberg, mails transported by cart
Hout Kraal to Philipstown, mails transported by cart
Humansdorp to George, mails transported by cart
    to Port Elizabeth, mails transported by cart
Imvani to Tsomo, mails transported by cart
Indwe to Cala, mails transported by cart
Jamestown to Aliwal North, mails transported by cart
    to Dordrecht, mails transported by cart
Jansenville to Mount Stewart, mails transported by cart

Kabousie to Stutterheim, mails transported by cart
Kalabas Kraal to Mamre, mails transported by horse
Kei Road to Butterworth, mails transported by cart
Kenhardt to Carnarvon, mails transported by cart
      to Draghoender, mails transported by cart
      to Upington, mails transported by cart
Kenilworth to Barkly West, mails transported by cart
      to Kimberley, mails transported by tram
Kimberley to Beaconsfield, mails transported by tram
      to Griquatown, mails transported by cart
      to Kenilworth, mails transported by tram
      to Kimberley Station, mails transported by cart
King William's Town to Fort Beaufort, mails transported by cart
      to Grahamstown, mails transported by cart
      to King Williams Town Station, mails transported by cart
Klaarstroom to Prince Albert, mails transported by cart
Klipdam to Winsorton Road, mails transported by cart
Knysna to George, mails transported by cart
      to Knysna Landing, mails transported by boat
      to Plettenberg's Bay, mails transported by cart
Kokstad to Harding, mails transported by cart
      to Maclear, mails transported by cart
      to Umtata, mails transported by cart
      to Umzimkulu, mails transported by cart
Krankuil to Petrusville, mails transported by cart
Kuruman to Vryburg, mails transported by cart
Ladismith to Laingsburg, mails transported by cart
      to Riverdale, mails transported by cart
Lady Frere to Queenstown, mails transported by cart
Lady Grey to Barkly East, mails transported by cart
      to Robertson, mails transported by cart
L'Agulhas to Bredasdorp, mails transported by horse
Laingsburg to Ladismith, mails transported by cart
Lower Paarl to Paarl Station, mails transported by cart
Maclean Town to Berlin, mails transported by cart
Maclear to Cala, mails transported by cart
      to Kokstad, mails transported by cart
      to Tsolo, mails transported by cart
Malmesbury to Darl;ing, mails transported by cart
      to Malmesbury Station, mails transported by cart

Mamre to Kalabas Kraal, mails transported by horse
Maraisburg to Cradock, mails transported by cart
    to Thebus, mails transported by cart
Maribogo to Setlagoli, mails transported by horse
Matjesfontein to Sutherland, mails transported by cart
Middelburg to Middelburg Station, mails transported by cart
    to Rosmead, mails transported by cart
Mier to Zwart Modder, mails transported by camels
Montagu to Ashton, mails transported by cart
Moorreesburg to Hopefield, mails transported by cart
Morokwen to Vryburg, mails transported by ox-cart
Mosita to Setlagoli, mails transported by horse
Mossel Bay to George, mails transported by cart
    to Mossel Bay Landing, mails transported by boat
    to Oudtshoorn, mails transported by cart
    to Riversdale, mails transported by cart
Mount Ayliff to Post St Johns, mails transported by cart
Mount Stewart to Jansenville, mails transported by cart
Murraysburg to Biesjespoort, mails transported by cart
    to Biesjespoort, mails transported by cart
    to Graaff-Reinet, mails transported by cart
Norval's Pont to Venterstad, mails transported by cart
O'okiep to Garies, mails transported by cart
Orange River to Hope Town, mails transported by cart
Oudtshoorn to Calitzdorp, mails transported by cart
    to George, mails transported by cart
    to Mossel Bay, mails transported by cart
    to Prince Albert, mails transported by cart
Paarl to French Hoek, mails transported by cart
Paarl Station to Lower Paarl, mails transported by cart
Pearston to Graaff-Reinet, mails transported by cart
    to Somerset East, mails transported by cart
Peddie to Breakfast Vlei, mails transported by cart
Petrusville to Krankuil, mails transported by cart
Philipstown to Hout Kraal, mails transported by cart
Piquetberg to Piquetberg Station, mails transported by cart
    to Porterville, mails transported by cart
Plettenberg's Bay to Knysna, mails transported by cart
Port Elizabeth to Humansdorp, mails transported by cart
    to Port Elizabeth Landing, mails transported by boat

        to Port Elizabeth Station, mails transported by van
        to North Jetty, mails transported by van
Porterville to Piquetberg, mails transported by cart
        to Porterville Road, mails transported by cart
Port Nolloth to Port Nolloth Landing, mails transported by boat
Port St Johns to Mount Ayliff, mails transported by cart
        to Umtata, mails transported by cart
Prieska to Britstown, mails transported by cart
        to Draghoender, mails transported by cart
Prince Albert to Klaarstroom, mails transported by cart
        to Oudtshoorn, mails transported by cart
        to Prince Albert Road, mails transported by cart
Queenstown to Lady Frere, mails transported by cart
        to Queenstown Station , mails transported by cart
        to Whittlesea, mails transported by cart
Raman's Drift to Steinkopf, mails transported by ox-cart
Richmond to Richmond Road, mails transported by cart
Riebeek West to Hermon, mails transported by cart
Riversdale to Heidelberg, mails transported by cart
        to Ladismith, mails transported by cart
        to Mossel Bay, mails transported by cart
Riverton to Riverton Road, mails transported by cart
Robertson to Lady Grey, mails transported by cart
Rosmead to Middelburg, mails transported by cart
Sea Point to Camp's Bay, mails transported by tram
        to Cape Town, mails transported by tram
Setlagoli to Maribogo, mails transported by horse
        to Mosita, mails transported by horse
Seymour to Alice, mails transported by cart
        to Fort Beaufort, mails transported by cart
Simonstown to Simonstown Station, mails transported by cart
Sir Lowry Road to Cape Town, mails transported by tram
Sir Lowry's Pass to Gordon's Bay, mails transported by cart
Somerset East to Cookhouse, mails transported by cart
        to Pearston, mails transported by cart
Somerset Strand to Strand Halt, mails transported by cart
Somerset West to Somerset West Station, mails transported by cart
Steinkopf to Raman's Drift, mails transported by ox-cart
Stellenbosch to Stellenbosch Station, mails transported by cart
Steytlerville to Barroe, mails transported by cart

Strand Halt to Somerset Strand, mails transported by cart
Strydenburg to Krankuil, mails transported by cart
Stutterheim to Kabousie, mails transported by cart
Swakopmund to Walwich Bay, mails transported by horse
Swellendam to Heidelberg, mails transported by rail
        to Swellendam Station, mails transported by cart
Table Bay to Table Bay Landing, mails transported by boat
Taungs to Taungs Station, mails transported by cart
Thebus to Maraisburg, mails transported by cart
Three Sisters to Wagenaar's Kraal , mails transported by cart
Tsolo to Butterworth, mails transported by cart
        to Maclear, mails transported by cart
Tsomo to Engcobo, mails transported by cart
        to Imvani, mails transported by cart
Tulbagh to Tulbagh Road, mails transported by cart
Umtata to Butterworth, mails transported by cart
        to Cala, mails transported by cart
        to Kokstad, mails transported by cart
        to Port St Johns, mails transported by cart
Umzimkulu to Kokstad, mails transported by cart
Uniondale to Avontuur, mails transported by cart
        to Willowmore, mails transported by cart
Upington to Kenhardt, mails transported by cart
        to Zwart Modder, mails transported by ox-cart
Vanrhynsdorp to Clanwilliam, mails transported by cart
        to Garies, mails transported by cart
Venterstad to Norval's Pont, mails transported by cart
Victoria West to Carnarvon, mails transported by cart
        to Victoria West Road, mails transported by cart
Vosburg to Britstown, mails transported by cart
Vryburg to Kuruman, mails transported by cart
        to Morokwen, mails transported by ox-cart
        to Vryburg Station, mails transported by cart
Wagenaar's Kraal to Three Sisters, mails transported by cart
Walwich Bay to Swakopmund, mails transported by horse
Wellington to Wellington Station, mails transported by cart
Whittlesea to Queenstown, mails transported by cart
Williston to Fraserburg, mails transported by cart
Willowmore to Uniondale, mails transported by cart
Windsorton Road to Klipdam, mails transported by cart

Worcester to Caledon, mails transported by cart
        to Worcester Station, mails transported by cart
Wynberg to Constantia, mails transported by cart
        to Hout Bay, mails transported by cart
Zwart Modder to Mier, mails transported by camels
        to Upington, mails transported by ox-cart

SEVEN

INDEX OF RAILWAY STATIONS 1862-1910

Abbotsdale, on the line from Cape Town to Eendekuil, opened on 12 November 1877.

Aberdeen Road, on the Graaff-Reinet line, opened on 3 February 1879. A telegraph office was opened in November 1882. Station master Charles Frank Robertson was appointed on 1 April 1909, salary £174 pa.

Achtertang, on the line from Rosrnead to Norval's Pont, opened on 17 December 1890. A telegraph office was opened in 1890.

Addo, on the line from Port Elizabeth to Rosmead, opened on 26 July 1875. A telegraph office was opened about 1885. Station master Alexander Forsyth, appointed 23 September 1909, salary £220 pa.

Adelaide, on the line from Blaney to Cookhouse, opened on 14 December 1903. A telegraph office was opened in 1904. Station master Mason Birbeck, appointed 1 November 1903, salary £232 pa.

Adendorp, on the Graaff-Reinet line, opened on 25 August 1879. A telegraph office was opened in 1883.

Albertinia Station, on the line from Cape Town to George, opened on 22 January 1906. A telegraph office was opened in 1906.

Albert Junction, on the line from Stormberg to Lady Grey, opened on 2 September 1885. The line from Stormberg to Springfontein was opened on 21 May 1892. A telegraph office was opened in 1891.

Alexandria, on the line from Port Elizabeth to Port Alfred, opened on 18 May 1909.

Alice Station, on the line from Blaney to Cookhouse, opened on 2 May 1904. A telegraph office was opened in 1905. Station master Edward Lewis, appointed 29 April 1904, salary £201 pa.

Alicedale Junction, on the line from Port Elizabeth to Rosmead, opened on 27 August 1877. The line from Port Elizabeth to Port Alfred was opened on 3 March 1879. Station master Arthur Edward Wayt, appointed 30 June 1908, salary £355 pa.

Aliwal North Station, on the line from Storrnberg to Lady Grey, opened on 2 September 1885. A telegraph office was opened in about 1885. Station master William Branfield, appointed 12 March 1897, salary £297 pa.

Aloes Station, on the line from Port Elizabeth to Rosmead, opened on 26 July 1875. Station master Stephanus Isaack Minnaar, appointed 17 September 1909, salary £252 pa.

Amabele Station, on the line from East London to Stormberg, opened on 15 April 1878. Line from Amabele to Butterworth, opened on 7 September 1904. A telegraph office was opened in 1907. Station master Horatio Edgar Jones, appointed 5 September 1904, salary £242 pa

Amalinda Station, on the line from East London to Stormberg, opened on 18 December 1876. A telegraph office was opened in October 1904.

Anenous Station on the line from Port Nolloth to Concordia, opened on 11 June 1887.

Artois Station, on the line from Cape Town to Artois, opened in 1904. A telegraph office was opened in 1902 for railway work only.

Arundel Station, on the line from Rosmead to Norval's Pont, opened on 16 October 1883. A telegraph office was opened in 1890.

Ascot Station, on the line from Cape Town to Ascot, opened on 28 May 1908.

Ashton Station, on the line from Cape Town to George, opened on October 1887. A telegraph office was opened in 1887.

Assegai Bosch Station, on the line from Port Elizabeth to Avontuur, opened on 15 June l906. A telegraph office was opened in 1906.

Atherstone Station, on the line from Port Elizabeth to Port Alfred, opened on 3 March 1879.

Avontuur Station, on the line from Port Elizabeth to Avontuur, opened on 1 January 1907, A telegraph office was opened in 1907 for railway work only.

Bailey Station, on the line from East London to Stormberg, opened on 15 October 1883. Station master Thomas Henry Lawrence, appointed 1 June 1908, salary £335 pa.

Bamboo Junction, on the line from Rosmead to Stormberg Junction, opened on 8 February 1892. A telegraph office was opened in 1904.

Bangor Station, on the line from Rosmead to Naaupoort. A telegraph office was opened in 1896.

Barkly Bridge Station, on the line from Port Elizabeth to Rosmead, opened on 26 July 1875. The line from Port Elizabeth to Port Alfred was opened on l8 May 1909. A telegraph office was opened in 1893. Station master Robert David Sparke, appointed 1 April 1909, salary £208 pa.

Barroe, also listed as Barroe Kraal, on the Graaff-Reinet line, opened on 1 August 1878. The line from Port Elizabeth to Rosmead was opened on 2 April 1883. Station master Robert Henry Jennett, appointed 9 August 1903, salary £186 pa.

Bathurst Station, on the line from Port Elizabeth to Port Alfred, opened on 1 December l884. A telegraph office was opened in 1897.

Beaconsfield Station, on the line from De Aar to Mafeking, opened on 28 November l885. A telegraph office was opened in about 1885. Station master James Quinlan, appointed 15 May 1903, salary £265 pa.

Beaufort Station. A telegraph office was opened in April 1880.

Beaufort West Station, on the line from Cape Town to De Aar, opened on 5 February l880. A telegraph office was opened in April 1880. Station master Frank Willie, appointed 1 June 1908, salary £335 pa.

Bedford Station, on the line from Blaney to Cookhouse, opened on 2 March 1903. A telegraph office was opened in 1905. Station master Alfred Henry Hann, appointed 1 June 1903, salary

£249 pa.

Bellevue Siding, on the line from Port Elizabeth to Rosmead, opened on 27 August 1877. A telegraph office was opened in October 1907.

Bellville, on the line from Cape Town to De Aar, opened on 13 February 1862. The line from Cape Town to Eendekuil was opened on 14 September 1876. Station master George Harry Ridout, appointed 7 July 1908, salary £280 pa.

Belmont Station, on the line from De Aar to Mafeking, opened on 28 November 1885. A telegraph office was opened in 1885. Station master JPG de Villiers, appointed 7 December 1901, salary £212 pa.

Berlin Station, on the line from East London to Stormberg, opened on 18 December 1876. A telegraph office was opened in January 1878. Station master Harry Blowen Pepper, appointed 22 July 1896, salary £232 pa.

Bethesda Road, on the Graaff-Reinet line, opened on 3 March 1898. A telegraph office was opened in October 1907.

Bethulie Bridge Station, on the line from Stormberg to Springfontein, opened on 21 May 1892

Biesjespoort Station, on the line from Cape Town to De Aar, opened on 14 May 1883. A telegraph office was opened in 1896.

Blaaubank Siding. A telegraph office was opened in 1898.

Blaauwater, on the line from Graaff-Reinet to Rosmead.

Blanco, on the line from Mossel Bay to Oudtshoorn. A telegraph office was opened in September 1881.

Blaney Station, also listed as Blaney Junction, on the line from East London to Stormberg, opened on 18 December 1876. The line from Blaney to Cookhouse was opened on 1 May 1877. A telegraph office was opened in January 1878. Station master Vincent Henry Begley, appointed 18 June 1904, salary £255 pa.

Blue Cliff Station, on the Graaff-Reinet line, opened on 22 September 1875. A telegraph office was opened in about 1885.

Border Siding, on the line from De Aar to Mafeking, opened on 1 December 1890. A telegraph office was opened in 1896.

Bosman's Crossing Station, on the line from Cape Town to De Aar, opened on 1 May 1862. A telegraph office was opened in 1894.

Bot River Station, on the line from Cape Town to Caledon, opened on 1 August 1902. A telegraph office was opened in 1902.

Bowker's Park Station, on the line from East London to Stormberg, opened on 15 October 1883. The line from Bowker's Park to Tarkastad was opened on 5 December 1900. A telegraph office was opened in 1897.

Brackenfell Siding, on the line from Cape Town to Eendekuil, opened on 14 September 1876. A telegraph office was opened on 1 March 1904.

Brakpoort Siding, on the line from Beaufort West to De Aar Junction. A telegraph office was opened in 1898.

Brakpits Station, on the line from Port Nolloth to Concordia, opened on 23 April 1889

Breede River Station, on the line from Cape Town to De Aar, opened on 14 June 1876. A telegraph office was opened in June 1878.

Britstown Station, on the line from De Aar to Prieska, opened on 1 April 1905. A telegraph office was opened in 1907. Station master John Florence, appointed 10 March 1904, salary £225 pa.

Brussels Siding. A telegraph office was opened in 1898.

Buhrmannsdrift Station, on the Mafeking local line, opened on 1 November 1904.

Burghersdorp Station, on the line from Stormberg to Lady Grey, opened on 19 March 1885. A telegraph office was opened in about 1885. Station master Ernest Henry De Bene, appointed 1 September 1902, salary £285 pa.

Bushman's River Station, on the line from Port Elizabeth to Rosmead, opened on 3 February 1879.

Butterworth Station, on the line from Amabele to Butterworth, opened on 17 December 1906. A telegraph office was opened in 1908. Station master Daniel Petrie, appointed 12 December 1906, salary £256 pa.

Caledon Station, on the line from Cape Town to Caledon, opened on 1 August 1902. A telegraph office was opened in 1907. Station master Jonathan Pitcher, appointed 1 August 1902, salary £289 pa.

Cambridge Station, on the line from East London to Stormberg, opened on 18 December 1876. A telegraph office was opened in 1904. Station master John Horne Storey, appointed 11 September 1903, salary £233 pa.

Cape Collieries, on the line from Rosmead to Stormberg Junction, opened on 8 February 1898.

Cape Town Docks, on the Cape Town Suburban line, opened on 11 May 1975

Cape Town Railway Office. A telegraph office was opened in January 1876.

Cape Town Station. The line from Cape Town to De Aar was opened on 13 February 1862. The Cape Town Suburban line was opened on 1 December 1905. Station master Joseph George Upham, appointed 28 March 1906, salary £180 pa.

Carlton Station, on the line from Rosmead to Naaupoort. A telegraph office was opened before 1888.

Carnarvon Station, on the line from Cape Town to Carnarvon, opened on 1 August 1906. A telegraph office was opened in 1907. Station master JG Upham, appointed 28 March 1906, salary £180 pa.

Cathcart Station, on the line from East London to Stormberg, opened on 3 November 1879. A telegraph office was opened in about 1903. Station master George Cooper, appointed 11 January 1899, salary £265 pa.

Centlivres Station, on the Graaff-Reinet line, opened on 22 September 1875.

Ceres Road Station, on the line from Cape Town to De Aar, opened on 3 November 1875. A telegraph office was opened in May 1876. Station master William Alexander McMurray, appointed 27 February 1905, salary £236 pa.

Chiselhurst Station, on the line from East London to Stormberg, opened on 18 December 1876

Cillies Station, on the line from Paarl to French Hoek, opened on 7 June 1904

Claremont Station on the line from Cape Town to Simonstown, opened on 19 December 1864. A telegraph office was opened in May 1876. Station master Albert William Bowers, appointed 23 April 1902, salary £247 pa.

Clumber Station, on the line from Port Elizabeth to Port Alfred, opened on 1 December 1884.

Coega Station, on the line from Port Elizabeth to Rosmead, opened on 26 July 1875. A telegraph office was opened in 1908. Station master Robert West, appointed 20 September 1909, salary £215 pa.

Coerney Station, on the line from Port Elizabeth to Rosmead, opened on 1 March 1876. Station master SJ Clark, appointed 1 June 1893, salary £264 pa.

Colesberg Junction, on the line from Rosmead to Norval's Pont, opened on 16 October 1883. A telegraph office was opened in about 1885.

Colesberg Station. A telegraph office was opened in about 1885.

Collett Siding. A telegraph office was opened in 1905.

Colonies Plaats Station, on the line from Graaff-Reinet to Rosmead.

Commadagga Station, on the line from Port Elizabeth to Rosmead, opened on 3 February 1879. Station master Ms Ina Longbottom, appointed 23 June 1903, salary £188 pa.

Concordia Station, on the line from Port Nolloth to Concordia, opened on 22 April 1889. A telegraph office was opened in 1894.

Constable Station, on the line from Cape Town to De-Aar, opened on 1 February 1878. A telegraph office was opened in June 1880.

Content Station, on the line from De Aar to Mafeking, opened on 1 December 1890

Conway Station, on the line from Port Elizabeth to Rosrnead, opened on 2 April 1883. A telegraph office was opened in 1908. Station master Rupert Stanley Higgs, appointed 24 January 1908, salary £216 pa.

Cookhouse Station, on the line from Port Elizabeth to Rosmead, opened on 2 March 1880. The line from Cookhouse to Somerset East was opened on 1 August 1882. The line from Blaney to Cookhouse was opened on 2 March 1903. A telegraph office was opened in March 1882. Station master Peter McNab Ramsey, appointed 17 September 1901, salary £300 pa.

Cradock Station, on the line from Port Elizabeth to Rosmead, opened on 1 June 1881. A telegraph office was opened in about 1885. Station master Joseph William Needham, appointed 18 September 1902, salary £360 pa.

Crawford Station, on the line from Cape Town to Ottery, opened on 1 February 1904

Cyphergat Station, on the line from East London to Stormberg, opened on 16 February 1884. A telegraph office was opened in 1885. Station master Leopold Pettifer, appointed 1 November 1906, salary £174 pa.

Darling Station, on the line from Cape Town to Hopefield, opened on 28 February 1903. Station master John James Paisley, appointed 19 December 1904, salary £216 pa.

Dassie Deur Station on the line from Port Elizabeth to Rosmead, opened on 1 June 1881. Station master Edmund Arthur Webber, appointed 17 February 1909, salary £226 pa.

De Aar Junction, also listed as De Aar, on the line from Naauwpoort to De Aar, opened on 31 March 1884. The line from Cape Town to De Aar was opened on 31 March 1884. The line from De Aar to Mafeking was opened on 3 November 1884. The line from De Aar to Prieska was opened on 1 April 1905, A telegraph office was opened in January 1884. Station master Charles Arthur Pennington, appointed 1 July 1908, salary £339 pa.

Debe Nek Station. A telegraph office was opened in 1908.

De Doorns Station, on the line from Cape Town to De Aar, opened on 7 November 1877. A telegraph office was opened in 1898.

Deelfontein Station, on the line from Cape Town to De Aar, opened on 31 March 1884. A telegraph office was opened in 1900.

Despatch, on the Graaff-Reinet line, opened on 22 September 1875. Station master John Smith, appointed 9 March 1906, salary £238 pa.

Diep River Station, on the line from Cape Town to Simonstown, opened on 15 December 1882

Dohne, also listed as Dohne Toll, on the line from East London to Stormberg, opened on 15 August 1878. Station master Alfred Burton Spenceley, appointed 22 November 1907, salary £230 pa.

Doorn River Station, on the line from Mossel Bay to Oudtshoorn

Dordrecht Station, on the line from Sterkstroom to Maclear, opened on 1 February 1896. A telegraph office was opened in 1896.

Dronfield Station, on the line from Kimberley to Warrenton.

Durban Road. A telegraph office was opened in May 1876.

Dwaal Station, on the line from Naaupoort to De Aar Junction.

Dwarsvlei Station, on the line from Graaff-Reinet to Rosmead.

Eagle Station, on the line from Amabele to Butterworth, opened on 1 November 1905

East London Station, on the line from East London to Stormberg, opened on 18 November 1876. The East London Suburban line was opened on 15 August 1878, and on 15 August 1878 the line was extended to the Landing Jetty. A telegraph office was opened in about 1885. Station master Frederick William Crosbie, appointed 1 February 1893, salary £360 pa.

Eendekuil Station, on the line from Cape Town to Eendekuil, opened on 15 November 1902. A telegraph office was opened in 1885.

Eerste River Station, on the line from Cape Town to De Aar, opened on 13 February 1862. The line from Cape Town to Caledon was opened on 21 October 1889. A telegraph office was opened in January 1876.

Egerton Station, on the line from East London to Stormberg, opened on 18 December 1876

Elgin Station, on the line from Cape Town to Caledon, opened on 1 August 1902

Elliot Station, on the line from Sterkstroom to Maclear, opened on 18 May 1905. Before that time it was known as Elliot Siding and was served by a telegraph office, which had been opened here in 1897 but for railway work only. In 1905 it was upgraded to a Station and its telegraph service was opened up to the general public. Station master Thomas William Wostenholm, appointed 18 March 1905, salary £180 pa.

Elsie's River Halt, on the line from Cape Town to December Aar, opened on 13 February 1862
Essex Station, on the line from East London to Stormberg, opened on 5 May 1880
Faure Siding, on the line from Cape Town to Caledon, opened on 21 October 1889. A telegraph office was opened in 1896.
Firgrove Station, on the line from Cape Town to Caledon, opened on 21 October 1889. Station master Peter Christian Brand, appointed 23 September 1909, salary £247 pa.
Fish Hoek Station, on the line from Cape Town to Simonstown, opened on 1 December 1890
Fish River Station, on the line from Port Elizabeth to Rosmead, opened on 2 April 1883. Station master William Henry Norman Ware, appointed 21 March 1909, salary £205 pa.
Fort Beaufort, on the line from Blaney to Cookhouse, opened on 17 October 1904. A telegraph office was opened in November 1894. Station master Charles Frederick James Brine, appointed 14 October 1904, salary £201 pa.
Fort Jackson Station, on the line from East London to Stormberg, opened on 18 December 1876. Station master Thomas Weir Wilson, appointed 17 October 1904, salary £201 pa.
Fourteen Streams Station, on the line from De Aar to Mafeking, opened on 1 December 1890. A telegraph office was opened in 1890.
Francistown Station, British South Africa Co, on the line to Rhodesia. A telegraph office was opened in 1897. Station master RM MacLean, appointed 15 July 1908, salary £274 pa.
Fraserburg Road, on the line from Cape Town to De Aar, opened on 11 August 1879. A telegraph office was opened in August 1879. Station master Richard Thomas Trevithick, appointed 9 October 1905, salary £226 pa.
Fraserdale Station, on the line from Cape Town to Ottery, opened on 1 February 1904
French Hoek Station, on the line from Paarl to French Hoek, opened on 7 June 1904. Station master William Hotten Martyn, appointed 1 July 1907, salary £235 pa.
Fullerton Siding. A telegraph office was opened in 1906.
Gamtoos Station. A telegraph office was opened before 1910.
George Station, on the line from Cape Town to George, opened on 25 September 1907. A telegraph office was opened in March 1908.
Gerracoop Station, on the line from Port Nolloth to Concordia, opened on 15 March 1893.
Glencairn Station, on the line from Cape Town to Simonstown, opened on 1 December 1890
Glenconnor Station, on the Graaff-Reinet line, opened on 1 May 1877. Station master Steven Thomas Matthews, appointed 1 October 1907, salary £220 pa.
Glenharry Station, on the Graaff-Reinet line, opened on 3 March 1898. Station master D Pettit, appointed 20 March 1906, salary £200 pa.
Good Hope Station, on the line from Uitenhage to Klipplaat
Goodwood Station. A telegraph office was opened in 1909.
Goudini Road Station, on the line from Cape Town to De Aar, opened on 16 June 1876 A telegraph office was opened in July 1876. Station master Lewis Walter Walter, appointed 1 July 1907, salary £235 pa.
Graaff-Reinet Station, on the Graaff-Reinet line, opened on 26 August 1879. A telegraph office

was opened in about 1885. Station master George Finlay, appointed 18 August 1906, salary £285 pa.

Grahamstown Station, on the line from Port Elizabeth to Port Alfred, opened on 3 September 1879. A telegraph office was opened in about 1885. Station master Frederick William Connock, appointed 24 September 1905, salary £300 pa.

Graspan Station, on the line from De Aar to Mafeking, opened on 28 November 1885

Greatberg Siding, A telegraph office was opened in 1904.

Great Brak River Station, on the line from Mossel Bay to Oudtshoorn

Greytown Station, on the line from East London to Stormberg, opened on 1 January 1879

Groot Drakenstein Station, on the line from Paarl to French Hoek, opened on 7 June 1904

Grootfontein Station, on the line from Cape Town to De Aar, opened on 4 November 1878

Haarlem Station, on the line from Port Elizabeth to Avontuur, opened on 1 January 1907

Haasfontein Station, on the line from Graaff-Reinet, opened on 1 August 1878

Halseton Station, on the line from Sterkstroom to Maclear, opened on 1 February 1896

Hanover Road, on the line from Naauwpoort to De Aar, opened on 31 March 1884. A telegraph office was opened in 1885. Station master John Micheal Keating, appointed 21 November 1901, salary £250 pa.

Hartenbosch Station, on the line from Mossel Bay to Oudtshoorn

Hebron Road, A telegraph office was opened in 1890.

Heidelberg Station, on the line from Cape Town to George, opened on 19 February 1903. A telegraph office was opened in 1906.

Helderberg Station. A telegraph office was opened in 1904.

Henning Station, on the line from Rosmead to Stormberg Junction, opened on 8 February 1892

Hermon Station, on the line from Cape Town to De Aar, opened on 1 September 1875. Station master Alexander McAdam, appointed 21 October 1907, salary £247 pa.

Heuvel Kraal Station, on the line from Oudtshoorn to Klipplaat

Hex River Station, on the line from Cape Town to De Aar, opened on 7 November 1877

Highlands Station, on the line from Port Elizabeth to Port Alfred, opened on 3 March 1879

Honeynest Kloof Station, on the line from De Aar to Mafeking, opened on 28 November 1885

Hopefield Station on the line from Cape Town to Hopefield, opened on 28 February 1903. Station master Edward Kitley, appointed 3 June 1908, salary £220 pa.

Hout Kraal Station, on the line from De Aar to Mafeking, opened on 3 November 1884. Station master Arthur James Ford, appointed 1 July 1908, salary £280 pa.

Houwater Station on the line from De Aar to Prieska, opened on 1 April 1905

Houwhoek Station, on the line from Cape Town to Caledon, opened on 1 August 1902

Hugo Siding. A telegraph office was opened in 1901.

Huguenot Station, on the line from Cape Town to De Aar, opened on 4 November 1863. A telegraph office was opened in 1907. Station master Richard Lidsey Andrew, appointed 11 July 1908, salary £270 pa.

Humansdorp Station on the line from Port Elizabeth to Avontuur, opened on 1 November 1905.

A telegraph office was opened in January 1906.

Humewood Road, on the line from Port Elizabeth to Avontuur, opened on 1 April 1906

Hutchinson Station, on the line from Cape Town to De Aar, opened on 14 May 1883

Hutchinson Station, on the line from Cape Town to Carnarvon, opened on 1 May 1905. Station master Henry David van der Schyff, appointed 5 July 1908, salary £200 pa.

Ida Siding, on the line from Sterkstroom to Maclear, opened on 17 August 1904. A telegraph office was opened in 1905.

Imvani Station, on the line from East London to Stormberg, opened on 5 May 1880. Station master Nicholas Gaston Forget, appointed 1 March 1902, salary £232 pa.

Inciba Station, on the line from Amabele to Butterworth, opened on 15 April 1905. Also known as Zigzag. A telegraph office was opened on 15 April 1905.

Indwe Station, on the line from Sterkstroom to Maclear, opened on 1 February 1896. A telegraph office was opened in 1896. Station master Albert Goodwin, appointed 13 March 1905, salary £223 plus £48 house allowance pa.

Isigidimi Station, on the line from Stormberg to Lady Grey, opened on 2 September 1885

Jan de Boers Station, on the line from Cape Town to De Aar, opened on 1 February 1878

Jeffrey's Bay Station, on the line from Port Elizabeth to Avontuur, opened on 1 November 1905

Kalabas Kraal Station, on the line from Cape Town to Eendekuil, opened on 25 September 1877

Kalk Bay Station, on the line from Cape Town to Simonstown, opened on 5 May 1883. Station master Thomas Bewick Cairns, appointed 21 July 1908, salary £247 pa.

Kariega Station, on the Graaff-Reinet line, opened on 6 February 1877. A telegraph office was opened in 1907.

Kei Road, on the line from East London to Stormberg, opened on 1 May 1877. A telegraph office was opened in January 1878.

Kendrew Station, on the Graaff-Reinet line, opened on 17 March 1879

Kenilworth Station, on the line from Cape Town to Simonstown, opened on 19 December 1864. A telegraph office was opened in 1891.

Kerk Siding. A telegraph office was opened in 1898.

Ketting Siding. A telegraph office was opened in 1903.

Kimberley Station, on the line from De Aar to Mafeking, opened on 28 November 1885. A telegraph office was opened in about 1885. Station master Samuel Henry Day, appointed 23 May 1903, salary £295 pa.

King William's Town Station, on the line from Blaney to Cookhouse, opened on 1 May 1877. A telegraph office was opened in about 1885. Station master Walter Edward Dickerson, appointed 19 August 1906, salary £330 pa.

Klaas Voogts River Station, on the line from Cape Town to George, opened in October 1887

Klapmuts Station, on the line from Cape Town to De Aar, opened on 4 November 1863

Klein Poort Station, on the Graaff-Reinet line, opened on 1 August 1878. Station master JE Rowlands, appointed 1 April 1909, salary £215 pa.

Kleinstraat Station, on the line from Cape Town to De Aar, opened on 7 November 1877

Klerk Siding. A telegraph office was opened in 1901.

Klipbank Station, on the line to Beaufort West

Klipheuvel Station, on the line from Cape Town to Eendekuil, opened on 25 September 1877. Station master Edward Gilbert Frost, appointed 23 October 1907, salary £223 pa.

Klipplaat Station, also listed as Klipplaat Junction Station, on the Graaff-Reinet line, opened on 3 February 1879. Station master WJ Williams, appointed 27 September 1909, salary £259 pa.

Klipplaat Junction, on the line from Klipplaat to Oudtshoorn, opened on 1 August 1902.

Knapdaar Station, on the line from Stormberg to Springfontein, opened on 21 May 1892. Station master Emil Calvin Schaefer, appointed 14 September 1903, salary £270 pa.

Knysna Station, on the Knysna Local line, opened on 14 July 1907

Koelenhof Station, on the line from Cape Town to De Aar, opened on 4 November 1863

Komgha, on the line from Amabele to Butterworth, opened on 7 September 1904. Station master Charles Henry Slogrove, appointed 9 September 1904, salary £174 pa.

Komgha Station. A telegraph office was opened in 1907.

Kookfontein Station, on the line from Port Nolloth to Concordia, opened on 15 March 1893

Kraaifontein Junction, on the line from Cape Town to Eendekuil, opened on 14 September 1876. A telegraph office was opened in December 1876. Station master Alexander McDougall, appointed 1 August 1905, salary £180 pa.

Kraaipan Station, on the line from De Aar to Mafeking, opened on 3 October 1894

Krakeel River Station, on the line from Port Elizabeth to Avontuur, opened on 1 October 1906

Krankuil Station, on the line from De Aar to Mafeking, opened on 3 November 1884. Station master Arthur Edward Sansom, appointed 15 September 1905, salary £200 pa.

Kromme River Heights Station, on the line from Port Elizabeth to Avontuur, opened on 3 September 1906

Kroomie Siding, on the line from Blaney to Cookhouse, opened on 17 October 1904. A telegraph office was opened in August 1905.

Kubusie Station, on the line from East London to Storrnberg, opened on 15 April 1878

Kuils River Station, on the line from Cape Town to De Aar, opened on 13 February 1862. A telegraph office was opened in October 1904.

Kweekwa Station, on the line from Cape Town to Carnarvon, opened on 1 May 1905

Lady Grey Station, on the line from Stormberg to Lady Grey, opened on 2 November 1905. A telegraph office was opened in about 1907.

Laingsburg Station, on the line from Cape Town to De Aar, opened on 4 November 1878

Lakeside Station, on the line from Cape Town to Simonstown, opened on 15 December 1882

La Motte Station, on the line from Paarl to French Hoek, opened on 7 June 1904

Lang Vlei Station, on the line from Cape Town to George, opened in October 1887

Lansdowne Station, on the line from Cape Town to Ottery, opened on 1 February 1904

Lebanon Halt, on the line from Cape Town to Caledon, opened on 1 August 1902

Le Roux Station, on the line from Klipplaat to Oudtshoorn, opened on 14 December 1903

Letjesbosch Station, on the line from Cape Town to De Aar, opened on 5 February 1880

Letts Kraal Station, on the line from Graaff-Reinet, opened on, opened on 3 March 1898
Loerie Station, on the line from Port Elizabeth to Avontuur, opened on 1 November 1905
Lonetree Loop, on the line from East London to Stormberg, opened on 18 December 1876
Longhope Siding. A telegraph office was opened in 1890.
Lootsberg Spur Station, on the line from Graaff-Reinet to Rosmead.
Lower Incline Siding. A telegraph office was opened in 1903.
Ludlow Station, on the line from Rosmead to Naaupoort.
Lyndoch Station, on the line from Cape Town to De Aar, opened on 1 May 1862. Station master CH Watts, appointed 1 July 1897, salary £235 pa.
Maclear Station, on the line from Sterkstroom to Maclear, opened on 29 August 1906
Madibi Siding, on the line from De Aar to Mafeking, opened on 3 October 1894
Macfarlane Station, on the line from Kimberley to Warrenton.
Maclear Station. A telegraph office was opened in 1907.
Mafeking Station, on the line from De Aar to Mafeking, opened on 3 October 1894. The Mafeking Local line was opened on 13 March 1897, and extended on 1 November 1904. Station master EL Barker, appointed 21 June 1907, salary £288 pa.
Maitland Junction. A telegraph office was opened in 1895.
Maitland Station, on the line from Cape Town to De Aar, opened on 13 February 1862. The line from Cape Town to Ottery was opened on 1 February 1904. A telegraph office was opened in 1904. Station master Walter James Donaldson, appointed 2 June 1908, salary £274 pa.
Malan Siding. A telegraph office was opened before 1910.
Malengo Station. A telegraph office was opened in 1910.
Malmesbury Station, on the line from Cape Town to Eendekuil, opened on 12 November 1877. A telegraph office was opened in about 1885. Station master Wallace John Biggerstoff Veary, appointed 20 July 1908, salary £280 pa.
Marais Siding, on the line from Klipplaat to Graaff-Reinet. A telegraph office was opened on 1 October 1907.
Matjesfontein Station, on the line from Cape Town to De Aar, opened on 1 February 1878. Station master Albert Jenkins, appointed 13 May 1909, salary £210 pa.
McIlish Station, on the line from Cape Town to Eendekuil, opened on 25 September 1877
Middelburg Road. A telegraph office was opened in about 1885.
Middelburg Station, on the Graaff-Reinet line, opened on 1 October 1897. A telegraph office was opened in 1898. Station master Matthew Galbraith Martin, appointed 21 May 1906, salary £246 pa.
Middledrift Station, on the line from Blaney to Cookhouse, opened on 14 December 1903. A telegraph office was opened on 1 June 1907.
Middleton Station, on the line from Port Elizabeth to Rosrnead, opened on 17 September 1879. Station master John Pears Anderson, appointed 1 September 1904, salary £203 pa.
Miller Siding, on the line from Klipplaat to Oudtshoorn, opened on 1 August 1902. A telegraph office was opened in 1907.

Milner Station, on the line from Cape Town to Ottery, opened on 1 February 1904

Milnerton Junction, on the line from Cape Town to Ascot, opened on 22 September 1904

Mimosa Station, on the line from Port Elizabeth to Rosmead, opened on 1 April 1876

Misgund Station, on the line from Port Elizabeth to Avontuur, opened on 1 December 1906

Mission Station, on the line from Cape Town to Caledon, opened on 1 August 1902

Mochudi Station, Bechuanaland Protectorate, on the line to Rhodesia. Station master FC Roodt, appointed 22 March 1906, salary £267 pa; William George Hopkins, appointed 19 September 1909, salary £238 pa.

Modder River Station, on the line from De Aar to Mafeking, opened on 28 November 1885. Station master David Campbell, appointed 28 September 1908, salary £220 pa.

Molteno Station, on the line from East London to Stormberg, opened on 16 September 1884. A telegraph office was opened in about 1903. Station master John Glaholm, appointed 14 September 1903, salary £270 pa.

Montagu Road. A telegraph office was opened in November 1877.

Moorreesburg Station, on the line from Cape Town to Eendekuil, opened on 9 September 1901. A telegraph office was opened in about 1908. Station master William Joseph Wilkins, appointed 1 November 1902, salary £214 pa.

Mortimer Station, on the line from Port Elizabeth to Rosmead, opened on 1 June 1881. Station master Alfred William Hemming, appointed 15 May 1906, salary £223 pa.

Mossel Bay Station, on the line from Cape Town to George, opened on 22 January 1906. A telegraph office was opened in about 1906.

Moster's Hoek Rail. A telegraph office was opened in 1907.

Mount Stewart Station, on the Graaff-Reinet line, opened on 1 August 1878. Station master Arthur Darby Kingwell, appointed 13 May 1906, salary £195 pa.

Mowbray Station, on the line from Cape Tovin to Simonstown, opened on 19 December 1864. Station master Benjamin Manning, appointed 26 June 1895, salary £290 pa.

Muizenberg Station, on the line from Cape Town to Sinonstown, opened on 15 December 1882. Station master Carl Abraham Soderlund, appointed 8 July 1908, salary £253 pa.

Mulder's Vlei Station, on the line from Cape Town to De Aar, opened on4 November 1863. The line from Cape Town to Eendekuil, opened on 14 September 1876. Station master Charles Henry Curtis, appointed 29 March 1907, salary £189 pa.

Murray Station, on the line from Graaff-Reinet to Rosmead.

Myburg's Siding. A telegraph office was opened in 1900.

Mynfontein Station, on the line from Victoria West Road to De Aar Junction.

Naauwpoort Junction, on the line from Rosmead to Norval's Pont, opened on 16 October 1883. The line from Naauwpoort to De Aar was opened on 31 March 1884

Nababeep Station, on the line from Port Nolloth to Concordia, opened on 15 March 1893

New Brighton Station. Probably on the Port Elizabeth Suburban line. A telegraph office was opened in 1910. Station master James Clarke, appointed 21 February 1907, salary £198 pa.

Nelspoort Station, on the line from Cape Town to De Aar, opened on 14 May 1883

Newlands Station, on the line from Cape Town to Simonstown, opened on 19 December 1864. Station master William Misselbrook, appointed 12 August 1905, salary £265 pa.

North End Station, on the line from Port Elizabeth to Rosmead, opened on 26 July 1875

Norval's Pont Station, on the line from Rosmead to Norval's Pont, opened on 17 December 1890. The line from Norval's Pont to the ZAR border was opened on 17 December 1890. Station master Charles Somerville Jarvis, appointed 1 December 1902, salary £328 pa.

Nuy Siding. A telegraph office was opened in 1896.

Nuy Station, on the line from Cape Town to George, opened in October 1887. A telegraph office was opened in November 1906.

Oatlands Station, on the Graaff-Reinet line, opened on 3 February 1879.

Observatory Road, on the line from Cape Town to Simonstown, opened on 19 December 1864. A telegraph office was opened in 1890. Station master Bartholomew Bathurst, appointed 25 August 1908, salary £232 pa.

Omdraaisvlei Station, on the line from De Aar to Prieska, opened on 1 April 1905. A telegraph office was opened in 1906.

O'Okiep Station, on the line from Port Nolloth to Concordia, opened on 15 March 1893

Orange River Station, on the line from De Aar to Mafeking, opened on 3 November 1884. Station master James Leonard Jacklin, appointed 29 January 1909, salary £232 pa.

Orchard Siding. A telegraph office was opened before 1903.

Osplaats Station. A telegraph office was opened in 1897.

Ottery Station, on the line from Cape Town to Ottery, opened on 1 February 1904

Oudtshoorn Station, on the line from Klipplaat to Oudtshoorn, opened on 1 March 1904. A telegraph office was opened in 1907. Station master Joshua Crosoer, appointed 21 July 1903, salary £285 pa.

Paarl Station, on the line from Cape Town to De Aar, opened on 4 November 1863. A telegraph office was opened in January 1876. Station master Ferguson John Knott, appointed 1 July 1908, salary £279 pa.

Paarl Station, on the line from Paarl to French Hoek, opened on 7 June 1904

Palapye Road, Bechuanaland Protectorate, on the line to Rhodesia. Station master Martin Hussey, appointed 29 May 1906, salary £278 pa.

Pampoenpoort Station, on the line from Cape Town to Carnarvon, opened on 1 May 1905. A telegraph office was opened, date not known.

Peelton Station, on the line from East London to Stormberg, opened on 1 May 1877. A telegraph office was opened in 1907.

Piquetberg Road. A telegraph office was opened in May 1876.

Piquetberg Station, on the line from Cape Town to Eendekuil, opened on 15 November 1902. A telegraph office was date of opening not known. Station master Andries Jacobus Rabe, appointed 26 May 1909, salary £192 pa.

Plewman Station, on the line from Naaupoort to Norval's Pont.

Plumstead Station, on the line from Cape Town to Simonstown, opened on 15 December 1882.

Station master John Henry Geary, appointed 24 August 1908, salary £226 pa.

Pokwani Siding, also given as Phokwani. On the line from De Aar to Mafeking, opened on 1 December 1890. A telegraph office was opened in 1900. Station master James Grierson, appointed 15 September 1909, salary £180 pa.

Port Alfred Station, on the line from Port Elizabeth to Port Alfred, opened on 1 December 1884. A telegraph office was date of opening not known.

Port Elizabeth Station, on the line from Port Elizabeth to Rosmead, opened on 26 July 1875. The line from Port Elizabeth to Avontuur was opened on 1 April 1906

Porterville Road, on the line from Cape Town to De Aar, opened on 1 September 1875. A telegraph office was date of opening not known. Station master Henry Cooper, appointed 1 February 1903, salary £294 pa.

Port Nolloth Station, on the line from Port Nolloth to Concordia, opened on 1 August 1886

Potfontein Station. A telegraph office was date of opening not known.

Pretorius Station, on the line from Graaff-Reinet to Rosmead.

Prieska Station, on the line from De Aar to Prieska, opened on 19 September 1905. A telegraph office was opened on 1 December 1906.

Prince Albert Road, on the line from Cape Town to De Aar, opened on 11 August 1879. A telegraph office was opened in August 1879.

Pudimoe Siding. A telegraph office was opened in 1898.

Queenstown Station, on the line from East London to Stormberg, opened on 5 May 1880. A telegraph office was opened in about 1885. Station master John Edward Yates, appointed 18 September 1902, salary £325 pa.

Ramathlabama River Station, on the Mafeking Local line, opened on 13 March 1897

Rendsburg Station, on the line from Naauwpoort to Norval's Pont.

Reapenberg Station, on the line from Cape Town to Ottery, opened on 1 February 1904

Redhouse Station, on the Graaff-Reinet line, opened on 22 September 1875. Station master William Cornelius Dalziel, appointed 1 November 1908, salary £223 pa.

Retreat Station, on the line from Cape Town to Simonstown, opened on 15 December 1882. Station master D Bailey, appointed 15 July 1899, salary £265 pa.

Rhenosterkop Siding, on the line from Cape Town to De Aar, opened on 14 May 1883. A telegraph office was opened in 1897.

Rhodes Station, on the line from Cape Town to Ottery, opened on 1 February 1904

Richmond Road, on the line from Cape Town to De Aar, opened on 31 March 1884. A telegraph office was opened in about 1885. Station master Alfred Thomas Castle, appointed 16 July 1904, salary £186 pa.

Riet Siding, on the line from Naauwpoort to De Aar Junction. A telegraph office was opened in 1896

Riversdale Station, on the line from Cape Town to George, opened on 19 February 1903. A telegraph office was opened in 1908.

Riverton Road, on the line from De Aar to Mafeking, opened on 1 December 1890. A telegraph office was opened in 1892.

Robertson Station, on the line from Cape Town to George, opened in October 1887. A telegraph office was opened in 1887.

Rondebosch Station, on the line from Cape Town to Simonstown, opened on 19 December 1864. Station master James Barry Munnik Long, appointed 8 July 1908, salary £280 pa.

Roode Hoogte Station on the Graaff-Reinet line, opened on 3 March 1898

Rosebank Station, on the line from Cape Town to Simonstown, opened on 19 December 1864. Station master James Pirrie, appointed 26 March 1898, salary £289 pa.

Rosmead Station also listed as Rosrnead Junction, on the line from Port Elizabeth to Rosmead, opened on 2 April 1883. The line from Rosmead to Stormberg Junction was opened on 8 February 1892. The line to Graaff-Reinet was opened on 1 October 1897. A telegraph office was opened in 1898. Station master GAF Linde, appointed 27 May 1906, salary £250 pa.

St James Station, on the line from Cape Town to Simonstown, opened on 5 May 1883. Station master William Heath, appointed 9 January 1906, salary £235 pa.

Saltaire Station, on the line from Port Elizabeth to Rosmead, opened on 3 February 1879

Salt River Station, on the line from Cape Town to De Aar, opened on 13 February 1862. The line from Cape Town to Simonstown was opened on 19 December 1864. Station master William Moore, appointed 1 November 1897, salary £330 pa.

Sand Flats Station on the line from Port Elizabeth to Rosmead, opened on 1 April 1876. Station master S Pettit, appointed 1 October 1901, salary £281 pa.

Sandfontein Station, on the line from Uitenhage to Klipplaat

Sapkamma Station, on the line from Uitenhage to Klipplaat

Saxony Station, on the line from Klipplaat to Graaff-Reinet.

Schoombie Station, on the line from Rosmead to Stormberg Junction, opened on 8 February 1892. Station master Henry Richard Heard, appointed 1 October 1907, salary £220 pa.

Sea Point Station, on the line from Cape Town to Sea Point, opened on 1 December 1905

Sheldon Station, on the line from Port Elizabeth to Rosmead, opened on 17 September 1879

Sherborne Siding, on the line from Rosmead to Naaupoort. A telegraph office was opened in 1886.

Simondium Station, on the line from Paarl to French Hoek, opened on 7 June 1904

Simonstown Station, on the line from Cape Town to Simonstown, opened on 1 December 1890. A telegraph office was opened in 1895. Station master Arel Hartoig Hansen, appointed 30 April 1909, salary £295 pa.

Sinksa Bridge Station, on the line from Mossel Bay to Oudtshoorn

Sir Lowry's Pass, on the line from Cape Town to Caledon, opened on 1 February 1890. Station master EC Pearce, appointed 28 April 1909, salary £223 pa.

Skead's Junction. A telegraph office was opened in 1897.

Slypklip Station, on the line from Kimberley to Warrenton.

Somerset East Station, on the line from Cookhouse to Somerset East, opened on 1 August 1902. A telegraph office was opened in 1902 for railway work only. Station master George Cawood

Nelson, appointed 5 July 1905, salary £256 pa.

Somerset Strand Station, on the line from Cape Town to Caledon, opened on 16 December 1905. A telegraph office was opened on January 1906.

Somerset West Station on the line from Cape Town to Caledon, opened on 21 October 1889. A telegraph office was opened in 1889 for railway work only. Station master P Hoal, appointed 29 April 1909, salary £238 pa.

Southernwood Station. This station served the suburb of Southern Wood, in East London, on the local Suburban line. Station master Henry Irvin, appointed 20 December 1907, salary £220 pa.

Springmount Station, on the line from Port Elizabeth to Port Alfred, opened on 18 May 1909

Spytfontein Station, on the line from De Aar to Mafeking, opened on 28 November 1885

Steenbrass Station, on the line from Cape Town to Caledon, opened on 1 August 1902

Stellenbosch Station, on the line from Cape Town to De Aar, opened on 1 May 1862. A telegraph office was opened in May 1876. Station master JO Rex, appointed 1 July 1908, salary £290 pa.

Sterkstroom Station, on the line from East London to Stormberg, opened on 15 October 1883. The line from Sterkstroom to Maclear was opened on 1 February 1896. Station master William Edward Jenvey, appointed 8 February 1907, salary £232 pa.

Steynsburg Station, on the line from Rosmead to Stormberg Junction, opened on 8 February 1892. A telegraph office was opened in 1891.

Stormberg Junction, on the line from East London to Stormberg, opened on 19 March 1885. The line from Rosmead to Stormberg was opened on 8 February 1892. A telegraph office was opened in 1891. Station master Henry Stanley Johnstone, appointed 14 September 1903, salary £268 pa.

Strikland Station, on the line from Cape Town to Eendekuil, opened on 14 September 1876

Surbiton Station, on the line from East London to Stormberg, opened on 3 November 1879

Swartkops Station, on the Graaff-Reinet line, opened on 22 September 1875

Swellendam Station, on the line from Cape Town to George, opened on 12 April 1899. A telegraph office was opened in 1899.

Taaibosch, on the line from Naauwpoort to De Aar, opened on 31 March 1884

Tafelberg, on the line from Port Elizabeth to Rosmead, opened on 2 April 1883

Tarkastad Station, on the line from Bowker's Park to Tarkastad, opened on 5 December 1900. A telegraph office was opened in 1900. Station master Samuel Wilmot Webster, appointed 10 May 1904, salary £198 pa.

Taungs Station, on the line from De Aar to Mafeking, opened on 1 December 1890.

Templeman, Station on the Knysna Local line, opened on 14 July 1907

Thebus Station, on the line from Rosmead to Stormberg Junction, opened on 8 February 1892. Station master William Samuel Jonathan Heath, appointed 16 January 1903, salary £235 pa.

Thirtythree Mile Siding. A telegraph office was opened in 1894.

Thomas River Station, on the line from East London to Stormberg, opened on 3 November 1879

Thorngrove Station, on the line from Port Elizabeth to Rosmead, opened on 1 June 1881

Thornhill Station, on the line from Port Elizabeth to Avontuur, opened on 1 November 1905

Three Sisters Station, on the line from Cape Town to De Aar, opened on 14 May 1883

Toise River Station, on the line from East London to Stormberg, opened on 1 January 1879. Station master Benjamin Ridgard, appointed 1 April 1997, salary £255 pa.

Toleni Station. A telegraph office was opened in May 1907.

Touws River Station, on the line from Cape Town to De Aar, opened on 7 November 1877. Station master ThomasMurphy, appointed 21 July 1908, salary £290 pa.

Triangle Station, on the line from Cape Town to De Aar, opened on 7 November 1877

Tulbagh Road, on the line from Cape Town to De Aar, opened on 1 September 1875. A telegraph office was opened in May 1876.

Tunnel Siding. A telegraph office was opened in 1896.

Tweedale Station, on the line from Naaupoort to Norval's Pont.

Tweefontein Siding, on the line from Cape Town to De Aar, opened on 7 November 1877. A telegraph office was opened before 1907.

Twentytwo Mile Station, on the line from Port Nolloth to Concordia, opened on 1 August 1886

Twee Revieren Station, also known as Two Streams Station, on the line from Port. Elizabeth to Avontuur, opened on 1 March 1906

Tylden Station, on the line from East London to Stormberg, opened on 5 May 1880. Station master Matthew Henderson, appointed 22 April 1907, salary £195 pa.

Ugie Station, on the line from Sterkstroorn to Maclear, opened on 18 March 1906.

Uitenhage Station, on the line from Graaff-Reinet, opened on 22 September 1875. A telegraph office was opened in about 1885. Station master Richard Elliott Tracey, appointed 27 September 1905, salary £314 pa.

Uniondale Road, on the line from Klipplaat to Oudtshoorn, opened on 15 April 1903. A telegraph office was opened in October 1908.

Valley Junction, on the Port Elizabeth Suburban line, opened on 15 December 1906

Van der Stel Siding, on the line from Cape Town to Caledon, opened on 1 February 1890. A telegraph office was opened on January 1906.

Vermaak Siding. A telegraph office was opened in 1894.

Victoria West Station. A telegraph office was opened in 1905.

Victoria West Road, on the line from Cape Town to Carnarvon, opened on1 May 1905

Vlakteplaats Station, on the line from Klipplaat to Oudtshoorn, opened on 1 August 1903

Vlottenberg Station, on the line from Cape Town to De Aar, opened on 1 May 1862. Station master Robert Bell, appointed 1 June 1893, salary £235 pa.

Voor Bay Station, on the line from Cape Town to George, opened on 22 January 1906

Vredenburg Station. A telegraph office was opened in May 1882.

Vryburg Station, on the line from De Aar to Mafeking, opened on 1 December 1890. Station master Alfred Box, appointed 19 September 1909, salary £248 pa.

Waku Station on the line from East London to Stormberg, opened on 5 May 1880

Walmer Station, on the Port Elizabeth Suburban line, opened on 15 December 1906

Warrenton Road, on the line from De Aar to Mafeking, opened on 1 December 1890. A telegraph office was opened in 1890. Station master John Charles Owens, appointed 21 June 1907, salary £238 pa.

Warrenton Station. A telegraph office was date of opening not known.

Waverley Siding, on the line from Bowker's Park to Tarkastad, opened on 1 December 1900. A telegraph office was opened in January 1904.

Wellington Station, on the line from Cape Town to De Aar, opened on 4 November 1863. A telegraph office was opened in January 1876. Station master Joseph Patrick Greenan, appointed 20 July 1908, salary £310 pa.

Wemmer's Hoek, on the line from Paarl to French Hoek, opened on 7 June 1904

Wildfontein, on the line from Naauwpoort to De Aar, opened on 31 March 1884

Willowmore, on the line from Klipplaat to Oudtshoorn, opened on 1 August 1902. A telegraph office was opened in 1902, but for railway work only. Station master Frederick Doyle, appointed 24 September 1909, salary £219 pa.

Windsorton Road, on the line from De Aar to Mafeking, opened on 1 December 1890

Witmoss, on the line from Port Elizabeth to Rosmead, opened on 1 June 1881. Station master Donald McKinnon, appointed 27 June 1901, salary £238 pa.

Wolvefontein, on the Graaff-Reinet line, opened on 1 August 1878

Woodstock, on the line from Cape Town to De Aar, opened on 13 February 1862. Station master Thomas Biggleston Shewring, appointed 1 October 1902, salary £244 pa.

Worcester, on the line from Cape Town to De Aar, opened on 16 June 1876. The line from Cape Town to George was opened in October 1887. Station master Thomas McNish, appointed 18 August 1906, salary £300 pa

Wynberg Station, on the line from Cape Town to Simonstown, opened on 19 December 1864. Station master Henry Crocker, appointed 22 October 1901, salary £300 pa.

Xalanga, on the line from Sterkstroom to Maclear, opened on 17 August 1904

Zwartkops Station, also listed as Zwartkops Junction, on the line from Port Elizabeth to Rosmead, opened on 26 July 1875. A telegraph office was opened on the same day. Station master Arthur James Knott, appointed 1 November 1898, salary £255 pa.

EIGHT

GROWTH OF RAILWAY INFRASTRUCTURE 1862-1910

1862, February 13: Cape Town to Eerste River, including stations at Woodstock, Salt River, Maitland, Elsie's River Halt, Belville and Kuils River

1862, May 1: Eerste River to Stellenbosch, including stations at Lyndoch, Vlottenberg and Bosman's Crossing

1863, November 4: Stellenbosch to Wellington, including stations at Koelenhof, Mulder's Vlei, Klapmuts, Paarl and Huguenot

1864, December 19: Salt River to Wynberg, including stations at Observatory Road, Rosebank, Newlands, Mowbray, Rondebosch, Claremont and Kenilworth

1875, May 11: Cape Town Docks to Main Line

1875, July 26: Port Elizabeth to Addo, including stations at North End, Zwartkops Junction, Aloes, Coega and Barkly Bridge

1875, September 1: Wellington to Tulbagh Road, including stations at Hermon and Porterville Road

1875, September 22: Swartkops to Uitenhage, including stations at Redhouse and Despatch

1875, November 3: Tulbagh Road to Ceres Road

1876, March 1: Addo to Coerney

1876, April 1: Coerney to Sand Flats, including a station at Mimosa

1876, June 16: Ceres Road to Worcester, including stations at Breede River and Goudini Road

1876, September 14: Belville to Mulder's Vlei, including stations at Strikland, Brackenfell and Kraaifontein

1876, December 18: East London to Blaney, including stations at Chiselhurst, Cambridge, Amalinda, Egerton, Fort Jackson, Lonetree Loop and Berlin

1877, February 6: Uitenhage to Kariega, including stations at Centlivres and Blue Cliff

1877, May 1: Blaney to Kei Road, including a station at Peelton

1877, May 1: Blaney to King William's Town

1877, May 1: Kariega to Glenconnor

1877, August 27: Sand Flats to Alicedale Junction, including a station at Bellevue

1877, September 25: Kraaifontein to Kalabas Kraal-, including stations at Mellish and Klipheuvel

1877, November 7: Worcester to Kleinstraat, including stations at Tweefontein, Hex River, De Doorns, Triangle and Touws River

1877, November 12: Kalabas Kraal to Malmesbury, including a station at Abbotsdale

1878, February 2: Kleinstraat to Matjesfontein, including stations at Jan de Boers and Constable
1878, April 15: Kei Road to Kubusie, including a station at Amabele
1878, August 1: Glenconnor to Mount Stewart , including stations at KIein Poort, Wolvefontein, Haasfontein and Barroe Kraa1
1878, August 15: East London to Landing Jetty
1878, August 15: Kubusie to Dohne Toll
1878, November 4: Matjesfontein to Grootfontein, including a station at Laingsburg
1879, January 1: Dohne Toll to Toise River, including a station at Greytown
1879, February 3: Alicedale to Cornmadagga, including stations at Bushman's River and Saltaire
1879, February 3: Mount Stewart to Aberdeen Road, including stations at Klipplaat Junction and Oatlands
1879, March 3: Alicedale to Atherstone, including a station at Highlands
1879, March:17 Aberdeen Road to Kendrew
1879, August 11: Grootfontein to Fraserburg Road, including a station at Prince Albert Road
1879, August 26: Kendrew to Graaff-Reinet, including a station at Adendorp
1879, September 3: Atherstone to Grahamstown
1879, September 17: Commadagga to Middleton, including a station at Sheldon
1879, November 3: Toise River to Cathcart, including stations at Thomas River and Surbiton
1880, February 5: Fraserburg Road to Beaufort West, including a station at Letjesbosch
1880, March 2: Middleton to Cookhouse
1880, May 5: Cathcart to Queenstown, including stations at Waku, Tylden, Imvani and Essex
1881, June 1: Cookhouse to Cradock, including stations at Thorngrove, Witmoss, Dassie Deur and Mortimer
1882, December 15: Wynberg to Muizenburg, including stations at Plurnstead, Diep River, Retreat and Lakeside
1883, April 2: Cradock to Rosmead Junction, including stations at. Baroda, Fish River, Conway and Tafelberg
1883, May 5: Muizenberg to Kalk Bay, including a station at St James
1883, May 14: Beaufort West to Hutchinson, including stations at Rhenosterkop, Nelspoort, Three Sisters and Biesjespoort
1883, October 15: Queenstown to Sterkstroom, including stations at Bowkers Park and Bailey
1883, October 16: Rosmead Junction to Colesberg, including stations at Naauwpoort Juncticn, Arundel and Colesberg Junction
1884, March 31: Hutchinson to De Aar Junction, including stations at Richmond Road and Deelfontein
1884, March 31: Naauwpoort to De Aar Junction, including stations at Wildfontein, Hanover Road and Taaibosch
1884, September 16: Sterkstroom to Molteno, including a station at Cyphergat
1884, November 3: De Aar Junction to Orange River, including stations at Hout Kraal and Krankuil

1884, December 1: Grahamstown to Port Alfred, including stations at Clumber and Bathurst
1885, March 19: Molteno to Burghersdorp, including a station at Stormberg Junction
1885, September 2: Burghersdorp to Aliwal North, including stations at Albert Junction and Isigidini
1885, November 28: Orange River to Kimberley, including stations at Belmont, Graspan, Honeynest's Kloof, Modder River, Spytfontein and Beaconsfield
1886, August 1: Port Nolloth to Twentytwo Mile
1887, June 11: Twentytwo Mile to Anenous
1887, October: Worcester to Ashton, including stations at Nuy, Lang Vlei, Robertson and Klaas Voogts River
1889, April 23: Brakpits to Concordia
1889, October 21: Eerste River to Somerset West, including stations at Faure and Firgrove
1890, February 1: Somerset West -to Sir Lowry's Pass, including a station at Van der Stel
1890, December 1: Kimberley to Fourteen Streams, including stations at Riverton Road, Windsorton Road, Content and Warrenton
1890, December 1: Fourteen Streams to Vryburg, including stations at Pokwani, Taungs and Border
1890, December 17: Colesberg Junction to Norval's Pont Bridge, including stations at Achtertang and Norval's Pont
1890, December 17: Norval's Pont Bridge to Bloemfontein, OFS
1892, February 8: Rosmead Junction to Stormberg Junction, including stations at Schoombie, Thebus, Steynsburg, Henning and Bamboo Junction
1892, February 20: Bloemfontein to Kroonstad, OFS
1892, May 7: Kroonstad to Viljoen's Drift, OFS
1892, May 21: Albert Junction to Bethulie Bridge, including a station at Knapdaar
1892, May 21: Bethulie Bridge to Springfontein, OFS
1892, May 21: Viljoen's Drift to Vaal River Bridge, OFS
1893, March 15: Anenous to Kookfontein
1893, March 15: Kookfontein to O'Okiep
1893, March 15: Gerracoop to Nababeep
1894, October 3: Vryburg to Mafeking, including stations at Kraaipan and Madibi Siding
1896, February 1: Sterkstroom to Indwe, including stations at Halseton and Dordrecht
1897, March 13: Mafeking to Ramathlabama River
1897, October 1: Rosmead Junction to Middelburg
1898, February 8: Bamboo Junction to Cape Collieries
1898, March 3: Middelburg to Graaff-Reinet, including stations at Roode Hoogte, Bethesda Road, Letts Kraal and Glenharry
1899, April 12: Ashton to Swellendam
1890, December 1: Kalk Bay to Sirnonstown, including stations at Fish Hoek and Glencairn
1900, December 5: Bowker's Park to Tarkastad, including a station at Waverley
1901, September 9: Malmesbury to Moorreesburg

1902, August 1: Sir Lowry's Pass to Caledon, including stations at Steenbrass, Elgin, Lebanon Halt, Houwhoek, Bot River and Mission

1902, August 1: Cookhouse to Somerset East

1902, August 1: Klipplaat to Willowmore, including a station at Miller

1902, November 15: Moorreesburg to Eendekuil, including a station at Piquetberg

1903, February 19: Swellendam to Riversdale, including a station at Heidelberg

1903, February 28: Kalabas Kraal to Hopefield, including a station at Darling

1903, March 2: Cookhouse to Bedford

1903, April 15: Willowmore to Uniondale Road

1903, August 1: Uniondale Road to Vlakteplaats

1903, December 14: Vlakteplaats to Le Roux

1903, December 14: Bedford to Adelaide

1903, December 14: King Williams Town to Middledrift

1904, Artois to Ceres Road

1904, February 1: Maitland to Ottery, including stations at Reapenberg, Fraserdale, Milner, Crawford, Lansdowne and Rhodes

1904, March 1: Le Roux to Oudtshoorn

1904, May 2: Middledrift to Alice

1904, June 7: Paarl to French Hoek, including stations at Cillies, Simondium, Groot Drakenstein, Wemmer's Hoek and La Motte

1904, August 17: Indwe to Xalanga, including a station at Ida

1904, September 7: Amabele to Komgha

1904, September 22: Milnerton Junction to Milnerton

1904, October 17: Alice to Adelaide, including stations at Fort Beaufort and Kroomie

1904, November 1: Mafeking to Buhrmannsdrift

1905, April 1: De Aar Junction to Omdraaisvlei, including stations at Britstown and Houwater

1905, May 1: Hutchinson to Pampoenpoort, including stations at Victoria West and Kweekwa

1905, May 18: Xalanga to Elliot

1905, September 15: Komgha to Inciba

1905, September 19: Omdraaisvlei to Prieska

1905, November 1: Inciba to Eagle

1905, November 1: Humewood Road to Humansdorp, including stations at Thornhill, Loerie and Jeffrey's Bay

1905, November 2: Aliwal North to Lady Grey

1905, December 1: Cape Town to Sea Point

1905, December 16: Van der Stel to Somerset Strand

1906, January 22: Riversdale to Voor Bay, including stations at Albertinia and Mossel Bay

1906, March 1: Humansdorp to Two Streams

1906, March 16: Elliot to Ugie

1906, April 1: Port Elizabeth to Humewood Road

1906, May 16: Fourteen Streams to Orkney, Transvaal Colony
1906, June 15: Two Streams to Assegai Bosch
1906, August 1: Pampoenspoort to Carnarvon
1906, August 19: Ugie to Maclear
1906, September 3: Assegaai Bosch to Kromme River Heights
1906, October 1: Kromme River Heights to Krakeel River
1906, December 1: Krakeel River to Misgund
1906, December 15: Valley Junction to Walmer
1906, December 17: Eagle to Butterworth
1907, January 1: Misgund to Avontuur, including a station at Haarlem
1907, April 25: Mossel Bay to George
1907, July 14: Knysna to Templeman
1908, May 28: Milnerton to Ascot
1909, May 18: Barkly Bridge to Alexandria, including a station at Springmount

NINE

FIELD-CORNET'S MAILS 1877-1910

The "*Cornet*" was originally a military rank in the Dutch army assigned to the standard bearer of a cavalry unit, and was derived from a "*corneta*", a word used by the Spanish to describe a cavalry flag. Its use was adopted by the Dutch whose flag bearers of a cavalry unit thus became known as the "*kornets*". In the 18th Century it began to be used by the Dutch administration at the Cape and, in 1798, it was applied it to a "*veldwachtmeester*", an officer in the civilian commando guard. At that stage the two terms were telescoped together and the title of a "*veld-cornet*" came into being.

When the British took over the colonial administration of the Cape of Good Hope in 1806 the position was retained as a civil post, and following the dissemination of Ordinance 22 of 1827 the Field-Cornet became an assistant to the Justice of the Peace. In 1848 his duties were extended to those of an Assistant Magistrate. Similar positions were established in the Dutch Republics after 1845 and in the Colony of Natal in 1846 (SESA 1972), although their duties and political outcomes differed substantially.

Originally Field-Cornets appointed in the Cape Colony were intended to serve a military role at a time when European settlement in the outlying districts was limited to scattered families of migrant pastoralist farmers vulnerable to attack by San stock thieves and confrontations with aggrieved Khoikhoi and Xhosa pastoralist farmers. Initially the post was an elected civilian position whose duties were primarily aimed at the organization of regional civil units into rapid-response military commandos.

However, once the borders of the Colony began to stabilize and a military pax was slowly enforced, their positions became increasingly administrative, often acting as officers of the peace, ad hoc magistrates, representatives of central government and law enforcement agents. The Dutch rural community commonly used its quarterly church gatherings of *nachtmaal* as the focus of many of its social activities, and the local Field-Cornet usually attended these meetings to read out and clarify the latest Government edicts emanating from Parliament in Cape Town, to discuss political issues of the day, and to settle minor disputes between neighbours.

After the 1850s they were employed extensively by the Department of Public Works in Cape Town whose project managers, engineers and quartermasters needed to be in regular contact with their head office. These work camps were also Convict Stations whose inmates were used as labourers to build and maintain the Colony's road building system.

Therefore, by the 1870s, the position of a Field-Cornet had become an integral part of a system of communication between Colonial management in Cape Town and its technical staff in the field. However, as the postal system became increasingly efficient, so then the duties of the Field-Cornet were gradually absorbed into the regular mail delivery system. By May 1910, when the Union of South Africa was legislated into being, there were still 540 Field-Cornets active in the Cape but finally, in 1916, their position was abolished and they were replaced by Justices of the Peace.

A
ACHTER ZWARTLAND, Malmesbury
ALLEMAN'S POORT, Wodehouse
ALTONA, Victoria West
ANTJE'S KRAAL, Prince Albert
ANYSBERG, Ladismith
ANYS RIVER, Sutherland
ARDYNE PARK, Tarka
AVONDALE, Bedford

B
BADEBABUTHA, Vryburg
BANK'S DRIFT, Kimberley
BASBERG, Philipstown
BASTARD'S FONTEIN, Carnarvon
BAVIAAN'S HOEK, Ceres
BEERFONTEIN, Aliwal North
BELLVILLE, Paarl
BELLEVUE, Stellenbosch
BIEDOUW, Clanwilliam
BIESJESDAL, Vryburg
BIESJESFONTEIN, Vanrhynsdorp
BIESJESPOORT I, Britstown
BIESJESPOORT II, Victoria West
BLAAUWKRANTZ, Albert
BLINDEFONTEIN, Piquetberg
BLOKZYNPLAATS, Calvinia
BLOEMFONTEIN, Fraserburg
BLOEMHOF, Hanover
BLOEM VLEI, Tembuland
BLOKZYNPLAATS, Calvinia
BLUE GUM HILL, Swellendam

BOKSPRUIT, Murraysburg
BOVENLANGVLEI, Clanwilliam
BOXMOOR, Uitenhage
BRAAKLEEGTE, Wodehouse
BRAAM RIVER, Uniondale
BRAKFONTEIN I, East London
BRAKFONTEIN II, Malmesbury
BRAKFONTEIN III, Philipstown
BRAKKIES, Vanrhynsdorp
BRAKVLEI, Hopetown
BREEKKERIE, Carnarvon
BRETBY, Kuruman
BUCK KRAAL, Peddie
BUFFELSFONTEIN, Willowmore
BUFFELSHOEK, Riversdale
BULTFONTEIN, Victoria West
BUSHMAN'S KRAAL, Tarka

C
CLARKSDALE, Wodehouse
CLEARWATER, Herbert
CLOETESPAN, Hopetown
COBHAM, Kuruman
COEGA, Willowmore
CORRENTE RIVER, Riversdale
CROMARTY, Griqualand East

D
DANKFONTEIN, Albert
DE HOOP, Uniondale
DE KIST, Aberdeen
DE RIET, Fraserburg

DE VLEI, Caledon
DICHAKING, Kuruman
DIKGAT, Namaqualand
DOEGA, Calvinia
DOWKOM'S KRAAL, Humansdorp
DOWNS No 1, Division of the Cape
DRIEFONTEIN, Murraysburg
DRIEHOEK, Clanwilliam
DRIEHOEKSFONTEIN, Murraysburg
DWAARS RIVER, Sutherland

E
EBENEZER, Jansenville
EENDEFONTEIN, Carnarvon
EIKEBOOM, Clanwilliam
ELANDSBERG, Sutherland
ELAND'S DRIFT I, Bredasdorp
ELAND'S DRIFT II, Uitenhage
ELAND'S DRIFT III, Uniondale
ELANDSFONTEIN I, Beaufort West
ELANDSFONTEIN II, Britstown
ELANDSHEUVEL, Hanover
ELGIN, Caledon
ELIBANK, Barkly East
ENGLAND, Vryburg
ERIN, Wodehouse
EWANRIGG, Komgha

F
FETCANI GLEN, Barkly East
FOLESHILL, Griqualand East
FONTEIN, Laingsburg
FONTEINTJIE, Colesberg

G
GAKWE, Vryburg
GAMALILO, Kuruman
GANNA PUNT, Calvinia
GANNIPAN, Carnarvon
GEELBEK, Malmesbury

GEMBOKSVLAKTE, Hopetown
GLEN ADELAIDE, Glen Grey
GLEN ELGIN, Caledon
GLEN GREY, Glen Grey
GLEN NORMAN, Caledon
GOEDMOEDSFONTEIN, Port Elizabeth
GOOD HOPE I, Beaufort West
GOOD HOPE II, Caledon
GOOD HOPE III, George
GOOD HOPE IV, Uitenhage
GONNAPAN, Carnarvon
GOUDINI, Worcester
GRASEN DALEN, Malmesbury
GROENWATER LOCATION, Hay
GROOTFONTEIN I, Beaufort West
GROOTFONTEIN II, Malmesbury
GROOTFONTEIN III, Kuruman
GROOTFONTEIN IV, Uniondale
GROOTFONTEIN FARM, Prince Albert
GROOT RIVER, Ladismith
GROOT VLEI, Beaufort West
GUNSTELLING, Molteno
GURRETY, Calvinia

H
HARRY'S GELUK, Vryburg
HARTEBEESTE VLAKTE, Kenhardt
HARTEBEESTFONTEIN, Humansdorp
HARTKLIP, Vryburg
HASTING'S, Peddie
HERBOUW, Graaff-Reinet
HILLSIDE, Uitenhage
HOEKSPLAATS, Victoria West
HOLM PARK, Komgha
HONEYGROVE, Cradock
HOTWEG'S KLOOF, Cradock

JI
INDOWANA, Griqualand East
JAGER'S KRAAL, Beaufort West

NINE: Field-Cornets

JAGT POORT, Richmond
JONKERSFOPNTEIN, Riversdale
KAAP VLEI, Namaqualand
(INDIGENOUS) KRAAL, Fraserburg
(INDIGENOUS) POORT, Hanover

K
KANG, Vryburg
KANOLVLEI, Clanwilliam
KAREEBOSCH, Murraysburg
KAREERDOORN, Carnarvon
KAREERDOORNS, Fraserburg
KAREEHOEK, Britstown
KAREEPOORT, Philipstown
KARNMELK RIVER, Swellendam
KAT HOEK, Bredasdorp
KELHAM, Peddie
KILMACHAIG, Tembuland
KLAVER VLEI, Malmesbury
KLEIN DOORN RIVER, Riversdale
KLEINFONTEIN, Steynsburg
KLEIN GOBE, Vanrhynsdorp
KLEINPLAATS, Vanrhynsdorp
KLEIN RIVER, Uniondale
KLEIN UMZIMVUBU, Griqualand East
KLEINZONDAGRIVIERSHOEK,
    Graaff-Reinet
KLIPFONTEIN I, Mossel Bay
KLIPFONTEIN II, Willowmore
KLIPHEUVEL, Namaqualand
KLIPARANI, Mafeking
KLIPDRIFT I, Caledon
KLIPDRIFT II, George
KLIPDRIFT III, Graaff-Reinet
KLIPFONTEIN I, Mossel Bay
KLIPFONTEIN II, Tarka
KLIPFONTEIN III, Vanrhynsdorp
KLIPFONTEIN IV, Willowmore
KLIPKOLK, Fraserburg
KLOVER VLEI, Malmesbury

KLUITJES KRAAL, Swellendam
KNAP VLEI, Namaqualand
KNEL, Steynsburg
KNOLVLEI, Clanwilliam
KNOFFALFONTEIN, Richmond
KOODOOSKLOOF, Aberdeen
KOORNLAND'S KLOOF, Clanwilliam
KOPPIESKRAAL, Calvinia
KORDAATSKUIL, Victoria West
KOUDE RIVER, Bredasdorp
KOURKAM, Namaqualand
KRAAIFONTEIN I, Murraysburg
KRAAIFONTEIN II, Namaqualand
KRIEGERSKRAAL, Bedford
KRIELSPAN, Mafeking
KRUIS PAD, Montagu
KRUIS RIVER, Victoria West
KWELEGA DRIFT, East London
KWESFONTEIN, Hanover
KYKOEDIE, Bredasdorp

L
LANDREY'S. King Williams Town
LANGEBERG, Malmesbury
LANGEFONTEIN, Humansdorp
LANGKUIL, Clanwilliam
LANGLAAGTE, Herbert
LANGVERWACHT, Robertson
LA POORTE, Beaufort West
LEEUFONTEIN, Philipstown
LEEUWENDAM, Malmesbury
LEEUWKUIL, Beaufort West
LEEUWSPRUIT, Wodehouse
LEMOENKLOOF, Britstown
LOERIESFONTEIN, Calvinia
LONGSLOPE, Cathcart
LOOTCLIFFE, Stutterheim
LYMORE LODGE Barkly East

M

MAGORAS, Hay
MALPAS, Barkly East
MANCAZANA, Stockenstrom
MARAISHOPE, Uitenhage
MATJESFONTEIN, Britstown
MATJESVLEI, Willowmore
MELKHOUTFONTEIN, Riversdale
MEURFONTEIN, Griqualand East
MIDDELVALLEI, Griqualand East
MIDDLE RIVER, Swellendam
MIDDLE WATER I, Hanover
MIDDLE WATER II, Prieska
MIDDLEWYK, Richmond
MIMOSA LODGE, Beaufort West
MODDERFONTEIN I, Cradock
MODDERFONTEIN II, Prieska
MODDERFONTEIN III, Somerset East
MODDERFONTEIN IV, Victoria West
MOOI PLAATS, Komgha
MOORDENAARS POORT I, Middelburg
MOORDENAARSPOORT II, Steynsburg
MORGENZON, Barkly East
MOUNT CARMEL, Barkly West
MOUNT CURRIE, Griqualand East
MOUNT TEMPLE, Kuruman
MOXAM, Griqualand East

N

NAAUWTE, Willowmore
NAROSIES, Calvinia
NELSPOORTJE, Prieska
NIEUWEDAM, Prince Albert
NIEUWEFONTEIN, Richmond
NIEUWEJAARSFONTEIN, Britstown
NOOITGEDACHT, Albert

O

OEST, Fraserburg
ONRUSTFONTEIN, Philipstown
ONVERWACHT, Riversdale
OORLOGSFONTEIN, Victoria West
OORLOGSPOORT, Aberdeen
OPKOMST, Uniondale
OPPERMAN'S KRAAL, Richmond
ORANGE GROVE, Herbert
OUDEMUUR, Clanwilliam
OUDEPLAATS, Richmond

P

PAARDEFONTEIN, Cradock
PAARDE KRAAL, Cradock
PALEN EN RIET VALLEI, Malmesbury
PALMIET, Albany
PIRIE, WARD 8, King Williams Town
PITSING, Griqualand East
PLAATJESFONTEIN, Hanover
PLOOYESFONTEIN, Hanover
POORTJE, Colesberg
PORTUGAL'S RIVER, Sutherland
PROGRESS, Vryburg
PYPFONTEIN, Murraysburg

Q

QUARIGAS, Montagu
QUANIGASFONTEIN, Roberson
QUARRYFONTEIN, Vryburg

R

RETREAT, Robertson
RHENOSTER HOEK, Tarka
RIETFONTEIN I, Beaufort West
RIETFONTEIN II, Carnarvon
RIETFONTEIN III, Fraserburg
RIETFONTEIN IV, Murraysburg
RIETFONTEIN V, Prince Albert
RIETFONTEIN VI, Willowmore
RIETKOPSKOLK, Carnarvon
RIETMONDT, Fort Beaufort
RIETPOORT, Jansenville

RIET RIVER, Montagu
RIETVLEI, Malmesbury
ROODEPUNT, Aberdeen
ROODEWAL, Sutherland
ROSSLYN, Barkly East
RUIGTE VLEI, Murraysburg
RUSTMYNZIEL, Wodehouse

S
SAFRAAN RIVER, Oudtshoorn
SAFT SIT, Prieska
SALT RIVER, Beaufort West
SCHILDERKRANTZ, Wodehouse
SCORPION'S DRIFT, Carnarvon
SECRETARIS KRAAL, Murraysburg
SILVER VALE, Komgha
SLANGVALE, Malmesbury
SMAL HOEK, Fort Beaufort
SMITH"S KRAAL, Sutherland
SOODHOEK, Humansdorp
SOUBATSFONTEIN, Namaqualand
SOUTH WINTERVELD, Richmond
SPES BONA, Ceres
SPIELMAN'S KRAAL, Uniondale
SPINNEKOP'S KRAAL, Fraserburg
SPIOENKOP, Prieska
SPREEUWFONTEIN, Laingsburg
SPRINGERSBAAILEEGTE, Fraserburg
SPRINGFONTEIN, Fraserburg
SPYTFONTEIN, Hanover
STERKFONTEIN, Tarka
STINKFONTEIN, Prince Albert,
STOFFKRAAL, Prieska
STRUISFONTEIN, Malmesbury
STUURMANS KUILEN, Hanover
SUNNYSIDE I, Herbert
SUNNYSIDE II, Wodehouse

T
TAAIBOSCHFONTEIN, Victoria West
TAAIBOSCHPOORT, Philipstown
TAFELBERG, Fraserburg
TARANTAAL, Swellendam
TARSUS, Cathcart
THE HALT, Gordonia
THOMAS GAT, Richmond
THORNHILL, Vryburg
TILNEY, Swellendam
TOVERWATER I, Murraysburg
TOVERWATER II, Uniondale
TRETYRE, Steytlerville
TREURFONTEIN, Griqualand East
TSAELINGWE, Kuruman
TSENIN, Kuruman
TWEEFONTEIN I, Fraserburg
TWEEFONTEIN II, Graaff-Reinet
TYGER HOEK, Uitenhage
TYGER VLEI, Carnarvon

U
UITKYK, George
UIJEN VLEI, Calvinia
UITHOEK, Clanwilliam
UMTAMVUMA DRIFT, Griqualand East
UPPER DWAAS, Uniondale

V
VAN DER LINDE'S DAM, Cradock
VAN RENSBURG, Alexandria
VAN ZYL'S KRAAL, Fraserburg
VARSCHFONTEIN, Beaufort West
VENTER'S VLEI, Philipstown
VENTNOR, Barkly East
VERLATENDAM, Hopetown
VERLATENFONTEIN, Steynsburg
VIEL SALM, Griqualand East
VINK RIVER, Robertson
VISCHGEWAGD, Steynsburg
VLAKFONTEIN, Hay
VLAKTEPLAATS, Worcester

VLOKSWERVER, Carnarvon
VOGELGEZANG, Bredasdorp
VOGEL RIVER, Bredasdorp
VOGELSTRUISBULT, Prieska
VOGELSTRUIS FONTEIN I, George
VOGELSTRUISFONTEIN II, Malmesbury
VOGEL VLEI I, Bredasdorp
VOGEL VLEI II, Mossel Bay
VREDENBURG, Somerset East
VROLYKHEID, Prince Albert

W
WARD GROENBERG, Paarl
WARD No 3, Alexandria
WARM KAROSS, Jansenville
WARWICKDALE, Barkly East
WATERFALL, Riversdale
WATERVAL, Ladismith
WATERVLEI, Paarl
WEGDRAAI, Kenhardt
WELBEDACHT, Clanwilliam
WELGELEGEN, Vryburg
WELGEVONDEN I, Prieska
WELGEVONDEN II, Steytlerville
WELTEVREDEN I, Aberdeen
WELTEVREDEN II, Malmesbury
WIEGENAARSPOORT, Beaufort West
WIJDPOORT, Hay
WILDEALSPUTS I, Britstown
WILDEALSPUTS II, Hay
WILDEBEESTKUIL, Britstown
WILDEFONTEIN, Aliwal North
WINDHOEK, Wodehouse
WINTERBERG, Murraysburg
WINTERHOEK, Graaff-Reinet
WINTERSFONTEIN, Somerset East
WITBERG, Hay
WITTEKLIP, Swellendam
WITTEKRANTZ, Beaufort West
WOLVEKOP, Richmond
WOLVEKOP, Victoria West
WOLWEDANS, Sutherland
WOODLANDS, Bedford
WOOLHOPE, Komgha

Z
ZANDHOEK, Humansdorp
ZEVEN VLEI, Piquetberg
ZONDAGS RIVIER HOOP, Graaff-Reinet
ZOUT HOOGTE, Tarka
ZOUTPAN I, Calvinia
ZOUTPAN II, Malmesbury
ZOUTPAN III, Riversdale
ZUUR ANYS, Humansdorp
ZWALUW KRANTZ, Murraysburg
ZWARTBERG, Namaqualand
ZWARTPUTS, Vryburg
ZWARTFONTEIN, Vryburg
ZWARTWATER, Malmesbury
ZWARTHEUWEL, Riverdale
ZWEMKUIL, Prieska

TEN

DEPARTMENTS OF POSTS AND TELEGRAPHS
INCOME: ANNUAL RETURNS 1873-1910

YEAR	*No of POs	PO Income	No of TOs	TO Income	Annual Income
1873	379		18		
1874	394		22	£13,668	
1875	402		37	£14,601	
1876			65	£25,949	
1877		£32,704	82	£27,634	£60,338
1878	572	£26,881	98	£44,432	£71,313
1879	588		101	£49,731	
1880	**585**	**£27,187**	**121**	**£60,829**	**£88,016**
1881	629		118	£91,426	
1882	608		128	£82,864	
1883	610		209	£76,539	
1884	612	£45,433		£78,628	£124,061
1885	607	£60,816		£87,452	£148,268
1886	618	£64,037	215	£80,116	£144,153
1887	623	£64,779	217	£87,925	£152,704
1888	635	£54,542	223	£110,081	£164,623
1889	649	£27,242		£142,419	£169,661
1890	**675**	**£46,708**	**268**	**£137,007**	**£183,715**
1891	694	£50,384	278	£137,524	£187,908
1892	718	£52,777	310	£151,120	£203,897
1893	752	£68,121	320	£162,500	£230,621
1894	797	£88,724	334	£159,388	£248,112
1895	839	£68,455	360	£188,159	£256,614
1896	888	£26,712	394	£252,910	£279,622
1897	934	£72,822	426	£285,213	£358,035
1898	942	£76,815	470	£262,192	£339,007
1899	969	£72,310	480	£263,347	£335,657
1900	**961**	**-£3,882**	**494**	**£382,146**	**£378,264**
1901	904	-£11,274	483	£548,852	£537,578
1902	963	£43,167	506	£500,257	£543,424
1903	1003	£118,885	528	£444,676	£563,561
1904	1013	£223,472	547	£340,647	£564,119
1905	1043	£186,644	558	£278,731	£465,375
1906	1060	£113,116	590	£265,668	£378,784
1907	1087	£157,528	595	£191,441	£348,969
1908	1065				
1909	1087				
1910					

ELEVEN

LIST OF LITERARY PUBLICATIONS PRINTED AND PUBLISHED IN THE CAPE COLONY PERMITTED TO USE THE NEWSPAPER RATE OF POSTAGE

The provisions of Section VIII of the Post Office Act No 4 of 1882 permitted any literary publications printed and published in the Cape Colony to be carried by the Postal Service to any place within the Colony at the current Newspaper Rate of postage, this being set at ½d for every four ounces or part thereof. This amplified the provisions of a previous Act, No 8 of 1859, which required that every book, pamphlet, newspaper or other printed work produced in the Colony should bear the "real name or names" of the author, or the publisher, as well as the name of the printer and his place of residence. The penalty for such an omission was prescribed at a sum not exceeding £100. For as long as publishers conformed to such regulations, they were permitted to use the postal service to deliver their journals to their subscribers. In such cases where the publication was addressed to any place outside the Colony, then a book rate of postage was applicable. On 1 August 1909 the following publications were permitted to make use of the Cape's newspaper rate of postage:

African Insurance, Banking and Commercial Gazette	Cape Town
African Monthly	Grahamstown
Agricultural Journal	Cape Town
Algoa Gazette	Port Elizabeth
Almanack voor de Nederduitsch Gereformeerde Kerk	Cape Town
Ayres' Seed Catalogue and Gardening Guide	Cape Town
Cape Church Monthly and Parish Record	Cape Town
Catholic Magazine for South Africa	Cape Town
Christelijk Strever	Stellenbosch
Christian Student	Stellenbosch
Church News	Cape Town
Church Chronicle	Cape Town
Commercial News and South African Storekeeper	Cape Town
Commercial Times	Cape Town

Dale College Magazine	King Williams Town
De Afrikander	Cape Town
Diocesan College Magazine	Rondebosch
Dun's Gazette	Cape Town
Educational News of South Africa	Cape Town
Farm and Stock	Port Elizabeth
Federal Leaflet Guild of Loyal Women	Cape Town
Friend	Cape Town
Gardens Messenger	Cape Town
Garlick's Fashion Gazettes and Journals	Cape Town
Gereformeerd Maandblad	Stellenbosch
Goede Hoop	Cape Town
Guild of Loyal Women	Cape Town
Huguenot High School Magazine	Paarl
Insurance	Cape Town
Journal of the Institute of Bankers in South Africa	Cape Town
Kerkbode	Cape Town
Kindervriend	Cape Town
Konigsbode	Stellenbosch
Lennon's Trade Journal	Cape Town
Licensed Victuallers' and Sporting Gazette	Cape Town
Lichtstralen	Stellenbosch
Masonic Education Fund of South Africa Annual Report	Cape Town
Missions to Seamen, Annual Report	Cape Town
Ons Taal	Paarl
Pickstone Brothers Catalogue	Paarl
Plain Talk	Cape Town
Postal and Telegraph Herald	Cape Town
Presbyterian Churchman	Cape Town
The Rhodian	Grahamstown
St Andrew's College Magazine	Grahamstown
St Barnabas Parish Magazine	Cape Town
St Cyprian's Magazine	Cape Town
St Michael and All Angels' Parish Magazine	Cape Town
St Paul's Church Magazine	Cape Town
Silver Leaves	Cape Town
Silver Leaves	Wynberg
South African Church Quarterly Review	Port Elizabeth
South African College Magazine	Cape Town
South African Commerce and Manufacturers' Record	Cape Town

South African Feathers	Cape Town
South African Medical Record	Cape Town
South African Municipal Journal	Cape Town
South African Photographic Journal	Cape Town
South African Railway Magazine	Cape Town
South African Sentinel	Kenilworth, Cape Town
South African Storekeepers Gazette and Grocers Record	Port Elizabeth
South African Trade Journal	Cape Town
De Staat	Cape Town
The State	Cape Town
Stemmen des Tijds	Paarl
Student's Quarterly	Stellenbosch
Sudafrikanisches Gemeindeblatt	Wynberg
De Unie	Cape Town
Victoria College Calendar, Stellenbosch	Cape Town
De Wekker	Stellenbosch
War Cry	Port Elizabeth
Wilsonies	Cape Town
Young Men's Journal	Cape Town
Zendingkerk	Cape Town

In order to qualify for this postage rate the publication had to consist wholly or in greater part of political or other news, or of articles relating thereto, or to other current topics with or without advertisements. The full title and date of publication had to appear at the top of the first page, and the whole or part of the title, and the date, at the top of every subsequent page. In addition to the above, the Post Office made special provision for the delivery of Christmas numbers of magazines which, owing to the seasonal nature of their content, were liable to a special rate of postage of 1d for every 2ozs or fraction of that weight.

In 1886 the following journals qualified for the festive postage rate: Christian Million, Christian World, Detroit Free Press, The Gardener's Magazine, Graphic, Illustrated London News, Illustrated Sporting and Dramatic News, Judy Almanac, Lady's Pictorial, Life, Moonshine, The Penny Illustrated, Punch Almanac, Society, Vanity Fair, Weekly Budget, and Whitehall Review.

TWELVE

NUMBER OF HOUSES PAYING DUTIES IN 1870

Soon after the introduction of Representative Government at the Cape in 1854, the political debate began to be dominated by the vexing issue of taxation. This was focused particularly upon the question of how to arrive at a formula that would levy a fair universal tax upon a population whose residents had vastly different concepts of wealth, income, infrastructural development and residential standards. This does not mean that the concept of a tax was not already in existence in rural southern Africa, and the practice of tithing and death duties were in existence long before the arrival of colonial administrators, but the imposition of a tax was never popular and, much like modern society, strategies for their avoidance were not uncommon.

The method that found most favour among colonial administrators was the application of a universal House Tax, which sought to tax a family according to the size and financial worth of its residence. This might have worked reasonably well in an urban environment where land ownership was a norm, but seldom achieved equality in a farming community which might still include hunter-gatherers, indigent refugees, pastoralist farmers and sedentary farmers whose concepts of land ownership did not conform to a cadastral system. As a result this method of taxation was subject to a wide range of housing types and never managed to achieve a fair rate of application. As a result it was subject to constant changes of interpretation.

The tabulation below has been used to show, in a general manner, the housing types that predominated in 1870 in the various Divisions of the Cape Colony at a time when colonial settlement was beginning to define itself into urban and rural areas. Working on the assumption that town or village dwellers had better access to an education that included more than just the basics of numeracy and literacy, it becomes possible to extrapolate the number of families per Division that might have belonged to a regular letter writing public and were thus potential clients of the postal system.

The numbers listed below have been broken down into groups according to their levels of taxation, from 5 shillings per annum to 30 shillings plus. In every Division most of the contributors are in the lowest bracket, while houses in the upper group are in a distinct minority. This is not only a guide as to the quality of housing generally available at the Cape at that time, but is also a rough indicator as to the social stratifications existing in Cape society, with a predominance of farmers and crafters at its core. Socially, its leading members would have been medical personnel and colonial administrators, and the role of a local teacher was probably filled in part-time by the local clergyman. It was this latter group that would have constituted, in the main, the members of the public most likely to have made use of the local post office.

Other indicators, that are not shown here, might have included census figures, literacy rates, and for a time, the number of indigenous residents forced to find employment on white-owned farms.

DIVISION	Year	5s	10s	20s	30s+	TOTAL
Albany	1870	2298	708	126	39	3171
Albert	1870	552	523	78	2	1155
Alexandria	1870	440	80	3		523
Aliwal North	1870	922	284	32	5	1243
Bathurst	1870	619	76	5		700
Beaufort	1870	341	182	44	7	574
Bedford	1870	1146	159	12		1317
Bredasdorp	1870	772	53			825
Caledon	1870	1811	161	9		1981
Calvinia	1870	269	122			391
Cape Division	1870	5527	2485	517	154	8683
Clanwilliam	1870	1291	96	2		1389
Colesberg	1870	1177	460	85	6	1728
Cradock	1870	1748	400	41		2189
East London	1870	973	40	3		1021
Fort Beaufort	1870	1217	240	16	2	1475
Fraserburg	1870	451	206	20		677
George	1870	1630	198	8	2	1838
Graaff-Reinet	1870	1984	513	32	6	2535
Hopetown	1870	294	211	19	1	525
Humansdorp	1870	804	204	13		1021
King Williams Town	1870	2114	318	15	14	2461
Knysna	1870	402	54	71		464
Malmesbury	1870	1312	382	37	2	1733
Middelburg	1870	939	221	11	1	1172
Mossel Bay	1870	612	69	10	3	694
Murraysburg	1870	152	107	30		289
Namaqualand	1870	1646	166	6		1818
Oudtshoorn	1870	2458	222	3		2683
Paarl	1870	2464	544	19	2	3029
Peddie	1870	805	46	3		854
Piquetberg	1870	769	172	14	1	956
Port Elizabeth	1870	1858	588	134	90	2670
Prince Albert	1870	748	219	17		984
Queenstown	1870	2220	320	24	1	2565

TWELVE: House Duties

DIVISION	Year	5s	10s	20s	30s+	TOTAL
Richmond	1870	408	210	28		64
Riverdale	1870	1492	172	4		166
Somerset (East)	1870	2000	266	25		2291
Stellenbosch	1870	1221	308	81	5	1615
Stockenstrom	1870	744	52	0		796
Swellendam	1870	1588	197	8		1793
Tulbagh	1870	591	224	16	2	833
Uitenhage	1870	1840	387	39	6	2272
Victoria East	1870	208	76	1	1	286
Victoria West	1870	508	279	50	12	849
Worcester	1870	698	238	34	1	971

ABBREVIATIONS

AN	Division of Aliwal North
APO	Army Post Office
Bas	Basutoland
BB	British Bechuanaland
BCA	British Central Africa
BONC	Barred oval numeral canceller
BP	Bechuanaland Protectorate
BSAC	British South Africa Company
CDS	Circular date stamp, generic
CGH	Cape of Good Hope
Comdt	Commandant, Dutch military term for a Commander
CT	Cape Town
DC	Double circle office date stamp, generic
DHO	Divisional Head Office
DRC	Dutch Reformed Church, used as NGK in Afrikaans
EL	East London
FAMP	Frontier Armed and Mounted Police
F-C	Field-Cornetcy
ft	Foot, Imperial linear measure where twelve inches made up a foot and three feet made up a yard, equals approximately 305mm
Garicp	Formerly known as the Orange River, derived from the Khoikhoi meaning a river
GB	Great Britain
GE	Griqualand East
GovP	Government Printer
GPO	General Post Office
GW	Griqualand West
HO	Head Office
HSRC	Human Sciences Research Council
ins	Inch, Imperial linear measure where twelve inches made up a foot, each equals 2.54mm
KEdVII	King Edward VII

KiGariep	Formerly known as the Vaal River, derived from the Khoikhoi "heig ariep", meaning "grey river"
Kim	Kimberley
KWT	King Williams Town
£	British pound, Imperial coinage usually abridged to £.s.d, meaning pounds, shillings and pence, where twelve pence made a shilling and twenty shillings made up a pound.
MOO	Money Order Office
MTO	Military Telegraph Office
NGK	Nederduitse Gereformeerde Kerk, used as DRC in English
NPB	Newspaper Branch
NPC	Newspaper Counter
Nyasa	Nyasaland
ODS	Office date stamp, generic
OFS	Orange Free State
OPO	Ocean Post Office
ORC	Orange River Colony
Ovp	Overprint
OVS	Oranje Vrij Staat, or Orange Free State
PA	Postal Agency
pc	Post Card
PE	Port Elizabeth
PFSA	Philatelic Federation of Southern Africa
PM	Postmaster
PMG	Postmaster General
PO	Post Office
POA	Post Office Agency
POC	Post Office Circular
POG	Post Office Guide
POS	Post Office Stone
PPC	Picture post card
PPHSSA	Postmark and Postal History Society of Southern Africa
PSC	Postal stationery card
PWD	Public Works Department
QV	Queen Victoria
R	Division of Robertson
RO	Railway Office
RTO	Railway Telegraph Office
SAJS	South African Journal of Science
SAP	South African Philatelist
SAPOM	South African Post Office Museum
SC	Single circle office date stamp, generic
SESA	Standard Encyclopedia of South Africa

SO	Sub-Office
Stn	Station
SWA	South West Africa
Swazi	Swaziland, today known as the Kingdom of Eswatini
TeO	Telephone Office
TEX	Telephone Exchange
TO	Telegraph Office
TPO	Travelling Post Office
Tvl	Transvaal
VOC	Vereenigde Oost-Indische Compagnie, or Dutch East India Company
VRS	Van Riebeeck Society
WWI	First World War
WWII	Second World War
ZAR	Zuid Afrikaansche Republiek, or the South African Republic

BIBLIOGRAPHY

ANONYMOUS. 1998. *Life at the Cape Over a Hundred Years Ago, by a Lady*. Cape Town: Struik.
AXELSON, Eric. 1969. *Portuguese in South-East Africa 1600-1700*. Johannesburg: Witwatersrand University Press.
BARNARD, Lady Anne. 1994. *The Cape Journals of Lady Anne Barnard*, 1797-1898. Cape Town: VRS.
BATTISS Walter W, JUNOD, Henri Philippe, FRANZ, Gottfried H, and GROSSERT, John W. 1958. *The Art of Africa*. Pietermaritzburg: Shuter & Shooter.
BENNETT, R. c1908. *Reminiscences of the Cape Government Telegraphs*. Cape Town: SA Newspaper Co Ltd.
BERRY, TB. 1966. *South African Post Marks*. Johannesburg, Philatelic Federation of South Africa.
BUCHANAN, Nora. 2008. *A History of the University of Natal Libraries*, 1910-2003. Unpublished PhD Thesis, University of KwaZulu-Natal.
BURMAN, Jose. 1984. *Early Railways at the Cape. Cape Town*: Human & Rousseau.
CAPE ALMANAC. 1801-1838 inclusive. Various publishers.
CAPE OF GOOD HOPE. *1838-1882. Post Office Civil Establishment Lists*. Cape Town: GovP.
  1865. *Petition of Mr JA le Sueur*, Postmaster General. Cape Town: GovP, 29 May 1865.
  1865. *Report of the Commission Appointed to Inquire into the System of Audit etc*. Cape Town: House of Assembly. (A21-'65) (CGH, A21-'85)
  1879. *Correspondence with Reference to the Transfer of Imperial Property to the Colonial Government*. Cape Town: Saul Solomon and Co.
  1881. *Military Posts and Works*, 1880. Cape Town: Saul Solomon and Co.
  1883. *Report of a Commission Appointed by His Excellency the Governor to Enquire into and Report Opon the Existing Conditions and Regulations of the Civil Service in this Colony*. G.110-'83. Cape Town: GovP.
  1906. *Instructions for the Guidance of Deputy Postmasters and Post Office Agents*. Cape Town: Cape Times Ltd.
CAPE OF GOOD HOPE GOVERNMENT GAZETTE. 1860a. *Gaol Supplies*: Queenstown. 9 October.
  1860b. *Gaol Supplies*: George. 9 October 1860.
COULTER, Jean. 1988. *They Lived in Africa*. Port Elizabeth: the Author.
DE VILLIERS, Simon A. 1971. *Robben Island*. Cape Town: Struik.
DUERDEN, Dennis. 1975. *The Invisible Present*. New York: Harper and Row.
DU PLESSIS, JD. 1947. *The Cape Malays*. Cape Town: Maskew Miller.
ELPHICK, Richard. 1977. *Kraal and Castle: Khoikhoi and the Founding of White South Africa*. Yale University.
EMMS, Merwyn. 1976. Fortifications of the Cape of Good Hope. LANTERN, 25:4, June 1976.
  1976. Murder Most Foul. Postel, November 1976.

1977. Adventure was Part of the Job. Postel, July 1977.

FRESCURA, Franco. 1982. The Barred Oval Numeral Canceller of the Cape of Good Hope of 1864. Post Office Stone 14(2), June 1982.

1983. The Experimental Dating and Obliterating Cancellers of the CGH. Post Office Stone, 15(3), September 1983. 3-21

1984. The Large Single Circle Canceller of the CGH. Post Office Stone, 16(4), December 1984. 3-7.

1995. Cetshawayo kaMpande: Some biographical notes. FORERUNNERS, Vol 9, No 2 (July-October 1995). 67-69. California.

2002. *The Post Offices of the Cape of Good Hope, 1792-1910*. Pretoria: The Archetype Press.

2003. Convict Stations and the Cape Post Office.. FORERUNNERS, Vol 16, No 2 (November 2002-February 2003). California.

2004. *The Cape Post Office During the South African War of 1899-1902*. Pretoria: Occasional Paper No 16, Postmark and Postal History Society of Southern Africa.

2005. The Cape General Post Office, 1792-1910. FORERUNNERS, Vol 19, No 1, (July-October 2005). California.

2006. Postmasters General of the Cape, 1792-1910. FORERUNNERS, Vol 19, No 2 (November 2005-February 2006). 53-57. California.

2007. The Cape Colonial Establishment, 1872-1910. CAPE AND NATAL PHILATELIC JOURNAL, Vol 11, No 4 (44), December 2007: 108-113.

2008. Women in the Cape Colonial Post Office. FORERUNNERS, Vol 21, No 3, (March-June 2008): 86-91. California.

2018. Felons, Forgers and Fences: South Africa's Undeclared War on Archives.. FORERUNNERS, Vol 31, No 2, (November 2017-February 2018): 45051. California.

2018. *Postal Cancellations of of the Cape, 1853-1910*. Johannesburg: Federation of South African Philatelists.

2018. A Survey of Post Office Stones Used at the Cape of Good Hope, 1601-1652. FORERUNNERS, Vol 32, No 1, (July-October 2018): 10-18. California.

GILL, Stephen. 1995. *A Guide to Morija*. Morija: Morija Museum and Archives.

GOLDBLATT, Robert. 1983a. *The Official Post and the Official or "Free" Letter Stamps of the Cape of Good Hope*. Johannesburg: Postmark and Postal History Society of South Africa, Occasional Paper 4.

1983b. *Postmarks of the Cape of Good Hope*. Cape Town: Reijger.

GOMM, Neville. 1997. The Post Office Stone. FORERUNNERS, 10:3 and 11:1, November 1996-June 1997.

GRANT, Maurice Harold. 1910. *History of the War in South Africa*. London: Hurst and Blackett.

GREEN, Lawrence G. 1949. *In the Land of Afternoon*. Cape Town: Howard Timmins.

HAGEN, Hemut S, and NAYLOR, Stan P. 1985. *Railway Stamps of South Africa*. Johannesburg: Philatelic Federation of Southern Africa.

HODGKIN, Jonathan. 1970. Jonathan Edward Hodgkin's Diary, 1894. Africana Notes and News, 19:3, 102-8.

JUNOD, Henri A. 1912. *The Life of a South African Tribe*. Neuchatel, Switzerland: Imprimerie Attinger Freres.

JURGENS, Adrian Albert. 1943. *The Handstruck Letter Stamps of the Cape of Good Hope from 1792 to 1853 and the Postmarks from 1853 to 1910*. Cape Town: The Author.

1945. *The Bechuanalands*. London: Royal Philatelic Society.

KILPIN, Ernest F. 1887. *The Cape of Good Hope Civil Service List, 1887*. Cape Town: Juta.

1892. *The Cape of Good Hope Civil Service List, 1892*. Cape Town.

1910. *The Cape of Good Hope Civil Service List, 1910*. Cape Town: Cape Times Limited.

LOVEDALE MISSIONARY INSTITUTION. 1895. *Reports for 1895*. Cory Library, Grahamstown.

1897. *Reports for 1897*. Cory Library, Grahamstown.

MATTHEWS, ZK. 1960. I*mvo Zabantsundu*. 3 June- 21 November 1960.

MEINTJIES, Johannes. 1980. George Vice, Founder of Molteno in Cape Colony. Africana Notes and News, 24:3, 107-9.

MOREE, PJ. 1998. *Met vriend die God geleide*. Zutphen.

NATTRASS, Jennifer. 1999. Prohibition Village. COUNTRY LIFE, SP 1999. 24-29.

NETHERSOLE, M, and FRESCURA, F. 1983. Typology of Cape Postal Markings. Post Office Stone, 15(4), December 1983. 5-31. See Type 5g1.

PERINGUEY, L. Inscriptions Left by Early European Navigators on their Way to the East.. Annals of the South African Museum, Vol XII.

PHILIP, Peter, 1981. *British Residents at the Cape, 1795-1819*. Cape Town: David Philip.

PLACE NAMES COMMITTEE. 1978. *Official Place Names in the RSA and in SWA*. Pretoria.

POSTMASTER GENERAL, CAPE OF GOOD HOPE.

1872-1884. *Report of the Postmaster-General*. Cape Town: GovP.

1885-1910. *Report of the Postmaster-General (Postal and Telegraph Department)*. Cape Town: GovP.

1895. *Report of the Postmaster-General (Postal and Telegraph Department)*. Cape Town: GovP.

POST OFFICE OF THE CAPE OF GOOD HOPE. 1882. *Post Office Circular No. 5*, 1 June 1882. Cape Town, Cape Times.

1894. *Post Office Circular No 149*, 1 May 1894. Cape Town, Cape Times.

1895. *Post Office Circular No 163*, 1 July 1895. Cape Town, Cape Times.

1902. *Post Office Circular No. 249*, 1 August 1902.. Cape Town, Cape Times.

c1903. *Instructions for the Guidance of Head Postmasters in the Cape of Good Hope*.

1905. *Post Office Circular No. 286*, 1 September 1905. Cape Town, Cape Times.

1906. *Post Office Circular No. 298*, 1 September 1906. Cape Town, Cape Times.

PUBLIC WORKS DEPARTMENT, CAPE OF GOOD HOPE. 1885-1910. *Report of the Department of Public Works*, Cape Town: GovP.

PULLAN, M. 1980. Hong Kong Study Circle Bulletin No 228, November/ December 1980.

PUTZEL, Ralph F. 1981. Early Cape Post Marks Pose Puzzles. SA Philatelist, February 1981.

1986. *The Encyclopedia of Southern African Post Offices and Postal Agencies* I. Cape Town.

1989. *The Encyclopaedia of South African Post Offices and Postal Agencies*. Tokai: The Author.

RADFORD, Dennis. 1979. *The Architecture of the Western Cape, 1838-1901*. Johannesburg: Wits.

RAPER, Peter E. 1987. *Dictionary of Southern African Place Names*. Johannesburg: Jonathan Ball.

2004. *New Dictionary of South African Place Names*. Johannesburg: Jonathan Ball.

RAVEN-HART, R. 1967. *Before Van Riebeeck*. Cape Town: Struik.

RHIND, David, and WALKER, Michael. 1996. *Historical Railway Postcard Journeys in Southern Africa*.

Cape Town: The Authors.

ROSENTHAL, Eric. 1957. *The Cape of Good Hope Triangular Stamp and its Story*. Cape Town: Balkema. Reprinted with an Addendum by Colin Rowe in 2009.

ROSENTHAL, Eric, and BLUM, Eliezer. 1969. *Runner and Mailcoach*. Cape Town: Purnell.

ROTH, Douglas. 1976. Jurgensiana. SAPhil, February 1976. 33.

SCHOONEES, Peter. 1991. *Inscriptions on Padroes, Pastal Stones, Tombstones and Beacons*. Cape Town: South African Cultural Museum.

SELLICK, WSJ. 1904. *Uitenhage Past and Present*. Uitenhage: Uitenhage Times.

SKOTA, Mweli TD. 1930. *The Yearly African Register*. Mr Paul Xiniwe. RL Lesson & Co. (p109).

SLATER, Lorna. 1982. *The Story of Sidbury, 1820-1920*. Port Elizabeth.

SOUTH AFRICAN PHILATELIST, June 1965 and February 1966.

SOUTH AFRICAN RAILWAYS MAGAZINE. November 1911, p1138. South African Railway Museum.

STANDARD ENCYCLOPEDIA OF SOUTH AFRICA (SESA). 1972. Cape Town: Nasionale Opvoedkundige Uitgewery.

STORRAR, Patricia, and KOMNICK, Gunther. 1984. *A Colossus of Roads: Thomas Bain*. Cape Town: Murray and Roberts.

SYMONS, JE. 1997. *The Macloutse Post Office and its Postmaster, Bechuanaland Protectorate 1892*. Davis, CA: Krone Publications.

TAYLOR, James. 2003. *Traditional Arab Sailing Ships*. London: The British-Yemeni Society, August 2003

THEAL, George McCall. 1907. *History of Africa South of the Zambesi before 1795*. London: George Allen & Unwin.

THOMPSON, Leonard. 1990. *A History of South Africa*. New Haven: Yale University Press.

TREDGOLD, Arderne. 1986. *Village of the Sea*. Cape Town: Human&Roussow.

TYLDEN, G. 1948. Majorobello. Africana Notes and News, 5:2, 49-50.

UNION OF SOUTH AFRICA. c1910. *Instructions to Postal Agents*. Pretoria: Union Post Office. 1933. *Instructions to Postal Agents*. Pretoria: The Government Printer.

VERSTAPPEN, P. 1982. *The Book of Surnames*. London.

WARNECK, Gustav. 1888. *Modern Missions and Culture: Their Mutual Relations*. Edinburgh: James Gemmell.

WELTZ, Stephan. 1989. *Postage Stamps and Postal History of the World*, Johannesburg, 22 February 1989.

WHIDDICOMBE, John. c1865. *Memories and Musings*.

YAP, Melanie, and MAN, Dianne Leong. 1996. *Colour, Confusion and Concessions*. Hong Kong: Hong Kong University Press.

www.ingramcontent.com/pod-product-compliance
Lightning Source LLC
Chambersburg PA
CBHW080411170426
43194CB00015B/2775